Business Ethics and Practice

SIMON ROBINSON AND PAUL DOWSON

The Chartered Institute of Personnel and Development is the leading publisher of books and reports for personnel and training professionals, students, and all those concerned with the effective management and development of people at work. For details of all our titles, please contact the publishing department:
tel: 020-8612 6204
e-mail publish@cipd.co.uk
The catalogue of all CIPD titles can be viewed on the CIPD website:
www.cipd.co.uk/bookstore

Business Ethics in Practice

Simon Robinson and Paul Dowson

Chartered Institute of Personnel and Development

Published by the Chartered Institute of Personnel and Development,
151, The Broadway, London, SW19 1JQ

This edition first published 2012

Typeset by Fakenham Prepress Solutions, Fakenham, Norfolk NR21 8NN

Printed in Great Britain by Bell & Bain, Glasgow

British Library Cataloguing in Publication Data

A catalogue of this publication is available from the British Library

ISBN 978 1 84398 272 2

The views expressed in this publication are the authors' own and may not necessarily
reflect those of the CIPD.

The CIPD has made every effort to trace and acknowledge copyright holders. If any
source has been overlooked, CIPD Enterprises would be pleased to redress this in
future editions.

Chartered Institute of Personnel and Development,
151 The Broadway, London, SW19 1JQ
Tel: 020 8612 6200
E-mail: cipd@cipd.co.uk
Website: www.cipd.co.uk
Incorporated by Royal Charter.
Registered Charity No. 1079797

Contents

Foreword

For too long the issue of ethics has been left at the margins of business education, seen either as a matter for externally imposed regulation (often in the face of corporate opposition) or for delegation to heads of corporate social responsibility whose internal status rarely matched their external projection. For many reasons this is now changing.

In the face of complex collective action problems – for example, sustainability and poverty reduction – corporations are being held to account both for what they do (eg emitting carbon) and for what they don't (monitoring labour standards among their suppliers). The possibilities of data sharing and social activism offered by the Internet and greater expectations of transparency have meant that companies have increasingly had to accept that they are operating in full public view. The 2008 economic crisis with its terrible and still unfolding impact on hundreds of millions of lives is rightly seen as, in large part, a failure of corporate culture and governance. Less dramatic, but perhaps of equal long-term significance, a variety of disciplines – particularly behavioural economics – have shattered the myth of *Homo economicus*. If all human beings are perfectly informed utility maximisers, then businesses can legitimately argue that their products are simply responding to expressed desire. But once we accept that human beings are subject to a whole range of cognitive frailties, which advertising and marketing are adept at exploiting, it then becomes much harder for businesses to claim that they are simply responding to, rather than actively shaping, our preferences.

This latter insight has already had a big impact on the food and alcohol industries which have had to accept at least some responsibility for what they encourage us to eat and drink. Other sectors are still in denial. For example, time and again the financial services sector has exploited our cognitive weaknesses (particularly short-termism) and information asymmetries to sell us dodgy, exploitative and even dangerous products.

Yet, on the upside, commercial brands have a huge potential to support us in making wiser choices and living better lives, and doing so in a way which adds to the business bottom line. Think of the global network of runners and joggers that has been created by Nike, or the way 'cradle to cradle' carpet manufacturer Desso has changed customer expectations in an industry which used to be an environmental black spot.

As pressures on corporations grow – as they undoubtedly will – companies and their stakeholders will have to engage in new and possibly uncomfortable debates. This will involve many practical issues but will also mean engaging with deeper philosophical questions. To commit to being a 'responsible' business is the beginning of a conversation not its end. That conversation will be hugely assisted if its participants have a grounding in the many dimensions and subtleties of the idea of responsibility. Which is why Simon Robinson and Paul Dowson have chosen just the right moment for a book which is not only clear and accessible but also provokes reflection and nuanced debate.

That business leaders see an understanding of concepts of ethics and responsibility as an essential part of their managerial toolkit is, right now, only an aspiration. But it is one that could be brought a step closer if today's budding business leaders were to read this book.

Matthew Taylor
Chief Executive
Royal Society of Arts

Acknowledgements

The authors would like to acknowledge the support of editorial staff at CIPD, in particular Katy Hamilton and Heidi Partridge. It takes discipline and empathy to get authors through a book of this size. We were the grateful recipient of both.

We would also like to acknowledge the many students who have helped us to reflect on and develop our thoughts on and teaching about ethics. There are no experts in this area, only a community of practice prepared to question and be questioned.

DEDICATION

I dedicate this book to my wife Angie Robinson who embodies all of Aristotle's virtues, but especially patience. It is my good fortune that she also embodies the core virtue of Aquinas, love.

I dedicate this book to my Father and Mother, David and Mary Dowson for underlining openness and conversation, whatever the challenge.

Authors

Simon Robinson. Professor of Applied and Professional Ethics, Leeds Metropolitan University

Educated at Oxford and Edinburgh Universities, Robinson became a psychiatric social worker before entering the Church of England priesthood in 1978. He entered university chaplaincy in Edinburgh and Leeds, developing research and lecturing in areas of applied ethics and business ethics. In 2004 he joined Leeds Metropolitan University.

He has written and researched extensively in business ethics, corporate social responsibility, the nature and dynamics of responsibility, equality, ethics and culture, and ethics and care.

Books include: *Agape, Moral Meaning and Pastoral Counselling; Their Rights, Advanced Directives; Case Histories in Business Ethics; Values in Higher Education; The Teaching and Practice of Professional Ethics; Employability and Ethics; Engineering, Business and Professional Ethics; Spirituality and Sport; Spirituality, Ethics and Care; Ethics for Living and Working; Ethics and the Alcohol Industry; Leadership Responsibility.*

He is co-general editor of the Peter Lang book series on International Studies in Applied Ethics.

Paul Dowson. Senior Lecturer, Leeds Metropolitan University

Educated at the Universities of East Anglia, Leeds, and Huddersfield as well as St John's (CE) College, Nottingham. Paul has a business background and gained his MBA from the University of Leeds in 1992. To pursue his interest in teaching he joined Leeds Metropolitan University in 2002. Paul describes himself as an 'Eriksonian', reflecting his leading research interest in applying the thinking of Erik Erikson to business and personal development. In 2005 he developed with Engage Mutual Assurance 'LifePlan', an innovative Corporate Responsibility (CR) programme aimed at defining personal and professional pathways for adults of all ages. He has been working and writing with Simon Robinson since 2004. In 2008 they launched the Responsible Engagement programme, which seeks to build student identity around taking responsibility for self, other and global concerns; as well as introducing them to CR.

Introduction

Writing a textbook about business ethics depends on why you want to write it and what you think business ethics is. This is why there are so many textbooks that each claim to have cornered the meaning and practice of business ethics. In this Introduction we want to explain why we have organised this book in the way that we have, and what the best way of using it is.

We do not claim to have captured everything about the meaning and practice of business ethics. Give us another decade and we might think about such a claim. We have rather three aims:

- to provide key tools for understanding and practising ethics in business. These will help you to talk confidently about ethical values, and to interrogate and develop practice effectively in the light of those values
- to provide critical reflection on practice and values in key areas of the business ethical environment. After the first four chapters we therefore look at leadership, the character and culture of the organisation, human resource management, relationships to the different professions within business, the relationships to consumers, and the wider social and physical environments
- to provide ways for you to practise ethics in the context of your business or your education and training for business.

The first aim looks straightforward, provided that we realise that tools do not do the job for us. They have to be used properly, and this means that we have to understand their point and how to use them well.

The second aim is simply one way of making sense of ethics in business. We could have focused on different ways, such as ethical issues like bribery and corruption, or key ethical values such as justice and freedom. Instead, we have chosen to show how such issues and values apply across different areas of ethical practice, as we shall see below.

The third aim might seem to be ambitious – after all, how can you practise being good? We address that question in the last part of the Introduction. Before we get to that, consider in fact how you might practise ethics. What would that look like? You might reflect also on whether you do that now, and if so, how, and how well.

THE CHAPTERS

Chapter 1 introduces students to ethics in practice, and definitions of business ethics. It examines different questions and critiques of ethics in business, and business ethics as a discipline in business studies. In particular it focuses on the ethical divide – the often negative view of ethics in the practice of business. It develops the reasons for thinking and behaving ethically in business. The final part of the chapter sets out reflective practice as the means for connecting business ethics with other aspects of business practice, and other subjects in the curriculum, including personal and professional development.

Chapter 2 examines ethical theory in practice. This covers normative ethical theories – theories that try to explain the basis of what is ethically good. It examines underlying worldviews, cultural and religious. It emphasises that theory is essentially connected to practice.

Chapter 3 examines descriptive theories of ethics – theories that show how we make ethical decisions, and what might enable or prevent such decision-making. It develops an ethical decision-making framework that enables individuals and organisations to handle core values in a complex and plural ethical environment, and introduces the idea of ethical thinking.

Chapter 4 begins with a case study of aspects of the credit crisis. It critically analyses the case in terms of responsibility, and details how the lack of responsible practice led to the breakdown described. From this it develops an analysis of the ethical environment, involving interactive dimensions: interpersonal, organisational, cultural, social, ecological and global. It argues that all aspects of this environment are involved in some way in the business practice over time, and concludes on an interactive fourfold bottom line of responsibility. The key ethical category of responsibility is analysed, forming the basis of ethical practice.

Chapter 5 focuses on the ethics of leadership and governance, critically examining the underlying theories and practice, and the centrality of ethics to leadership.

The book then begins to explore the different aspects of the ethical environment.

Chapter 6 focuses on the emergence of the ethical perspective in the business organisation through the development of codes, culture and character. Key elements of responsibility are worked through in each area.

Chapters 7 and 8 focus on the organisation: first employees in general (human resources), and then the ethical perspectives of different professions. These chapters also raise the question of how far management is a 'true profession', and how business relates to the ethical perspectives of the different professions.

Chapters 9 and 10 focus on immediate external stakeholders including customers, competitors and suppliers.

Chapters 11 and 12 examine the social environment and the responsibility of business. The first of these focuses on civil society, giving examples in local and global contexts, and noting how business can relate to and develop social capital. It also examines the relationship of business to shareholders and NGOs. The second looks at the relationship of business to government. In both these chapters we help the student explore the way in which hard cases, such as the alcohol and tobacco industries, take the executive's ethical argument beyond a narrow view of business ethics to consideration of core political and philosophical principles such as freedom and responsibility.

Chapters 13 and 14 complete the analysis of the ethical environment, focusing first on the global context and then on the natural environment and sustainability.

KEY THEMES

We aim to weave several key themes throughout these chapters.

Values and principles

These are the 'big ideas' of ethics, and include values such as equal respect, justice and human rights. We show how such values have to be addressed in every aspect of business, whatever the size. Justice, for instance, is a key part of human resources, focusing especially on procedural justice – where practices in the firm have to be seen to be fair. It is also a key part of working globally. Many multinational firms have to operate in areas where there is a strong sense of injustice, and where the firm may be accused of contributing to that injustice. Justice is also part of personal development and the virtues, and how one develops the capacity for justice. It is important to know how to handle the concept and practice of justice across the working environment.

Another example is human rights, which apply to the workplace as much as to global politics. So how should business respond to the challenge of human rights in the different areas? Similarly, what does equal respect mean in each of these areas?

If you need to develop these or any other theme for an essay, for instance, simply look in the index, and it will enable you to track these themes across the different areas.

Practice

Ethics is focused in practice. Ethical theory is only useful if it explains what we can see. We therefore want to see what ethics looks like. We provide examples of how businesses have successfully and unsuccessfully developed ethical practice. These and other exercises show how one might think about and practise ethics, aiming to develop your own ethical perspective in business. All behaviour that we see reflects some view of values. The key questions are, do we know what that is, and can we effectively justify it?

Difference

Ethical big ideas always lead to debate. This is partly to do with the perspective of different cultures and partly different views within one's own culture. The differences become more marked the more we get down to details of ethical practice. So we have to decide how we deal with those differences. One culture might argue that it is best to put the interest of families first – with family as a key value. Another culture may argue the importance of equal treatment for all, regardless of family or national links. When it comes to hiring policy or contract decisions it is important know how such differences might be handled.

One argument is that we should tolerate different views just because they are different. Another argument is that some things are more important than difference, such as human rights and justice. Good ethical practice finds a way of working through these issues. A theme throughout the book is that of the ambiguity of difference. It may be important to respect the humanity of the different other, but their value system might be problematic and require to be challenged.

Difference is also important in ethics as a function of learning. Engaging different values causes us to reflect on, challenge and develop our own understanding and practice.

Joined-up ethics

If ethical values are focused in practice, it is important to see the connections that ethics makes across different areas. First, ethical decision-making shares much the same framework as other decision-making frameworks in business, and connects to different areas of expertise within Business Studies, such as governance, leadership, marketing, business strategy, and human resources. The key aspects of this book can thus be used across the business curriculum.

Second, business ethics links up through the category of responsibility with 'cognate' areas such as citizenship (civic responsibility), volunteering, employability (with core ethical virtues relating to workplace skills), enterprise (with capabilities such as creativity), and personal and professional development.

Third, business ethics connects with other areas of ethics and wider philosophical concerns, from political ethics to social and global ethics. This bridges the gap between personal, professional and political.

Fourth, the same ethical tools are relevant to small and big business. There may be different emphases but it is still about embodying responsibility in the context of different environments.

Fifth, ethics is both reactive, facing dilemmas, but also proactive, involving planning that may avoid dilemmas.

All of this demands synoptic thinking – the capacity to see the overarching picture and how the different aspects connect.

Ethical mapping

The image of making a map is very apposite for ethics. In one sense maps are always developing over time, in response to differences in the physical terrain and to the sense we make of that terrain. The general shape of the ethical map may remain much the same, but there are also many different perspectives, depending on culture, context, role and function.

Business ethics involves a continual task of mapping ethical meaning, working out what is of value and how we embody that value, and thus enabling others to take the ethical journey.

Responsibility

Perhaps the central ethical category in business ethics is responsibility. Corporate social responsibility (CSR) has tended to stress triple-bottom-line reporting, and thus targets and measurement of effects. It also focuses on the responsibility of business as distinct from other institutions.

Responsibility as a key ethical category that applies whatever the context involves the practice of:

- ethical agency – being responsible as an individual and corporation for what we think and value, and how that affects our practice and the wider social environment. This means that responsibility is both about an awareness of the environment, of our effect on it, and the values that cause us to respond to it
- accountability to – knowing who we are accountable to and how to give a critical account to them
- liability for – working through shared responsibility for our social and physical environment, and planning for that. This requires the exercise of the 'moral imagination', the capacity to develop creative ethical planning. The more responsibility is shared and effectively negotiated, the more possibilities multiply.

Even just a lack of awareness of that environment can lead to poor strategic decisions and significant negative effects on that environment, as the credit crisis of 2007–8 showed.

Ethics in all this is essentially a shared enterprise in all business contexts.

Adult ethics

At various points in the book we note that ethics is focused in critical rational reflection. This involves not only intellectual reflection but also an awareness of the underlying relational dynamics, which often arouse strong feelings.

There are three areas that may involve such feelings. The first is around the taking of responsibility. Associated with this is the fear of standing out or taking risks. We note research that confirms that a majority of people prefer to deny or avoid responsibility.

The second is associated with the dynamics of ethical critique. Often, questioning one's values is seen as a threat to identity, thus questioning the worth of the organisation or person. This is associated with the early stages of human development, when the child is unable to distinguish between the self (with associated personal worth) and the actions of the self. It is a critique that can be associated with parental injunctions and lead to a response 'from the child' of resentment or anger. We note case studies such as Nestlé and Nike where ongoing debates, even between organisations, have been fuelled by such a dynamic. This dynamic can also be connected to ethical bullying, where values are imposed on an unthinking workforce.

A third area lies not so much where we have to control or handle negative feelings but where positive feelings reinforce practice. It is often focused in the good feelings associated with service or success. Even here, though, there has to be a critical stance towards those positive feelings. In some of the case studies, such as Enron, strong positive feelings were developed by the firm around values but were not based in reality or integrity.

In contrast to the child dynamic of these three areas is the adult response, involving an awareness of the underlying dynamic: a focus on action rather than person, cultivating virtues that enable responsibility to be taken, and developing the capacity to question, challenge, and accept questions about values and practice.

THE DANGERS OF CLOSED ETHICS

Related to the issues of difference are closed ethics. By this we mean ethics that are based and operate in the boundaries of a particular organisation, and take no account of wider ethics. Such organisations tend to avoid critical questioning and deny wider responsibilities. Throughout the book we therefore note the importance of guarding against the imposition of a closed ethical viewpoint, requiring instead critical dialogue that can test what we think and are aware of, and that can generate creative and imaginative responses to the wider environment.

Ethical heroes

If ethics is essentially embodied, not simply found in dusty books, we should be able to find examples of good embodiment, people who stand out as ethical heroes, and as such are worth emulating. Please note that heroes are not perfect. The ancient Greek myths were full of heroes who were flawed, such as Herakles (better known as Hercules), but they embodied key values or virtues. You will find several good examples of people and organisations such as Arthur Andersen, Anita Roddick and Johnson & Johnson throughout the book. These are people or organisations that have embodied responsibility and integrity. We would encourage you to reflect on your own ethical heroes.

PRACTISING ETHICS

Returning to the third aim, this book is the basis of a learning experience that aims to help you practise some of the core capacities we have noted above. Core to this are the key ethical tools of ethical theory – the ethical decision-making framework, ethical thinking, and ethical virtues, from responsibility to the moral imagination. These enable synoptic and mature thinking, which ultimately joins up how we think about and respond to the social and physical environment. Each of these tools requires practice and development, especially of responsibility.

Learning in the book is therefore based on reflective practice, and thus the idea of a learning cycle where we reflect on practice, the context of that practice, the underlying values and purposes used in such practice, and then how we can develop that practice in the light of those values.

Most of the chapters thus begin with practice or a history of practice and an analysis of the values and how they can be embodied or how there has been a failure to identify or embody them.

If you work through the different exercises and case studies, you will begin to develop the key aspects of responsibility and related capacities including:

- practice in knowing what you think, and what values you and your corporation hold and the capacity to question them
- practice in awareness of the social and physical environment, and the effect of your and your corporation's actions on them
- practice in giving an account of values and how they are embodied in practice
- practice in developing plans for shared responsibility to be put into practice.

The capacities associated with the practice of responsibility include critical thinking, synoptic thinking, practical wisdom (the capacity to reflect on the good), empathy (deeper awareness and understanding of the self, others and the wider environment), accountability, the capacity to plan and negotiate responsibility, and moral imagination (the capacity to see how the common good can be embodied in practice). The practice of these elements remains key in all different business contexts, from public organisations to NGOs to SMEs to large corporations.

Dotted around the text are boxes that invite you to practise one or more of these things. These include:

Scenario. This focuses on difficult decisions, where available options all have negative consequences, referred to as dilemmas.

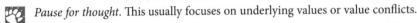 *Pause for thought.* This usually focuses on underlying values or value conflicts.

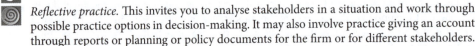 *Reflective practice.* This invites you to analyse stakeholders in a situation and work through possible practice options in decision-making. It may also involve practice giving an account through reports or planning or policy documents for the firm or for different stakeholders.

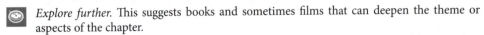 *Explore further.* This suggests books and sometimes films that can deepen the theme or aspects of the chapter.

There are also *Case studies.* These involve a detailed historical narrative, inviting you to reflect on synoptic thinking in the story – how all the different elements of ethical meaning are connected, or not. Again you may be asked to imagine yourself as part of that story. These exercises often require working with other students, or discovering, analysing and developing data related to the case.

ONLINE RESOURCES

- Lecturer's guide – practical advice on planning and delivering business ethics lectures, with feedback on in-text features
- PowerPoint slides – build and deliver your course around these ready-made lectures, ensuring complete coverage of the module
- Student's guide – practical advice for students with feedback on in-text features

For online resources, please visit **www.cipd.co.uk/orl**

TALKING ABOUT ETHICS

Given the increased concern for ethics in business it is clear that the more successful you become in business, the more you will be asked to give an account of your or your firm's view of ethics. Increasingly, these questions may even begin at job interviews, where firms want to see what ethical maturity is in evidence. As you work through this book, keep in mind how you will communicate your ethical position clearly and succinctly. In an interview, for example, you might be asked about the values of the corporation you want to join, what you think about them, and how they relate to the values you hold.

A SUMMARY OF HOW TO USE THIS BOOK

UNDERGRADUATES

- Identify the core ethical tools that are developed in the first chapters.
- Practise the tools in the different contexts the book focuses on.
- Consciously develop your ethical identity so that you can give an account of your ethics, personally and professionally, to colleagues, partners and stakeholders.

BUSINESS PEOPLE

In addition to the practice of the core ethical tools and the key modes of responsibility (relevant to all businesses great or small) the book gives particular examples of how to develop areas such as ethical codes and culture, management planning and reporting mechanisms. These elements can fit easily into professional strategic thinking and planning.

Key to all use of this book is that you look to take responsibility for ethics, its core values and practice. Too many cases show evidence of failed business organisations that have established codes and reporting mechanisms but without developing their ethical capacities, not least awareness and imagination. Ethics in business is lived, not paid lip-service, and business ethics in practice does make a difference.

ON THE EDGE

The striking cover of this book shows a polar bear on the edge of an ice-floe, focusing on the next step that will provide a pathway to survival.

It reminds us that humanity is on the edge, trying to work out how it will sustain its depleted environment, discovering pathways together.

As we write this book the world economy is on the edge of a second disaster that could affect millions of lives. The search for pathways there is not just about economic survival but about discovering ways that embody the responsibility absent in the crisis itself.

And, in a sense, ethics in business is always on the edge, shaping pathways which sustain meaning and purpose in an uncertain environment.

The tools and strengths that we point to in the book can contribute to shaping those pathways in practice.

Simon Robinson and Paul Dowson,
November 2011

CHAPTER 1

'Are we still the good guys?' – Introducing Ethics in Business

LEARNING OUTCOMES

When you have completed this chapter you will be able to:

- understand the misconceptions about ethics
- understand how ethics is practice-centred
- understand the history of business ethics and how it involves a dialogue between values and practice.

INTRODUCTION

'Are we still the good guys?' is a quote from Cormac McCarthy's book *The Road* (Vintage, 2007:65), which also features later in this chapter.

This chapter is intended to help you to begin to engage more with ethics, and place ethics in the context of professional reflective practice.

- It examines the case of David Sharp, introducing and contrasting the ethical challenge to individuals and to business.
- It explores the misconceptions about ethics, noting the practice-centred nature of ethics.
- It outlines professional reflective practice and how it relates to ethical value.
- And it sets out a brief history of business ethics, noting the implications of that history to the study and practice of ethics in business.

EVEREST ETHICS

CASE

In 2006 David Sharp returned to Everest, determined to conquer it. In 2003 and 2004 he had been part of unsuccessful attempts. The extent of Sharp's determination can be gauged by the fact that he lost several toes in his first attempt. The story of what happened to him in 2006 involves some speculation. It is believed that he did reach the top, climbing by himself and with a limited supply of oxygen. During the descent he ran out of oxygen, and eventually died from exhaustion and cold, while sheltering beneath a small outcrop on the crest of the north-east ridge. Sharp had collapsed while he was still clipped on to a fixed line used by climbers on that route, and he was just under 1 metre (3 feet) from it. Before he died, as many as 40 people passed by him. Most of these were members of two climbing teams from Himex, a company specialising in mountain ascents, and a following Turkish team. A few members of these teams did stop to ascertain his condition, and to attempt either to comfort him or help him in some way. Reports suggest that the first ones to do this stopped on their descent. Some, in their ascent claimed not have seen him. With the encumbrance of climbing gear and goggles even things close might be missed. Others suggest they thought that Sharp was in fact the corpse of an Indian climber who had died there in 1996, a well-known 'feature' of the climb. It would, however, have been diffcult for climbers not to realise that something was wrong given his proximity.

 PAUSE FOR THOUGHT

Each of the climbers had to make a decision as they unhooked themsleves from their safety line to go round Sharp and then rehook themselves. What would your decision have been? How would you have made that decision? When asked to account for your thinking and actions, how would you justify them?

Now compare your thinking with that of two of your student colleagues. Are you convinced with their argument? If not, why not?

Finally, listen to your colleagues' assessment of *your* arguments. Do they confirm your thoughts and feelings? Do they challenge your thinking in any way? If so, how?

There was international outrage about the decision to leave Sharp to die.

This was best expressed by Sir Edmund Hillary, one of the first two men to climb Everest, who argued that the culture of mutual care in the climbing community was being driven out by the combination of personal ambition in a high-risk pursuit and commercialisation. (For a 2003 interview with Hillary on the commercialisation of climbing Everest, visit http://news.bbc.co.uk/1/hi/world/south_asia/2938596.stm.)

Faced by a dying man, most of the climbers thought it was more important to get to the top of the mountain. They were acting under what has been called the 'bystander effect', by which individuals avoid getting involved and asking questions they don't want to know the answers to. McCoy (1983), referring to a similar case, argues that this can occur when ambitions to achieve an objective are such that they cloud ethical awareness. It is also argued that the highly successful commercial organisation Himex reinforced this. It was the firm's job to ensure that its customers achieved their ambition in safety – anything else was secondary.

Hillary's argument was amplified by the media (http://www.timesonline.co.uk/tol/life_and_style/article640130.ece?token=null&offset=12&page=2). Many journalists argued that a rescue could have been attempted had the Himex teams been stopped on the way up – if, in other words, the head of Himex, Russell Brice, and his team leaders had chosen not to give the customers what they had paid for.

In response, Brice argued that the proper thing to do was not to rescue Sharp. His argument asserted that any attempt to rescue him might have put his customers at risk. He prided himself on a strong safety record, having never lost a customer. Moreover, he calculated that rescue at the point of descent would not have been feasible. In any case, given the condition of the man, a rescue attempt would have been futile, and would have endangered up to 20 people.

REFLECTIVE PRACTICE

You are now down the mountain, several thousand feet below Sharp and in radio contact with the climbing group leaders. If you were Chief Executive Officer of Himex, what difference would it make to your decision? What would you do, and how would you account for your thinking and your actions?

Compare your thinking with that of your neighbour.

Is ethics in business the same as personal ethics? What are the differences? Do they change your view about what is right to do in this situation? If so, why?

Compare your thoughts with two other students', and assess each other's views.

From the response of Brice it becomes clear that there is a difference between personal and business ethics. The ethical choice of the individuals faced with Sharp was direct and immediate. The choice in one respect was simple: to do what one could or to walk on by. It could be argued, then, that the role of the business person was more complex, involving responsibility for the safety of several different stakeholders, and for a business and all who depended on it, not just the one man mutely appealing for help. The response of Hillary, of course, suggests otherwise. His argument is that there is a simple choice. You either do the right thing, respond to the dying man, or you do the business thing. By definition, he suggests, business avoids doing the right thing. It is primarily concerned with making money and will do whatever it takes to achieve that. The implication is either that business is value-neutral or that its objectives do not take account of ethical issues. The ethical issues are thus always secondary – something that you can attend to if you have the time and the resources.

We might already be able to hear the cynical laughter accompanying that old line, 'Business ethics? But isn't that an oxymoron (involving terms that are contradictory)?'

THE ETHICAL DIVIDE

At this point the business person must be careful. It is too easy to concede the ethical high ground and to say something like 'We can see the problems but just cannot afford to be ethical.' In the red corner we then have the champions of ethics – those who will tell us what ethics is really about. In the blue corner we have the business leaders who are suspicious of the ethical thinkers, and so of ethics. The job comes first.

Business ethics has to bridge this divide, often caused by how we view ethics. We therefore begin with an analysis of the underlying misconceptions about the meaning and practice of ethics.

CONCEPTIONS OF ETHICS

Preaching

Ethics is about a series of prescriptions, telling people what they should and should not do. Some argue that it is therefore wrong to try to teach ethics. Teaching would then be telling people what to think when the task of education should be to enable critical dialogue that develops independent thinking, or alternatively to simply train potential managers in practical skills.

Theorising

Ethicists, especially philosophers, do not know anything about the issues faced by people in business. As Vardy (1989: 196) puts it, they 'live in a secure and problem-free environment removed from business realities'. Lurking beneath this argument is a large gap between theory and practice. The ethicist is someone who will work in theoretical and even ideal terms; the business leader is someone who has to get his or her hands dirty on occasion.

Specialising

Ethics is a specialism. It involves having to learn a whole set of new ideas including handling complex concepts. In the light of that, business people simply do not have the time to get involved seriously. A variation of this is the argument in higher education that business ethics is itself a specialism, and not one essential to the practice or teaching of business. Business ethics might thus be at best an option in the curriculum.

Being kind

This is an argument that starts with the view that ethics is really about altruism, putting the other first. But, the argument goes, business cannot be about that – it has to be about the interest of the corporation, and without that self-centredness the business would not be sustainable. A well-known variation on this is Carr's (1996) argument that the business leader leaves his 'normal' ethics at the office door and enters into the equivalent of a game in which the rules are very different. Like poker, the 'game' requires competition, deception, and so on, and all the players understand this.

We now address each of these conceptions.

MISCONCEPTIONS

Ethics is not about preaching

Strictly speaking, ethics is the systematic study of how to behave in the right way and how we decide what is right in a situation and what is good overall. Business ethics is a form of applied ethics which focuses on decisions made and practice carried out in business. *Business ethics* involves the exploration of:

- the underlying ethical values of business, including those of any particular profession or position in business, such as accountancy or managers. It is important to note the different ethical perspectives that may be held by these different groups
- how any values might be embodied in the corporation. This includes the development of codes of ethics
- particular ethical perspectives/policies in areas such as corporate governance, corporate responsibility or workplace relationships
- underlying ethical theories that seek to explain the basis of what is ethically good. The study of ethical theory is sometimes referred to as *meta-ethics*
- underlying values, worldviews and different social and cultural contexts of the areas in which business operates. Any of these may affect our view of what is ethically right or wrong
- how to make ethical decisions as a part of everyday business decision-making in a variety of contexts
- how to make an ethical argument. Ethics is not just about asserting an opinion. Any argument has to be crafted and coherent if it is to justify actions. The better the business leader is at this, the better he or she will be at handling challenges
- how to develop the capacities to make such decisions. It is one thing to work out what to do, and another thing to have the capacity to put it into practice.

Ethics and morality: what is the difference?

Many philosophers hold that there is no difference between the two concepts, and use the terms 'ethics' and 'morality' interchangeably. Some, however, place a great emphasis on maintaining a distinction. Some philosophers, such as Nietzsche (1966), draw a contrast between morality as system of rules or moral obligations accepted as the cultural norm, and ethics as involving the freedom to work out for oneself what is right or wrong. Nietzsche sees morality as essentially imposed, encouraging a slave mentality, and ethics as the practice of free agency.

Grayling (2008) argues that ethics properly refers to 'either the organised philosophical study of the concepts and principles involved in systems of morality, or it is the set of principles, attitudes, aims and standards adopted by individuals or organisations by which they live and act'. In the first of these, ethics involves the systematic philosophical enquiry into principles or practices. The second sense involves the ethics of the organisation of which one is a part (including any ethical codes and culture).

In this book we use the terms 'morality' and 'ethics' interchangeably.

The importance of theory

One can understand the reluctance of some business leaders to get involved with academic ethicists. It is a particular form of a general suspicion of academics. The argument is, however, not well built. First, it first relies on the stereotype of the academic as someone only concerned with abstract ideas (see McCall Smith, 2003). In fact, academics are more and more concerned about practice, and perhaps above all about bringing critical dialogue to practice. That means dialogue which rigorously challenges both ideas and practice.

The second part of the argument involves a false division between theory and practice. Although it is possible to distinguish theory from practice, the term 'theory' describes a belief or principle that guides action or assists comprehension or judgement, or describes a set of statements or principles devised to explain a group of facts or phenomena. In other words, theory is devised to make sense of practice, experience or phenomena. The root of the word is an ancient Greek verb meaning 'to see'. The test of any theory, then, is that it should help you make sense of practice.

It may be objected that practitioners do not spend much time on ethical theory. But that is not entirely true. Brice, the CEO of Himex, *was* making an ethical argument. He believed that it was important to measure outcomes The issue was not about whether it was ethical, but rather about whether it was *good* ethics – whether he could justify his ethical position, and if so, how. Not only was he making an ethical argument about the right thing to do, he was couching that ethical argument in the light of a particular ethical theory, a way of thinking about what is good. For him, an ethical decision involved trying to maximise the good for the most people on the north face of Everest – something that involved calculating the risks to any rescue party (see Chapter 2). It is also about having the courage to make a decision based on this approach.

Hillary's and Brice's positions were simply different views about ethics. Hillary was arguing that ethics is built on principle – in this case, the principle of saving life. Brice was arguing that ethics is about consequences and how any action affects all the people involved. In this sense the business person cannot avoid being drawn into the ethical debate. Someone will always ask for an account of how decisions have been taken. So rather than avoid theory, the business person should be at home with the ideas and know how to use them well.

Philosophical perspective

The gap between theory and practice parallels that between intellect and practical skills. We tend to assume that intellect is not related to practice.

So what is the intellect, and do you have one?

Aristotle, philosopher of ancient Greece (384–322 BCE), saw the intellect as connected directly to practice. He argued therefore that there were five intellectual virtues or capacities (Aristotle 2004):

- scientific knowledge (*epistēmè*), or empirical understanding
- artistic or technical knowledge (*technè*), knowledge of how to make or do things
- intuitive reason (*nous*), the capacity to discern first principles of understanding, sometimes referred to as common sense
- practical wisdom (*phronēsis*), the capacity to reflect on the good and act in accordance with that
- philosophical wisdom (*sophia*), a combination of intuitive and scientific knowledge.

Ethical thinking as part of everyday life

It is easy to imagine that ethical thinking is so highly specialised that we rarely get involved in it, or that we have to develop highly specialised knowledge.

 PAUSE FOR THOUGHT

Have you taken an ethical decision in the last 24 hours? If so, what did it involve?

Did you realise that you were taking an ethical decision?

How often do you take ethical decisions?

The truth is that we are involved in ethical thinking at several points in our normal day. When your child demands a larger portion of pudding, for example, your response will begin to work out why he shouldn't have so much. You might argue that such large portions will make him greedy, and so affect both his character and his weight. You might argue that the guiding principle of the family is equality – you all get the same portion, young or old. This then sparks off an ethical debate about the nature and application of justice. Is it really fair to give Grandma the same portion as a growing boy who needs more energy?

The subsequent dialogue can then begin to establish that 'This is how and why we do these things in this family.' Ideas like justice, fairness and freedom are common in day-to-day dialogue, often without our realising that these are ethical values that help us to decide what is right or wrong – not unlike Monsieur Jourdain in the comedy play *Le bourgeois gentilhomme* by Molière (2007). In the play, M. Jourdain comes into money and wants to learn to be a 'gentleman'. He is told by his philosophy teacher that he must learn the skill of speaking prose if he is to achieve this. The word 'prose' is new to him, but when he begins to practise it, he realises that he has been speaking it all his life.

Such ethical values are also commonly used in many organisations, not least in universities (see *Reflective practice: Student values* below). Consider first what the core ethical values of higher education are.

REFLECTIVE PRACTICE

Student values

Being part of higher education involves core ethical issues and values, including:

- the problem of plagiarism, a word that in English is derived from a late Latin noun meaning 'kidnapping'. It is wrong to use someone else's ideas or words as if they are yours

- fairness in marking. There are many efforts to ensure that student assignments are fairly marked, including anonymising scripts

- fair recruitment. How do we decide between accepting students for university who have similar qualifications?

- ethics in research. For instance, are research participants able to give informed consent to their involvement?

What other ethical issues or values are important for the student? How are they discussed in your institution, and where are they referred to the institution's website?

  If you are based in a business workplace, what are the values that are part of your institution? Is it important for your business to show fairness to employees? How are such values talked about or expressed in workplace conversation?

Without concern for fairness, academic freedom and other values, the very project of higher education would collapse. Applied ethics are thus not extra to the job of universities: they are rather at its heart. The point is that we are not always aware that we are thinking about and practising ethics. The issue then is not whether we think about ethics but rather how best we may think ethically. This means being clear and being able to justify the view of ethics that we have. Chapter 2 looks at the underlying theories of ethics, and Chapter 3 looks at how we make ethical decisions and how we think/argue ethically. Much of this is about clear thinking.

Specialism

The idea that business ethics is a specialism that is somehow sealed off from other academic and practical areas is simply false. As noted above, handling ethical ideas is part of everyday life. Actively reflecting on ethics and how we practise it simply helps us to do it better and to integrate it more effectively into everyday life. Core to this activity is making connections around ideas, values and practice. Far from being a narrow sub-discipline, or focused purely in narrow ethical dilemmas (ethical challenges that cannot be easily resolved), business ethics connects to many different but related areas, including:

- different views of what ethics means, and what are important underlying values
- different roles and purposes that may have particular perspectives on ethics – for example, manager and accountant, engineer and manager, finance director and chairman of the board
- related ideas, including corporate social responsibility, health and safety, diversity.

Throughout this book we will be making connections between ethics and these different areas.

Being kind

Paying attention to ethics is not the same thing as demanding that business be altruistic (focused primarily on the interest of others). Some would argue that this should be the case and that business ought to transfer from a paradigm focused on shareholder value to one that is focused on altruism. However, much of ethics is about self-care and sustainability. Without self-care it is hard to see how any concern for others can be fulfilled. Self-interest as such is not unethical. The issue is about what is proper concern for business and how self-care can be balanced with wider care, for society and the environment. The debate over this runs throughout this book.

Reasons for being ethical

This balance is reflected in the different reasons that support attention to ethics, based in self-interest, mutual interest and the common good.

Self-interest
- The management of reputation. Effective business depends upon trust. Trust is built through the practice of integrity (see Chapter 6). This in turn can minimise external regulation.
- Ethical focus can actually enable greater awareness and more effective decision-making (see Chapter 3).
- Attention to purpose, justice and values can engender a more motivated and creative workforce (see Chapter 7).
- Be sure your sin will find you out (Numbers 32:23). This comes from the book of Numbers in the Old Testament and is part of the Jewish Wisdom tradition. In other words, it is based on practical wisdom. It is easy to imagine that we are invisible and that we cannot be seen. Hence, Plato's story of the ring of Gyges (Plato, 2007). Gyges is a shepherd who discovers a ring that makes him invisible. If you are invisible, do you have to be good? The answer is twofold. First, you are not invisible to yourself. This about living with yourself and thus about integrity (see Chapter 6). As Frasier (radio psychiatrist in the TV comedy show of the same name) says, 'Ethics is about what you do when nobody is looking' (see Frasier, 'A word to the wise guy', http://www.youtube.com/watch?v=xDaSFqHfkao). Second, the truth is that we operate in a world where we are seen by somebody – if not now, then later. This is true most of all in relation to our IT-dominated environment. As we shall see, most of the corporate ethical disasters, such as Enron, involved firms assuming that their practices would not be seen.

Mutual interest
- Business is part of a complex network of stakeholders with mutual interests, accountability and values. It is in the interest of all to develop ethics and responsibility together. There is an argument that developing ethical meaning and practice across the industry, or with wider stakeholders, improves ethics and the effectiveness of the corporation.
- Stakeholders, not least political and non-governmental organisations (NGOs), can cause negative pressure that could affect the firm's output (see Chapter 11).

The common good
- Business relates to a wider environment that it shares responsibility for with other groups, professional and voluntary (Chapters 6 onwards). The business is seen here as a part of its community and the wider world. It is responsible for its effects on that world, and in one sense is the local and global citizen. As such it must be aware of any negative effects of its practices *and* of any positive effects it might have.
- Responsibility is also shared for the future (see Chapter 14).

The name of the game

All of these considerations make the idea that business can operate a set of rules, like a game, that do not relate to wider ethical values or concerns hard to sustain. Within business there are some professions which, far from relying on the poker rules of Carr noted above, are actually about transparency. Accountancy, for instance, aims to give a true account of the financial situation, however bad it is, and whatever pressure there is. Marketing and PR also have professional bodies who bring with them ethical codes. All of these professions are accompanied by a much wider ethical perspective that holds business practice to account. This includes, as stakeholders, their own professional bodies. In the wider global context too, it is clear that business cannot cocoon itself around narrowly defined rules of a game. Business is connected with the wider global context and culture (see Chapter 2). Faced by a supply chain in which there is an abuse of human rights, the business leader has to decide what to do and has to justify his or her action (see Chapter 10). In the light of the glare of the media and the concern of the stakeholders it becomes difficult to suggest that ethics do not apply to business.

At the least this requires attention to ethics in business. In the debate about the fate of David Sharp, Hillary was trying to assert his view of ethics over the business leader's. At that point, the very last thing the business leader could do was to let go of the ethical debate and concede a lack of ethics. Who is going to trust a manager who cannot justify his or her practice ethically?

INTEGRATING ETHICS IN A COMPLEX AND PLURAL BUSINESS WORLD

Most of the discussions around business ethics assume a clarity about what business actually is. The problem is that any large business is not simple. It is complex and involves a number of different stakeholders (people and groups that have an interest in the business), including the different professions such as accountancy and the communication professions. This means that business ethics is not focused in one group or role, as compared to medical ethics, which is focused in the doctor, or nursing ethics. Business ethics involves different professional ethics, corporate ethics, and in some cases wider social and environmental ethics. Being in business, then, demands being able to handle a critical conversation between the different ethical perspectives.

Sometimes this involves long-term planning to include all the different perspectives (Armstrong *et al*, 1999). Sometimes the ethical challenge is addressed at your role as a professional within a business. Sometimes you are simply faced with a dilemma. In the Challenger case (see Chapter 8) it involved conflict between engineers, managers and political advisers. Sometimes the ethical challenge asks for an individual response. More often it calls for a critical conversation with colleagues, stakeholders or board members.

Effective business ethics, then, provides the awareness, capacities and skills to handle these conversations and decisions. Inevitably, this means that ethics is not simply about individual rational decision-making. It is also more holistic, bringing together practice, relationships, ideas (theory) and values (often built around identity). Thus, at the heart of ethics is the integration of these dimensions. One of the most useful integrative ideas for the professional has been Schön's concept of reflective practice.

REFLECTIVE PRACTICE

The process of reflective practice can be best seen as a recurring learning cycle involving several phases, summed up by Kolb's learning circle (Kolb, 1984):

- *articulation* of a narrative in response to experience
- *reflection* on and *testing* of its meaning
- *development* of the meaning
- *response*, leading to a new experience.

Donald Schön (1983) develops this further. He famously argued against a simplistic view of professional development. Much of the professional education of the old school assumed that there was a standard body of knowledge that would be learned in professional schools. This knowledge would be applied to a range of issues. The old view of the medical profession, for instance, was one of paternalistic doctors applying their expertise without consulting the patient. The problem with this approach is that:

- it can encourage a view of professional practice which is largely about achieving targets
- it can lead to the attempt to apply knowledge in an unreflective way, and thus to impose expertise.

Schön noted, through observation of a range of different professions, that in practice there was a response which led not to an imposition of knowledge but rather a 'reflective conversation with the situation'.

What emerged was a process like this:

- an analysis of the situation in order to work out what the problem might be and what issues are involved
- 'appreciative' or value systems that help to find significant meaning in the situation
- overarching theories that might provide further meaning
- an understanding of the professional's own role in the situation, both its limits and its opportunities
- the ability to learn from 'talkback', involving reflective conversation about the situation
- the treatment of clients by the professional as reflective practitioners.

In a sense Schön is simply developing the idea of what it is to be a professional in any context, including business and related professions. A professional in this sense is someone who knows what he or she is doing, develops meaning and learns in relation to practice, and understands how he or she affects clients and the wider community, including the profession.

This partly builds on the work of Illich (1977), who questioned the role of the professional in society, not least in the way that society has become dependent upon professions such as doctors. Such dependence was negative, partly because it led to the individual not taking responsibility and partly because, through lack of awareness, it led to personal and public disasters. In medicine this led to iatrogenic illness (illness caused by the doctor) and very public disasters such as the Alder Hey case (news.bbc.co.uk/2/hi/1136723.stm) in which organs were stripped from dead babies for research without the consent of the parents.

Schön concludes that the technical skill of the professional could not and should not be exercised without taking into account the relational context.

Gibbs (1988) provides another simple framework that takes account of the emotions as well as ideas in reflection:

- *Description*: what happened?
- *Feelings*: how did you feel about the situation?
- *Evaluation*: what was good or bad about the situation?
- *Analysis*: what sense can you make of the situation?
- *Conclusion*: what else could you have done?
- *Action plan*: if this arose again, what would you do?

Schön and Gibbs do not systematically draw out the ethical dimensions of or values behind reflective practice. However, two things are clear. First, the reflective practice framework is one that applies to all disciplines associated with professional practice. It is especially associated with the development of best practice. Second, there are strong underlying ethical values in reflective practice. These include:

- the person's taking responsibility for his or her own ideas and values, and how they relate to practice
- responsiveness to the situation, enabling dialogue with the client and stakeholders
- awareness of the professional's role and limitations
- respecting the autonomy of the client
- the value of continued learning.

Each of these can be seen as an ethical value, of importance in determining the right action. The first two involve key aspects of responsibility, and these are examined in Chapter 4. The third is critical to the development of leadership, examined in Chapter 5. The fourth is seen by many as the core ethical value, and we return to that throughout the book. The fifth is both ethical and functional. It is hard to take the best decisions if you are not up to date with the issues. This suggests that an ethical business person will also be the most competent.

Reflective practice, then, connects directly to ethical decision-making, awareness of the situation, understanding core values and any conflicts, and working through options and planning (see Chapter 3).

BUSINESS ETHICS: A HISTORY

De George (2005) argues that the history of business ethics is made up of three aspects: ethics in business, the history of the discipline of business ethics, and what has become known as the business ethics movement.

ETHICS IN BUSINESS

Reflections on rules about ethics in business have been around for a long time. The Code of Hammurabi (1700s BC) prescribes prices and tariffs, and sets down rules of commerce and harsh penalties for non-compliance (Goodin, 1985). Aristotle (2000) focuses on commercial relationships in the context of household management. He reflects on matters of justice in commerce and trade, and condemns usury (charging high interest on borrowed money), greed and the pursuit of wealth for its own sake. Many of Aristotle's views are taken up by Aquinas, although the latter accepts the possibility of charging interest for a good end. Trade and business were also central to the Reformation, which was responsible for the development of a work ethic tied to religion. Ethical meaning and the purpose of business in particular were central to business practice.

During the Enlightenment this intimate connection between business and ethics began to loosen. The focus now moved to economics, the basis of the market (Smith, 1993; Locke, 1980) and the development of capitalism. In turn this was critiqued by Marx (2008). At this point business was not perceived to be independent of the market. Business *per se* was not the focus of ethical reflection, which was rather the context of business.

The later twentieth century then saw more religious critique of business, not least on the part of the Roman Catholic Church (John Paul II, 1981, 1991). It was not capitalism as such that was the subject of the critique, for the intention was more to argue the importance of operating this system in a way that promoted the common good.

In the twenty-first century these debates have taken on a global dimension. Increased globalisation has shown that business is often connected intimately to the market but also to the global political context of the market. Thus, cases such as Shell in the Niger Delta are as much about social, political or environmental ethics as about business ethics *per se*. Such high-level cases are parallelled by domestic cases such as Enron in which the kind of reflections that Aristotle makes are shown not to be out of date.

Ethics in business is, then, alive, controversial and contentious. It cannot be ignored.

BUSINESS ETHICS AS AN ACADEMIC DISCIPLINE

Into this boiling-pot business ethics has entered as an academic discipline.

It began to emerge in the 1960s, partly as a result of the strong wave of social ethics in the USA and the UK. This led to a strong critique of politics and any centres of power that might reinforce injustice. Social theology and philosophy were thus increasingly involved in this area (see Stackhouse *et al*, 1995). The area did not begin to take shape with applied ethics courses analogous to medical ethics, however, until the incursion of philosophers into the field. This led to the first conferences in business ethics and the development of ethics networks in Europe and in the USA (the European Business Ethics Network, the Institute of Business Ethics and the Society of Business Ethics).

As the field grew, it became very different from general courses on society and business, providing an explicit ethical framework for business. At the same time its reception by business itself was cool (Vardy, 1989). This contrasted sharply with the medical profession who embraced the concern for professional ethics as a key part of what it meant to be a profession. As a result, competence in ethical thinking was deemed to be central to professional practice. In one medical school in the UK (the University of Leeds) in the 1990s, ethics was therefore fully integrated into the teaching, and involved the first lecture for medical students on ethics. Teaching was focused on combined input from medical practitioners and philosophers, and the medical practitioners took pride in developing an ethical competence (see Inter-disciplinary Ethics Applied Centre, www.idea.leeds.ac.uk).

There was a considerable increase in business ethics courses, often focused on business schools, not least at Harvard, and in business ethics journals. It did not, however, receive the same input from practitioners as did medical ethics, in which medical academics and practitioners alike would write in journals and be involved in teaching. The business world often viewed philosophers and theologians as lacking awareness of the reality of business and as groups who were essentially critical of business (Vardy, 1989).

This debate has heightened in the twenty-first century, not least around the relationship between business schools and business and about the professional identity of business. Ghoshal (2005) argued that business, as taught in business school, was too focused on science and on technique and not enough on value. Khurana and Nohria (2008) argued that management should be like a 'true profession', such as medicine and law. A true profession, it is argued, is built on core values such as service (see Chapter 8).

THE BUSINESS ETHICS MOVEMENT

The third element that De George argues for involves the practical development in corporations of ways of articulating ethical values and embodying ethical practice. This has included the development of social responsibility policies, corporate ethics codes, ethics training programmes, ethics committees and officers, and the inculcation of an ethical culture within the firm. The latter is often characterised as a twentieth-century phenomenon, although examples such as the Quaker movement occurred much earlier (Cadbury, 2010). One example of the movement in the mid-twentieth century is Scott Bader, who gifted his company to his employees in 1951. Here ethics, with ideas such as justice, fairness and equality, was worked through in terms of democracy. Another example, from 1943, was the development of manufacturers Johnson & Johnson's 'credo', a statement of belief that provided the basis for an ethical culture involving regular reflection on codes and practice.

From the 1960s there was a gradual development of business ethics across business in response to media concern, public pressure, organisations' own view of ethics, and legislation. Public pressure, for instance, was expressed through the economic boycott on Nestlé goods in response to the corporation's marketing of baby-milk substitute in developing countries (see Chapter 13). Public pressure was fuelled by media exposés and led to the development of a code of practice agreed by the wider industry and developed by the World Health Organisation.

Wider concerns about equality and safety led to legislation both in the USA and the UK, and forced human resources and management to develop policies around discrimination, equal opportunity, and equal pay. Environmental and human rights legislation focused business further on areas that had never been seen as part of its concern, from being responsible for discharge of effluent (see Chapter 14) to respecting religious rights at work (see Chapter 7).

All of these areas confirmed that business ethics was a matter of continued dialogue and debate: businesses were continually being challenged by social issues. Often the debate was about who should regulate – in other words, who should decide on matters of value and practice and ensure compliance. This led to the development of legislation in several other areas such as the oil, chemical and the defence industries (see Chapters 12 and 14).

The result was increased effort from most large companies to incorporate into their organisations the basic ethical structures, from ethical committees to corporate ethics officers, to ethics training programmes and the means of enabling whistleblowing (informing managers of unethical or illegal practice).

All of this debate inevitably reinforced the global context of business ethics, making it difficult to restrict ethics simply to the workplace or work projects. Work projects by definition involve social and environmental contexts, and thus questions of how social ethics relate to business ethics. So, for instance, legislation was developed in the 1970s to prevent bribery and corruption in foreign dealings (see Chapter 13), leading to agreements among the Organisation for Economic Co-operation and Development (OECD) countries.

In the case of South Africa, this led to companies becoming actively involved in working against the repressive regime. The Sullivan Principles (see Chapter 12) were developed as a guideline for how companies might take affirmative action against apartheid legislation and to lobby the South African government for change. Public pressure was on these firms to withdraw from South Africa, and taking on the Sullivan Principles provided a means of both doing business and acknowledging the ethical problems of doing business in this context. In all this the companies became a political 'player'.

The global focus has been further sustained by the development of several global bodies who have formed voluntary codes in relation to developing and monitoring business ethics (see Chapter 13). These include the Caux Round Table (www.cauxroundtable.org) and the United Nations Global Compact (http://www.unglobalcompact.org/). An off-shoot of the Compact and the European Foundation for Management Development (EFMD) has been the Globally Responsible Leadership Initiative (www.grli.com) which focuses on developing leadership responsibility with business and business schools.

More recently a series of scandals involving, notably, Enron, Arthur Andersen, WorldCom and several organisations in the 2007/8 credit crisis have led to more legislation. In the USA the Sarbanes-Oxley Act of 2002, for instance, involves action such as a requirement that the CEO and CFO certify the fairness and accuracy of corporate financial statements (with criminal penalties for deliberate violations). It also requires a code of ethics for the corporation's senior financial officers, and increased public disclosure. Response to the firms involved in the credit crisis still has to be worked through (see Chapter 4). These and the global projects have focused more and more on the ethical category of responsibility. Self-monitoring of adherence to a corporation's stated principles and self-adopted standards is becoming more common, and some companies have voluntarily adopted monitoring of their practices, policies and plants by independent auditors. At its heart is the idea of the 'triple bottom line', involving financial, social and environmental corporate reporting. Other popular reporting mechanisms include corporate environmental sustainability reports and social audits, often part of indices that compare how different firms are operating. The focus on responsibility has led to stakeholders becoming more involved in the debate, from those involved in the supply chain to the shareholders (see Chapter 10).

THE WIDER CONTEXT OF ETHICS: HAVE WE LOST THE COMPASS?

All of these developments around business ethics have taken place in a wider conversation about ethics in general. At one level this has continued in academic disciplines such as philosophy and theology for well over two millennia. Something of this is discussed in the next two chapters where we look at the foundations of ethics.

There is also the wider context of how society has viewed and practised ethics, and this has involved real changes. Some people argue that Western society as a whole has lost any clear sense of ethical meaning. They argue that there has been a social breakdown:

- a breakdown of any shared sense of moral meaning and, in particular, adherence to the so-called 'grand narratives' of the last century and before. These are the 'stories' which claimed some universal truth and which influence whole generations (Lyotard, 1979). For example, in England before World War I there were the grand narratives of the Empire and Christianity. The first of these saw the Empire as a force for good, both civilising the world and enabling technological progress. Christianity, especially focused in the Church of England, was seen as the basis for most social meaning and support. Each Church of England parish thus looked after the parishioners from birth, through marriage, to death. The war and ensuing economic and health crises broke down those set views

- a breakdown of patterns of behaviour and institutions such as marriage and the family, caused partly by increased wealth and mobility, and changes in cultural attitudes. This has led to a massive increase in the divorce rate, an increase in cohabitation rather than marriage, and the increasing acceptance legally and culturally of single-sex partnerships
- a greater awareness of cultural and religious diversity within society, caused by increased migration and global awareness (Markham, 1999). This has led to a greater acceptance of ethical plurality – ie that ethical meaning is based in many different cultures and can lead to very different practices
- a greater acceptance of a liberal view of ethics. Such a view argues that one can do anything so long as it does not affect another negatively. There is a strong emphasis in this on the autonomy of the individual. It means that the individual person has the right to govern himself or herself and to work out his or her own value and belief systems (Perry, 1992).

This can easily lead to *ethical relativism* – the acceptance that there is no formal agreement about ethics. It is based either in the authorship of the individual or in one the many different cultures or communities in society. The only thing that binds that together then becomes an agreement to tolerate the different views – unless, that is, they lead to the harm of another.

In respect of formal ethics, this has all led to several things. Firstly, there was a move against any foundations for ethics. One simply worked things out for oneself. Secondly, in applied and professional ethics especially, there was a focus not upon foundations or underlying meaning but rather on ethical problems. The ethical dilemma was a puzzle that had to be solved, and this meant developing the tools to solve it. Ethics became a case-centred technical exercise.

So, from the certainty and uniformity of ethics based in power and religion, ethics had swung to quite the opposite pole, where the freedom of the individual to work out one's own ethical view point was paramount – and in applied and professional ethics the focus was on the working of that out.

Traditionalists see this as the loss of an ethical compass. Those who advocate the freedom to find one's own ethical meaning see it as the gaining of a compass that is properly used by the individual. The first of these accuses the freedom 'party' of basing ethics simply on desire, with no rigorous thinking. The freedom party accuses traditionalists of simply imposing ethical meaning. Famously, Nietzsche (1966) argued that this traditional view was an ethics of 'the herd' – that is, an ethics where no one thinks for himself or herself.

 PAUSE FOR THOUGHT

The changes in how we think ethically have led some to argue that we are less ethical than we used to be (see Trevino and Brown, 2004).

Do you think that is the case? If you do, where is the evidence?

IMPLICATIONS OF THE HISTORY

The brief history of business and wider ethics shows several things:

- Business ethics in its widest sense is well established. More people and groups are debating this and developing explicit and systematic practice than ever before.
- Business ethics involves ongoing dialogue between the three areas of De George's history. They sum up practice, value and meaning, all of which have to be worked on. As De George (2005) puts it, 'It is a vibrant, complex enterprise developing on many levels, with the three strands I've mentioned intertwining in complex, dynamic and fascinating ways.' This also means that business ethics will always involve a diversity of very different perspectives and narratives. It thus involves critical challenge, and constant reflection and development.
- Business ethics has to be explicit – it cannot be simply assumed. Firstly, by being explicit it looks to ensure that there is some sense of shared understanding across business, industry, stakeholders and the wider environment. Secondly, we have to know when we have crossed the line (see the case of the MPs' expenses below). Old certainties may have changed in what is called the post-modern era, such that the old compass does not appear to work. Nonetheless, there is need for an ethical map. Ethics is about making a map, and much of this book is about helping to develop the tools of map-making.
- Involved in such ethics is also ambiguity. In the Sharp case, none of the views was wholly right or good. Brice was concerned about both profit and people. Hillary championed both care and risk. Even strong ethical ideas, such as love, are not always good. People have done bad things in the name of love.
- Business ethics cannot be confined to a narrow area of expertise, and is not separate from general decision-making. Ethics is therefore connected to the development of management, strategy, human resources, leadership and all aspects of business, both in response to explicit dilemmas and in recognition and development of values at the centre of any practice.

CONCLUSIONS: CROSSING THE LINE

As the Sharp case showed, it is often difficult to know what you would do until you are faced by a situation, and there is a sense in which we never feel quite ready for that kind of challenge. This raises two questions:

- How can we be 'ready' to respond ethically?
- How can we develop a sense of ethics in the long term, not just when faced by an immediate or extreme challenge?

The two, of course, are connected. Neither Hillary's nor Brice's response to Sharp came out of the ethical blue. On the contrary, they both came out of a deep sense of values, and as such they both came out of a value narrative – the story that we tell to show what our ethical understanding is.

The value narrative of any person or organisation shows the journey taken. For Brice and Hillary everything depended not upon the immediate dilemma they were faced with but rather a series of decisions that preceded it. Hillary looks back to time of a climbing community of care. But where is the evidence for that, and where were the questions to remind climbers of it? Was there a written code? Was there a professional body? It may just be that this was the real ethical problem – that everyone assumed that there was a high ethics of care on the mountain but nobody had taken responsibility for maintaining it. The story of the journey was unclear.

As for Brice, how did all his thinking connect to the values and mission of his business? He clearly had a concern for safety on the mountain, and a good record. So how did those examples differ from the response to Sharp? Had there been a movement away from a concern for the safety of all on the mountain, to just the safety of his clients? If so, how might that have happened? What had his ethical journey involved?

There were many ethical questions to be asked in both these narratives well before that most difficult question asked by the presence of Sharp. This suggests that it is precisely the asking of those questions as part of the ongoing practice of any organisation that is important. Asking questions is core to the book *The Road*.

Are we still the good guys?

In Cormac McCarthy's book *The Road*, now a DVD, a man and his son are on a journey to the south of the USA. It is a time of chaos after a nuclear disaster, and they hope that the south will provide safety. Along the way the boy asks his father, 'Are we still the good guys?' The father is clear that they are, and that for him this involves defending his son against some very scary people. 'This is what good guys do.' But does that involve threatening or killing an old man who they meet? Does it involve abandoning others who are in danger? The story shows how things can change quickly, and that without noticing it the ethical line can be crossed, if the question is not asked. This is what the book means by the importance of 'carrying the fire'.

 The Road (2010) DVD, Icon Home Entertainment: http://www.youtube.com/watch?v=JaYvISSTyG4&feature=related

---

Many of the ethical 'disasters' in the first decade of the twenty-first century were characterised by the lack of awareness about when the ethical line was crossed. Many Members of Parliament, for instance, were initially not clear what line they had crossed when the expenses scandal was revealed by the *Daily Telegraph* (2010) ('MPs' expenses: Our MPs still aren't getting the message', *Daily Telegraph*, 5 February 2010).

The most recent example of this is the hacking scandal in the UK newspaper the *News of the World*.

CASE

THE END OF THE *WORLD*

The *News of the World* was closed down in July 2011 following revelations that stories were obtained through phone hacking, including the phones of murder victim Milly Dowler and victims of the 7/7 London bombings. (http://www.ctv.ca/CTVNews/TopStories/20110709/ news-of-the-world-reporters-readies-last-edition-110709/.)

Phone hacking is illegal under the Regulation of Investigatory Powers Act, 2000. The negative response of the public when it was used in situations involving vulnerable victims was massive, leading directly to the closure of the paper.

The response of leaders and managers involved with the *News of the World* was one of shock. Although stories about phone hacking had been around in 2006 and 2009, the assumption had been that these involved one or two rotten apples

and these had been dealt with. As Rupert Murdoch (CEO of News International, the parent company of the *News of the World*) is quoted as saying (10 October 2010), 'We have very, very strict rules. There was one incident more than five years ago. The person who bought the bugged conversation was immediately fired. If anything was to come to light – and we have challenged those people who have made allegations to provide evidence – we would take immediate action' (http://image.guardian. co.uk/sys-files/Guardian/documents/2011/07/21/hackingtimelinegraphic.pdf).

The *News of the World* editors and staff were also very clear that the ethics of the paper were of the highest. Indeed, these were informed by the professional ethics of journalism, to reveal the truth in the public interest. Thus, the final edition of the *News of the World* was made up largely of headlines of campaigns they had run, not least with respect to justice and paedophiles (http://www.bbc.co.uk/news/magazine-14098482).

At the time of writing, the case is ongoing: various formal inquires are about to begin around police corruption and journalistic ethics. Many of the questions are about the media industry and how it was run.

Questions

1 When did the *News of the World* cross the ethical line?

2 When did the senior management realise that a line had been crossed?

3 Why did it take several years for the management to realise it?

4 How did managers believe they had drawn the line?

5 What was the ethical line that they crossed? What is wrong with hacking, and why?

6 If you had been the CEO of News International or *News of the World*, how would you have drawn the line?

7 How would you have made sure it was not crossed?

As the inquiries into the events at the *News of the World* continue, begin to build up answers to these questions.

This case shows how difficult it can be to establish ethics in any large business. Did the ethical rules provide a clear line for all in the business? What was the ethical identity of the *News of the World*? It might be argued that it was concerned less about truth and more about headlines that would sell the paper. The focus was therefore increasingly on celebrity scandal.

There was little attempt to question practices on the ground. In contrast to the rotten apples argument, there is increasing evidence that phone hacking and payment to police had become normalised as a means of obtaining the necessary headlines. The contrast of such normalised behaviour with the assertion of ethical rules suggests that there was no mechanism within the business for questioning or monitoring the values or practices of the organisation. So it would be perfectly possible for an editor to say that he or she did not actually commission any phone hacking, but for a phone hacking culture to develop.

The next three chapters begin look at how business can develop the ethical tools that ensure that the ethical questions are asked and ethical practice is monitored. First we examine normative ethical theory and the worldviews that inform that. Then we look at ethical decision-making and the ways in which ethical practice is developed and sustained. Thereafter we look at the ethical environment and how the responsibility for that environment can be fulfilled individually and collectively.

REFERENCES

ARISTOTLE (2000) *Politics*. London: Penguin Classics.

ARISTOTLE (2004) *The Nichomachean Ethics*. Translated by Barnes, J. and Thomson, J. A. K. London: Penguin Classics.

ARMSTRONG, J., DIXON, J. R. and ROBINSON, S. (1999) *The Decision-Makers: Ethics for engineers*. London: Thomas Telford.

BIRCH, S. and ALLEN, N. (2010) 'How honest do politicians need to be?', *The Political Quarterly*, 81(1): 49–56.

CADBURY, D. (2010) *Chocolate Wars*. London: Harper.

CARR, A. Z. (1996) 'Is business bluffing ethical?', in Rae, S. B. and Wong, K. I. (eds) *Beyond Integrity: A Judeo-Christian approach*. Grand Rapids, MI: Zondervan: 55–62.

DE GEORGE, R. T. (2005) *A History of Business Ethics*. Markkula Center for Applied Ethics, Santa Clara University. Available at: http://www.scu.edu/ethics/practicing/ focusareas/ business/conference/presentations/business-ethics-history.html.

GIBBS, G. (1988) *Learning by Doing: A guide to teaching and learning methods*. London: F.E.U.

GHOSHAL, S. (2005) 'Bad management theories are destroying good management practices', *Academy of Management Learning and Education*, 4(1): 75–91.

GOODIN, R. E. (1985) *Protecting the Vulnerable*. Chicago: Chicago University Press.

GRAYLING, A. C. (2008) 'Is there a real difference between the words "moral" and "ethical"?', *Prospect Magazine*, 29 June.

ILLICH, I. (ed.) (1977) *Disabling Professions*. London: Marion Boyars.

JOHN PAUL II (1981) *Laborem Exercens*. Rome: Vatican Press.

JOHN PAUL II (1991) *Cenesimus Annus*. Rome: Vatican Press.

KHURANA, R. and NOHRIA, N. (2008) 'It's time to make management a true profession', *Harvard Business Review*, 86(10): 70–7.

KOLB, D.A. (1984) *Experiential Learning: Experience as a source of learning and development*. Upper Saddle River, NJ: Prentice Hall.

LOCKE, J. (1980) *Second Treatise of Government*. London: Hackett.

LYOTARD, J. F. (1979) *The Postmodern Condition*. Manchester: Manchester University Press.

McCALL SMITH, A. (2003) *Portuguese Irregular Verbs*. London: Polygon.

McCARTHY, C. (2007) *The Road*. London: Vintage.

McCOY, B. H. (1983) 'The parable of the sadhu', *Harvard Business Review*, 61(5): 103–8.

MARKHAM, I. (1999) *Plurality and Christian Ethics*. Cambridge: Cambridge University Press.

MARX, K. (2008) *Capital*. Oxford: Oxford University Press.

MOLIÈRE (2007) *Le bourgeois gentilhomme*. Paris: Larousse.

NIETZSCHE, F. W. (1966) *Beyond Good and Evil*. Translated by Kaufmann, W. New York: Vintage.

PERRY, M. (1992) *Gods Within*. London: SPCK.

PLATO (2007) *The Republic*. London: Penguin.

SCHÖN, D. (1983) *The Reflective Practitioner*. New York: Basic Books.

SMITH, A. (1993) *An Inquiry into the Nature and Causes of the Wealth of Nations; The theory of moral sentiments*. London: Hackett.

STACKHOUSE, M. L., McCANN, D., ROELS, S. and WILLIAMS, P. (eds) (1995) *On Moral*

Business: Classical and contemporary resources for ethics in economic life. Grand Rapids, MI: William B. Eerdmans.

TREVINO, L. and BROWN, M. (2004) 'Managing to be ethical: debunking five business ethics myths', *Academy of Management Executive*, 18: 69–81.

VARDY, P. (1989) *Business Morality.* London: Marshall Pickering.

CHAPTER 2

Normative Ethical Theory

LEARNING OUTCOMES

When you have completed this chapter you will be able to:

- describe, analyse and critique rational theories of ethics
- describe, analyse and critique non-rational theories of ethics
- describe, analyse and critique underlying cultural worldviews that influence how we see the good
- describe, analyse and critique the use of religion in ethics.

INTRODUCTION: PREAMBLE ON ETHICAL THEORIES

Most of us tend to switch off at the mention of the word 'theory'. As we noted in the first chapter, theory is often associated with abstract thinking and thus is perceived as the opposite of 'practice'. Properly understood, however, *theory is about providing experience or practice with meaning*. Scientific theories seek to provide convincing explanations about physical phenomena. The theory of evolution, for instance, seeks to explain how the animal world has developed. Such is its status that it has now become accepted by most scientists (Dawkins, 2010). Like any theory, however, it is conceivable that it could be disproved.

For ethics there have been many different kinds of theory. These can be divided into normative theories, which try to provide the basis for right and wrong, and descriptive theories which look at how we think about and practise ethics. This chapter focuses on normative theories. The West has been dominated by two rationalist theories: utilitarian and deontological. Strictly speaking, these are not two discrete theories but rather two theoretical schools that have had different expressions down the history of ethics. For our purposes we will sum up the major elements of these theories. We also examine the non-rational theories – in particular, virtue ethics. Beneath all of these we will look at underlying worldviews that inform our idea of what is good.

The important point is that if you look behind any major argument in the news you will find ethical theories, and often worldviews, sometimes well set out and understood, sometimes ill-focused. A good example is big bonuses.

FAT CATS AND DIRTY RATS

One report (Storey and Dash, 2009) noted that nine banks in the USA that were bailed out in the credit crisis, having lost over $81 billion, were by late 2009 paying over $39 billion in bonuses. A year later and the issue is still not resolved (http://www.guardian. co.uk/business/2010/feb/24/rbs-bonuses-ukfi-approval).

Amidst accusation and counter-accusation there is still no agreed approach to how it should be resolved. Is it right to pay out big bonuses?

SCENARIO

Radio interview

Group exercise: Your firm has been asked by BBC Radio Four to join a phone discussion chaired by John Humphrys to talk about the argument against big bonuses. You have 10 minutes before the phone rings to choose who will go on air, and with your colleagues, to work out the best arguments against big bonuses so you can present briefly and precisely. In small groups prepare your brief.

Share your arguments with the wider class, and discuss.

On the radio programme is a former economic adviser to Mrs Thatcher, and this is the argument he sets out.

The bankers' defence
- Banks should be free to decide on their own bonus policy, provided they are not harming others.
- There is a limited market of people who are capable of fulfilling the core positions. There therefore has to be a compensation package that will attract the best, and retain them. In a post-credit-crunch speech Brian Griffiths (2009) accordingly argued that if there is government regulation of compensation, it would cause the best leaders to leave the country.
- The financial leaders deserve this high recompense because of the nature of the job. Leadership at this level is highly stressful. It involves long hours and the continued responsibility for a large workforce, for the effect of the company on a wider environment, and for a market situation that is by its very nature difficult and combative. There are very particular qualities needed to respond rapidly and effectively to crises. It takes a special leader to survive the demands of that situation.
- The big bonuses are necessary to ensure the success of the firm. Griffiths (2009) expands on this, arguing that it is reasonable to pay the CEO several million pounds in pay and bonuses if his or her actions lead to several hundred million pounds profit. This provides a good outcome for the shareholders, to whom the CEO is primarily accountable.
- The effect of the success of the banks goes beyond the firm, creating wealth for the wider society. This is largely expressed in the 'trickle-down theory' – ie that wealth creation eventually trickles down to the lowest-paid – which argues that the market is the most effective way of relating information and for making the best of the resources in society. So over time, it is argued, the market has increased prosperity and equality. A slightly wider argument suggests that the banking system is critical to the economic well-being of society through the creation of jobs, the payment of taxes, the creation of money with overseas partners, and so on. Some writers assert that it is a small step from this positive view of banking to argue that because of such financial and material well-being banking should take its place alongside other professions that serve society (Caldecote, 1990). After the credit crunch a similar line of argument has emerged, to the effect that the identity of business should be seen in terms of a 'true profession' (Khurana and Nohria, 2008). This is explored in more detail in Chapter 8.

We now examine the ethical theories that underlie these arguments.

RATIONALIST THEORIES

At the heart of these arguments are a number of ethical theories, and we begin with what are called rationalist theories – that is, theories based on rational arguments.

UTILITARIAN THEORY

This theory suggests that we find the meaning of ethics by looking at the consequences. In particular, something is right if it maximises the good, producing the greatest good for the greatest number (Mill, 1993). The greatest good is the greatest happiness. The classic scenario of this theory centres on the obese potholer.

> **SCENARIO**
>
> ### The good of the majority
>
> Twenty-six potholers (cavers) are trying to get out of a deep cave that is rapidly filling with floodwater. As they rush towards the cave exit, the largest member of the group tries to crawl through first and gets firmly stuck. However hard they try, his friends cannot move him.
>
> The group decides that they must sacrifice their friend so that the remaining 25 can live, and they place dynamite close by him to widen the exit. They do not purposively intend to kill him ... but even if that does happen, their action will be right, because it will maximise the good for the majority.

The stress in all this is the maximisation of social goods and, in particular, happiness. The bankers' defence relies heavily on this theory. The utilitarian approach argues that economic growth and wealth are key to the happiness and well-being of all. The efficient handling and distribution of this wealth depends upon an efficiently functioning banking system. The banks, in turn, need investment bankers to make a good profit. The most effective incentive for bankers is big bonuses. In this way, the paying of big bonuses ultimately makes everyone happier. Of course, some people are unhappy about big bonuses. But the happiness of the majority, it is argued, outweighs this. The biggest investors in the stock market, for example, are pension funds. They are the biggest kind of investor ahead of mutual funds, insurance companies, currency reserves, sovereign wealth funds, hedge funds, or private equity. At one point it was estimated that pension funds worldwide held over US $20 trillion in assets (*The Economist*, January 2008: economist.com).

There are several different kinds of utilitarianism, including:

- *act utilitarianism*, focusing on the act that is likely to produce the most good
- *rule utilitarianism*, focusing on sets of rules or codes that would produce the most good. The bankers' argument seems to fit into this category. As a rule, the argument goes, it is right to pay big bonuses because of their effect on the finance system and the wider happiness of society.

Difficulties with utilitarian theory

There is no doubt that the likely consequences must be examined in any attempt to decide what is right to do. Trying to base all ethical judgements solely on this theory, however, is problematic.

- What is the happiness that Mill argues for? He suggests that the good of happiness involves the higher, not the base, pleasures. But what are the criteria for deciding what a higher pleasure is, and why it is good? In any case, who decides? The theory does not help in actually defining what is good. A higher pleasure might be defined by some as high culture, by others as survival, and by yet others as psychological well-being.
- Any definition of happiness or the good may well depend on different cultural views – and how do you decide between them? What is good for one group may not be good for another. In relation to the bankers' arguments, what is good for Western pension funds may not be good for the global community. Is there any evidence of the finance system helping the developing world?

- The stress on consequences can easily lead to the end justifying any means. Can it be right to kill the populations of two entire cities in order to end World War II? Can it be right to accept or give bribes to keep a workforce employed? Can it be right to use torture in order to save lives? In the last example, Walzer (1973) offers the ticking bomb scenario, in which a terrorist knows where a bomb is due to go off shortly in a populous city. Many would argue that torture was right if it saved several thousand people. One person suffers, but a lot of others live on happily as a result. Many are uncomfortable with this. Torture might be justified in such an extreme case, but, argues Walzer, torture remains wrong. Defence against torture remains enshrined in human rights codes across the globe, because it says something about how we should treat human beings, regardless of consequences. It is therefore often argued that torture is one of the few things that cannot have exceptions. It is *always* wrong. Ironically, this could give rise to another level of utilitarian argument, along the lines that unless we make a stand on torture it could give a sign globally that it is acceptable, leading to increased suffering. At the very least such examples raise real problems for the theory.
- The stress on the good for the majority can easily lead to the oppression of the minority. Just because something will benefit 50.5% of the population does not make it good, and might in any case disadvantage the 49.5%.
- It may not be possible to assess the consequences with any precision. One of the problems about the global warming arguments is that science cannot give an absolute picture of the consequences. Sarewitz (2004), in relation to climate change, thus argues that politicians should not rely on science to tell them what to do. The politicians have to take responsibility for settling on the values they believe are critical for the good stewardship of the environment, one of the most important being the precautionary principle. This means that even if you are not sure, you take the precaution of trying to sustain the environment. In the case of the bankers it is simply not possible to assess the consequences clearly. There is evidence that the global finance system is interconnected and contributes to wealth in some ways across the world. However, the connection of this to big bonuses is problematic. Examination of consequences historically in this area suggests something quite different. The big bonus system before the credit crisis led to the pursuit of immediate profit, with no consideration of the mid- or long-term health of the organisation or the wider finance system. In this light, big bonuses contributed directly to the breakdown of the wider system (Sun *et al*, 2010) – quite the opposite of the claims of the bankers' defence. Furthermore, there is no evidence that suggests that investment bankers would leave if faced by smaller bonuses. Simply to say 'This is how the system works' is not enough. Research on wider leadership experience once more suggests something different. There is little evidence of many better jobs that would attract leaders away. There is evidence of available leaders who would take the job for considerably less pay (Kolb, 2006). Many alternative approaches have simply not been tested across industry, such as hiring leaders from within the firm, or recruiting from different countries. Another approach would be to change recruiting practice such that, for instance, candidates bid against each other, and the lowest salary estimate-bid wins. In short, the idea of a limited market has little substance and there may be several other ways of attracting leaders that have not been tested. Empirical work in the area of wider leadership makes depressing reading when it comes to even assessing the role of the CEO. Increasingly, the assumption about the effectiveness of leaders has been questioned. Khurana (2002: 23) argues that the evidence points to 'at best a contingent and relatively minor cause-and-effect relationship between CEOs and firms' performances'. Across the piece, research points to no correlation between CEO pay and corporate performance (Shaw, 2006). With respect to financiers, the point about their importance, or uniqueness, is at the very least contested. Some have argued that the defence of bonuses relies simply on an inflated and unsustainable view of leadership (Conger, 2005).

- In all, the use of utilitarian theory comes close to the *slippery slope fallacy*: 'Believe me, if you supertax the bonuses, then you will lose the people who are making you money.' A fallacy is an argument that is not logically coherent (see Chapter 3 for details). In this case it is not coherent because those consequences do not necessarily follow.

Summing up

It is important to estimate consequences, but we cannot rely entirely on utilitarian arguments. The stress on utilitarianism in the bankers' arguments is not well worked out – there is insufficient evidence to support their view of how big bonuses lead to good consequences for the most people.

Because of the uncertainty about defining what is good, it could be argued that that utilitarianism is not an ethical theory at all, but rather an important element in ethical decision-making.

DEONTOLOGICAL THEORIES

The theory that most immediately stands against a simple utilitarianism is the deontological (based on *deon*, the ancient Greek for 'what is required', and thus 'duty'). The deontological approach to ethics argues that duty or principles are the base of ethics rather than consequences. Right actions, according to Immanuel Kant (1964), are prescribed by principles, such as to keep promises, be truthful, be fair, avoid inflicting suffering on others, return the kindness of others. Kantian ethics is thus about doing the right thing regardless of whether it makes one happy – quite the opposite of Mill's view. Kant also notes duties specific to the self, such as to do no harm to the self, and to develop one's character and skills.

Kant suggests that these duties:

- embody respect for persons
- apply without qualification to all rational persons
- are universal principles.

What makes a person worthy of respect is the capacity to be rational, to develop the good that will enable the person to do his or her duty, and to fulfil key purposes. This respect involves treating people as ends in themselves, as having their own purpose and capacity. This in turn means treating people not as a means to our own ends. Coercion and manipulation of different kinds exhibit disrespect in these terms, such that the other is regarded as only useful for what they can do for you.

This leads to certain key moral imperatives. Kant contrasts these – referred to as 'categorical imperatives' – with non-moral imperatives, which he refers to as 'hypothetical'. *Hypothetical imperatives* are commands that are based on a condition, such as 'If you want to get fit, exercise regularly.' *Categorical imperatives* have no such conditions. It is simply wrong to cheat, or to break a promise. These are basic principles which are true without any reference to conditions or consequences.

Such principles also have to be able to apply universally, and Kant argues that most common principles pass this test. 'Promises should be kept', for example, applies in all situations. If we did not keep promises, the very meaning of the word would be brought into question.

For Kant this points to a view of ethics that is based upon absolute principles. The authority for such principles does not come from some outside source, such as God, but from their rational foundation. Beauchamp and Childress (1994) suggest four major principles in professional ethics: respect for the autonomy (self-governance) of the client, justice (treating all parties fairly), beneficence (working for the good of the client), and non-maleficence (avoiding harm to the client).

A deontological approach to the big bonus issue would focus on such principles as:

- fairness – a fair day's wage for a fair day's work
- avoiding cheating
- respect for work colleagues
- consistency.

This provides a powerful basis for ethics. Once again, however, it is difficult to see it as an exclusive foundation to ethics. It makes sense to stress the responsibility and duty of the person, however,

It is difficult to see how principles can be absolute – that is, without exception. The principle of promise-keeping is justified by saying that if people do not keep promises, the meaning of promise-keeping is eroded. But that is only true if promises are broken regularly. It is possible to say that, all things being equal, promises should be kept, the reason being that they form the basis of a contract. However, it may be possible that a person has to break a promise because of some greater concern. For example, a person may have promised another to maintain confidentiality, only to realise that the other person involved is a murderer who could kill again. Equally, it could be that a person is not able to keep a promise. For example, a person may promise to support a particular project but lose the resources, personal or financial, to do anything about it. In both those situations it could be argued that it is wrong to keep a promise. This applies to any great principle. It is very difficult to find a principle that does not have a potential exception to it.

 PAUSE FOR THOUGHT

What are the principles that inform your practice?

What are the principles that inform the practice of your workplace?

What are the principles embodied in the planning and practice of your management?

Can you think of any principle that has no exception, one that can apply in every situation?

Absolute principles have the danger that they discourage the taking of responsibility for working things out in context. This can lead to a lack of awareness of the situation, so that the principles are applied uncritically.

The idea of reason as the basis for respecting another person excludes human beings who are unable to reason intellectually, not least the severely learning-disabled. The very word 'person' is as much a word that expresses value as it is a description. There is therefore a real danger of excluding some humans from that respect if it is at all conditional – ie if respect is based upon some particular aspect or property of the person. It would, for example, exclude people with a severe learning disability from respect.

The general nature of principles requires that details be worked through in practice. In other words, it is hard to know just what they mean until one can see how they relate to a case. This suggests that any principle might have several very different meanings. A good illustration outside the world of business is the case of the conjoined twins from Gozo.

CONJOINED TWINS

In 2001 conjoined twins Jodie and Mary were in a Manchester hospital, the centre of a debate about whether they should be separated or not.

Jodie was a bright, alert baby. She had a functioning heart and lungs. Her legs were set wide apart but could be rectified by surgery. The probability was that separated from Mary, Jodie would be able to lead a relatively normal life, probably walking unaided, probably attending school and probably being able to have children. For Mary, things were very different. Her face was deformed but more importantly she had no effective heart or lung function. She lived only because of her physical attachment to Jodie. For Jodie, separation meant the expectation of a normal life; for Mary it meant death.

At first the debate seemed to be between a utilitarian view from the medical staff and subsequent judicial process, who favoured

separation, and the view of the family Christian leaders, who favoured no action, based on five key principles, including the sacredness of human life, and the absence of a duty to preserve life if extraordinary means have to be used.

The hospital took this to court, and it went to appeal. The judges at appeal accepted the main principles but argued from them exactly the opposite conclusion. The sacredness of human life, they argued, required that the twin who had the chance to survive should be given that chance. The weaker twin would be likely to die whatever decision was taken. Hence, they knew that the twins should be separated. Lee (2003) suggests that the conflict was not so much between different values as one found *within* such broad values. When applied to a case such as this the broad principles may point to different and possibly conflicting conclusions, depending on context.

Just as the principle respect for life can lead to different conclusions in practice, principles such as equality or freedom can have different meanings. Often the key ethical debate is about what they do mean. Once such principle is justice.

Justice

In the case of the big bonuses the key principle being claimed by both sides was justice. Behind much of the debate is the meaning of justice, and of merit or desert in particular. The most obvious ethical point around desert is that there should be reward for success. Bonuses would then be based upon agreed results. Strikingly, however, in practice bonuses have often been paid out despite poor results. Of course, there may be several criteria for judgement, including:

- the physical output for the worker, including hours spent at work
- the skills and capacities that are needed for the job, and the required training
- the difficulty, stress, danger or unpleasantness
- the responsibility taken on by the leader
- the creative capacity in achieving the outcome required by the shareholders or board.

The first problem with such a list of criteria is to determine which of them should be used and how they are to be assessed. Connected to that is the problem of how to tie pay levels to levels of desert. It is hard, on the face of it, to determine what these levels might be without comparing the proposed remuneration with not just that of similar workers but also that of other leaders and members of the organisation. At this point the calculation takes us into justifying why the leader's reward should be so much higher than the average worker's. Why should the differential not be a ratio of four to one, such as Plato suggested of levels of wealth between neighbours (Plato, 2005)? Tawney (1930), among others, argues that inequality is acceptable provided that the differential is not too great. Part of the argument for this is the positive effect on the organisation, stressing a more equal sense of respect for all members.

Different sides focus on the criteria that they think should apply. Sometimes they also use very different meanings of the same principle.

To Nozick (1972), for instance, justice demands a focus on merit (based on the high responsibility of the workers) and the freedom of the firm to decide what it wants to pay. He also argues that market mechanisms should not be interfered with. If they are interfered with, to skew the results towards big bonuses, this is unjust: the moral equivalent of theft.

Another view of justice involves fair distribution, not simply desert. This leads to Rawls' (1971) view of justice. Rawls argues for relative equality. Inequality is acceptable provided that it leads to greater equality overall. This view suggests that there is no freedom for firms to determine what compensation they want to pay. On the contrary, firms are part of a wider society to which they are accountable. The banks and other financial institutions are intimately connected both as a sector and in relation to the government.

The credit crisis introduces another element to ideas about justice. Once the governments had to bail out the banks when they had failed, any criterion relating to the level of bonuses should have changed. The use of public money means that the public have a direct stake in how the banking firms reward their leaders. The firms in question do not have the freedom to decide what the criteria should be but should consult the key shareholders.

All views of justice concur that the firm and wider society need to work through a compensation philosophy (see Chapter 7 for more detail) so that they can give a clear account of their practice. Process – how we arrive at an ethical judgement (procedural justice) – is thus as important as principle. Even a fundamental principle such as justice can then mean several things and must be worked out in practice.

PAUSE FOR THOUGHT

Which of the two major ethical theories informs your ethical practice?

Which of the two might best inform ethics in business, and why?

Summing up so far

Utilitarianism and deontological theories are important perspectives about ethics, and must be involved in ethical decision-making. For instance, it is thus possible to accept fundamental principles without making them absolute (applicable in the same way in all situations). However, taken as single ethical theories, offering one narrative to explain ethics, they raise more questions than they present answers. So philosophers have turned to other theories to supplement them.

NON-RATIONALIST THEORIES

Several non rationalist approaches to ethics stress additional aspects to be taken into account, in particular intuitionism, feminism, discourse ethics and virtue ethics. 'Non-rational' means that they involve more than simply rational calculation.

INTUITIONISM

Against the two examples of rational foundations to ethics, Hume (1975) had little time for the place of reason as a foundation of ethics. We must rather look to the heart, the passions. Reason could provide the rational justification of means, but nothing can provide a rational justification of ends. The promptings of the heart are no excuse for ignorance, and reason has to guide our understanding of the world and the possibilities of that world, but intuition is very much at the base of what we determine to be good. Hume's position suggests that reason and emotion are critical parts of any foundation of ethics. The importance of acknowledging feeling in decision-making is reinforced by Goleman's work on emotional intelligence (1996). Nonetheless, intuitionism does have problems. It is hard to build ethics purely on feelings. How would we distinguish which feelings were right and which wrong without rational criteria?

FEMINIST ETHICS

This approach has close parallels with the feminist ethics of care and with a good deal of pastoral theology over the last two decades which stresses care, empathy and trust as the basis of the ethical response (Robinson, 2008). Feminist writers contrast justice with care (Koehn, 1998). Justice, they argue, is solution-driven and based upon power. It assumes that there is 'right' solution to any ethical dilemma. In contrast, care as the foundation of ethics is concerned not simply to solve ethical dilemmas but rather to understand the underlying relationships and what is needed to bring people together. Feminist ethics therefore has a lot in common with conflict resolution approaches, looking to involve all parties in working out the ethical response. This is an ethics which looks to develop trust and is dependent upon key attributes such as empathy and care. Feminist ethics shares with critical theory (Western, 2007) a concern to analyse the power dynamic of any ethics. A feminist view of the big bonus issue would note the way in which present leaders of the finance industry have attempted to impose an uncritical ethical narrative about justice, based ultimately on their own self-interest. They would also note underlying gender and other inequalities. For many the idea of applying an ethics of care to business would seem to be the opposite of good management. Caring institutions are associated with public policy such as healthcare. However, we speak of 'customer care' or 'employee care' in the context of business.

 PAUSE FOR THOUGHT

What does it mean to care for your customers? What does such care involve in practice?

What does it mean to care for employees? Could this form a basis for business ethics?

DISCOURSE ETHICS

Awareness of this reflection and plurality has also led to a greater stress on the need for dialogue in order to discover ethical meaning. Habermas (1992) suggests that ethical meaning emerges from dialogue, enabling reflection on values and the discovery of shared norms. Getting the process right for such dialogue is thus of the highest importance, and Habermas suggests basic conditions for this, including respect for the other. Benhabib (1992) goes further, noting that although the dialogue may reveal shared moral meaning, the conditions of dialogue themselves already embody moral meaning, not least respect for those we are in dialogue with (Benhabib, 1992). So although dialogue is important in sharing and testing ethical meaning, the dialogue itself depends upon core principles.

VIRTUE ETHICS

Perhaps the most important ethical theory to challenge the two rationalist ones in the last three decades has been virtue ethics. Alasdair MacIntyre (1981) was responsible for the re-emergence of ethics built around virtue. He suggests that we must choose between Aristotle and Nietzsche. Aristotle places ethics in a community of shared meaning (1969). Nietzsche (2003) suggests that the traditional moral language no longer binds us. Indeed, he argues, such language tended to impose meaning on society, robbing the individual of the freedom to determine his or her own values. He therefore argues that it *should* no longer bind us.

McIntyre argues for Aristotle. Ethical meaning, he suggests, is situated in a community of practice, and is communicated not through principles but stories, including community ritual, which sum up the key virtues of the community. And it is virtues that are at the heart of ethical meaning. In Aristotelian terms virtues are dispositions for action which occupy the mean, or middle, not the extreme. Courage, for instance, lies between the two extremes of cowardice and foolhardiness. Underlying the virtues is the *telos*, the end, the purpose, which involves well-being or happiness. In all this, the approach is to get the character right, and good ethical practice follows from this. Unlike Kant, who saw the good decision as a matter of the will, not a matter of emotions and therefore of inclinations, Aristotle believed that the ethically correct person acted out of the inclinations that the virtues gave him or her. Such virtues are learned through practice. We examine more closely what might be the key virtues in business and the professions in Chapter 6.

How, then, would this approach fit the debate about bankers' bonuses?

This takes us back to the insight that all theories of justice demand an account of how that justice is served. Thus, as Harris notes, 'Each theory produces a central requirement that the *process* governing executive selection and/or compensation be just; otherwise, higher levels of executive pay cannot be justified' (Harris, 2006: 83). Increasingly, this line of argument has led to the notion that a 'compensation philosophy' should be developed for every major company, such that underlying values can be set out and discussed. Such a philosophy embodies the narrative of shared values, showing how the criteria for salaries and bonuses fit with those values. It also provides an ongoing basis for transparent critical conversation around leadership and justice. Inevitably, this takes compensation away from narrow economic criteria into the broader culture and ethos of the firm. The 'philosophy' becomes the narrative of the firm, aiming to show us what good practice looks like.

This develops a much richer understanding of what fairness means to employees and how perceptions of fairness affect their attitudes and behaviours. In turn, it incorporates issues related to trust, work relationships, and ethics. A corresponding implication is that compensation systems also play important social and symbolic roles in organisations and, through these roles, pay systems effect a variety of important outcomes such as employee commitment and performance. Research suggests that high-performing organisations create and nurture relational exchanges that are based upon trust, mutuality, care and respect (Rousseau, 1995). In light of the role that compensation systems play in employment relationships, it follows that they have an important part in developing such a culture. This in turn leads to shared values and a culture that act as a focus to commitment and effort – something confirmed by research on the importance of organisational justice for understanding the non-economic effects of compensation systems (Greenberg and Cropanzano, 2001), suggesting that fairness is central to employment relationships. Bloom (2004) sums up much of this research as confirming three things. First, the workforce is concerned about the basis of any view of fairness – hence the importance of compensation philosophy. Second, there is a concern for procedural justice: justice has to be seen to be done. Third, this ties into interactional justice for the whole organisation.

As the narrative of compensation and justice is developed, then, it enables all in the firm to practise the core virtues, not least the virtue of justice, the capacity to be fair. At the heart of all this is reflection on the core meaning and purpose of the organisation in relation to its employees and the wider society and environment.

Solomon (1988) contrasts this view of human well-being 'as focused on the meaningful community' with a more individualised approach: an 'impoverished idea of *Homo economicus* who has no attachments or affections other than crude self-interest and the ability to calculate how to satisfy that interest vis-à-vis other people' (Solomon, 1988: 118).

This reflection on core purpose is key to Aristotle's vision. It involves the intellectual virtue of *phronēsis*, practical wisdom. This is the capacity to reflect on the good, including purpose, and work through how it is embodied in practice. As we shall see later, the need to review the purpose of business has been an important theme since the credit crisis. We revisit practical wisdom, and how it can be developed, in Chapter 6.

Virtue ethics is an important move forward in ethical theory, but has its problems. First, it does not really get over the problem of how to handle ethical relativity – the idea that there is no shared understanding of ethics. If each community is the basis for ethical meaning, there can then be no sense of shared ethics beyond that community. Second, and connected, community-based ethics excludes any sense of justice that applies to all. This is exemplified by universal human rights – the belief that certain rights apply to all regardless of their culture or community. Action which abuses those rights is perceived as unjust. Third, virtue ethics assumes a community which has single voice and view of the good. In fact, all communities have many voices, with very different perspectives.

Nonetheless, virtue ethics takes us beyond the unthinking use of principles or consequences to owning how we think, what our identity is, and what this requires of us. The practice of core virtues in enabling reflection and dialogue then becomes critical. All of this points to an ethics which is about thinking flexibly, not simply about applying principles or finding clear solutions.

Figure 2.1 The branches of ethical theory

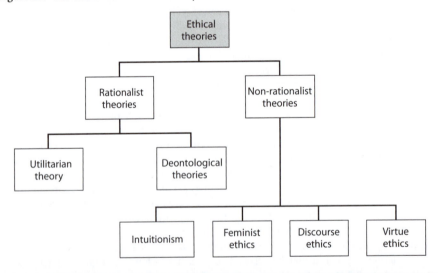

WORLDVIEWS

Most of the rational ethical theories are dominated by the question 'What is right or wrong?' Underlying that is another question: 'What is good?' And the answer to that depends upon the worldview that one holds. Worldviews are simply views of the world that give an explanation of what life is about and what is of value in that world. A worldview might involve a view of how the world was created (cosmology), of the nature of the world as it is, and how all the different parts relate (ecology), or of the role and value of humanity in that world (anthropology). In recent years the global warming debate has been dominated by a worldview that stresses the interconnectedness of the social and physical environment. This in turn has concluded that humanity has to take more responsibility for the environment and that it is not ethical to waste resources. Feminist ethics is based in a view of the world that has similar interconnectedness. The ethics itself then emphasises the notion of people working together for the good.

Iris Murdoch (1972), philosopher and novelist, argued against ethics as focusing simply on narrow views of obligation – ie on 'what it is right to do' in any situation. It also has to articulate what the good life is, 'what it is good to be' (Taylor, 1989: 5). And this requires not just reason but a vision of the good, and thus imagination. Critical moral consciousness, a real awareness of all who were involved in any situation and of the issues that came from those relationships, was a key part of this. Murdoch stressed the importance of a person taking responsibility for his or her ethical reflection and decision-making, but argued that it required more focus on the underlying meaning and how that connected to broader view of the good. For her, therefore, narrative and story become a key vehicle for ethical reflection. All this places value, and an awareness of what values one holds and why, before reasoning and action.

This applies directly to the debate about bonuses. At its most crude, beneath the right and wrong of bonuses are assumptions about human nature, and thus about what actually motivates people to work well. In fact, the wider data about the attraction and retention of leaders suggests that financial compensation is not the only criterion (Milkovich and Rabin, 1991). Top leaders in the armed forces and higher education, for instance, have jobs no less difficult than bankers, and find reward in the nature of the activity. It might be argued that although a banker's job is no less demanding than a general's, it is less pleasant, with fewer intrinsic rewards. The argument for big bonuses assumes that, in Longley's words, 'People are not driven hard enough to honest graft and creative industrial enterprise simply by an appeal to the common good' (quoted in Robinson, 1992: 13). However, many leaders in business argue the contrary – that motivation is more than financial. Although the intrinsic rewards of service through caring professions may be greater than those of business, there is no reason why a significant sense of intrinsic reward should not be discovered through a focus on the positive purpose of business.

This is clearly there in many different cultural worldviews around business. A good example is that of the Islamic scholar Fetullah Gülen. Gülen ties in the purpose of business to a strong sense of stewardship based in creation theology (Robinson, 2008b). Humanity is called to take responsibility for the created world. This sense of stewardship is then lived out in any profession, so that business people are seen as living the responsibility to respond to God in their profession. At the heart of this is the idea of *hizmet* or service. The business person has to provide evidence of such service. The theme of this approach is one of business as a vocation valued by society, in which business takes responsibility with others. A similar worldview comes from Jonas (1984), who argues for the importance of stewardship based on the worldview of a fragile physical environment that depends on the concerted efforts of all for it to be sustained.

 PAUSE FOR THOUGHT

What is your worldview? How does it inform your view of the good?

What are the dominant worldviews in the West?

What are dominant worldviews in the developing world?

Often worldviews are implicit or assumed. In the West, for instance, there is a strong consumerist worldview (Miles, 1998). This is built around individual choice and the freedom to choose. The worldview of nature as interconnected stresses rather a view of community, or people working together. Worldviews are thus not simply statements of fact. They involve major ethical values such as freedom, community or equality. They provide the value framework through which we view the world, what we believe about the world.

Any person or group may have several different worldviews or may have worldviews that appear to conflict with other worldviews. So how do we judge between different worldviews? Each worldview has to be tested against reality.

- Does it lead to harm, physical or psychological? Some worldviews, for instance, lead to the exclusion of others who do not agree.
- Does it lead to good ends, such as resolving conflict? As noted above, there is good evidence for instance that genuine working together leads to positive workplaces and greater productivity. Underlying the bankers' defence is a much broader worldview about freedom, the nature of society and the effects of the bankers' work – that big profits make wealth which will benefit society by 'trickling down' – all of which is contestable (Robinson, 1992).
- How far is the worldview engaging the major values, such as freedom, equality and community? Stress on only one of these will tend to lead to a narrow worldview, such as individual freedom against equality. We return to that in Chapters 3 and 4.

Worldviews, then, are not right in themselves. Simply because I believe something about the world does not make this view good. It is possible for any worldview to be used to a bad end, and therefore – as Bauman (1989) notes – it is important to be aware of different worldviews and to critically engage them.

To illustrate this we turn at this point to perhaps the most prevalent basis for worldviews globally: those involving transcendence.

TRANSCENDENT WORLDVIEWS

Transcendent worldviews are mostly expressed in religion. Some would argue that religion has no place in applied ethics. However, the majority of the world in some way bases its ethics on religion.

The first thing to say is that religion, like ethics, has many different approaches. The two broad theoretical bases are natural law and care (ethics based in love, care or compassion), and these provide what is sometimes a competing view of ethics, even within religion.

Natural law

Natural law is based in the idea of creation. In the Abrahamic religions (Christian, Jewish and Islamic) it is argued that God created the world and that his purposes are revealed in that creation. Those purposes are what show us the good at the base of ethics. The obvious example is to do with sexuality. Natural law argues that God created man and woman as sexual beings for the purpose of procreation. From that it is argued that homosexuality, for instance, does not fulfil God's purposes and is therefore ethically wrong.

There are real problems with natural law. As David Hume (1975) argues, we cannot simply say that something is right or wrong because of what it is. You cannot base a prescription about what you should do on a description of how things are. It is an important example of an ethical fallacy (see Chapter 3). It makes a logical leap without any real evidence of what is good or bad. Of course, natural law thinkers would argue that they are not basing their ethics in a description but rather on the purpose behind the description – that is, God's purpose in creation. But who decides what God's purpose is? Historically, it has been those in power who have decided what is good. At different points in the history of religion those in power have decided that order is paramount, allowing them to accept slavery, exclusively male leadership, and so on. This led to powerful ideas that were used to support the status quo. There is debate within the religions about this, some arguing that natural law can only give general guidance (like general ethical principles) and others arguing that the real basis of religious ethics is compassion, love or care.

Care

Different religions have different ethical emphases, and there were – and are – different viewpoints about what ethics is within each religion. Nonetheless, there is broad agreement among religions about the core ethical attitude, summed up in love and respect for common humanity: the so-called 'golden rule'. Some of the versions of that include:

- *Christian* – 'Treat others as you would like them to treat you' (Luke 6:31); 'Love your neighbour as yourself' (Matthew 22:39)
- *Hindu* – 'Let not any man do unto another any act that he wisheth not done to himself by others, knowing it to be painful to himself' (*Mahabharata*, Shanti Parva)
- *Confucian* – 'Do not do unto others what you would not want them to do to you' (*Analects*, Book xii:2)
- *Buddhist* – 'Hurt not others with that which pains yourself' (*Udānavarga*, v.18)
- *Jewish* – 'What is hateful to yourself do not do to your fellow man. This is the whole Torah' (Babylonian Talmud, *Shabbath* 31a)
- *Muslim* – 'No man is a true believer unless he desires for his brother what he desires for himself' (Hadith 13 of 40, Imam An-Nawawi).

As noted above, it seems at first sight to be a complete contradiction to talk about care and business. The first is purely about care – giving, and so on; the second is about management control and contract. However, it all depends on what you mean by 'care'. The concept of *agapē* (the Christian idea of unconditional love), for instance, is nothing to do with romantic love (Robinson, 2001). It provides the basis of unconditional care and commitment. In other words, it is about commitment to people and projects over time. At the very least this reinforces research on areas such as leaders which suggests that commitment of leaders over time leads to good results for business (see Chapter 6). At the same time *agapē* is not about unthinking care. Along with ideas like empathy it actually involves critical distance. It is very hard to care properly for another without a dispassionate distance that enables us not to become over-involved. Without that, it becomes hard to really see the other.

Of course, ideas like care do not tell us what is right, as such. This is an ethics which demands that you are always trying to work out what love means in any situation. Love or compassion provides the ethical attitude, and what this means in practice has to be rationally worked out.

Critique

Many religious worldviews are based in key religious texts. However, it is not easy to discern the voice of God in scriptures that are a product of their culture, expressed through laws, rules, songs and stories. Alongside any simple command of love are many worldviews based in different cultures. The difficulty with religion and cultural context is neatly summed up in the following excerpt from an amusing open Internet letter.

Dear Dr Laura, . . .

A letter posted on the Internet to Dr Laura, a hard-line Christian broadcaster who argued that homosexuality is wrong, based on Leviticus 18:22. The writer 'accepted' Dr Laura's view on homosexuality, but wanted some clarification on some of the other Old Testament laws. These included injunctions against wearing garments made of two different kinds of thread, and punishments for blasphemy and cursing.

I would like to sell my daughter into slavery, as it suggests in Exodus 21:7. In this day and age, what do you think would be a fair price for her?

Leviticus 25.44 states that I may buy slaves from the nations that are around us. A friend of mine claims that this applies to Mexicans, but not Canadians. Can you clarify? Why can't I own Canadians?

I have a neighbour who insists on working on the Sabbath. Exodus 35:2 clearly states that he should be put to death. Am I morally obliged to kill him myself?

These different texts from the Old Testament all reflect worldviews of different cultures which it is difficult for many to simply apply to the twenty-first century. A culture in the West based upon tolerance and care has a very different worldview.

None of this is to subvert religious ethics. Nonetheless, it shows that any religious command must be interpreted and critically tested, not accepted regardless of context or reason. Ethics cannot therefore be simplistically dependent on religion. Plato pointed to this as early as in his dialogue *Euthyphro*. In effect, he asks, is something right because God says so, or is it right independently of God's command? If it is the first, then how do we know that is not simply based upon the whim of the divine? If it is the second, judgements about what is ethically right depend upon rational criteria, and ethics becomes independent from God. Of course, the power of this dilemma is only a problem if you believe that ethics should be based on upon obeying God's commands uncritically. Even care has to be critically tested (Schweiker, 1995).

Some religious thinkers (such as Nazir Ali, 2011) endeavour to argue that there is a clear difference between religious ethics and secular (non-religious) ethics. Others (Markham, 1994; Ramadan, 2009) argue that both secular and religious ethics involve a plurality of cultures (with differences within the religions), that there is often a mixture of these worldviews in society and organisations, and that awareness of the different worldviews helps us to test and critique our own.

PAUSE FOR THOUGHT

Michael Nazir Ali (http://www.telegraph.co.uk/news/uknews/immigration/6989284/Bishop-Michael-Nazir-Ali-immigrants-should-accept-Britains-Christian-values.html) argues that the ethical identity of the UK is built on Christian values, and that the UK should acknowledge its debt to these values.

Is this true?

Can you identify a value in society that is specifically and exclusively Christian?

Religion can provide a strong basis for motivation and working together. It can also reinforce the importance of holding a worldview and its critical examination. Religion thus has a part to play in ethics, including business ethics (Stackhouse *et al*, 1995). However, religion is rarely 'pure'. It always is expressed in a wider cultural context, and may work with or reinforce wider cultural views of ethics. It is also not free from problems related to any institution, not least the felt need to defend or impose itself. Historically, it has imposed ethics and attempted to dominate views of the truth. For religion to be involved in applied ethics it has to be open to the same critical conversation as any other group.

Business and *kyosei*

A good example of worldview and religious ethics working with business is in the concept of *kyosei*. This comes from the Eastern religion and philosophy of Confucianism. It is one of the key ideas adopted by the Caux Round Table, an international group of businesses dedicated to developing ethics and responsibility (www.cauxroundtable.org). Canon, one of the member companies of this group, sees it as its core philosophy and speaks of it thus (www.mydigitalcameraworld.com/DC/ compact/canon):

> The corporate philosophy of Canon is *kyosei*. A concise definition of this word would be 'living and working together for the common good', but Canon's definition is broader: 'all people, regardless of race, religion or culture, harmoniously living and working together into the future'.

Core ideas of this philosophy include (Brooks and Brooks, 1998):

- a belief in the principle of reciprocity and the golden rule
- an understanding of humanity's fundamental interconnectedness and the fact that our actions have an impact both in immediate and in far-reaching ways, often not easily seen
- valuing the 'middle path' – this may take the form of practising moderation, such as taking only calculated risks in business; it also includes the need for balance between self-interest and altruism
- valuing character and virtue of the individual and the organisation more highly than personal gain or corporate profits – this principle is the most difficult, but nonetheless can have positive effects on the success of the business, as noted above
- the importance of constant learning and growth – improvement by learning (*kaizen*) is seen as central to the nature of humanity, once more requiring that all views of theory, fact or value should be tested
- a preference for simplicity – this is linked to a belief that the elegance of simplicity is more likely to bring us into harmony with others and with the planet.

This provides a clear framework for practice.

CONCLUSION

In this chapter we have introduced some of the major tools that help us to develop an ethical map. First, we looked at two core rational theories of ethics. Both were seen as important but could not be the only way of deciding what was right. Second, we looked at non-rational theories. These go beyond the rational theories and look to the wider relationships involved in any ethical decision and with that to the development of character and virtue. Again these cannot act as the exclusive bases for ethics but are necessary in developing ethical practice. Third, we looked at worldviews and how they inform ethics. These too have to be critically examined to ensure that they do not lead to negative ends, but can provide major ethical values for business practice.

From this we conclude that the most effective ethics, in the sense of both determining what is right in any particular situation, and what is the basis of the overall good, is one that uses all these aspects – principles (based in critical worldviews), a study of consequences (based on the past as well as the future), a concern for character and virtues, and a concern for the involvement of all parties in working through the ethical response (ethics as essentially not isolated but social). The case of big bonuses shows how theories have to be engaged and tested, and ultimately worked through into the philosophy and practice of the organisation.

This approach to ethics is one of balance, between:

- individual and group ethical decisions – personal ethics and professional ethics
- local and global. It is important to have ethics based in the community of practice, but some things – like human rights and justice – apply globally (see Chapter 13)
- rational, affective (to do with emotions and identity) and social. Ethics is more than individual and rational
- West and East: the division between West and East is often characterised as between the rational individual and the collective and affective community. The two worlds are equally important in ethics
- theory, value and practice. The three work together in ethics. There are no value-free theories, and no values that do not have a theory to give them meaning. They test each other, and are tested by practice.

The overall conclusion is that understanding ethical theory matters to business practice and the study of business practice:

- *Kyosei*, as quoted by Canon, reminds us that business has an ethical identity in society, like any of the major professions who have developed core moral codes. Evidence of ethical thinking is a key part of developing trust with stakeholders.

- Business people take on the role of ethical agents every day. Consider the following scene from an actual board meeting of a university.

Theory in practice

The CSR director is arguing for an ethical investment policy that ensures long-term investment in appropriate firms. The finance director replies that this is not possible because the foundation rules state the need to have any investment monies available at short notice. The CSR director argues that ethical investment is key to the CSR policy. The finance director then replies that perhaps they cannot afford to be ethical.

In fact, the first position is built around principles and the second is built around awareness of consequences and the need to sustain the institution. Both involve key ethical theories. The discussion moved on to accept the need for both perspectives and for developing ways in which they could be honoured, such as through ethical investment consultants.

The more business practitioners understand the ethics they are talking about, the better – and more ethical – decisions will be.

- Business people, especially leaders and managers influence and develop ethical positions whatever they do. It is important to understand both how they are doing this and how to handle ethical challenges that come from inside and outside the organisation. The better the grasp of theory, the better the business will able to react, acknowledging the ethical force of any argument and being able to critique that argument.
- The better the grasp of ethical theory and how it informs practice, the better the business person will be able to develop practice that does not end in disasters, such as happened to the *News of the World* or Enron.
- Faced by complex ethical cases, a grasp of ethical theory will enable managers effectively to manage the substantive ethical issues and the ethical perspectives of the stakeholders. A good example in terms of complexity and the ways in which to handle it is the case of child labour (see Chapter 7), which seems at first to be based on a simple principle but requires careful reflection about values and context.

Alongside any views of theory, then, comes the process of how we make ethical decisions and plan from an ethical perspective. This is examined in the next chapter.

EXPLORE FURTHER

Books

Beauchamp, T., Bowie, N. and Arnold, D. (2012) *Ethical Theory and Business*.

London: Pearson Education.

Thompson, M. (2005) *Ethical Theory*. London: Hodder & Stoughton.

DVDs

Touching the Void (2004 MGM). A film about the ethics of mountaineering.

REFERENCES

APPIAH, K. A. (2006) *Ethics in a World of Strangers*. London: Penguin.

ARISTOTLE (1969) *Nicomachean Ethics*. London: Penguin.

BAUMAN, Z. (1989) *Modernity and the Holocaust*. London: Polity.

BEAUCHAMP, T. and CHILDRESS, T. (1994) *Principles of Biomedical Ethics*. Oxford: Oxford University Press.

BENHABIB, S. (1992) *Situating the Self*. London: Polity.

BLOOM, M. (2004) 'The ethics of compensation systems', *Journal of Business Ethics*, 52: 149–52.

BROOKS, E. B. and BROOKS, A. T. (1998) *The Original Analects*. New York: Columbia University Press.

CALDECOTE, R. (1990) 'A bias against business', in *Wealth Creation and Christianity*. Industrial Christian Fellowship, June: 7.

CONGER, J. (2005) 'O Lord, won't you buy me a Mercedes Benz?: How compensation practices are undermining the credibility of executive leaders', in Ciulla, J., Price, T. and Murphy, S. (eds) *The Quest for Moral Leaders*. Cheltenham: Edward Elgar.

DAWKINS, R. (2010) *The Greatest Show on Earth*. London: Black Swan.

GOLEMAN, D. (1996) *Emotional Intelligence*. New York: Bantam Books.

GREENBERG, J. and CROPANZANO, R. (2001) *Advances in Organisational Justice*. Stanford, CA: Stanford University Press.

GRIFFITHS, B. (2009) http://www.guardian.co.uk/business/2009/oct/21/executive-pay-bonuses-goldmansachs

HABERMAS, J. (1992) *Moral Consciousness and Communicative Action*. London: Polity.

HARRIS, J. (2006) 'How much is too much? A theoretical analysis of executive compensation from the standpoint of distributive justice', in Kolb, R. *The Ethics of Executive Compensation*. Oxford: Blackwell.

HUME, D. (1975) *Enquiries Concerning Human Understanding and Concerning the Principles of Morality*. Oxford: Oxford University Press.

JONAS, H. (1984) *The Imperative of Responsibility: In search of an ethics for the technological age*. Chicago: University of Chicago Press.

KANT, I. (1964) *Groundwork of the Metaphyics of Morals*. Translated by Paton, J. New York: Harper & Row.

KHURANA, R. (2002) *Searching for a Corporate Savior*. Princeton, NJ: Princeton University Press.

KHURANA, R. and NOHRIA, N. (2008) 'It's time to make management a true profession', *Harvard Business Review*, 86(10), October.

KOEHN, D. (1998) *Rethinking Feminist Ethics*. London: Routledge.

KOLB, R. (2006) *The Ethics of Executive Compensation*. Oxford: Blackwell.

LEE, S. (2003) *Uneasy Ethics*. London: Pimlico.

MARKHAM, I. (1994). *Plurality and Christian Ethics*. Cambridge: Cambridge University Press.

MacINTYRE, A. (1981) *After Virtue*. London: Duckworth.

MILES, S. (1998) *Consumerism: As a way of life*. London: Sage.

MILKOVICH, G. and RABIN, B. (1991) 'Executive performance and firm performance', in Foulkes, F. (ed.) *Executive Compensation*. Boston, MA: Harvard Business School Press.

MILL, J. S. (1993) *Utilitarianism*. Oxford: Oxford University Press.

MURDOCH, I. (1972) *The Sovereignty of the Good*. New York: Schucker.

NIETZSCHE, F. W. (2003) *Beyond Good and Evil*. London: Penguin.

NOZICK, R. (1972) *Anarchy, State and Utopia*. New York: Basic Books.

PLATO (2005) *The Laws*, Book V. London: Penguin.

RAMADAN, T. (2009) *Radical Reform: Islamic ethics and liberation*. Oxford: Oxford University Press.

RAWLS, J. (1971) *A Theory of Justice*. Cambridge, MA: Harvard University Press.

ROBINSON, S. (1992). *Serving Society: The responsibility of business*. Nottingham: Grove Ethics.

ROBINSON, S. (2001) *Agape, Moral Meaning and Pastoral Counselling*. Cardiff: Aureus.

ROBINSON, S. (2008a) *Spirituality, Ethics and Care*. London: Jessica Kingsley.

ROBINSON, S. (2008b) 'Fetullah Gülen and the concept of responsibility', in Yurtsveer, E. (ed.) *Islam in the Age of Global Challenges*. Washington, DC: Rumi Forum.

ROUSSEAU, D. (1995) *Psychological Contracts in Organizations*. Thousand Oaks, CA: Sage Publications.

SAREWITZ, D. (2004) 'How science makes environmental controversies worse', *Environmental Science and Policy*, 7(5): 385–403.

SCHWEIKER, W. (1995) *Responsibility and Christian Ethics*. Cambridge: Cambridge University Press.

SHAW, W. (2006) 'Justice, incentives and executive compensation' in Kolb, R. (ed.) *The Ethics of Executive Compensation*. Oxford; Blackwell.

SOLOMON, R. (1992) *Ethics and Excellence*. Oxford: Oxford University Press.

STACKHOUSE, M. L., McCANN, D., ROELS, S. and WILLIAMS, P. (eds) (1995) *On Moral Business: Classical and contemporary resources for ethics in economic life*. Grand Rapids, MI: William B. Eerdmans.

STOREY, L. and DASH, E. (2009) *New York Times*, 30 July.

SUN, W., STEWART, J. and POLLARD, D. (eds) (2010) *Reframing Corporate Social Responsibility*. Bingley: Emerald.

TAWNEY, R. H. (1930) *Equality*. London: Allen & Unwin.

TAYLOR, C. (1989) *Sources of the Self*. Cambridge: Cambridge University Press.

WALZER, M. (1973) 'Political action: the problem of dirty hands', *Philosophy and Public Affairs*, 2(2), Winter: 160–80.

WESTERN, S. (2007) *Leadership: A critical text*. London: Sage.

CHAPTER 3

Ethical Decision-Making

LEARNING OUTCOMES

When you have completed this chapter you will be able to:

- understand and critically evaluate Kohlberg's and Erikson's descriptive theories of ethics
- critically evaluate the idea of a descriptive theory of ethics
- understand and critically evaluate the organisational context of ethical practice
- understand and apply approaches to ethical decision-making
- understand what mature ethical thinking involves.

INTRODUCTION

This chapter aims to examine how we 'do' ethics. First, it looks at descriptive theories of ethics. Unlike normative theories of ethics, these are not concerned with philosophical reflection on the meaning of ethics but rather with how we make our decisions and what we need in order to make such decisions. These theories involve both theories of moral development and theories of cultural causation. The chapter then examines a framework of ethical decision-making, built around the Colombian rain forest case.

PAUSE FOR THOUGHT

You may not have thought about this before, but how do you make an ethical decision? Do you have an informal method that you use to work out what is the right behaviour?

Compare and contrast your answer with an answer from another student/colleague.

You will be asked to repeat this activity after working through the chapter.

CASE

THE COLOMBIAN RAIN FOREST

A Western civil engineering firm with links into a Colombian private university was asked by the Colombian government to lead a project with the aim of meeting the technological needs of a tribal community in the remote rain forest. After a long and difficult journey the engineers, with a number of students, reached the village and agreed that the most urgent priority was an adequate supply of water. The nearest water supply was a large river about 800 metres (half a mile) from the village, and some 15 metres (50 feet) lower than it.

The crops on which the villagers depended required a regular and large supply of water, which was not always easily available during the drier parts of the year, although the river does just continue to flow during these times. The journey to the river was not pleasant, involving wading through a swamp. The swamp area had been increasingly used as a latrine by the tribe. The swamp area was also infested with mosquitoes and was the source of disease. Nonetheless, this area comprises an environment that includes important flora and fauna, including two rare animals.

The village, of course, had no electricity supply, and there was only rudimentary infrastructural technology. Housing conditions, in huts made of timber and willow reeds, were very poor. Illness and deformity were common, and the villagers had virtually no contact with the outside world.

The culture, however, was an attractive one. Honesty was a key virtue, and the villagers were accustomed to working hard to keep together body and soul. The corporate spirit of the villagers was very strong, supported by a lively belief system and frequent community rituals.

It seemed unlikely that anyone would attempt to support or further assist the village once the project was completed.

This case was originally detailed by John Cowan, Professor of Engineering Education at Heriot-Watt University in 1985.

Questions

1 How would you make decisions about this situation?

2 Work out the steps of your method. Sharing your method with two colleagues, work out together with them a method of ethical decision-making that you are all comfortable with. Explain to yourselves why that method is fit for its purpose.

3 Then share it with the class, and see if you can all agree on a decision-making process. *We will return to this case below in the decision-making framework.*

IT'S EASY TO BE ETHICAL!

Trevino and Brown (2004) refer to a newspaper article (from the Minneapolis-Saint Paul *Star Tribune*, 28 June 2002) with the headline 'Corporate ethics is simple – If something stinks, don't do it.' Such thinking advocates other approaches, including the well-known *light of day test*. The best form of this, when faced by a problem that seems to be ethical, is to imagine what your mother or your children would say if you were part of this practice and were in the headlines in tomorrow's papers. This can be intensified in the *consequence test* – namely, what would the consequences be for me or the business if I got involved?

Such tests are useful tools to bear in mind but they do not get us very far. First, they are not really tests at all but rather precautionary perspectives that remind us that we might be found out. Second, all they tell us to do is not to get involved. But what if not getting involved leads to making the unethical practice even worse, which in turn leads to a disaster for the firm and for clients of the firm, such as what happened with the *Herald of Free Enterprise* or even Enron? And what if my mother or partner were to read the headlines about the subsequent enquiry and saw that I had not done anything about the practice when I could have? Would she think I am a moral coward? A warning does not help us in deciding what is actually right to do. Third, what if my ethical sense of smell is not very good? I might be aware of a practice and consider it strange but note that the practice seems to have been accepted by colleagues and line managers.

PAUSE FOR THOUGHT

Abu Ghraib

In the Abu Ghraib gaol scandal of 2006 (see Robinson, 2011), a number of US military personnel were found guilty of abusing prisoners. In the cold light of day this is torture. They believed that it was an accepted part of the culture in a very difficult situation where they feared for their lives, and where even the medical officers seemed part of the practices. Higher up the command chain was the attempt to view some practices not as torture but rather as legitimate 'aggressive interrogation' – something claimed to be legitimised in response to the direct threat to the USA of 9/11. In other words, this was a form of moral justification that influenced the culture. The ordinary soldiers saw everyone doing this and thus assumed that it was all right. They did not 'smell' a thing.

What would make you question someone's practice?

Can you think of a time when a practice at work did not 'seem right'?

How would you want to respond to that?

Fourth, and connected, the way in which the 'smell test' is set out assumes that ethics is about an immediate ethical dilemma, and that it involves responding to that dilemma. Not only may it not be obvious to the person that there is a dilemma, in the light of the culture, but the ethical issues may not be about immediate decision-making, or even about wrongdoing as such, either. The engineers in the Colombian case above clearly had decisions to make that were not about simple ideas of right or wrong but about major values and what was good for all involved in that situation. At its most basic was the question: should they have been there in the first place? Even just the presence of a Western engineering firm runs the danger of negatively affecting a finely balanced culture. In the tribe's case this was one that did not view mortality as negative, compared to the engineer's culture which feared it.

Fifth, it assumes that ethical decision-making is individualist – that it merely requires the individual to make up his or her mind. But even the reflection up to this point in the chapter seems to indicate that ethical decision-making cannot simply be about one person. By definition there are many people who might be involved who radically affect both the ethical meaning and the practice.

Making an ethical decision, then, is not simple, and this chapter now explores what influences ethical decision-making, beginning with descriptive theories of ethics.

DESCRIPTIVE THEORIES OF ETHICS

Descriptive theories of ethics are concerned with describing the moral beliefs, opinions and values of individuals or social groups. Claims in descriptive ethics are not about what makes something right or wrong (good or bad) but rather about how people think about ethics in practice. Ethical reasoning and decision-making are therefore empirically observed, and theory is derived from that. Here we shall examine two well-known stage theories of development by Lawrence Kohlberg and Erik Erikson – a stage being a period in a person's development at which they exhibit typical behaviour and establish particular capacities. Kohlberg argued for six stages in moral development. Building on Piaget's (1965) work, his theory suggests that the key to moral development is the development of cognitive capacities. In comparison, Erikson, building on Freud, proposed eight stages of development.

KOHLBERG'S STAGES OF MORAL DEVELOPMENT

Kohlberg argued that the process of attaining moral maturity was lengthy.

He based his stage theory upon research and interviews with groups of young children. A series of moral dilemmas were presented to children, who were then interviewed to determine the reasoning behind their judgements of each scenario. The following is one example of the dilemmas Kohlberg presented (Kohlberg, 1969).

> In Europe, a woman was near death from a special kind of cancer. There was one drug that the doctors thought might save her. It was a form of radium that a druggist (pharmacist) in the same town had recently discovered. The drug was expensive to make, but the druggist was charging ten times what the drug cost him to make. He paid $200 for the radium and charged $2,000 for a small dose of the drug.
>
> The sick woman's husband, Heinz, went to everyone he knew to borrow the money, but he could only get together about $1,000. He told the druggist that his wife was dying and asked him to sell it cheaper or let him pay later. But the druggist refused, arguing that he had spent time and money developing this drug and so was entitled to the full fee. So Heinz became desperate, breaking into the man's store to steal the drug for his wife. Should the husband have done that?

Kohlberg pointed altogether to three dilemmas (see below) – that of Heinz, that of the druggist (should he charge what he was owed, or should he make an exception?), and that of the trial judge (should he be lenient or go by the letter of the law?). He was not interested so much in the answer to the question of whether Heinz was wrong or right, as in the *reasoning* for the participants' decision. The responses were then classified into various stages of reasoning in his theory of moral development.

An ethical dilemma

An ethical dilemma is a situation involving an apparent conflict between ethical imperatives. To obey one would result in going against another. In the first chapter, for instance, the head of Himex had to deal with two imperatives: to respond to the needs of David Sharp or to respond to the potential threat that his clients were under. The conflict for Heinz was 'Do I care for my wife, and thus commit theft? If I commit theft, she will get better – but I may go to prison!'

In ethical decision-making below we examine whether dilemmas are always real and how conflicts can be handled.

On the basis of his research, Kohlberg identified six stages of moral reasoning grouped into three major levels. Each level represented a fundamental shift in the social–moral perspective of the individual. The three levels are each divided into two stages.

Level I: Preconventional morality
- *Stage 1 – Obedience and punishment orientation*
  In Kohlberg's Stage 1 the child assumes that powerful authorities hand down a fixed set of rules which he or she must obey without question. Kohlberg calls this thinking 'preconventional' because children do not yet see themselves as members of society. Instead, they see morality as something external to themselves – something adults impose upon them.
- *Stage 2 – Individualism and exchange*
  At this stage children recognise that there is not just one right view that is handed down by the authorities. Children at both stages focus on punishment, but perceive it differently. At Stage 1, punishment is tied up in the child's mind with wrongness; punishment confirms that disobedience is wrong. At Stage 2, in contrast, punishment is simply a risk that one naturally wants to avoid. Stage 2 still involves preconventional reasoning because the children speak as isolated individuals rather than as members of society.

Level II: Conventional morality

- *Stage 3 – Good interpersonal relationships*
  This is seen by Kohlberg as occurring at the beginning of the teenage years, when the children see ethics as more complex. They believe that people should live up to the expectations of the family and community and behave in 'good' ways. This is conventional thinking because it assumes that the attitude expressed would be shared by the entire community.

- *Stage 4 – Maintaining the social order*
  At Stage 4 the respondent focuses on society as a whole. The emphasis is on obeying laws, respecting authority, and performing one's duties so that the social order is maintained. Stage 4 subjects understood the purpose and function of laws for society as a whole, and so could frame an argument about laws.

Level III: Postconventional morality

- *Stage 5 – Social contract and individual rights*
  A core motivation in Stage 4 is to keep society functioning. However, a totalitarian society might be well-organised but have little moral content. At Stage 5, people begin to ask the underlying question about what makes a good society. Critical theory is introduced, and one's own and other societies are tested. They recognise that different social groups within a society will have different values, but they believe that all rational people would agree on two points. First, all would want certain basic rights, such as liberty and life, to be protected. Second, they would want some democratic procedures for improving society.

- *Stage 6 – Universal principles*
  Stage 6 respondents also saw themselves as working out a conception of the good society. Certain individual rights must be protected and disputes should be settled democratically. Democracy, however, does not always result in outcomes that are just. A majority, for example, may vote for a law that hinders a minority. The moral reasoning behind this requires empathy, seeing the situation through the eyes of the different participants. This enables an impartial response similar to Rawls' view of justice as fairness (Rawls, 1971). Laws are evaluated in terms of their coherence with basic principles of fairness rather than upheld simply on the basis of their place within an existing social order.

Summary

The stages move from a simple acceptance of authority through to a reasoning about the nature of authority and the underlying ethical principles of society. According to Kohlberg, the stages form an invariant sequence: no stage is ever skipped. This was confirmed in longitudinal studies.

The sequence for the stages of moral development are universal – that is, occurring across all cultures. Cross-cultural research shows that individuals in 'technologically advanced' societies move rapidly through the stages of moral development, whereas in isolated communities few go beyond Stage 3. This seems to indicate that greater awareness of different ethical perspectives assists moral development.

Criticisms

There are several criticisms of Kohlberg's theory.

- *Care and the community* – Gilligan (1982) argues that the theory is incomplete, not least because it devalues the morality of care and the community. Kohlberg, as a member of the educated, elite, white, male, Western culture viewed individual autonomy and justice as the premier moral values. In effect he equated ethics with justice, ignoring other possible core principles, such as equality of respect and compassion and care. Gilligan views this as partly a gender issue. Feminist ethics argues that care is at the centre of ethics, and that this looks to work through ethical issues not in an individualistic way but through the sharing of responsibility by members of the community. She argues that there was a difference between male and female respondents, the latter stressing shared responsiveness. This involves more affiliative ways of living, tying ethics to real, ongoing relationships rather than abstract solutions to hypothetical dilemmas. For males, advanced moral thought revolves around rules, rights and abstract principles.

- *Culture* – Non-Western and tribal societies, and historically the lower classes in the West, also frequently see the community as more important than the individual. According to Kohlberg's upper-class Western view of moral reasoning, communitarian morality is doomed to rest forever at a lower stage of development. This view disregards the possibility that communitarian morality may be as advanced as individualist morality, if not more so. It also places Western culture at the top of the scale, with little room for cross-cultural inclusion.

- *Empirical methodology* – Some critics claim that the use of hypothetical situations skews the results because it measures abstract rather than concrete reasoning. When children (and some adults) are presented with situations out of their immediate experience, they turn to rules they have learned from external authorities for answers, rather than to their own internal voice. Young children therefore base their answers on rules of 'right' and 'wrong' they have learned from parents and teachers (Stages 1 and 2). Gilligan (1982) noted that if young children are presented with situations familiar to them, on the other hand, they often show care and concern for others, basing their moral choices on the desire to share the good and maintain harmonious relations, placing them in Stage 3 or 4 (which Kohlberg claimed was impossible at their age). It is difficult then to see how the idea of an invariable sequence can be sustained. It may be that individuals and groups locate themselves in different stages depending upon the context, any major crises causing access to higher or lower stages.

- *Descriptive theory* – Such concerns raise the question of whether the stage theory is genuinely descriptive. The interpretation of the data seems to be based on values already accepted by Kohlberg – that is, autonomy and cognitive decision-making. The height of these values is about standing out for universal justice, based in Rawlsian and Kantian ethical theory, for which there is hardly any empirical confirmation. It would thus seem to be connected to, if not based on, normative ethical theory.

- *Practice and principle* – Does moral reasoning necessarily lead to moral behaviour? Kohlberg's theory is concerned with moral thinking, but there is a big difference between knowing what we ought to do and motivation to action. Even if the moral stages of Kohlberg's theory do indicate moral thinking, there is little empirical indication how this affects behaviour.

Kohlberg's stage theory thus has important elements but does not take full account of the complexity of moral decision-making. To do that requires a greater understanding of the effects of aspects such as culture and gender on the decisions taken.

ERIKSON ON ETHICS

Erik Erikson is best known for his eight stages of human development and has been primarily associated with developmental psychology. In his book *Childhood and Society* (Erikson, 1950) he argued that alongside the stages of psychosexual development presented by Freud were psychosocial stages of ego development ('ego' denoting a firm sense of who one is and what one stands for) in which the individual had to establish new orientations in himself or herself and towards the social world.

According to Erikson, the eight stages are genetically determined, each stage centring on a crisis involving two conflicting personality outcomes. A positive outcome resulting from *adaptation* to the stage's crisis or challenge resulted in the creation of specific virtues. Alternatively, the result of the stage's challenge might be a negative outcome resulting from *maladaptation*.

Erikson's psychosocial virtues (hope, will, purpose, skill, fidelity, love, care and wisdom) are the fruit of adaptation and essentially represent various human qualities of strength gained through contestation. They constitute the basic properties of a strong, vital, healthy and whole person (Conn, 1977).

'Generativity' was Erikson's term for inter-generational enrichment, and it constitutes the primary task in adult life (Friedman, 1999):

- Erikson implied that adults were wired to care for the next generation and to seek to leave behind a legacy of that care. In *Insight and Responsibility* he writes, 'Generativity, as the instinctual power behind various forms of selfless "caring", potentially extends to whatever a man [or a woman] generates and leaves behind, creates and produces' (Erikson, 1964).
- The prime generative encounter for many adults is parenthood. However, this is only the most obvious expression of an instinctual ability to care for and to teach (in its widest sense) the next generation. Business leadership would also fall in this category.
- The short-circuiting of this innate potentiality results in an aberration whereby the adult can slip into self-absorption and effectively become his or her own infant or pet (Erikson, 1964).

'Mutuality' is about interdependence and denotes active relationships in which dependence on one another produces individual and cumulative strengths:

- People are born with the need for regular and mutual affirmation of this kind; and failure of this basic reciprocity and trust produces the most far-reaching failure, undercutting all development (Erikson, 1964).
- Mutuality underpins the well-known golden rule which in terms of mutuality would say that it is best to do to another what will strengthen you even as it will strengthen them – that is, what will develop the other's best potentials even as it develops your own (Erikson, 1964).

'Leeway' is Erikson's term for the freedom to be oneself and to grant such freedom to others:

- In Erikson's thinking, we might speak of the leeway of play and childlikeness, bound up with their liberating content of originality, creativity and abandon.
- There is genuine life and movement to leeway and it contrasts with a certain stagnation and rigidity that can prevail in adult settings, including the workplace.
- In Erikson's thinking it is important to differentiate childlikeness – here encouraged and positive to human development – from 'infantilisms' present in the mass market, bureaucratisation, consumerism and convention, all stifling to development and characterised by over-compliance.

It is important to appreciate that Erikson's stage theory is not an individualist model; neither does the individual pass from stage to stage in a constant, uninterrupted and linear fashion. As Friedman (1999) emphasises, progression along the life-cycle is not so much an individual but an *inter-generational* process in which individuals in one stage assist those in others.

Healthy development is therefore a shared responsibility, and the virtues emerge as Erikson suggests through the 'interplay of successive and overlapping generations, living together in organised settings' (Erikson, 1964). Living together, Erikson continues, means more than an incidental proximity. Rather, the individual's life stages are 'cogwheeling', as Erikson described it, with the stages of others. This moves the individual along the life-cycle as they move others. It constitutes what Erikson called an 'integrated psychosocial phenomenon' (Erikson, 1964).

The organised settings which Erikson describes, include an expanding series of institutions that meet the individual as he or she grows up and moves into the adult order – the family, school and society (including employment settings). They might also include a number of life arenas which Erikson regularly referenced: love, the workplace, home life, friendship and citizenship (Erikson, 1964). The virtues created by the dealings of the generations with each other flow both in and out of the institutions. Without the virtues, Erikson warned, institutions wilt and become 'sick' (Erikson, 1964).

Figure 3.1 Erikson's eight stages of psychosocial development, each with its crisis and favourable outcome (virtue)

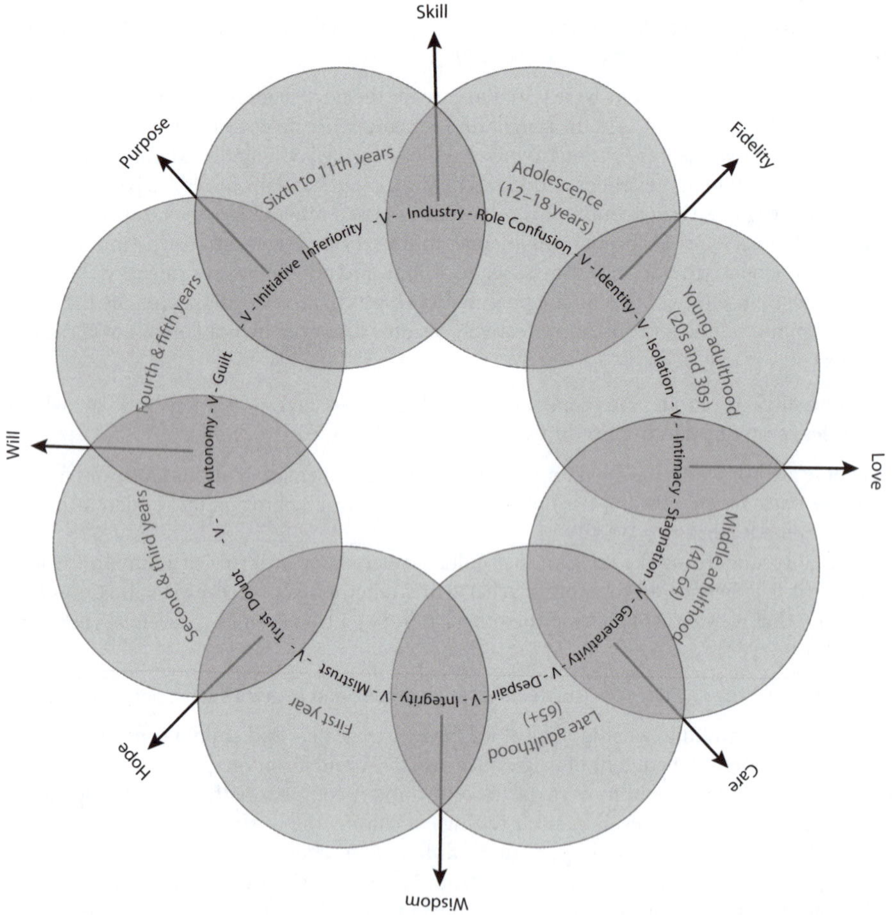

As a descriptive theory, Erikson's thinking sees positive and negative aspects of development. On the one hand, he stresses positive human development, expressed in such concepts as generativity, mutuality and leeway, all with their potential to take human development in a healthy direction. On the other hand, there are forces at work that threaten to at least derail, and at worst destroy, human flourishing. In this category is Erikson's concept of *pseudospeciation*. As the name suggests, the idea is that humanity has been inclined to substitute a false (and necessarily incomplete) version of mankind for the reality that we are all actually one species. The pseudo-species mentality is reflected in people's endless capacity to subdivide themselves into groups – ethnicities, classes, nationalities, ideologies, creeds, religions and suchlike – each group believing that they represent the correct fulfilment of human possibilities. In this way pseudospeciation *de facto* creates 'other' and, as Erikson highlights, 'As long as the core of any collective identity is a pseudo-species idea, it is going to be oppressive' (Erikson, 1973).

Erikson notes the superiority accompanying the pseudo-species mentality. Many groups, Erikson argues, 'provide their members with a firm sense of God-given identity – and a sense of immortality'. As for the 'outsiders', such is the need for groups to believe their superiority that outsiders are seen as strange (Erikson, 1966).

Much of Erikson's theory to this point underlies his view of ethics. For Erikson, ethics represented the endgame of development and had to be differentiated from the lesser states he called 'morality' and 'ideology'. He said it was important 'to learn to understand and to master the difference between infantile morality, adolescent ideology and adult ethics' (Erikson, 1964). Returning to our presentation of the life-cycle, because of – as Roazen puts it – a 'developmental lag' (Roazen, 1976), an ethical outlook does not automatically result simply from ageing. Moral learning and obligation Erikson identified as an aspect of childhood. Ideological experimentation and conviction he associated with adolescence. However, ethical consolidation was an adult task (Erikson, 1975).

Erikson also specifically referenced the development of an ethical orientation. 'Ethical' for Erikson in this context meant 'a universal sense of values assented to with insight and foresight, in anticipation of responsibilities' (Erikson, 1970). This marks out the ethical orientation as essentially and predominantly conscious, in contrast to the less mature moral orientation that goes before (Conn, 1977).

This led Erikson to call for a worldwide ethics, characterised by a greater consciousness of what any generation owes to every other one (Roazen, 1976). In contrast to the propensity to slip into a pseudo-species mentality, this was about struggling to assert a universally inclusive identity. The best leaders, for Erikson, were those who realised the potential for more inclusive identities (Evans, 1967).

For Erikson, mature ethical thinkers avoid judging and controlling others, moralising and blaming. Instead, they are principled and hold positive, life-affirming values. They maintain the world positively, holding it in trust for future generations and treat others as worthy, equal beings (Hoare, 2002). It is tempting perhaps to view oneself as ethical and principled, even in the light of Erikson's high-sounding definitions. But for Erikson, ethics were about *doing* something. Insight was worthless unless it led to responsible action; and principles had to be worked out in practice to meet the ethical test. Just as Kohlberg's descriptive theory of ethics was anchored in the normative theory of Kant, and Gilligan's in feminist theory, Erikson's stresses virtue ethics theory, with the importance of developing key virtues in community.

 PAUSE FOR THOUGHT

Why do you think grown adults are not always mature in their dealings with others? What are the implications for ethics?

Looking at Erikson's profile of an ethical adult, do you know any? Do you think they're a rare breed or encouragingly prevalent? What is the difference between moralising and being ethical?

Erikson's theory and the critiques of Kohlberg argue that ethical decision-making is not individualist but takes place in a social context. It is the study of this context, especially the organisation of business, that has much to say about how wider culture influences ethical decision-making.

THE ORGANISATIONAL CONTEXT OF ETHICS

Some research has found that principled individuals are more likely to behave in a manner consistent with their moral judgements, and they are more likely to resist pressures to behave unethically (Thomas, 1994). However, the work environment often creates pressure that makes it difficult both to recognise the need to make ethical decisions and to put them into practice. This is partly because the business context involves more complexity. There are more stakeholders involved, and with that more consequences to take into account. Something of this takes place at whatever level you are in business.

Sometimes, however, the social context radically affects how any action is actually perceived. Trevino and Brown note how surrounding behaviour can lead individuals to interpret ethics in the light of that. They give an example of it from a news item in the USA (Trevino and Brown, 2004):

> Police in New Britain, Connecticut, confiscated a 50-ft-long pile of stolen items, the result of a scavenger hunt held by the 'Canettes', New Britain High School's all-girl drill team. According to the *Hartford Courant*, police, parents, and school personnel were astonished that 42 normally law-abiding girls could steal so many items in a single evening. But the girls had a hard time believing that they had done anything wrong. One girl said: 'I just thought it was a custom … kind of like a camaraderie thing, [and] if the seniors said it was OK, and they were in charge, then it was OK!'

More serious examples of the effect of organisation and environment on ethical decision-making include the abuse of prisoners at the Abu Ghraib gaol in Iraq, described above (Robinson, 2011). This involved military police in the gaol based in Iraq being ordered to 'soften up' prisoners ready for interrogation. The result was a series of major abuses, leading to humiliation, injury and death.

Analysis of this suggested several major factors that affected ethical decision-making negatively (Zimbardo, 2007). First, there was little evidence of any practice of reflexivity. In the army this is institutionalised. The institution depends on unquestioning obedience. Trevino and Brown (2004) note that most adults in industrialised societies are at the 'conventional' level of cognitive moral development, and less than 20% of adults ever reach the 'principled' level at which thinking is more autonomous and principle-based. In practical terms, this means that most adults are looking outside themselves for guidance in ethical dilemma situations, either to significant others in the relevant environment (eg peers, leaders) or to society's rules and laws. Trevino and Brown (2004) conclude that this means that most people want to be led when it comes to ethics.

The experiments of Milgram (2005) revealed that almost 70% of participants accepted the direction of authority figures even where the action of the participant seemed to be causing risk to another person's life. Milgram wanted to look into the clash between authority and individual conscience. The experiment involved participants who controlled what they believed to be an electric current attached to a person they could either see or hear. They could see that what they perceived was pain in the other (who was actually an actor simulating pain) was being caused by their actions. However, they did not consider themselves responsible for this pain. The 'actor' was seen as partly responsible, because they got the questions wrong, in an experiment that the participant was told was about the relationship between pain and learning. More importantly, the experiment director was a figure of authority who assumed overall responsibility, both for the practice and the ideas and values behind it. Few of the participants took responsibility for critically questioning either the values or the practice.

When asked why they engaged in unethical conduct, employees often say, 'I had no choice' or 'My boss told me to do it' (Trevino and Brown, 2004). In terms of leadership, Hinrich (2007) has noted how easily this can lead to 'crimes of obedience', committed through simply following the orders of the leader. The assumption of the follower in such cases is that the leader is responsible for any values held and any decisions based on those values. In effect, the follower accepts no responsibility for testing ideas and values, and does not hold the leader to account for them. Sometimes, this thinking is moved on to the system, rather than the leaders *per se*. The dynamic is that we have to follow the system. Systemic thinking also tends to suspend critical thinking, easily leading to what Goodpaster (2006) refers to as 'teleopathy' – allowing secondary targets to distance oneself from any concern for the common good. Typically, if a junior member of a work team raises an ethical issue, the leader then reframes the issue, focusing on the needs of policy, saying that this is the leader's responsibility (Trevino and Brown, 2004). The system will function and achieve its end, without the need for humans in that system to take responsibility for their thoughts or actions. T. S. Eliot (1942) sums this up when he refers to attempts to make 'systems so perfect that no one will need to be good'.

Second, not only is there an assumption of the need to obey, the ethical environment is in turn justified by statements of value and purpose. Thus in the Milgram experiment the man with the white coat referred the participant to the vision that this project was helping to understand better the very nature of learning. It might also be justified by the language that is used. In the Abu Ghraib case the underlying purpose was the defence of the USA. At all costs 9/11 must not happen again. Any aggressive actions were set in this view of the greater good.

Third, this leads to use of language that either redefines the ethical meaning or obscures it. In the case of Abu Ghraib, torture was redefined. The White House legal adviser listed over 20 acts of 'aggressive interrogation' that were deemed acceptable (Robinson, 2011). Later court appeals affirmed that this was torture. The language used in the orders to the prison guards was intentionally not specific and euphemistic. Phrases like 'soften them up' gave an indication of aggression without actually saying what should be done. This led the guards to feel that aggression was acceptable and that they could do what they saw others doing.

The obscuring of ethical reality reaches its height in the rise of the Nazi Party. One example of this is the memo of Willy Just, an engineer in the Third Reich (cited in Bauman, 1989: 197).

> Memo:
> A shorter, fully loaded truck could operate much more quickly. A shortening of the rear compartment would not disadvantageously affect the weight balance, overloading the front axle, because a correction in the weight distribution actually takes place automatically through the fact that the cargo in the struggle toward the back door during the operation always is preponderantly located there. Because the connecting pipe is quickly rusted through by the fluids, the gas should be introduced from above, not below. To facilitate cleaning, an eight- to twelve-inch hole should be made in the floor and provided with a cover opened from the outside. The floor should be slightly inclined, and the cover equipped with a small sieve. Thus all fluids would flow to the middle, the thin fluids would exit during the operation, and the thicker fluids could be hosed out afterwards.

Neutral words, such as 'cargo', and the stress on technical solutions obscure the reality of the experience of people being murdered in the gas trucks on the Eastern Front. The memo aims to improve the efficiency of that killing. This points to the development of cultures that cause the employee to see things in an instrumental way rather than retain a wider awareness of issues. Trevino and Brown (2004) note the example of Dennis Gioia, who was recall coordinator at the Ford Motor Company in the early 1970s. The company decided not to recall the Ford Pinto despite the dangerous positioning of the petrol tank, which was causing fires that were killing the occupants of vehicles involved in low-impact rear-end collisions. Gioia operated in a situation of information-overload in which he saw thousands of accident reports. His criteria for deciding recalls were technical. The incoming information about the Pinto fires did not penetrate a process that was designed to look at other issues, and it did not initially raise ethical concerns. He and his colleagues in the recall office did not recognise the issue as an ethical one.

Trevino and Brown (2004) note that if the use of language can obscure the ethical issues, it can also influence moral awareness. For example, if the words 'stealing' music (rather than downloading) or 'forging' documents (rather than signing) were used, the individual would be more likely to think about these issues in ethical terms.

Jones (1991) found that the moral intensity of an issue influenced the recognition that it *was* an issue. Moral intensity is marked by the seriousness of any consequences and by social consensus. An individual is thus more likely to identify an ethical issue if it involves potentially harmful consequences and if others in the group view the issue as ethically problematic.

Fourth, clearly, another aspect that affects decision-making is the thought of adverse consequences. A good case in point is the whistleblower. Whistleblowing occurs when an employee brings to the attention of higher management – or even of an authority outside the firm – an activity or usage that is questionable (Borrie and Dehn, 2002). Research suggests that people who take principled stands, such as those who are willing to report a peer for unethical behaviour, are perceived as highly ethical while, at the same time, highly unlikable (Trevino and Victor, 2004). Whistleblowers are frequently ostracised or fired, leading to a fear of negative consequences (Miceli and Near, 1992).

Underlying many of these factors is the dynamic of individuals taking their ethical cue from the surrounding culture, and especially where unethical behaviour is associated with success. Nearly a third of respondents to one US business ethics survey (Trevino and Brown, 2004) said that colleagues condoned the ethically questionable practice of a leader who achieved success.

All of these considerations suggest the importance of developing an explicitly ethical culture, but also a critical culture, in which the ethical views are not accepted without question. In Chapter 6 we return to how such a culture can be developed.

AN ETHICAL DECISION-MAKING FRAMEWORK

The stress on descriptive theories of ethics does not of itself solve the problem of what is right or wrong. Descriptive ethics can, however, begin to help us work out how to think ethically and make decisions that take account of the key issues. James Rest (1994), for instance, develops Kohlberg's thinking, arguing for a complex, multiple-stage decision-making process. This involves:

- moral awareness (taking in the situation and the key ethical issues)
- moral judgement (deciding that a specific action is morally justifiable)
- moral motivation (the commitment or intention to take the moral action)
- moral character (persistence or follow-through to take the action despite challenges).

To explore ethical decision-making further we now return to the case study at the beginning of the chapter. This was an actual case. Analysis of the facts as outlined shows key elements for an ethical decision-making framework, involving data-gathering, value clarification and management, option assessment, planning with stakeholders, and audit.

DATA-GATHERING

The starting place of ethics is reflection on the situation. For the engineers in this case this meant reflecting on the story in order to identify:

- the purpose of being involved
- who else was involved
- the main needs that required response. Was there one or many? If many, what was the priority – and how do you decide on that?
- the technical issues surrounding those needs
- the ethical issues around indentifying and responding to the needs.

The immediate problem for them was the lack of clarity about who was the client. The government had commissioned the action, and the university was funding the student involvement, but the tribe was the party who would directly benefit, or not, from the work. It was clear that clarification was needed. It was also clear that the data-collection stage is not purely technical. It is about finding out about the perspectives and needs of the clients and also about the other groups or areas affected in the situation. For the government this would be a major publicity opportunity. It was being criticised for its lack of concern for the rain forest and the inhabitants. It wanted this to demonstrate the care of the government. For the civil engineering company and the university, getting this right could affect any future developments they hoped to be involved in. At the centre of it all was a tribe whose views were not clear. How would Western, so-called developed, culture affect them? How can one speak of enabling the tribe to develop an informed decision in this situation? Most of these questions can be faced in the context of the professional developing a relationship of trust with the tribe. This would crucially involve working with government representatives and would have to stay focused on the immediate problem, with a clear statement about the limitation of resources. Surrounding all this was the rich environment of the rain forest, which was under threat. The environment itself could be seen as a stakeholder, having an interest in the engineering response.

Core to all data-gathering is clarity about the expectations of stakeholders – which means that it is important to work with stakeholders even at this stage.

VALUE CLARIFICATION

The second stage of ethical decision-making is the clarification and working through of the values involved. In this case there are clearly several different kinds of values that the engineers had to be aware of.

Personal ethical values

An engineer may have particular concerns for the environment or for the health and well-being of groups in the undeveloped world. Some students who have responded to this case have been so concerned about the plight of the tribe that they argued that the engineers should look to develop a proper healthcare system for the tribe. The question then emerges how personal values relate to any case. In some cases personal values may be worthy, but not part of the role of the engineer. In other cases the personal values may supersede professional values. Some engineers might therefore find it difficult to work in contexts where there is potential for abusing the rights of stakeholders. Either way, it is important to identify any personal values and how they might relate to the situation.

Professional ethical values

Professional moral values can be divided into fundamental and procedural principles.
- Fundamental principles/values of the profession include *non-maleficence* and *beneficence* (Beauchamp and Childress, 1994). These are very broad principles, meaning, above all, do no harm; seek to do good. Interpreting them in the situation then becomes important. In this case it meant that the engineers had to ensure that they did not adversely affect the lives of the tribe in terms of either their culture or their health or environment. And it applied to the environment as a whole. Again, this would have to be worked through with the other interested parties.
  Another basic principle suggested by Beauchamp and Childress is *respect for autonomy* (self-governance). This can be seen in two ways. Firstly, in a negative sense it involves not interfering with the freedom of the clients to decide for themselves. Secondly, in a positive sense it refers to enabling the clients to make their own decision. Respecting the tribe's autonomy then involves respecting any decision they come to. The tribe might, for instance, politely decline any offer of help – in which case the engineers would have to inform their other 'clients', the university and the government, that the project, for all its importance, could not be successfully undertaken. Positive respect for autonomy would involve a careful discussion with the tribe leaders to work through things that the engineers had to offer. This would include the limitations of any offer, such as insufficient resources to maintain any sophisticated technology over a long period. Some engineers

in responding to this case felt that the very fact of the Western group's being there altered the dynamics of the situation and would inevitably affect the culture and environment for the worse.

A final basic value is of *justice*, such that the engineers treat all stakeholders fairly.

- Procedural principles are the important values which inform the professional's engagement with the situation, and are really instruments of the basic principles. *Confidentiality* is often essential for respecting the autonomy of the client. Such confidentiality must be formally established. How would that work through the case above, where so many stakeholders and possible clients are involved? *Informed consent* is also essential to positive respect. In addition, Beauchamp and Childress (1994) argue for cost-benefit analysis and risk-benefit analysis as ways of assessing consequences in the light of the basic principles.

A summary of professional principles

Fundamental principles

- Respect for the autonomy of the client
- Justice
- Beneficence
- Non-maleficence

Procedural principles

- Confidentiality
- Informed consent or decision-making
- Cost-benefit analysis
- Risk-benefit analysis

David Seedhouse (1998: 128ff) argues against such principles. This reminds us that any view of ethics is contested. He suggests that the fundamental principles are not clear enough. There are, for instance, many different views of justice. However, Seedhouse misses the point of such principles. They must be quite general, in order to give some idea of values that can be shared across different areas. At the same time the clearer meaning of the principle emerges as one engages with the situation. The procedural principles also help to give meaning. What is clear is that principles cannot be applied in an unthinking way – ie without reference to the situation.

Public ethical value

This involves two things. First, the values of all the different groups must be considered. In this case it involves the values of the engineers, the government, the university, the tribe, and so on. A second view of public values centres on values that underlie public life, focused on the idea of the common good. In this case such values included community, freedom and health.

Value conflict

Once values are clearly articulated, there may be value conflict or value congruence. Value conflict may emerge in terms of a dilemma, as noted above, involving no simple solution. Conflicts may be between values of different areas – such as personal, professional or public – or between different professional values. In the Colombian case the values of health and safety seemed to be in conflict with the values of sustainability (of culture and environment). Response to value conflicts requires first some attempt at prioritising them. Which do you think was more important?

In the Challenger case (see Chapter 8) the values of safety should have been paramount, rather than the political values. The virtue of practical wisdom (*phronēsis*) noted in the last chapter is critical to this. Reflection on end or purpose helps the manager or leader to focus on core values. The test of such a decision is whether the manager can give a justification for the choice of value to the stakeholders. In medicine, the value of patient autonomy has to be held in balance with professional views of what is in the best interest of the patient. However, patient autonomy remains more fundamental.

Second, values may be equally important and have to be held together. The professional principles of justice and equal respect for autonomy have to be held together, as do values of social care and institutional sustainability, noted in the Sharp case (Chapter 1). In the Colombian situation the autonomy of the tribe had to be held in balance with the sustainability of the social and physical environment, and the health of the community.

Third, any sense of dilemma may be more apparent than real, as Gilligan noted above. It may involve values that are focused in cultural attachments but which negatively affect the wider environment. It is important therefore to critically test any values and enable parties to question why they are important.

REFLECTIVE PRACTICE

Make a list of the stakeholders in the Colombian case.

What were their important values?

Make a list of all the ethical values in the case, and order them in terms of priority. How would you justify such an ordering?

Are there any value conflicts? If there are, how would you deal with them?

IDENTIFYING OPTIONS AND PLANNING

Any options will be dependent upon limitations and resources. These can only be identified through analysing, first, the capacities of individual 'actors', and then the resources in relation to the potential partnerships. Options will increase in relation to the different partnerships. At the base of this will also be exploration of responsibility, owned by individual actors, or shared between actors. Without negotiation of that responsibility, the options could not be put into practice. The key ethical category of responsibility is explored in detail in the next chapter.

Option assessment

Any response has to take account of the ethical issues, the various possible options in the light of the issues, the core values, bringing together value and principles, the constraints and possibilities, and the possible consequences and how they might affect the social and physical environment.

In the Colombian case there were three broad options: to do nothing, to develop an intermediate technological solution that would fully involve the tribe, or to develop a more sophisticated solution that would require high maintenance. The engineers on the spot decided, with the tribe, for the middle option, in the form of basic wooden piping and an Archimedean screw, because it would mean:

- minimal interference with the values of the tribe
- the tribe's retaining its autonomy and independence
- the tribe's retaining its strong community
- positive effects on the health of the tribe
- no major imbalance with other tribes in the area
- minimal interference with the environment.

PAUSE FOR THOUGHT

How far were the professional values fulfilled in this solution?

How far were the interests and values of the other stakeholders fulfilled?

AUDIT

Audit builds on the learning circle and reflective practice noted in the first chapter. It involves careful reflection prior to the next stage of development. Typically, large firms audit their financial, social and environmental practices. This is examined in detail in the final chapters.

REFLECTING ON PRACTICE

Of course, the deadlines of work mean that embodiment of values cannot be 'perfect', and the fitting of values to practice will be a matter of ongoing reflection. Indeed, in the light of such constraints, any ethical response may involve choosing the best of several difficult options. Nonetheless, the use of a framework that is understood and accepted by colleagues can enable rapid critical reflection on the immediate situation. Clearly, such a framework may not be used in detail for every situation. Moreover, the experienced reflective practitioner may well use the framework without consciously working through it in a serial way. However, it provides a means of making ethical sense of any situation.

It embodies and reinforces a view of ethics that is dialogic, participative, collaborative and transformative, and therefore directly relevant to employability.

In the light of that, four other things are of note about the ethical process:

1 If the process of dialogue is key to ethics, it cannot be simply about immediate problem-solving. On the contrary, the ethical outcome will be tied to the developing dialogue and involvement of others. Timing will thus be appropriate to the dialogue and situation.

2 The ethical process is essentially a learning process – learning more about the situation, stakeholders, values and possibilities. It will also include learning about the self.

3 This works against any idea of ethical perfectionism. Ethical perfectionism has several elements to it. First, it assumes that there is only one right solution to a problem. In fact there may be many different solutions that embody ethical value. This is one of Gilligan's critiques of Kohlberg. Second, it assumes that we can reach perfection in ethics. Whitehead (1989) in his learning theory suggests that this is never possible. On the contrary, each individual – and by extension every group – is a 'living contradiction': a mismatch of values and practice. Historically, this is exemplified in the way that often very morally upright people in the nineteenth century had little problem with child labour (Gallop, 2010). They only began to learn when campaigners such as Shaftesbury faced them with their actions and they saw that these were at odds with beliefs and values, including beliefs about children. It was as much about awareness (of the data or situation) as about the values. Whitehead argues that only once we experience that contradiction is there motivation to change. This idea of living contradiction is different from hypocrisy. Hypocrisy is when we *pretend* to hold certain beliefs and values, but don't really have them. Hypocrisy involves deception or even lying. Ethical decision-making involves minding that gap between values and practice that is there for everyone in some way. This is important in the development of ethical culture in business and in the claims that business might make of its ethics and how business is judged by others.

4 If ethical decision-making involves this kind of reflection, then it must also involve feelings as well as cognitive reflection. Seeing values and beliefs at odds with action creates an affective (emotional) as well as cognitive dissonance. All values are related to feeling precisely because we form some commitment to them. They are important to identity (Cowan, 2005). It is this feeling that motivates change.

ETHICAL THINKING: FALLACIES

In forming arguments about what you think is right or wrong, it is essential to pay heed to empirical and logical thinking. The first means that any data has to be properly collected and assessed. This data and the associated values act as the premise which forms the basis for your conclusion.

Even when an argument has a good premise it can be weakened by poor logic – and poor logic can easily go unnoticed. Faults in logic are often referred to as fallacies. Below are a number of common fallacies that are used in ethical arguments and that should be watched out for. It is particularly easy to slip up and utter a fallacy when you feel strongly about an issue. A conclusion may seem so obvious to you that it leads to a lack of attention around reasoning or how evidence is handled. Knowing what the major fallacies are can help you strengthen your ethical argument. It is important to know that fallacious arguments are common and can be powerful and persuasive if you are not watching out for them.

The most common fallacies include:

Ad hominem
This literally means that the argument is addressed to the person, not the issue. For example, 'X's argument is wrong because he is a Marxist.' The fact that X is a Marxist does not make his argument wrong. The argument must be judged on its own merit. In the final chapters there are many good examples of this fallacy used for and against business (see especially the Nestlé case study in Chapter 13).

Slippery slope
Another example of fallacious thinking in ethics is the *slippery slope argument*. This kind of argument describes something that will happen in the future if some action is allowed to happen. The classic versions of this are applied to ethical issues across the board, including changes in legislation on drugs and euthanasia. If you allow hard drugs to be legalised, it will lead to the complete breakdown of society. If you allow euthanasia, it will lead to the killing of elderly people who feel they are a nuisance.

The problem with this argument is that the conclusions simply do not follow. It is possible, for instance, to put in place safeguards which ensure that euthanasia is properly practised. The dire end that the slippery slope argument predicts may or may not happen. However, the fear that it might can give the argument a sense of authority.

The slippery slope fallacy is one version of the *non sequitur* ('it does not follow') fallacy, which involves an argument that endeavours to link two or more logically unrelated ideas together as if they were related.

Weak analogy
Many arguments rely on an analogy (a deduction based on comparison) between two or more objects, ideas or situations. The argument goes that if A is like B and B is wrong, then A must also be wrong. Everything then hangs on the analogy, which may or may not be valid. One version of weak analogy is moral equivalence, in which relatively minor problems are compared with much more serious issues or vice versa. For instance, mandatory seatbelt laws might be compared to the oppression of Nazi Germany.

Appeal to authority

We often try to strengthen arguments by referring to respected sources who support them. For example, we may refer to the writings of Gandhi to support the idea of human equality. However, simple appeal to Gandhi is irrelevant unless he can provide clear argument or empirical support for the importance of this moral idea. Appeals can also be made to popular views ('If 90% of the people think that bankers are wrong, then they must be') or to pity ('It is wrong to tax corporations – think of all the good they do for the community').

CONCLUSION

This chapter has examined some descriptive approaches to ethics. Stage theories show the importance of personal development, moving from a view of the person as influenced by the social context to more autonomous decision-making, based on rational reflection. Gilligan and others argue that this focuses on two extremes: the person who simply follows rules, and the person who thinks for himself or herself. Between those, argues Gilligan, is a social approach to ethics that is not just about individual decision-making but about people working together for any ethical response. The conclusion of that debate is that ethics is about *both* thinking for oneself *and* working out the response with others. The decision-making framework confirms, for instance, that data-gathering is more effective if the data is gathered from all stakeholders. The chapter has also shown that descriptive ethical theories assume, and are based in, normative ethical theories. Kohlberg is thus focused in Kantian theory, Gilligan in feminist theory, and Erikson strongly relates to virtue ethics theory. All this suggests that ethical thinking is focused in personal maturity, and the marks of 'adult ethics' are summed up below.

It also suggests that ethics is both about responding to difficult dilemmas often faced by the individual, and about how values are handled in day-to-day decision-making and planning. In turn, this emphasises the importance of a culture that makes ethical values and thinking explicit as part of any vision and value statement, so moving the debate from a narrow view of ethics into one which examines the responsibility of the individual and the corporation.

THE MARKS OF ADULT ETHICAL THINKING

- Awareness and maintenance of fundamental ethical principles, such as the right to life or respect, and the capacity to stand up for them.
- Rational thought that can critically test and justify ethical principles and estimate consequences.
- No attempt to impose an ethical perspective, claim the moral high ground or polarise ethical positions. This involves staying focused on the situation and ethical issues, not on underlying psychological dynamics.
- Critical engagement with ethical plurality inside and outside the organisation.
- The embodiment of core virtues which emphasise balanced thinking, such as courage and practical wisdom.
- Appreciation of the limits of knowledge, the ongoing process of learning.
- Working with others to find an ethical response focused on the common good.

MATURE ETHICAL THINKING AND INTERACTIONAL ANALYSIS

The identification of ethical thinking with maturity is brought out by two theorists, Eric Berne and Erik Erikson. This is not to suggest that such thinking is a product of *biological* maturity.

Eric Berne's well-known theory of transactional analysis (often abbreviated to 'TA') identifies three ego states all of which operate in every adult person:

- child

- parent
- adult.

The transaction or interaction between two people – one providing the transactional stimulus and the other the transactional response – where each will be in one of these three ego states, forms the basis of Berne's theory. Which ego state the individual occupies is evident in what the words are and how they are being delivered, and in the non-verbal signs accompanying those words (that is, body language including facial expressions).

Child represents the emotions and feelings the individual has stored from childhood, from birth to about the age of five. A particular situation will activate these emotions and feelings in either the agent (the transactional stimulator) or the (transactional) respondent. The observed stimulus or response will be characteristically childish – for example, 'You always blame me for everything!' (Berne, 1964). Berne said: 'Everyone carries a little boy [or girl] around inside of him [her]' (Berne, 1964).

Parent again represents recollections (or recordings) from the first five years, of the actions and words of the parent (or of those who assumed a parent-like role). These too are stored into adulthood and activated, this time being adopted and utilised by the child-become-grown-up. Like the child, 'Everyone also carries his [her] parents around inside of him [her]' (Berne, 1964).

Berne argues that 'So-called "mature" people are people who are able to keep the *adult* in control most of the time.' This is the third of the ego states and effectively regulates and objectively processes the other two states.

Applying Berne to ethics, his ego states explain why and how 'grown-ups' are not always adult, least of all in their interactions with others. It also provides a simple yet useful tool for recognising where ethical thinking is coming from in the self and the other. Arguments based in the parent ego state, for example, will look to encourage a compliant child response, possibly even dependency, and so unthinking and uncritical ethics. Arguments that are largely from the child ego state may aim to avoid taking responsibility. The child ego state might also see the other as parent, a figure of oppression who must be resisted – thus moving into *ad hominem* arguments.

Fallacious arguments tend to come from the child or the parent ego state, without engaging the adult. If these are at play in any ethical discussion, the dialogue is often accompanied by strong feelings (as may be expressed in 'I resent him trying to treat me like a child').

Mature ethical thinking recognises feelings but operates from the adult ego state, drawing attention to the different aspects of the ethical decision-making framework. Faced by the child–parent dynamic the aim would be to keep returning to that framework, helping those involved to access their adult ego state.

 REFLECTIVE PRACTICE

Look back over this chapter, thinking about what you felt as you read it.

Once you have reviewed the chapter, how would you now make an ethical decision? How has your method developed?

Compare and contrast your answer with that of another student/colleague.

EXPLORE FURTHER

Books

Geschwindt, S. (2007) *Am I Right? Or am I Right?: An introduction to ethical decision-making*. London: Trafford.

Fraedrich, J. and Ferrell, O. (2012) *Ethical Decision-Making for Business*. Los Angeles: South-Western College Publishing.

REFERENCES

BAUMAN, Z. (1989) *Modernity and the Holocaust*. London: Polity.

BEAUCHAMP, T. and BOWIE, N. (1989) *Ethical Theory and Business*. Englewood Cliffs, NJ: Prentice Hall.

BEAUCHAMP, T. and CHILDRESS, T. (1994) *Principles of Biomedical Ethics*. Oxford: Oxford University Press.

BERNE, E. (1964) *Games People Play*. London: Penguin.

BORRIE, G. and DEHN, G. (2002) 'Whistleblowing: the new perspective', in Megone, C. and Robinson, S. (eds) *Case Histories in Business Ethics*. London: Routledge: 96–106.

CONN, W. E. (1977) 'Erik Erikson: the ethical orientation, conscience and the golden rule', *Journal of Religious Ethics*, 5(2): 249–66.

COWAN, J. (2005) 'The atrophy of the affect', in Robinson, S. and Katulushi, C. (eds) *Values in Higher Education*. Cardiff: Aureus.

ELIOT, T. S. (1942) *The Complete Poems and Plays*. London: Faber & Faber.

ENTINE, J. (2002) 'Shell, Greenpeace and Brent Spar: the politics of dialogue', in Megone, C. and Robinson, S. (eds) *Case Histories in Business Ethics*. London: Routledge: 59–96.

ERIKSON, E. H. (1950) *Childhood and Society*. Harmondsworth: Penguin.

ERIKSON, E. H. (1959) *Identity and the Life Cycle: Selected papers*. New York: International Universities Press.

ERIKSON, E. H. (1964) *Insight and Responsibility: Lectures on the ethical implications of psychoanalytic insight*. New York: W. W. Norton & Co.

ERIKSON, E. H. (1966) 'The ontogeny of ritualisation', in Loewenstein, R., Newman, L., Schur, M. and Solnit, A. (eds) *Psychoanalysis – A General Psychology: Essays in honour of Heinz Hartmann*. New York: International Universities Press.

ERIKSON, E. H. (1970) 'Reflections on the dissent of contemporary youth', *International Journal of Psycho-Analysis*, 51: 11–22.

ERIKSON, E. H. (1973) *In Search of Common Ground: Conversations with Erik H. Erikson and Huey P. Newton*, with an introduction by Kai T. Erikson. New York: W. W. Norton & Co.

ERIKSON, E. H. (1975) *Life History and the Historical Moment*. New York: W. W. Norton & Co.

EVANS, R. I. (1967) *Dialogue with Erik Erikson*. New York: Harper.

FRIEDMAN, L. J. (1999) *Identity's Architect: A biography of Erik Erikson*. Cambridge, MA: Harvard University Press.

GALLOP, A. (2010) *Victoria's Children of the Dark*. London: History Press.

GILLIGAN, C. (1982) *In a Different Voice: Psychological theory and women's development*. Cambridge, MA: Harvard University Press.

GOODPASTER, K. (2006) *Conscience and the Corporate Culture*. London: Wiley Blackwell.

HINRICH, K. (2007) 'Follower propensity to commit crimes of obedience', *Journal of Leadership and Organisational Studies*, 4(1), August: 69–76.

HOARE, C. H. (2002) *Erikson on Development in Adulthood*. Oxford: Oxford University Press.

JONES, T. (1991) 'Ethical decision-making by individuals in organisations: an issue contigent model', *Academy of Management Review*, 16: 366–95.

KOHLBERG, L. (1969) 'Stage and sequence: the cognitive developmental approach to socialisation', in Goslin, D. A. (ed.) *Handbook of Socialization, Theory and Research*. Chicago: Rand McNally.

MICELI, M. and NEAR, J. (1992) *Blowing the Whistle*. New York: Lexington Books.

MILGRAM, S. (2005) *Obedience to Authority*. New York: Pinter & Martin.

PIAGET, J. (1965) *The Moral Judgement of the Child*. New York: Free Press.

RAWLS, J. (1971) *Justice as Fairness*. Oxford: Clarendon.

REST, J. (1994) 'Background: theory and research', in Rest, J. and Narvaez, D. (eds) *Moral Development in the Professions: Psychology and applied ethics*. Hillsdale, NJ: Erlbaum: 1–26.

ROAZEN, P. (1976) *Erik H. Erikson: The power and limits of a vision*. New York: Free Press.

ROBINSON, S. (2011) *Leadership Responsibility*. Oxford: Peter Lang.

SEEDHOUSE, D. (1988) *Ethics: The heart of healthcare*. London: Wiley Blackwell.

THOMAS, S. J. (1994) 'Moral judgment and moral action', in Rest, J. and Narvaez, D. (eds) *Moral Development in the Professions: Psychology and applied ethics*. Hillsdale, NJ: Erlbaum: 199–211.

TREVINO, L. and BROWN, M. (2004) 'Managing to be ethical: debunking five business ethics myths', *Academy of Management Executive*, 18: 69–81.

TREVINO, L. and VICTOR, B. (2004) 'Peer reporting of unethical behavior: a social context perspective', *Academy of Management Journal*, 35(1): 38–64.

WHITEHEAD, J. (1989) 'Creating a living educational theory from questions of the kind, "How do I improve my practice?"', *Cambridge Journal of Education*, 19(1): 41–52.

ZIMBARDO, P. (2007) *The Lucifer Effect*. London: Rider.

CHAPTER 4

Whose Responsibility? The Ethical Environment

INTRODUCTION

Chapters 2 and 3 introduced the debates about theories underlying ethics in business. Emerging from these were two themes. Firstly, ethics in business is more than rational theory: it also involves consideration of identity, purpose, feelings and virtues. Underlying that is narrative about worldview, informing ideas of the good, of value. As we see in Chapter 14, this becomes important in working in different cultures. However, it also raises the issue of what the nature of business is, and how it fits into the social and physical environment. In this chapter we examine that ethical environment and the related and central ethical category of responsibility, and how we respond to that environment. We develop that analysis by looking at responsibility in relation to the credit crisis of 2007/8. We focus on the moral agency of the corporation, the limits of corporate responsibility, and how this relates to responsibility as shared and negotiated. We also critically examine arguments for responsibility as an ethical theory, and end on a case that demonstrates the plurality of business and how this relates to the idea of multiple responsibilities. We conclude that responsibility is a core ethical category for business, not least in its capacity to connect different areas and contexts of ethical practice.

CASE

THE CREDIT CRISIS

The causes of the credit crisis in 2007/8 were many, and cannot be covered in detail here. However, there is general agreement about who was involved and what the major causes were.

First, at the heart of the crisis was the sale of mortgages by commercial banks to subprime lenders. The subprime lender is someone who is less likely to be able to pay the mortgage instalments because of poor credit history, low income or lack of collateral. This led to the systemic ignoring of factors that would affect the capacity to repay the loans. Generally within a year the subprime loans were sold in the secondary loan market. This had the effect of passing on the risk associated with the loans to other institutions.

Second, the investment banks who bought these loans then transformed the mortgages into mortgage-backed securities ('collatoralised debt obligations', or CDOs) that could be sold on. These innovative instruments aimed to share the risk surrounding loan repayments. They were also very complex, and in many cases this obscured the actual risk to the buyer.

Third, behind much of this was lack of supervision and regulation of financial markets across different countries. This allowed inadequate standards around underwriting loans, and poor monitoring of the problems emerging in the loan market. None of this was helped by lack of consistency of regulation between countries. Some regulators feared that too close supervision might affect the interest of banks based in their country and thus affect their national interests. In general, regulatory bodies were reluctant to focus on how the market as a whole was developing, preferring to focus on particular institutions.

Fourth, the role of government associate bodies also, in some cases, became part of the dynamic. The US government, for instance, was partly responsible for subsidising credit expansion in the US housing market through the government-sponsored enterprises Fannie Mae and Freddie Mac. This was part of a strongly egalitarian policy to help the less wealthy to buy their homes. Although concern was expressed within these institutions, the senior management continued to make large purchases of subprime loans. They were under pressure to meet goals set by the Department of Housing and Urban Development. Private investors soon entered this growing market, and with the rise of interest rates in 2004 many of the customers were unable to meet their mortgage payments, and house prices dropped alarmingly.

Fifth, reinforcing all this were the credit rating agencies – companies that assign credit ratings for issuers of debt obligations and debt instruments themselves. Competition between these credit rating agencies resulted in rating inflation. Evidence suggests that the more complex was the instrument, the higher was the rating produced by the agencies (Skreta and Veldkamp, 2009). This further encouraged the use of CDOs.

Sixth, the organisations who bought the debts failed to use any appropriate risk models. Indeed, their appetite for risk was encouraged by bonus systems for investment managers. This led to a short-term focus on immediate profit.

Finally, the focus on short-term profitability was reinforced by the priorities of bank shareholders. The average holding period for shares until the mid-1960s was almost seven years. Today it is less than a year in professionally managed funds. Aggressive shareholders like hedge funds prompted banks to a short-term focus on maximising shareholder value.

The effects of this crisis have been far-reaching, and are still being calculated. The International Monetary Fund estimated that the resulting global economic downturn has cost governments worldwide more than US $10 trillion to bail out the banks, with a massive adverse knock-on effect for employment, public spending and general well-being (http://news.bbc.co.uk/1/hi/8177814. stm).

ANALYSIS

We could view this story as simply a technical one and not an ethical one. These things happened for certain technical reasons and will be solved by technical, economic means. We simply have to be better bankers. However, even from the brief overview it is clear that alongside any technical concerns are ethical issues, not least about responsibilty.

The banks decided that the primary good was shareholder value. This meant that they were less concerned about capital requirements – what was left in the bank in case customers wanted their cash. The Basel Committee on Banking Supervision (http://www. bis.org/bcbs/) sets global levels for capital requirements, focusing on how banks manage risk, but banks in their attempt to increase profits sought to find ways of getting around the Basel requirements.

The banks were not clear about the context or history of their industry, and thus had no appreciation of what the consequences of their actions might be. Part of this involved not understanding the context, and part involved not understanding the history. Since the 1970s there had been over 120 bank-centred crises globally. Most of these followed booms in house prices and markets. Carroll and Mui (2008) note the example of Green Tree Finance who, in the 1990s, offered mortgages on mobile homes. The financial mismatch should have been obvious given that the average life of a mobile home did not exceed 15 years, and average length of mortgages sold was 30 years. No one, however, questioned the ever-increasing flawed loans. When problems began to occur with loan repayments in 1999, Green Tree Finance succeeded in selling the company to Conseco. Conseco subsequently became bankrupt. The leaders of the finance industry in 2008 made no attempt to examine the history of a sector that had made the same mistakes that led to the credit crunch. The only difference was that the early mistakes were restricted to individual corporations.

The lack of awareness extended to the products themselves. This was evidenced in different ways. There was no attempt critically to assess the sale of derivatives, in terms of theory or practice. Tett (2009) notes how attempts even to question practice, as a journalist, were dismissed out of hand. Repeatedly, firms made the mistake of buying into practices that were not thoroughly understood or that involved judgements outside their expertise. AIG, for instance offered credit-default insurance on mortgage-backed securities that it didn't understand. Merrill Lynch decided it would use instruments developed by Goldman Sachs to invest its own capital in what were subsequently revealed to be 'toxic' loans. Once again, the examples from the past might have warned against such a lack of critical thinking. Conseco in 1999 had a successful track record of taking over companies, all of which were insurance-based. The corporation had no understanding or experience of the mortgage business, however. The result was an inadequate understanding of the business model that it had taken on when buying Green Tree Finance. Despite this, Conseco increased its mortgage business. This continued up to the point of collapse. The only criterion for taking this firm on was that it made money.

The firms did not perceive any connection with the wider industry. They thus did not see that they were accountable to that wider industry. Recent work from the Institute of Chartered Accountants in England and Wales (ICAEW, 2007) has emphasised that the finance professions are part of a wider finance industry. At the very least this demands a framework of trust and transparency, ensuring a commitment to the future of the industry. By extension, clear and truthful information becomes critical for the wider financial markets. Participants in the markets depend upon accurate information to make choices. Accurate information is also necessary if any organisation is to plan effectively and sustainably. In turn, such information is necessary if public policy is to be effective. In effect, the ICAEW is arguing that the functioning of the whole financial system relies upon the practice of integrity. By extension, any wider financial services will be accountable to the wider financial system, not least because the financial services cannot operate in a system that has collapsed.

There was a lack of awareness of the wider community. The thinking of leaders was insulated. Merrill Lynch and WaMu, for instance, built large portfolios of mortgage-related securities that were based on the assumption that housing markets were localised, and thus that failure in one area would not affect other areas. The credit crisis showed, however, that markets were interconnected, and thus that leaders had to be aware of the possible effects of any practice.

The lack of realism was also reflected in the attitude to risk. Companies such as LTCM and AIG claimed that their portfolios and securities were risk-proof. Even disregarding the subprime base of the securities, the very idea of a financial instrument's being risk-free is problematic. Much of the belief in the lack of risk was founded in the mathematical modelling that was behind the development of the CDOs (see Lanchester, 2010: 97). This showed that by selling on the debts the firm was no longer responsible for ensuring repayments of the debts, so reinforcing little sense of responsibility beyond the immediate – and no sense of shared responsibility – for the industry or the wider community. Behind this there was another, equally naïve, assumption: that things would not go wrong. LTCM, for instance, thought that even in the event of problems it could always unwind its projects in an orderly fashion. In fact, all buyers disappeared at once. The same thing happened to Merrill Lynch, WaMu and others. The market unfolded so quickly that nobody would buy their debt portfolios.

The lack of any critical thinking was also evidenced all through the business chain, not least in the way the original mortgage businesses approached their customers. Companies actively encouraged mortgage customers to make decisions that were not based in realistic and responsible thinking.

REASONS

There might be several reasons for this lack of responsibility, from greed to the conceptual and structural reinforcement of the behaviour.

Greed

The first and most popular is to see the practices as generated by greed (Williams, 2009). Rather than virtue, this suggests vice. Greed is indeed one of the so-called seven capital vices, or deadly sins:

- lust – excessive desire of a sexual nature
- gluttony – over-indulgence and consumption, to the point of wasting resources
- greed – excessive desire for possessions, status or power
- sloth – a failure to use one's talents, resulting in inertia and inactivity
- anger – more precisely, uncontrollable rage
- envy – resentment of those who have what one desires
- pride – confidence in one's own superiority, together with an excessive love of oneself and one's capacities.

There is a long history to this idea, developed in moral theology and writers such as the early fourteenth-century poet Dante (1995). Dante's view of these vices is central to the thriller film *Seven* (DVD, Warner Home Video, 1995).

Some have famously tried to argue that such vices are 'good', because in some ways they may lead to good ends.

PAUSE FOR THOUGHT

Greed is good

Gordon Gekko (played by Michael Douglas) in the Twentieth-Century Fox film *Wall Street* (1987) argues that greed is good precisely because it fuels wealth creation. This argument also goes back a long way (1714), as exemplified in Bernard Mandeville's *Fable of the Bees* (2007). The fable shows that the self-concern of the bees leads to the production of honey, something enjoyed by others beyond the hive. Through this Mandeville argues that private vices can lead to public good. The vice of greed can lead to increased wealth for all.

Do you think that greed is acceptable? If it is, why do you think so?

Two things characterise such vices: excess and a loss of control. These tend to lead to clouded or narrowed awareness of the wider social environment, resulting in poor judgement. A vice such as sloth involves a lack of motivation and even depression, making it difficult to respond to the social environment. Pride can be seen as an acceptable attitude, expressed as reasonable pride in one's abilities or in the actions of one's organisation. It becomes a vice when focused exclusively on one's own achievements, to the exclusion of others. Focus on that pride leads once more to a lack of awareness of the social and physical environment, and ultimately to poor judgement in respect of the self, and to bad decision-making.

Greed is precisely a focus on the pursuit of self-interest such that there is no awareness of the surrounding environment or of the consequences of actions. It could be argued that the leaders in the credit crisis displayed greed and pride. In contrast, it should be pointed out that a *lack* of personal greed does not of itself lead to an ethics based purely on the interest of others. It is possible to be properly focused in self-interest and also be aware of the surrounding social and physical environment (see Chapter 1 on the reasons for ethics in business).

Rationalising and denial

In relation to the credit crisis there was a general defence of the practices noted above, leading to the denial of responsibility. At one level this involved the ideas that what was being done was not against the law, and that others were doing the same thing. A development of this argument appears from Goldman Sachs. At the time of writing (although in fact since then resolved), Goldman Sachs were being sued by the US Securities and Exchange Commission. The charge was one of fraud, based upon a hedge fund which asked Goldman Sachs to put together a collateralised debt obligation (CDO). The hedge fund subsequently bet, successfully, that the CDO would fail. There is no denying that something like this happened. For some time thereafter the kind of arguments used to rebuff the accusation were that this is simply what happens in the bond market, as distinct from the stock market, and that the people who lost money were all part of this risk business and understood the risks. At one level the argument was close to the long-ago expressed view of Albert Carr (1968), that business really is not about ethics (see Chapter 1). Everyday ethics are left at the office door. The point, so the argument goes, is that everyone in business knows what the 'game' is about – competition and deception, and much that requires us to suspend 'normal' ethics. Once one begins what is analogous to a game, one simply uses the rules of the game to gain personal advantage. Allied to the idea of an alternative ethics of game rules is the argument that the only people who have been harmed are those who have chosen to play the game, and thus, by implication, those who chose to risk what resources they had. In this light, greed and deception are simply a part of the game.

There are problems with such an argument in this case. First, it is not clear that the analogy to games rules actually holds. The idea that one can determine the content of a

CDO and then bet on it involves an activity that is far from a game of chance. Games of chance are characterised by a level of fairness. All have a similar chance to win; no one knows what the deal will give them. In the Goldman Sachs case there was no level playing field. The bet was fixed.

Second, of equal difficulty, is the idea that those who bet on the various deals will harm only themselves if things go wrong. This is clearly false. At the very least those who are involved in the bond market are connected to the firms that they work for. The fallout from the credit crisis amply demonstrated that failure in the area directly and adversely affected colleagues and co-workers. Extending beyond that are the shareholders large and small who invest in the finance organisations. If we suspend 'normal' ethics in favour of the rules of the risk business, then what might those rules actually be, who polices them and who might ensure that none of this affects people who have mortgages, and the housing industry, the non-speculative side of banking, the finance and banking industry, the governments who have bailed out the industry, and so on? The credit crisis showed that they are connected to all these groups and more, and share responsibility for global financial well-being. Minimally, this requires greater regulation in the bond market, to mirror the stock market, and probably dividing the speculative side of banking from other banking operations. Regulation in this sense would be to remind the firms involved that responsibility cannot be 'suspended'.

Third, one reason why many of the finance institutions practised in the way they did was because it was culturally and financially reinforced. In particular, the culture of remuneration reflected and determined the key values of the organisations. General remuneration and the large bonuses were tied directly to immediate profits (see Chapter 2). This reinforced a focus that that was concerned less with the nature of the product and more with profit. The dynamic was already there in examples such as Green Tree Finance, a firm that continued to deal in flawed loans because remuneration was tied directly to an increase in the number of mortgages. Key to the later subprime lending crisis was also the connection of immediate remuneration to the generation of flawed loans. These of course were then turned into securities and sold on. Remuneration was thus tied directly to a single and flawed means of making money. This clearly signalled that the firm was responsible for nothing but making money now – not for any effect of that decision on the firm a year or more down the line, or effect on the wider social environment.

In effect, then, the finance industries, reinforced by governments, had sealed themselves off from the wider social environment.

THE ETHICAL ENVIRONMENT

All of this points to a social and physical environment that is the context of any decision-making in business. Brown (2005) suggests that this environment involves five dimensions:

- cultural
- interpersonal
- organisational
- social
- natural.

The cultural dimension of the social environment is all about meaning. Culture is the expression of meaning and value through words, process, ritual, form (including art) and practice. In Chapter 6, for instance, we explore how Barcelona FC has developed their own culture and how it relates to their local and national culture. Culture rarely involves a single narrative. Many different parts of society assert some sense of meaning and value, but none can assert moral meaning for all. Core differences in culture then need to be properly addressed through critical dialogue.

The interpersonal level for Brown is about the different relationships that individuals and organisations have. All have different elements because we are all involved in multiple relationships. In the workplace one is not only a worker but also a citizen and a family member. Often the workplace recognises both of these aspects of identity. So, for instance, leave is provided for parental duties.

The organisational level looks to develop meaning and practice at the level of the organisation. This involves developing the values and purpose of the organisation and aligning practice to them.

The social level looks at the operation of the corporation beyond its boundaries. The corporation is part of many wider different groupings. Manufacturers of alcohol, for instance, are part of a much wider alcohol industry. At one level they compete with other members of that industry. At another level they are part of a wider identity that interrelates to other organisations. The alcohol industry relates to politicians in pursuit of a fair base for competition. It relates to the wider society through advertising regulation groups. It also contributes to the development of such regulation. It relates to wider groups through the concern for health. As we shall see in Chapter 6, the abuse of alcohol has become a problem for many countries, leading to significant health and economic problems. The issue is, then, how the industry responds to the needs in society and to the claims and demands of the different groups. Wetherly and Otter (2011) argue that there are legal, political, technological and economic environments. We examine these in more detail in later chapters as part of the social and cultural environment.

At the fifth level the firm has to make decisions about how it will respond to the global and physical environment. Linked to this and to the social environment is the issue of sustainability. How can these environments be sustained?

In each of these domains the firm and wider industry have to make decisions about how they respond to the different relationships and the needs expressed by the different groups involved. Several things can be noted about this environment:

- It is plural. There is therefore a need to handle very different domains at the same time.
- The domains are inevitably ambiguous. They may be both important to one and also a threat. The physical environment thus sustains individuals and organisations, but if care is not taken, it can threaten them.
- Our relationship with the domains is interactive, our actions affecting the environment and the groups and persons who are part of it.
- Key to any relationship with the environment is responsivity – working out how one should respond to that environment.

At the heart of this is the key ethical category of responsibility. Who is responsible for the different aspects of the organisational, social and physical environment? Business has to work out how it should relate to those environmental aspects, and thus what its responsibility involves. This raises issues about the identity and purpose of business, and how it might begin to determine its responsibilities. In short, the 'ethical environment' is the wider environment within which business operates, and all the related questions about the duties, effects, meaning and responsibilities involved in the relationship of business to that environment. These are precisely the questions that the finance industry did not address, or addressed in a narrow and exclusive way.

We begin our exploration of this by examining the meaning of responsibility.

RESPONSIBILITY

Much of the work in business studies and responsibility has focused on the concept of corporate social responsibility (CSR). For a time this was very much about the relationship of business to the community. This has developed further into what has been called the 'triple bottom line' approach, which emphasises the importance of giving an account of the firm's relation to the social and physical environment as well as of the financial state of the firm. Alongside this has been an emphasis both on the complexity of the external environment and on the need to include the internal (organisational) environment in any view of responsibility, not least in terms of the health, safety and well-being of the staff (see Chapter 11). The concept of responsibility itself, however, goes beyond even these concerns.

Schweiker (1995) suggests that there are three interrelated modes of responsibility, the first two of which originate in Aristotle's thinking: imputability, accountability and liability.

IMPUTABILITY

Imputability is simply about making a causal connection – the imputing of a cause that is responsible for something. There are strong and weak views of this. The weak views (McKenney, 2005) simply refer to the causal connection between the person and any action. Person A has caused, or was responsible for, action B. Such a view does not help in determining just how much the person is actually involved in, and therefore fully responsible for, the action. A stronger view then suggests that to be fully responsible for something necessitates a rational decision-making process. Taylor (1989) argues that this decision-making constitutes a strong valuation that connects action to deep decision-making. The owning of the thoughts and the related decision is what constitutes the moral agency and identity of the person or group. Closely connected to this is the concept of moral or retrospective responsibility which focuses on blame for actions. Responsibility, however, is not simply about finding blame but rather empowering an organisation and its members to acknowledge their values and practice, in effect developing rational agency, being responsible for ideas, values and practice.

- *Ideas* – This demands clarity about the concepts that are used, and the capacity to justify them rationally. We can hardly be said to be responsible for our thoughts if we cannot provide some account of and justification for them. Core to this is some understanding of purpose. Any account and justification of thoughts and actions also demands openness to critical intellectual challenge. We saw in the credit crisis that there was little, if any, understanding of the CDOs. The mathematical formula that provided the basis for the risk-free status of CDOs was understood by few. The only concept that the leadership was clear about was profit.
- *Values* – This demands the capacity to appreciate the values that underlie thoughts and action. It is not just that they are coherent, it is also that they have distinct meaning and levels of significance, such that one prefers one practice to others. Even at this stage, responsibility involves a comparison with other practices and their values. Deciding upon one's own values or the values of the organisation thus does not take place in social isolation or apart from the core relationships to the social and physical environment. This also engages feelings, not least because values connect to purpose and identity and thus any sense of self-worth. Responsibility around feelings requires two things. First, it demands that responsibility be taken for the feelings. It might be thought that by definition one cannot control feelings. When you feel afraid, for instance, the feeling takes you over: it controls you. However, psychotherapeutic research supports the idea that although feelings may arise spontaneously, we nonetheless are responsible for what we do with them (Robinson, 2008). Second, it demands responsibility for critically examining those feelings, and the underlying worldviews that may be responsible for keeping those feelings in place.
- *Practice* At the heart of the third focus is social awareness, of the effects of one's actions, and thus the connection between oneself and the other, whether in the social or the physical environment. In business, for instance, does one fully understand the practice of an organisation and the effect that this might have on the wider social and physical environment?

None of this prescribes a particular response. What it does demand is awareness of what one is doing, how that fits into the purpose of the organisation and how that affects the internal and external environment. In other words, there is a relational context to agency that goes beyond the individual self and that demands awareness and responsiveness. The relationality is also about being answerable to the self.

Critically, then, the idea of responsibility includes responsibility for meaning in practice. Taylor (1989) argues that self-interpretation is key to identity. Mustakova-Possardt (2004: 245) sums up responsibility for both worldviews and awareness of the social and physical environment in the idea of 'critical moral consciousness'. This involves:

- a moral sense of identity
- a sense of responsibility and agency
- a deep sense of relatedness on all levels of living
- a sense of 'life meaning or purpose', linking to underlying beliefs.

These connect:

- core intellectual values, not least the development of rational agency
- ethical values, which include core principles such as justice and respect
- spirituality, here used as a generic term pointing to underlying beliefs about the world, sometimes expressed in terms of worldviews
- competency values, not least professional and technical skills and values – from communication to teamwork, to concern for excellence.

At one level this requires the development of vision and value statements in organisations. It also requires a critical relationship to those statements. This is partly to enable the organisation and its members to fully understand them. Simply to state values and adhere to them is not to understand them. To understand them requires a critical reflection on the values in relation to the community of practice and any idea of purpose. In the case of Enron, employees typically learned their values as a mantra, often having them printed out on their desk in case their manager came by. They did not fully understand what the ideas or values involved or what the impact of them was on practice. The leaders of Enron were similarly focused in developing a closed community, with little understanding of what they were doing outside of the narrow business community. Critical questioning was avoided. This is further emphasised by Heath and Norman (2004). Learning lessons from disasters such as the Enron case, they argue that the real problems emerge when managers keep their actions secret from the shareholders. The shareholders are thus not able to be part of a conversation about values, purposes and ways in which the business is run. They argue that when business is not transparent, responsibility is easily lost at all levels. Responsibility is worked out through dialogue between all stakeholders and shareholders.

In contrast, manufacturers Johnson & Johnson – famous for their proactive 'credo' (see Chapter 6) – also held regular sessions to review and challenge the basic ideas. It is this process, and not simply the establishment of the credo, that enabled management there to respond so effectively and rapidly when faced by the poisoning crisis involving Tylenol (Rehak, 2002). The leadership and workforce understood and 'owned' the values and were used to critically reflecting on their meaning in practice.

The leadership in the credit crisis showed a lack of agency, often not understanding the purpose, the practice, or the effects of that practice.

ACCOUNTABILITY TO

The second interconnected mode of responsibility is accountability to another. This focuses on the ethical environment. Typically, we have different kinds of accountability, depending on the kind of relationship we have with people or groups. This is usually 'contract' relationships, formal or informal. The contract sets up a series of mutual expectations. At one level, these are about discernible targets that form the basis of any shared project, and without which the competence of the person cannot be assessed. At another level, there are broader moral expectations of how one should behave in any contract. This would reflect the importance of openness and transparency in relationships and other such behaviours that provide the basis for trust. Any contract can be modified and developed by the parties, so that contracts between shareholders and executives, for instance, need not be confined to a single purpose. The contract also sets up the sense of answerability to another. I owe, and thus give, an account to that person or group of my thoughts and actions, thus connecting imputability to accountability. This may involve several different kinds of accountability relationships, from family to community, to work organisation, to profession.

Many writers argue that accountability in business is best understood through stakeholder theory. Stakeholders were initially defined as individuals or groups who were critical to the survival of an organisation, especially business, including employees, customers, lenders and suppliers (Freeman, 1984). This has been further developed to 'any individual or group who can affect or is affected by the actions, decisions, policies, practices or goals of the organisation' (Carroll and Buchholtz, 2000) This widens stakeholders to the government, the community, and beyond. For multinational corporations this becomes even more complex. Arguments surrounding this are examined in more detail in Chapter 11.

LIABILITY FOR

Moral liability (as distinct from legal liability) goes beyond accountability into the idea of wider responsibility *for* projects, people or places. Each person or group has to work out moral liability in context, without necessarily an explicit contract. Working that out demands an awareness of the limitations of the person or organisation, avoiding taking too much responsibility, and a capacity to work together with others and to negotiate and share responsibility. This is responsibility *for* people and projects in the past, present and future. Most relationships involve a mixture of accountability and liability. A good example is a doctor, who is both accountable for and to the patient. Once again this can have a strictly legal sense or a wider moral one encompassing the broadest possible view of stakeholders, from those directly affected by any business or project to the social and natural environment in which it operates. Like accountability, it involves multiple responsibilities.

This takes the complexity of the business environment even further, leading to developments in corporate responsibility, seeing business as itself a stakeholder in wider society and thus having more to do with corporate citizenship. Feminist ethics, in particular, point to a web of stakeholder relations that stress connectivity, interdependence, power sharing, collective action and conflict resolution. Business is a part of society and its identity is established through how it relates to society, not least in its conduct with those who are affected by, and who affect, it. Just as dialogue is required for moral agency, dialogue is required in working out a creative and feasible response to the wider social and physical environment.

This begins to move responsibility into a more practice stance, such that it provides the basis for another ethical theory based on responsibility itself.

RESPONSIBILITY ETHICS

In post-Holocaust ethics, writers such as Bauman (1989) reflect on the experience of the Holocaust (the industrialised murder of over 6 million Jews in World War II). The Holocaust happened because of the way in which certain groups of people were excluded from humanity. Responsibility for the other was, in these cases, denied. This denial was exacerbated by management techniques such as the division of labour, which further distanced any sense of responsibility. Rationality in all this was focused on efficiency, not response to the wider environment. The basis of ethics, Bauman argues, then has to be inclusive awareness and appreciation of the other. Ethics thus *begins* with taking responsibility for the other, and the rest is how that responsibility is worked out, with others. Levinas (1991) sees ethics as beginning with the 'face' of the other. It is a short step then to saying that 'Everyone is really responsible to all men, for all men and for everything' (Dostoevsky, 1993: 41).

Arendt tempers this, concluding 'that in one form or another, men must assume responsibility for all crimes committed by men and that all nations share the onus of evil committed by all others' (Arendt, 1991: 282). Here, Arendt does not necessarily mean strict moral liability for the ethical mistakes of others, but more the sense that humankind must take collective responsibility for learning from those mistakes.

As a theory of ethics this does not literally mean we have to be responsible for everything. Rather, one begins with the attitude of responsibility. This cannot be totally fulfilled by the one person. So, for Bauman, 'the moral self is always haunted by the suspicion that it is not moral enough' (Bauman, 1989: 81).

Bauman argues that unless one begins from an attitude of universal responsibility or responsibility to the whole, in addition to any individual or role responsibility, we run the danger of excluding others from the moral realm. The unconditional nature of this takes us back to the Holocaust where people with 'difference', from disabilities to different cultures, were deemed to be outside the accepted circle. No one took responsibility for them, or for defending them. This is neatly summed up in the lines of Pastor Martin Niemöller quoted below.

Alongside this it is important to have a critical pluralism, allowing for different perspectives to critically question any view of value. Bauman thus notes of the Milgram experiments (see Chapter 3), 'A most remarkable conclusion flowing from the full set of the Milgram experiments is that pluralism is the best preventative medicine against morally normal people engaging in morally abnormal actions' (Bauman, 1989). The idea of having only one moral viewpoint embedded in a community which cannot be questioned tends to lead to denial of responsibility both for people outside that community and of responsibility for relationships within the community.

Pastor Niemöller's 'First they came ...'

Pastor Niemöller recorded that during the rise of the Nazi Party, different groups of people were gradually taken away without anyone feeling responsible enough to stand up for them.

...
Then they came for the Jews
And I did not speak out
Because I was not a Jew
Then they came for me
And there was no one left
To speak out for me

Martin Niemöller was a Lutheran pastor who stood out against the Nazi oppression and survived Dachau concentration camp: http://www.hmd.org.uk/ resources/poetry/first-they-came-pastor-martin-niemoller.

A more satirical take on responsibility comes from Tom Lehrer's song about Wernher von Braun, the former Nazi scientist who worked on the development of rockets in the USA (*The Complete Tom Lehrer*, 2010, Sbme/Shout Ent.):

'Once the rockets are up,
Who cares where they come down?
That's not my department,'
Says Wernher von Braun.

CRITIQUE

There are several problems with the extreme form of this theory:

- There is the danger that it could lead to taking too much responsibility, and thus shifting business away from core purposes (this debate is developed further in Chapter 11).
- The way in which Levinas and others characterise the 'other' as the basis of ethics ignores reality. It is not reasonable to simply be drawn into caring for the other. The 'other', as we have noted, is always ambiguous, capable of both bad and good, and as such, care has to be taken how one responds.
- The relationship with the other is also mutual, which requires a balancing of concern for the self and the other. The self is also 'another'.
- Perhaps most importantly, the other in any social environment is also someone who is the bearer of responsibility. They are not simply the bearer of need, but have an interactive part to play in a relationship (see Chapter 11 for a more detailed development of this in relation to stakeholder theory).

Any theory that is based in responsibility thus has to focus on the way in which universal responsibility – responsibility for the common good – is shared and negotiated.

This is something that requires all three modes of responsibility working together.

SHARED AND NEGOTIATED RESPONSIBILITY

If universal responsibility is to be genuine, it has to be shared, involving an attitude of mutual responsibility for the whole, and a willingness to share the practice of responsibility. This relates directly to all levels of decision-making. Even at the level of data-gathering it is therefore critical to work together with other groups (see Chapter 3) if there is to be the fullest awareness of the situation.

Research in families and family social policy has noted the importance of negotiating responsibilities in developing and maintaining ethical meaning. Finch and Mason (1993) concluded that a majority of families did not work from principles or any predetermined value base but from a negotiation of responsibility which involved three things:

- identifying the stakeholders in any situation
- analysis of the stakeholders in terms of power and responsibility, so enabling a full appreciation of constraints and resources in the situation
- a negotiation of responsibility. This does not simply look to the development of goods for all stakeholders. Rather, it accepts the premise of mutual responsibility and enables its embodiment in the light of shared values and the capacities of the stakeholders. It thus enables a maximisation of resources through collaboration. Far from stakeholders' passively accepting benefits from business, it involves all in the practice of responsibility. The process of negotiating responsibility includes all stakeholders in this practice. It does not prescribe what that responsibility will be, but does enable the parties to own and develop that responsibility.

Much of this is tied to identity and self-image. Often in the area of corporate ethics a group will take on too much responsibility precisely because it sees itself as the only one genuinely responsible for the common good (see the Brent Spar case study in Chapter 11).

WORLDVIEW: STEWARDSHIP

Behind the idea of shared responsibility is a worldview, and Caldwell *et al* (2008) argue for the idea of stewardship. This focuses on the recognition that resources are not totally owned by the leader or the group, and that he/she and it act as custodian or steward to use these resources for a greater good. Caldwell *et al* suggest that stewardship is found in covenant thinking rather than in a contract of accountability. Covenant thinking is about a broader commitment over time to the wider environment. It tends to begin with this concern and then see how it can be fulfilled, and who is best to do that.

Compared to this, a contract is specific, calculative and limits relationships, and can be put to one side if the terms of the agreement are broken. It would be very easy to polarise the two approaches to agreements and so set up a battle between covenant and contract. Both are needed in working through responsibility. Covenant provides the long-term commitment, and contract involves working through how it can be achieved.

Stewardship is expressed strongly in theological and philosophical terms. The theology of Fethullah Gülen (see Chapter 2) shows how God makes human beings accountable to him for the stewardship of his creation. Jonas (1984), a philosopher from a Jewish background, aims to provide a philosophical rather than theological justification for responsibility for the whole global environment (see Chapter 14).

Responsibility in all this is based on an identification with the environment and an acute awareness of mankind's role in relation to that. Niebuhr thus writes, 'What is implicit in the idea of responsibility is the image of man – the answerer, man engaged in dialogue, man acting in response to action upon him' (Niebuhr, 1963).

RESPONSIBILITY AND POWER

Core to responsibility in this are issues about power:

- Business can have great power. For big business this can mean negative effects on the ethical environment. Jonas (1984) stresses the effects of technology on the wider environment, something well illustrated by the extractive industries (see Chapter 13). Awareness of that power demands *reactive responsibility*, being prepared to mitigate the effects of business.
- Power can be channelled most effectively when it is shared for the common good. This involves *proactive responsibility*, working together for responsibility-centred planning.
- Power can be used to dominate, to avoid questioning, to deny responsibility and to prevent responsible practice, as in the case of Enron (see Chapter 5).

RESPONSIBILITY AND VIRTUE

In the light of all this, responsibility can be seen as a virtue (Ladd, 1991), the capacity to take responsibility, reactive and proactive. This applies to the corporation as agent, and to different players within the corporation.

Equally, other virtues might be seen as necessary for the development of responsibility. Focusing on the Aristotelian virtues of justice, courage, temperance, patience and practical wisdom (*phronēsis*), it could be argued that these enable responsibility to be taken. Courage, for instance, is central to the capacity to take responsibility in the face of pressures to conform to bad practice. Courage is also necessary for speaking out, or in extreme cases for whistleblowing. *Phronēsis*, an intellectual virtue, involves reflection on and appreciation of purpose, and the relation of this to practice. Aquinas (2006: IIaIIae 47.6) develops this further with his view of practical wisdom. He argues that it involves awareness of the past and the lessons that must be learned from the past (*memoria*), awareness of the present and its environment (*docilitas*) and awareness for the future (*solertia*). This involved taking responsibility for present awareness and for the future, and thus for possible consequences of one's actions – something that was absent in the practice of the banks. See Chapter 6 for a longer consideration of virtues in the business practice.

Responsibility ethics then focuses on the lived nature of ethics, the individual and organisation taking responsibility for meaning and practice. This contrasts with the idea of compliance (Reynolds, 2011), the non-engaged fulfilling of rules. Such responsibility is central to the work of the Globally Responsible Leadership Initiative Foundation (http://www.grli.org/) which seeks to focus on the development of such responsibility both in the workplace and through education.

FREEDOM

Philosophy has linked responsibility closely with freedom (Fischer and Ravizza, 2000). This debate has especially been around the first mode of responsibility, imputability, and includes issues such as: how far can someone be held to be responsible? How far are individuals really free to make decisions and so to be responsible for their actions? Isn't much of our thinking and action in some way determined, such that we do not have free will? This might involve psychological determinism (the way I was brought up) or situational determinism (things that make it difficult for me to have a choice). Strawson (1962) argues that it is possible to have determinism but also to be responsible for one's thoughts (compatibilism). In one sense this is core to the human experience. Many things affect how we think, but rational decision-making has to take them into account when making a choice.

 PAUSE FOR THOUGHT

Freedom matters

To see how freedom is not simply a 'philosophical issue', go back to the case of Willy Just (Chapter 3). Did Just have a choice? Some would argue that he did not. Had he refused to write his memo, he and his family might have been killed by the Nazis. His choice was therefore determined by things outside himself. Nonetheless, he did have a choice – that is, several alternatives: to plan long-term to escape from Germany to real safety, to work with others to subvert the development of gas trucks, to continue to work and to use the work as a cover for long-term projects against the Third Reich (such as saving Jews). A good example of the practice of this responsibility is Oskar Schindler (see *Schindler's List*, DVD, Universal Studios). Schindler, a German businessman, used his power and networks to provide work for Jews, preventing their deaths.

The argument here is that we always have a choice, and that choice is dependent on exercising the three modes of responsibility: working out values, how these affect actions and how actions affect others, what we owe to whom and how we might share responsibility. In the end the choice may be to do nothing. That is still a choice for which we take responsibility.

Other issues of freedom occur throughout this book, particularly in Chapter 11, where Friedman argues for the negative freedom of the businessperson, and in the workplace culture where freedom is located in autonomy, the capacity to govern oneself. Freedom is another of those ethical big ideas that we often do not think about until we have lost it, and it is frequently behind ethical debates in business.

A RESPONSIBLE BUSINESS: CORPORATE MORAL AGENCY

Can a firm actually be responsible? That is, can a firm be a responsible agent, capable of making responsible decisions? This has both ethical and legal implications, not least because where there is wrongdoing there is the need to discover who is responsible – individual leaders within the firm, the leadership governance structure, or in some sense the firm itself.

Among others, French (1979) argued that the nature of corporations is quite distinctive compared to other kinds of organisations, because of their rules of governance and hierarchical structure. Initially, French reached three main conclusions:

- corporations exhibit intentionality
- corporations are capable of exhibiting rationality regarding their intentions
- corporations are capable of altering their intentions and patterns of behaviour.

As a result, he concluded that corporations can be seen as 'fully-fledged moral persons', accompanied by the privileges, rights and duties normally accorded to moral persons.

There has been sustained crticism of this view. The major criticism has been that it is not possible to view the corporation as a person. Once a philsophical debate about the meaning of personhood begins, it takes the debate into wider definition problems. For instance, a Kantian would argue that a person should be viewed as an end in his or her self. It is hard to speak of a corporation in this way. Subsequently, therefore, the debate focused on the idea of agency, and whether one could actually speak of the firm as having intentions or whether this is simply board members coming to a consensus.

French's response was to focus on the term 'agent' rather than 'person', and to claim that Stanford Professor of Philosophy Michael Bratman had developed a convincing view of group intentionality, subsequently developed by Arnold (2006). Bratman argues that it is possible for groups to have intentions on the following lines:

> Intentions are expressed and understood not simply in terms of 'mental states', ideas that I want to do something. They are expressed in decision-making and planning.

It is possible, then, for a group to develop an intention through shared decision-making and through planning. Individuals within the group may not agree fully with the intention, or may be doing different tasks to achieve the intention of the group. However, they express the intention of the group as a whole. Bratman uses the example of the large family who agree on the intention to take their parents on a trip for their fiftieth wedding anniverasary, with all the planning involved. Individuals in such a project work to fulfil the intention of the group.

In addition we may note Taylor's (1989) point that decision-making individually and as a group establishes purpose and indentity. Identity, by extension, is a function of relationships, and any relationships to the social and physical environment set up issues of responsibility. This posits a view of agency that does not need to rely on seeing corporations as 'persons' but can see corporations as having decision-making and planning processes that establish identity and responsibility in relation to the social and physical environment. Such thinking is embodied in the UK's Corporate Manslaughter and Corporate Homicide Act (Matthews, 2008).

THE LIMITS OF RESPONSIBILITY

Milton Friedman is often seen as one of the foremost modern advocates of the free market and limiting the responsibility of the manager and the corporation. In relation to the debate about responsibility and business his argument is simple (Friedman, 1983). The role of business is the creation of wealth, and the prime responsibility of business is thus to make a profit for its owners, usually the shareholders. In this, the executive director acts as an agent (defined here as someone who works on behalf of another) serving the interests of 'his principal' – ie the owners. The interest of the principal is profit maximisation, and involvement in any activities in the community outside this sphere would be a violation of trust and thus morally wrong. Friedman does not argue against the social involvement of the company as such, rather simply that the company, and the owners especially, can decide to do what they think is fit. There is no moral or legal obligation on the company to be more socially involved, and the company can follow its own ends, so long as they are legal. We look critically at this view in Chapter 11.

The practice of responsibility comes together in the case study of the computer game.

PRACTISING RESPONSIBILITY: COMPUTER GAMES

CASE

Following the success of a computer game based upon a scenario set in the frozen north, a certain computer software development company was commissioned by the client company to develop a second game. This time the client – a multimedia global firm – wanted increased shock value, and the inclusion of the explicit death of young children. An added incentive towards this was that if the computer company agreed to it, there would be a more immediate release of monies outstanding from the first game. The manager of the software firm and his engineering staff were uneasy about this request – although initially a little unsure why they felt such unease. They sensed that there might be wider issues about how such games affect players and about how their firm might be perceived.

As a result of discussions with his staff the manager decided that it was important to clarify the situation. He wrote to his client's legal department and asked if they would confirm in writing that the company wished him to develop a second game, and that it was their intention that this game should involve increased horror and the death

of children. No such confirmation was received. The money owed to the software development company was rapidly released, and the new game made, without the two additions.

Questions

1 Why did the legal department respond in this way, do you think?

2 There were two businesses involved in this case. Does the social responsibility of each of them differ, and if so, why?

3 Who are the important people in this case who might be affected by the decisions of these two companies?

4 In the light of your answer to the question above, how would you have responded to the request of the commissioning company?

5 Imagine that you are on the board of the computer games firm. Because of this problem you have been asked to draw up a new policy on the responsibilities of the firm. What would be the main things you would include?

The computer firm case was deceptively complex. It did not involve one company surrounded by stakeholders. Firstly, there were two companies involved, each of which was a stakeholder in the other's business. For the commissioning company this was a minor but potentially lucrative relationship. For the computer firm this was a potentially critical deal that would help to keep it alive.

Secondly, each company had some very different stakeholders, with different and sometimes conflicting values. The commissioning company, for instance, had a strong line in family entertainment. The game, however, was targeted at late adolescents. This could potentially spoil the company's family image. In recent times, there had also been an increase in customers from different cultures, including the Muslim world, with a strong family ethic. Up to this point, responsibility to any possible customers would seem to coincide with self-interest. There is little point in trying to sell to one group in a way that would actually affect the company's reputation with other potential customers. It may, of course, be that there are wider responsibilities to children and families. Are they the firm's responsibilities? What is the effect of violent games on younger people? Research is inconclusive about this. The precautionary principle might well apply here, then. If you are not sure what negative effect your project might have on children or the wider society, or how that might reinforce other negative social changes, the precautionary principle suggests that the firm exercises precaution and does not become involved in gratuitous horror.

Alternatively, it might be possible for such a company to be involved in developing further research around this area. At the very least there are questions about what the wider social responsibility of the company might be.

For the computer games company these questions are a little different. There are responsibilities to the owner and the employees. However, as computer engineers many employees were part of a wider professional body of engineers. That profession is itself a stakeholder in the sense that any decision made by computer firm might affect the standing of computer engineers in wider society. Recent work on the responsibility of engineers emphasises the importance of maintaining the integrity of the profession. The profession itself has a real concern about the effects of any computer games on the wider society.

All of this takes the firm into a critical dialogue. The dialogue began within the firm, the directors and employees all feeling uncertain about accepting the contract but not clear how they should respond. The dialogue continued with the commissioning firm, trying to clarify precisely what was meant. If the dialogue had continued, it might have led the games company to explore whether the use of horror or the death of children in a computing game was necessarily wrong. It is possible to see these, for instance, as being used in the context of a game with a moral framework by which those who kill the children or who allow that slaughter to happen can be brought to justice. It might be possible then to take the contract and develop a game based in a broader ethical context, thus contributing to a wider social responsibility. This would move away from polarised and fragmented thinking such as simply denying responsibility for the possible effects of the game or passing responsibility to the government (for age regulation) or to parents.

Once the firms move into dialogue, they have to take responsibility in the three modes noted above: they have to be clear about what their purpose, values and actions are, be able to give an account of those, and be clear about the responsibility involved.

The commissioning company clearly did not want to give an account of its original commission. So it gave no reply to the letter. To do so would have meant it taking responsibility for what had been requested, and this could have had a negative effect on its reputation.

ROLE RESPONSIBILITIES AND THE NATURE OF BUSINESS

The computer games case study once more demonstrates the plural responsibilities in any situation in business. Any corporation may have facing them responsibilities that relate to roles or relationships. The case outlined included:

- professional responsibilities, informed by a view of the identity of the profession, expressed in terms of its purpose
- corporate responsibilities – in this case, to the workers in the firm and external stakeholders
- wider civic responsibilities in relation to the effects of any project
- responsibilities to the common good
- personal responsibilities, in relation to the individuals' culture outside the workplace.

These different responsibilities reinforce the point that business is by nature not homogenous but is rather made up of a good number of different professions and specialisms, each of which has an ethical perspective. This is explored in more detail in Chapter 8.

Ethics based on responsibility provides a way of holding all of these different elements together. First, it provides an attitude of universal responsibility – responsibility as shared. Second, it is a both/and ethics. As a professional engineer, for instance, I am responsible to my profession and my firm, and society, and so on. The finance director in the case above was responsible for his professional area of work, and for the direction of the corporation, and for the relationship of the business to society. Hence the need to fulfil a plural accountability. Third, as Bauman noted, acknowledgement and engagement with this plurality, within and outside the firm, provides the critical dialogue that works against closed ethical systems which attempt to dominate others, and provides ways of most effectively working through responsibility in practice.

Taking responsibility works with both ethical theory and the ethical decision-making process, enabling the understating of ideas, values, practice and the effect of practice. Core to this is the capacity to ask simple questions of clarification (as expressed in the letter to the legal department). The understating emerges through critical dialogue that assesses the importance of the different values, and analyses the different options (increased through shared responsibility).

CONCLUSION

This chapter has explored the key ethical category of responsibility in relation to the ethical environment. It has examined:

- the meaning of the term 'responsibility'
- arguments for a wider sense of shared responsibility, including responsibility as a key ethical theory
- ways of negotiating responsibility.

We found that the financial crises of 2007/8 showed a lack of responsible practice in the finance industry in all the three modes, being unaware of its environment and purpose (and even with CDOs not knowing what it was actually doing); not being accountable to any group other than the shareholders; and not being prepared to share responsibility for the wider social environment.

Responsibility has often been perceived as reactive – reacting to events – and thus associated with apportioning responsibility and blame. The wider sense of responsibility is proactive, involving planning and then involvement of stakeholders in the practice of taking responsibility. This includes members of the corporation itself.

Central to this is a view of plural responsibility, the members of the corporation being responsible both for their area and for the whole, taking individual and collective responsibility. The working out of responsibility therefore demands reflection at individual and corporate levels, and critical dialogue at these levels and between the different stakeholders. This also takes responsibility beyond a focus on simply giving an account of the effect of the corporation on society and the environment. Just as important is an account of purpose and values, of how the corporation thinks about and values the environment.

Although an extreme form of responsibility ethics is hard to maintain, the importance of responsibility as a foundation for practical ethics remains. There are several reasons for this :

- As an ethical category it bridges the gap between large and small business. There is no one way of fulfilling responsibility. It has to be worked out in context and in relation to the different stakeholders.
- It links core ethical theories normative and descriptive, and core virtues.
- It links cognate concepts and practices such as citizenship and volunteering (civic responsibility), applied ethics (professional and business responsibility) and sustainability (social and environmental responsibility, examined more closely in Chapter 14).
- It links core rational business skills with ethical meaning (not least in the first mode of responsibility), and thus links responsibility to employability (see Chapter 6).

All of this suggests that although ethics may at any one time involve a decision to be taken by an individual, it also involves much longer-term thinking, planning and responsiveness, requiring that shared responsibility be taken in the three modes above. Responsibility thus further develops virtue ethics. The ethics is lived, embodied – not simply taken from principle or code.

To show how this responsibility can shape the actions and culture of a firm we now examine ethics in relation to leadership and governance and the development of ethical culture.

Figure 4.1 An overview of responsibility in practice

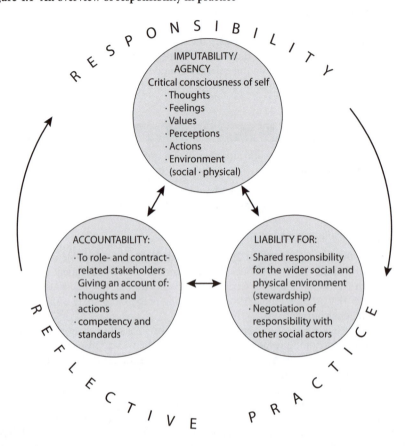

EXPLORE FURTHER

Books

Bauman, Z. (1993) *Postmodern Ethics*. Oxford: Blackwell, for an important reflection on the ethics of responsibility.

Reynolds, J. (2011) *Ethics in Investment Banking*. Basingstoke: Palgrave.

DVDs

The Inside Job (2011, Sony), for a detailed narrative of what happened in the credit crisis.

REFERENCES

AQUINAS, T. (2006) *Summa Theologica*, Volume II, Part II-II (*Secunda Secundae*). Charleston, SC: Bibliobazaar.

ARENDT, H. (1991) 'Organised guilt and universal responsibility', in May, L. and Hoffman, H. (eds.) *Collective Responsibility: Five decades of debate in theoretical and applied ethics*. Lanham, MD: Rowman & Littlefield.

ARNOLD, D. (2006) 'Corporate moral agency', *Midwest Studies in Philosophy*, 30(1): 279–91.

BAUMAN, Z. (1989) *Modernity and the Holocaust*. London: Polity.

BROWN, M. (2005) *Corporate Integrity*. Cambridge: Cambridge University Press.

CALDWELL, C., HAYES, L., BERNAL, P. and KARRI, R. (2008) 'Ethical stewardship – implications for leadership and trust', *Journal of Business Ethics*, 78(1/2), March: 153–64.

CARR, A. (1968) 'Is business bluffing ethical?', *Harvard Business Review*, January/February: 143–53.

CARROLL, A. B. and BUCHHOLTZ, A. B. (2000) *Business and Society: Ethics and stakeholder management*, 4th edition. Cincinnati, OH: South-Western College.

CARROLL, P. and MUI, C. (2008) 'Six lessons we should have learned already', *Harvard Business Review*, September: 8–91.

DANTE (ALIGHIERI) (1995) *The Divine Comedy*. London: Everyman.

DOSTOEVSKY, F. (1993) *The Grand Inquisitor*. Indianapolis: Hackett.

FINCH, J. and MASON, J. (1993) *Negotiating Family Responsibilities*. London: Routledge.

FISCHER, J. and RAVIZZA, M. (2000) *Responsibility and Control*. Cambridge: Cambridge University Press.

FREEMAN, E. (1984) *Strategic Management: A stakeholder approach*. Boston, MA: Pitman.

FRENCH, P. (1979) 'The corporation as a moral person', *American Philosophical Quarterly*, 16: 207–15.

FRIEDMAN, M. (1983) 'The social responsibility of business is to increase its profits', in Donaldson, T. and Werhane, P. (eds) *Ethical Issues in Business*. New York: Prentice Hall.

HEATH, J. and NORMAN, W. (2004) 'Stakeholder theory, corporate governance and public management', *Journal of Business Ethics*, 53(3): 247–65.

HINRICH, K. (2007) 'Follower propensity to commit crimes of obedience', *Journal of Leadership and Organisational Studies*, 4(1), August: 69–76.

ICAEW (2007) *Reporting with Integrity*, London: ICAEW.

JONAS, H. (1984) *The Imperative of Responsibility*. Chicago: Chicago University Press.

LADD, J. (1991) 'Bhopal: an essay on moral responsibility and civic virtue', *Journal of Social Philosophy*, 32(1).

LANCHESTER, J. (2010) *Whoops!* London: Penguin.

LEVINAS, E. (1991) *Entre Nous: On thinking of the other*. New York: Columbia University Press.

MANDEVILLE, B. (2007) *The Fable of the Bees*. London: Penguin.

McKENNNY, P. (2005) 'Responsibility', in Meilaender, G. and Werpehowski, W. *Theological Ethics*. Oxford: Oxford University Press.

MATTHEWS, R. (2008) *Blackstone's Guide to the Corporate Manslaughter and Corporate Homicide Act 2007*. Oxford: Oxford University Press.

MILGRAM, S. (2005) *Obedience to Authority*. New York: Pinter & Martin.

MUSTAKOVA-POSSARDT, E. (2004) 'Education for critical moral consciousness', *Journal of Moral Education*, 33(3): 245–70.

NIEBUHR, H. R. (1963) *The Responsible Self*. New York: Harper & Row.

REHAK, J. (2002) 'Tylenol made a hero of Johnson & Johnson', *New York Times*, 23 March.

REYNOLDS, J. (2011) *Ethics in Investment Banking*. Basingstoke: Palgrave.

ROBINSON, S. (1992) *Serving Society*. Nottingham: Grove.

ROBINSON, S. (2002) 'Nestlé and international marketing', in Megone, C. and Robinson, S. (eds) *Case Histories in Business Ethics*. London: Routledge: 141–58.

ROBINSON, S. (2008) *Spirituality, Ethics and Care*. London: Jessica Kingsley.

ROBINSON, S. and KENYON, A. (2009) *Ethics in the Alcohol Industry*. Basingstoke: Palgrave.

ROBINSON, S., DIXON, R., MOODLEY, K. and PREECE, C. (2007) *Engineering, Business and Professional Ethics*. London: Heinemann Butterworth.

SCHWEIKER, W. (1995) *Responsibility and Christian Ethics*. Cambridge: Cambridge University Press.

SHEEN REPORT (DEPARTMENT OF TRANSPORT) (1987) The Merchant Shipping Act 1984, *MV Herald of Free Enterprise* – report of court no. 8074. London: HMSO.

SKRETA, A. and VELDKAMP, L. (2009) 'Ratings shopping and asset complexity: A theory of ratings inflation', *Journal of Monetary Economics*, 56(5): 678–95.

SOLOMON, R. (2005) 'Emotional leadership, emotional integrity', in Ciulla, J., Price, T. and Murphy, S. (eds) *The Quest for Moral Leaders*, Cheltenham: Edward Elgar: 28–44.

STOREY, L. and DASH, E. (2009) *New York Times*, 30 July.

STRAWSON, P. F. (1962) 'Freedom and resentment', *Proceedings of the British Academy*, 48: 187–211.

TAWNEY, R. H. (1930) *Equality*. London: Allen & Unwin.

TAYLOR, C. (1989) *Sources of the Self*. Cambridge: Cambridge University Press.

TETT, G. (2009) *Fool's Gold*. London: Little Brown.

TITMUSS, R. (1970) *The Gift Relationship*. London: Penguin.

VOGEL, L. (2006) 'Natural law Judaism? The genesis of bioethics in Jonas, Strauss, and Kass', in Schweiker, W., Johnson, M. and Jung, K. (eds) *Humanity Before God*. Minneapolis: Augsburg: 209–37.

WETHERLY, P. and OTTER, D. (eds) (2011) *The Business Environment*, 2nd edition. Oxford: Oxford University Press.

WILLIAMS, R. (2009) Cardiff Lecture, available from *Times Online* on http://www.timesonline.co.uk/tol/news/uk/article5863259.ece [accessed 7 March 2011].

CHAPTER 5

Leadership and Governance

LEARNING OUTCOMES

When you have completed this chapter you will be able to:

- describe, analyse and critique different theories of leadership
- describe, analyse and critique different views of ethical leadership
- describe, analyse and critique unethical leadership practice, as exemplified in the Enron case
- describe, analyse and critique key ideas of governance and the place of ethics in governance.

INTRODUCTION

In this chapter we explore what it means to be an ethical leader. A case study on Enron examines unethical leadership. We then look at the meaning of leadership and how ethics relates to it. In particular we examine the ethical problems around the trait theory of leadership, and the value-centred transformational, servant, and transactional leadership theories. We finally focus on governance as a key means of leadership, its ethical base, and how it might be developed. The chapter ends with a case study on ethical leadership and the Body Shop.

 ## PAUSE FOR THOUGHT

Do you think of yourself as a leader? Do you want to be a leader? Consider situations in which you have led a group. What did leadership involve for you? Was the leadership given to you, or did you assume it? How did it feel to lead?

What are your experiences of being led? Were they positive or negative, and in what ways?

Who is the best leader you have experienced, and in what way was he/she the best?

 ## REFLECTIVE PRACTICE

Think of three examples of leadership that you would aspire to. In a learning group of four students, share and analyse these examples to work out why you thought they were valuable. Do the examples model ethical behaviour? If they do, can you come up with some sort of definition of what ethical behaviour is?

ENRON AND LEADERSHIP

In 2001 the Enron Corporation suffered the biggest corporate failure up to that time. At that stage, it was the seventh largest company in the USA, and had been valued at $70 billion by the stock exchange. At the heart of the failure was massive fraud. This involved

- non-transparency in its financial reporting to shareholders and analysts

- the use of mark-to-market accounting. Enron became the first non-financial company to use this method of accounting. It required that income from any long-term contracts should be estimated at the present value in any future net cash flows. This led to false and misleading reporting. Perhaps the most famous example of this was the long-term deal signed with Blockbuster to develop on-demand video entrainment for several US cities. The profit on the deal was estimated at $110 million. Despite the fact that the project was not viable, and Blockbuster pulled out of the deal, Enron still calculated and formally recorded the future profits

- special-purpose entities – companies created by Enron to hide the debts of the main company.

In terms of leadership, Enron was a striking example in the corporate world of cult dynamics (Sherman, 2002: 25). Cults associated with New Religious Movements (INFORM, http://www. inform.ac/) tend to emphasise three elements:

- charismatic leadership, involving the leader as the centre of faith, and the source of truth

- an overarching vision, based very much on emotion that seeks to drive forward and inspire the members of the organisation

- the promotion of a culture characterised by conformity and fear.

All three elements together form a leadership framework that in Enron should have raised ethical questions.

Activity

Watch the DVD *Enron, the Smartest Guys in the Room* (Lionsgate, 2007).

Reflection

What does this film tell you about leadership? What are the main ethical problems in the way in which the Enron leaders operated?

CHARISMATIC LEADERSHIP

Enron's leadership worked hard to create the mystique of charisma around themselves. This involved several things:

- Leaders developed an identity of male power and authority. Often they would use *Star Wars* analogies. Jeff Skilling, the CEO, referred to himself at one point as Darth Vader, and to his traders as storm troopers (Schwartz, 2002). This reinforced the leader as successful, individualist and standing out against weaker opposition.
- The leaders were seen as the source of all information. As a result, leadership could not be questioned and a culture of compliance rather than questioning was developed. At the heart of this cult dynamic were policies that controlled information flow. This had the effect of reinforcing the authority of Enron's leaders. The leaders were deemed to be solely responsible for the direction of the organisation and the probity of the practice.
- To reinforce that sense of probity they developed a code of ethics referred to as RICE (Respect, Integrity, Communication and Excellence). Kenneth Lay, the chair, wrote: 'We want to be proud of Enron and to know it enjoys a reputation for fairness and honesty,

and that it is respected … Let's keep that reputation high' (quoted in Cruver, 2003: 333). The code was, however, used as a dramatic device to convince stakeholders of the ethical image of Enron. In fact there was little conversation around ethics in the day-to-day functioning. One report, for instance, notes that executives involved in a power plant in Mumbai paid the local government officials to suppress legitimate opposition (Human Rights Watch, 2002). On another occasion the power was shut down in the state of California in order to inflate prices.

- The code reinforced belief in the leadership. It focused on the good image of the leader, intending to convince stakeholders that whatever was said about the firm, the leaders were essentially good and trustworthy.

The success of the system is evidenced by the fact that the media for several years did not begin to question the leadership, and academics had little critical to say. Staff at the Harvard Business School produced several case studies on Enron, uniformly praising its successes and commending its business model to others.

PAUSE FOR THOUGHT

What caused external bodies not to be critical?

All of this led to an inflated view of the leaders – one that they bought into themselves. This in turn led to the development of narcissism (self-love) and *hubris*, an overweening sense of pride that makes the leader believe that he or she has no limitations. The effect of this was to cause the leader and those around him to lose touch with the complexities of the business environment.

THE VISION OF ENRON

Reinforcing the charismatic leadership was the development of a compelling vision. This provided the basis of identity and belief, enabling the members to believe in themselves and in the corporation. The vision involved:

- the strong ethical identity noted above
- a vision of continual growth ending in Enron's eventually becoming the world's largest company. This included the development of a series of 'big ideas' culminating in the unfurling of a huge banner at the company's main entrance, proclaiming its latest vision – 'FROM THE WORLD'S LEADING ENERGY COMPANY – TO THE WORLD'S LEADING COMPANY'
- a strong sense of identity and purpose. This included inculcating an air of privilege and uniqueness among those who belonged to Enron (Lalich, 2004). Employees developed a strong feeling of purpose and even destiny. They belonged to a special organisation and were themselves special: the brightest and the best. This strong sense of excellence made for an intensely stimulating environment, many wondering how they could ever bear to work anywhere else (Cruver, 2003). Emotionally and intellectually intense recruitment and initiation procedures all reinforced this sense of specialness
- the reinforcement of this feeling of excellence by images of the employees being at war with those outside the organisation. It generated a need to strive ever harder to maintain levels of excellence, requiring high levels of commitment. Success, excellence and stimulating vision were thus all connected, and focused on developing both a committed and a conforming workforce. This led to a very strong work – even sacrificial – ethic by which it was common for middle managers to work over 80 hours a week
- a concomitant polarisation in thinking – that the Enron vision was right, and all

others wrong. The result was that there was no appreciation of values, accountability or responsibility outside the firm.

Both the areas of leadership and vision thus focused on a belief in the leaders rather than in ideas or even in the values of the firm, and on the strong sense of belonging that reinforced the members' sense of worth. What kept all that in place was the development of a culture that was both conformist and based in fear.

PROMOTING A COMMON CULTURE

At the heart of cult dynamics is a mixture of individualised care leading to a strong sense of identity and belonging, alongside a fear of being rejected. To stay in the community one has to both conform and work hard. At first sight, then, the member feels accepted unconditionally, only to find that belonging is conditional upon thinking the right thoughts and doing the right thing (Robinson, 2008).

Fusaro and Miller (2002: 51) note that despite all the effort that Enron expended in selecting and hiring the right people, 'it was quick to fire them'. This was embodied in the appraisal system, known as 'rank and yank'. A performance review committee rated employees twice a year. This led to the establishing of three groups:

- A: Members of this group were highly motivated. They were to be challenged and were awarded huge bonuses.
- B: Those in this group were to be encouraged and affirmed.
- C: Those in this bottom category were given until their next review to improve, and the bottom 15% were fired. Those just above that 15% were placed on warning that they would be next if they did not improve.

A cut-throat culture was thus created (Kets de Vries, 2001). In order to feel safer – in order to survive – those who were most vulnerable had to become aggressive, the employees forming alliances to work against the more vulnerable. It was in each employee's interest that someone other than themselves received a poor rating.

Employees were thus continually disoriented, being viewed as the cleverest, but branded as 'losers' if their performance review failed, and fearful of being fired at any time. This lowered employee confidence but reinforced confidence in the leaders, and reinforced the imperative to strive harder. In the light of this, no dissent was tolerated. Indeed, bad news was not tolerated. That same dynamic was there at the core of the fraud which systematically covered up the bad news of deficits.

Cruver (2003: 37) notes that alongside this were the trappings of a common culture including the development of common vocabulary around targets and change, similar dress code, and major rituals, such as events for all the workforce that revealed the 'next big idea', which reinforced common identity and faith in the leaders. In effect, the culture aimed to regulate people's identities and thus control the organisation through producing individuals with an acceptable range of values, behaviours, attitudes and emotions.

SUMMING UP

The leaders of Enron had in effect replaced any consideration of general ethical values with the development of a closed value system. The core values were around the increase of shareholder value and the creation of a successful business empire. A closed ethical system is one that sees the narrow interests and identity of the organisation as fundamental to ethical meaning. In the light of that the leadership felt justified in:

- psychologically abusing employees, through the development of a culture of fear, showing a lack of respect for their dignity and autonomy
- allowing actions that led to negative consequences for all the stakeholders, including customers, such as closing down the California power grid. One of the great debates

about leadership ethics is whether the leadership should be allowed to do things that are ethically problematic for the good of the company (see *Dirty hands* below)

- developing a culture of deceit. Vision and values were not open to critical testing. Alongside the ethical statements was an ethical parallel universe embodied in the practice of the leaders that was dominated by aggressive values and virtues associated with a narrow view of success. High shareholder value became the key value, and involved any means acceptable to achieve that.

All of these were in some sense abuses of the power of leadership. The leaders had created a culture in which these were not seen as abuses of power but as legitimate means of developing the corporation.

Dirty hands

Dirty Hands (*Les mains sales*) is a play by Jean-Paul Sartre written in 1948. The extract below was translated and quoted by Laurie Calhoun in an issue of *The Independent Review* in 2004.

'You cling so tightly to your purity, my lad! How terrified you are of sullying your hands. Well, go ahead, then – stay pure! What good will it do, and why even bother coming here among us? Purity is a concept of fakirs and friars. But you, the intellectuals, the bourgeois anarchists, you invoke purity as your rationalisation for doing nothing. Do nothing, don't move, wrap your arms tight around your body, put on your gloves. As for myself, my hands are dirty. I have plunged my arms up to the elbows in excrement and blood. And what else should one do? Do you suppose that it is possible to govern innocently?'

The words from Sartre's play are about leadership. In effect he is saying, 'Get into the real world – no one can lead without getting his hands dirty.'

One response is to argue that Sartre has not begun to tell us what he means by dirty hands. If this means that a leader has to get involved in difficult decisions that may have bad consequences, such as laying off employees, then this does not call for ethically improper behaviour. If he means that leaders have to do things that are not ethical in order to achieve their required ends, he has not begun to make the case for this.

 PAUSE FOR THOUGHT

Could you make a case for moving into unethical behaviour to achieve your firm's targets?

Where would you draw the line as a leader?

Would you lie to an employee to ease a difficult situation?

Would you condone a manager's signing off an engineering safety check without proper inspection in order to keep the project up to speed?

Would you condone the small falsifying of figures to keep your firm's share value up?

At what point would the leader cross the line and take others with him or her?

You are in a leadership role in a medium-sized business. One of your managers is heading off to make a final-round presentation for a bid for a lucrative consultancy contract. You wish him good luck and he responds by saying that he does not need luck. He shows you a copy of an internal confidential document about making effective bids from the firm he was making the bid to. He had taken it from the top of a cabinet in the waiting room before he went for the first-round presentation.

Discuss with your learning group the options you would have as leader, which option you would take, and why. Would you:

- pull out of the bid?
- discipline the manager?
- allow it go ahead?
- pretend you had not heard what he said?
- phone your opposite number in the firm you are bidding to, and own up?
- stop your manager and ask him to account for what he said?

What other options might there be, and what would effects of these be?

Source: suggested by an ICAEW presentation at the Centre for Applied Ethics Conference, Kingston University, 2008

DEFINING LEADERSHIP

Thus far we have looked at how leadership can lead to the abuse of power within the firm and to negative consequences for the firm. The ethical problems can be viewed in relation to several of the ethical theories:

- as a lack of respect for the workforce and stakeholders, with little acceptance of the common good (deontological)
- as limiting good consequences only to the firm and shareholders (utilitarian)
- as developing a narrow community or practice which ignores key ethical virtues (virtue ethics).

But why should leaders be ethical? Isn't their task to simply fulfil the aims of their organisation?

Much of the debate about ethical leadership then comes back to the definition and purpose of leadership. Pye (2005) suggests that there are several thousand different definitions of leadership in academic literature. In that case it is not surprising that the very concept of leader is contested. Attempts have been made to narrow the term to ideas around the core actions of a leader – not least the simple idea that a leader gives direction. Covey (2002), for instance, argues for the meta, macro and micro aspects of leadership activity.

- meta leadership – is to do with the vision of the organisation. This establishes the direction it is going in
- macro leadership – focuses on strategy, organisation and process. This works out how the organisation is going to get there
- micro leadership – is about relationships, the use of power and how people relate to leadership. This is how we enable people to work together to make the journey.

All three levels of leadership involve change and enabling others to take responsibility for change (Rost, 1991).

This seems to be a reasonable starting point. However, none of these elements is straightforward. All have major questions around them that are ultimately about value and purpose. At the meta level, who decides on the vision and purpose? Should the leader be concerned primarily with the sustainability of the organisation or with wider concerns of the society and the environment? In all of this, how does the leader deal with the many conflicts of value and interest that will test the vision?

At the macro level, how far do strategies and process relate to the core meaning of the vision and purpose? Macro leadership will have to establish targets, but do targets always fulfil the visions, and can targets take away from the core values?

SCENARIO

Targets and health

As the manager of a hospital, what would your most important targets be – to keep down expenditure, to cut down on waiting times, to keep wards clean, to maximise patient 'throughput', to increase the efficiency of staff? The list is endless.

How do those targets relate to the core vision of healthcare, to do with enabling health and well-being?

If health and well-being is partly dependent on the communication of care and attendant qualities ('Care and compassion are what matters most': National Health Service Constitution), how does that square with cutting down staff contact time, or making staff focus on measurable targets, such that attention to patients becomes secondary?

The issue is put starkly by the NHS Ombudsman who, in a report in 2011 about the care of the elderly in the NHS, says: 'I have collated this report because of the common experiences of the patients concerned and the stark contrast between the reality of the care they received and the principles and values of the NHS.'

Read the report at http://www.ombudsman.org.uk/care-and-compassion/home

---

The micro level then raises the questions of how the leader handles the demands of very different relationships. At the heart of this are issues about power. If the leader is someone in authority, how should he/she use that authority? In extreme circumstances can the leader be excused the abuse of power? Does followership mean compliance, and if so, does that diminish the autonomy and engagement of the follower? Can leaders legitimately manipulate followers in the interest of the vision? Underlying those debates are questions about the purpose and nature of authority and leadership.

In the light of all these questions Ciulla (2004) argues that ethics is very much at the heart of leadership. There is no value-neutral view of leadership, and any approach or style is built upon values that have to be justified and may well be challenged. Traditionally, however, leadership has been seen to do with individual leaders and how they exercise their authority to achieve core objectives, regardless of ethical value. This centres on the theory of leadership traits.

LEADERSHIP TRAITS

Trait theories have their root in Hippocrates and his classification of personality types according to the four 'humours'. Yukl sums up the core traits of the leader (Yukl, 1999: 215) in relation to his/her:

- energy level and stress tolerance
- self-confidence
- locus of control
- power motivation
- achievement orientation
- need for affiliation

- emotional stability and maturity
- personal integrity.

Yukl's work is a summary of other research focused on effective leadership. Effective leaders are those who have shown high levels of these characteristics. This seems to give these traits something of a scientific basis, thus often forming a basis for training and development.

The trait theory of leadership is most often based on two aspects of leadership: the 'great man' and the functionalist approach. The first refers to the innate capacities that make up the exceptional person, mostly perceived as male, and which enable that person to lead. This has a long history going back to Aristotle and Plato and the belief that leaders have to be charismatic and of superior intelligence. The second focuses on the core functional capacities. The functions themselves are often developed in relation to particular views of humanity. McGregor (1960), for instance, in a model that is still used by many business schools, puts forward two theories of humanity underlying leadership models. One sees humanity as essentially negative – wishing to avoid responsibility and work. The role of the leader then is to coerce or cajole followers into working. The other sees human beings as basically positive, and looks to give them as much freedom and responsibility as possible in an organisation. This leads to two different styles of leadership, each of which demands certain traits.

CRITIQUE OF TRAIT THEORY

There are problems with the trait approach.

Despite the summaries noted above, there are in fact many different view of traits, all commonly contested. Western (2008) notes that even when lists of common traits are developed, their meaning is open-ended, leading to debate about what they actually mean in context. His list includes ideas such as dominance, self-confidence, and extroversion. Not only do they need further explanation, they raise issues about values. Each of these feeds into the 'great man' myth – the idea that leadership can only be practised by individuals of an elite group. This in turn assumes that leadership involves working with followers who are less able and who must follow their leader. The underlying worldview is one of individualism and fragmentation, and there is no attempt to justify this or defend it against a more interactional worldview. This again presents a picture of leadership that encourages obedience and not autonomy, raising questions around workplace democracy and what constitutes respect for a workforce. Critical theory (Western, 2008) suggests that the 'great man' theory is tied to the taking and asserting of power. It implies that the individualist view of leadership can encourage unethical behaviour, such as lack of respect for the workforce. Characteristically, it can also lead to poor ethical decision-making and planning, such that powerful individual leaders are unaware of the wider ethical environment and its issues.

The trait and competency versions of this theory assume that there is a clear understanding of the role of leadership, and that it is something about a leader of an organisation who ensures the successful pursuit of its aims and objectives. Much of the literature about the trait theory is therefore based on empirical work with individual leaders who have been successful, and that largely in the context of business (Western, 2008). Such an empirical aspect gives it the impression of being scientifically based. However, there is little that is scientifically convincing about choosing what is a narrow sample of leadership. The results simply confirm that leaders who operate in a narrow business context lead in a way that utilises individualistic traits. The surveys ask no critical questions about the role of leader, and so cannot expect to find anything different from the old charismatic paradigm. This pseudo-scientific approach asserts a value-neutrality that is unjustified. On the contrary, argues Ciulla (2004), leadership has to work with values, both in relation to the organisation and to external stakeholders. This demands clarity about ethical meaning, and about mediating ethical meaning in relation to other groups (see also Calas and Smircich, 1988; Ghoshal, 2005).

The trait theory assumes a one-size-fits-all-shapes-and-contexts leadership model. None of this shows any evidence of critical reflection about diversity of leadership. A good example is the UK National Health Service (NHS), which has developed a competencies framework (Western, 2008). The framework underlines the idea of leadership as essentially individualist, pointing to generic competencies that are associated with success. However, it is not clear that a generic model can fit the many different professional groupings in the NHS. The very different contextual differences between the leader of a surgical unit, a charge nurse on a busy accident and emergency ward, and a chief finance officer have to be considered. Western argues that the descriptions of leaders can easily become so open-ended as to be of little practical use. Perhaps even more striking is the point that leadership in such a context has to relate to a plurality of professions. Any leader may find that a leader from another profession is either in authority above them or that he or she may have to work with other leaders who are on the same level and who have different focuses. The same applies to any business, where different professions, from accountancy to engineering, may have different perspectives about vision, values and objectives. Leadership in this view is part of interactional relationships, not something above them. This becomes critical when we come to governance, with strong arguments for the importance of dispersed leadership and the need for different perspectives.

All of this suggests that ethics should be at the heart of leadership (Ciulla, 2004), the leader shaping ethical awareness with the firm. None of this says that the great man theory and related ideas are totally wrong. On the contrary, this theory and its associated emphasis on individual leadership may prove important in context.

But how should the leader deal with such value and purpose? Two theories argue for the importance of leadership that develops the ethical tone of the organisation and the ethical capacities of its members: *transformational leadership* and *servant leadership*.

TRANSFORMATIONAL LEADERSHIP

The founding advocate of this approach was James Burns (1978), with later developments by writers such as Bass (2005). Burns argued for a view of the leader as essentially moral. Figures such as Hitler, by definition, fall outside leadership discourse. Burns attempts to establish that the purpose of the leader is by definition transformational, enabling the organisation to change and respond to change. He distinguishes *transformational leadership* from *transactional leadership*.

- Transactional leadership is primarily about getting the job done. Transactional, or modal, values are thus about the means of any process, and include responsibility, fairness, honesty, promise-keeping and honouring commitments. Central to this leadership are processes that enable the development of consensus, and Burns argues that the transactional approach to leadership values consensus over purpose.
- Transformational leadership focuses on the ends, not the means. This involves development that can be painful and conflicting. It is not focused on happiness *per se* or achieving agreements that compromise core values. Burns goes on to argue that the ends in question are key moral ends that transcend the interests or purpose of any particular group. These include justice, freedom, and equality. Ethically, he looks to the leader to focus on universal principles that operate in terms of the greater good. Every leader is faced by the need to respond to universal ethical values. The classic example of such leadership is given as Gandhi. He elevated the aspirations – and with them the life chances – of a whole nation, effecting social change that led to independence. These outcomes were based on core values of freedom and equality, and provided the basis for collective purpose that could be shared.

Not surprisingly, this is not a simple task. In practice, at one level it involves meeting the needs of the group or the followers. Burns uses Maslow's hierarchy of needs, stressing the primacy of core physical needs, including safety and shelter, to argue that the leader must address the basic needs first. This is essential if the higher-level social needs of the followers, including social identity and self-actualisation, connected ultimately with higher values, are to be met. Burns (1978) argues that the transformational leader should:

- expand the followers' understanding and profile of needs
- transform the followers' view of self-interest: this will enable followers to see that concern for others is a key part of their own interest
- increase the confidence of the followers
- elevate the expectations of followers
- enable a fuller appreciation of the leader's intended outcomes
- enable behavioural change
- motivate followers to higher levels of personal achievement, seen in terms of Maslow's self-actualisation (see also Turner *et al*, 2002).

At the heart of this, the leader is enabling the members of the group to develop moral maturity. Burns ties this into Kohlberg's stages of moral development (see Chapter 3). All this suggests that transformational leadership is associated with this level of moral maturity and that such leaders are better able to make decisions around value and purposes. In turn, it is argued, this leads to more effective leadership:

- The focus on values and rationality means that the transformational leader is better able to receive and take in the widest possible data, different perspectives of that data and different possible options, thus leading to better leadership decisions.
- The approach leads to the development of a better, more effective and responsive organisation. The appeal to higher motives accesses more effective motivation. Burns describes the transformational leader as one who 'looks for potential motives in followers, seeks to satisfy higher needs, and engages the full person of the follower' (1978: 20). The effect of all this is to enable group members to develop into responsible leaders, becoming fully moral agents.
- Transformational leadership in this way can cause change not merely in the organisation but also change in wider society, so it fits into the concern in business and beyond for social responsibility as a key part of the identity of the organisation.

IMPOSING VALUES

Burns' approach is strongly deontological, involving the assertion of basic universal principles. The focus on taking people on such a journey led initial critics to be concerned about the possibility that, far from empowering followers, this might involve manipulation, if not coercion, making employees believe in the leader's values. In response to that, later advocates of transformational leadership (such as Bass and Steidlmeier, 2004) distinguish *pseudo-transformational leadership* (based on attempts to dominate the values of the organisation) from *authentically transformational leadership*.

Authentic transformational leadership

Authentic Transformational Leadership (ATL) involves four elements:

- Idealised influence
  ATL provides charismatic leadership centred on universal values. This contrasts with pseudo-transformational leadership, which is focused in grandiose visions and aggrandisement.

- Inspirational motivation
  ATL centres on positive values, such as harmony and altruism, whereas pseudo-transformational leadership tends to focus on fear, defence and insecurities. Bass refers to such leaders as false Messiahs. They give the appearance of offering charismatic

leadership that leads to motivation and fulfilment but do not actively engage the followers in personal or moral development.

- Intellectual stimulation
  The key to ATL involves an 'open architecture dynamic' into the discussion of vision, evaluation and implementation. Such leadership encourages critical conversation and debate around vision and practice. For Bass and Steidlmeier this means both openness to world views that underlie the moral vision, so they write of 'spirituality', and a strongly implied emphasis on the need to develop rational reflection, so that all can rationally defend the values of the organisation.

  Pseudo-transformational leadership is not tolerant of the dynamic of critical conversation, and does not get involved in developing the intellectual capacity of organisation members. The Enron case exemplifies all these elements.

- Individualised consideration
  ATL focuses on how the individual can develop, involving the provision of coaching and mentoring. In a real sense this involves enabling followers to develop as leaders. Such leadership would involve both contributions to the organisation as a whole and ways in which the individual could represent the organisation beyond its boundaries, such as the development of corporate responsibility projects. In contrast to this, the pseudo-transformational leader would look to maintain the dependence of the followers, setting up child–parent relationships that discourage autonomy (self-governance).

FURTHER CRITIQUES OF TRANSFORMATIONAL LEADERSHIP

There is no doubt that there is much of importance in the model of transformational leadership. However, there remain several criticisms:

- It is not clear that leaders have to create a vision that will transcend the interests of the individual. Keeley (2004), for instance, found that successful leaders reflect the many interests and values of the different stakeholders. Effective listening in this was seen to be more important than communicating a vision. This ties in strongly with the development of stakeholder theory in business, suggesting that all organisations have to deal with many different stakeholders, internally and externally, and that this involves handling not simply plural interests but also different views about the values and purpose of the organisation and beyond.
- It is not clear that leaders should be effecting change in the way Burns argues for – ie striving to change values. Change is a given in any institution, and is often imposed on the organisation. Some argue (Keeley, 2004) that the most effective way of handling this is through reflection on the values already held in common by the members of that community, using them as the basis for working together.
- Research (Keeley, 2004) suggests that charisma is not necessarily central to leadership. On the contrary, charisma can easily subvert the capacities in lower levels of management through diminishing their responsibility and authority in relation to the leader.
- The rigid distinction between transactional and transformational values is unhelpful. Bass and Burns both accept the need for some transactional aspects to leadership, but dominated by transformational values. However, transactional values are more significant than Burns allows. First, the values of fairness, responsibility, trust and promise-keeping, for instance, would be seen by Kant and other deontological ethicists as central to the higher moral project. Fairness, for instance, relates directly to justice (Rawls, 1971). Second, transaction is not simply about pursuing self-interest. Transaction may involve the negotiation and development of responsibility, and as such would seem to be essential in working through what higher, general, values and principles mean in practice (see Chapters 2 and 4).

Underlying many of these criticisms is the view that the transformational model, despite the attempts to distinguish authentic leadership, runs the danger of not genuinely respecting the autonomy of followers. Keeley (2004), for instance, argues that such leadership assumes that collective ends are more legitimate or morally powerful than individual ends. It is the leader who has the understanding of the common good, and this understanding should be communicated to the follower who, of his or her own free will, accepts the core values. This sets up a paternalist relationship: the leader knows what the core values are and he or she has to communicate them to the follower, who is not aware of them and must develop the awareness. This is reinforced by the use of such terms as 'prophet' and 'messiahship'. But who is to say what the core values are? Western (2008) argues that this involves imposing values and the engineering of culture. In effect, he is arguing that the transformational leadership approach imposes values as much as the charismatic, individualist and elite leadership model.

Enteman (1993) argues, further, that at any time different moral values may take precedence, involving such imperatives as the sustainability of the firm and of related stakeholders.

SERVANT LEADERSHIP

Closely related to the transformational approach is that of servant leadership. Once again this strikes out against the heroic and individualistic view of leadership. Greenleaf (1977) developed the idea through a reading of Herman Hesse's story *Journey to the East* (2003). Central to the story is Leo, a servant who carries the bags and does all the essential chores. Over time it becomes evident that Leo gives to the group a sense of coherence and well-being, not least through his presence and singing. When Leo inexplicably disappears, the group loses its coherence and direction. It becomes clear to the leading character that Leo was in fact the leader of the group.

As Ciulla (2004: 71) points out, this is a simple but radical shift, principally because it questions the paradigm of leaders and follower, such that leaders take the function often associated with followers – that of servant. In one sense, this marks it out very clearly from the transformational model and suggests that the prophet and messiah idea of that model speaks to power and authority. Servanthood involves putting the needs of those who are being led first. The paradigm is Christian: the stress is on Christ's servanthood (the Gospel of Mark 8:27–30).

This model focuses on a change in mindset to 'an understanding and practice of leadership that places the good of those led over the self-interest of the leader' (Laub, 2004: 5). It moves away from a concern with organisational interests, and even from a concern for the customers. These issues are not unimportant, but under servant leadership they become peripheral. Laub argues that this is what makes servant leadership distinctive from transformational leadership. The success of the group and its members will emerge from this focus on the followers. Researchers such as Alimo-Metcalfe and Alban-Metcalfe (2005) argue the importance of providing empirical research on the success of servant leadership.

All this takes any assessment of leadership beyond simple task fulfilment and into monitoring whether real service has been achieved, and just what is involved in servant leadership. It becomes clearer in the six key behaviours of servant leadership that Laub (2004) sets out: valuing people, developing people, building community, displaying authenticity, providing leadership, and sharing leadership.

Greenleaf (1977) adds to this ten core characteristics of the servant leader: listening, empathy, healing, awareness, persuasion, conceptualisation (the capacity to develop a vision), foresight (the capacity to understand and learn from the past, and apply these lessons to the present and future), stewardship, commitment to the growth of people, and building community.

Neither of these lists of attributes or behaviours systematically sets out the meaning of servant leadership. Nonetheless, it is clear ethically that the idea goes beyond the universal principles of Burns to principles centred in altruism and care, virtue ethics, and in a worldview of stewardship.

CRITIQUES OF SERVANT LEADERSHIP

Polleys (2002) argues that there is no theoretical base to the concept. Moreover, she suggests that it is not possible to build any theory. This should come as no surprise. The concept is based first and foremost in value and a particular worldview, as distinct from any academic theory. Empirical research has then aimed to provide support for the model in practice, not least because many criticisms suggest that it is not practical in the context of leadership that demands difficult and swift decision-making.

The lack of theory makes it difficult to provide a substantive analysis of the term. This leads to a view of leadership that is based in a strong ethical principle – service – but does not rigorously think this through. Ultimately, the idea of service requires at least some idea of the good being served. Even Hitler's henchmen would have seen themselves as servants to others and a greater cause.

The good behind the idea of service is best expressed in the concept of *agapē*, unconditional care in the Christian tradition (Robinson, 2001). As noted in Chapter 2, this can be an important, even foundational, ethical idea, but is not sufficient. Feminist writers (Robinson, 2001) note how, historically, women became oppressed by models of unconditional service.

The emphasis on care and service can lead to an ethics that is polarised and imbalanced. More even than transformational leadership there is too great a stress on altruism, to the exclusion of self-interest. As we noted in the first chapters, concern for others has to be balanced with concern for self and with organisational sustainability.

TRANSACTIONAL LEADERSHIP

Rost (1991) attempts to balance the different ethical elements through the idea of transactional leadership. He defines leadership as 'an influence relationship among leaders and followers who intend real changes that reflect their mutual purposes' (Rost, 1991: 102). He contrasts influence with institutional authority. Influence is multi-directional; authority is top-down with one direction. Influence is based on persuasion, not coercion. This requires several things:

- effective contractual relationships, involving acceptance of responsibilities legitimated by contract – Rost casts followers as active, not passive, subordinates, empowered by contract
- multiple leadership, varying in different contexts. Active followers have many roles that shift dynamically and are all part of a complex system, not a fixed hierarchy. This is increasingly so in more complex organisations. It accepts that organisations may have several different purposes.

This leads to constant interactive relationships, responding to change. Rost (1991) accepts that all leadership involves transformation of some kind but argues that it is important to guard against unethical means. Contract and negotiation are the best way of maintaining autonomy and integrity among all the parties. This highlights power relations, and the negotiations necessary among people of unequal power and different agendas. Followers are significantly involved in negotiating any exchange or transaction that results in a decision or a course of action, and this theory acknowledges that followers could influence the leader. Leadership then becomes a social system characterised by mutual feedback between leaders and followers (Rost, 1991: 30).

There is no doubt that a contract can be a means of developing equality and freedom. At one level it protects the individual from coercive or abusive leadership (negative freedom).

At another level it enables the members of the organisation to develop a voice (positive freedom). However, the contract can also be used in negative ways to oppress the follower and discourage initiative. Important as good contractual relationships are, there thus has to be some elements of the transformational approach: leaders and followers working through the meanings of core values in practice.

Ethical leadership has to deal simultaneously with a number of different perspectives and hold them together. First, leadership should ensure creative enterprise that will drive a project forward while keeping it under prudent control. Second, it should be sufficiently knowledgeable about the workings of a project to be accountable for its actions, yet be able to stand back from the day-to-day management and retain an objective long-term view. Third, leaders should be sensitive to the pressures of short-term issues and yet be informed about broader, long-term trends. Finally, the leader is expected to be focused upon the sustainability of the project while acting responsibly towards the members of the project or organisation, partners and society and the environment.

To keep all of that together requires dispersed leadership, in effect sharing the responsibility of leadership. For Alimo-Metcalfe and Alban-Metcalfe (2005) this takes leadership into a more complex arena, requiring the development of strong virtues of leadership in enabling all these things to be held in tension through the group. In particular, these authors list six factors that emerge from research with leaders in healthcare trusts in the UK:

- valuing individuals – this involves genuine concern for the well-being and development of others, based in inclusivity
- networking and achieving – this involves enterprise, developing networks inside and outside the organisation, and inspirational communication: this is based in a strong sense of connectedness
- enabling, through delegation and empowerment
- acting with integrity, involving honesty and openness
- being accessible – behind this lies a sensitivity to the needs of others
- being decisive, and being able to take risks.

The authors suggest that there are good ethical reasons for this approach and that it also leads to success. Decisiveness and the capacity to take risks, for instance, are the sign of a robust entrepreneurial organisation.

The work of Peter Senge (1990) fits well with this view of the ethics of dispersed leadership. He focuses on the capacity of the organisation to learn. A genuine learning organisation looks to enable a continued reflection between its vision and reality. Importantly, leadership becomes more a function of stewardship: leaders are not focused on absolute control but rather on enabling the organisation to be accountable and aware of the social and physical environment. In one sense, then, it is clear that the leader enables the ethical tone of the corporation. Trevino and Brown (2004) argue that this is not because of any myth about the ethical charisma of the leader providing a model. It is rather specifically about how the leader enables ongoing reflection on core values and purpose.

Trevino and Brown contrast such behaviour with unethical managers who set out high values but in fact practise deceit, and 'ethically silent' managers who reveal no moral understanding. The problem with 'ethical silence' is that no behaviour is ethically neutral. As Tawney (1930) argued, all behaviour, especially decisions, embodies value and thus indicates an ethical position. For the leader not to make this ethics clear runs the risk of ethical and organisational confusion.

The task of the ethical leader, then, is to help the organisation think about, articulate and test ethical values, and to embody the core virtues that enable this. In that sense the leader embodies the core values. We explore this in more detail in the next chapter.

ETHICS AND GOVERNANCE

The role of leadership has increasingly focused on the governance of the firm, and specifically on how the leadership is organised in the board, maintaining an ethical vision with the sustainability of the corporation. The charismatic model of leadership has tended to see the CEO acting also as the chair and as a result dominating the board. Increasingly, however, there is increasingly a stress on dispersed leadership in the board and beyond.

Underlying the views of corporate governance have been three major theories: agency theory; stewardship theory; stakeholder theory;

- Agency theory – The term 'agency' here is used very differently from the concept of rational agency noted in Chapter 4. Here, the agent (CEO or MD) is seen as a self-interested operator hired by the principals (the owners/shareholders) to fulfil their objectives of increasing shareholder value. Governance then would involve finding ways of controlling the agent, through reward or regulation (Bowie and Freeman, 1992).
  There is little foundation to this theory, other than the assertion of the underlying worldview which seeks to defend the freedom of the executive to maximise shareholder value (an argument examined more closely in Chapter 11). It also relies on an individualist view of leadership, with all its problems.
- Stewardship theory – Stewardship, as already noted (see Chapter 4), focuses on shared responsibility and value. The steward then is seen as acting on behalf of a corporation whose values and purpose he or she believes in. Stewardship theory, like servant leadership, can lack realism. It does not consider the possibility that there may be several different purposes of the business, or how it will handle different views. In relation to governance it also suggests a strong level of trust should be given to the CEO who sees himself or herself as steward, even advocating that the CEO should also be chair of the board. This runs the danger of uncritical acceptance of the CEO's power.
- Stakeholder theory – The stakeholder theory of governance maintains that stakeholders should be involved in some way. As noted in Chapter 4, this suggests that there are other indications of good performance than shareholder value and takes account of the social and environmental context. The major limitations of this theory to governance are questions of how it handles conflicts between stakeholders, in terms of both their needs and their responsibilities.

Nonetheless, the stakeholder model is increasingly the focus for governance. This is partly because the business crises of the late twentieth and early twenty-first century – such as Enron – had such a negative effect on stakeholders. In response to those crises, two approaches emerged: the legal and the principled. The first of these was represented by the Sarbanes-Oxley Act of 2002.

THE SARBANES-OXLEY ACT, 2002

This approach to governance relies on legal regulation, and can be summed up as 'comply or else'. The Act (SOX) included:

- penalties for corporate fraud and prison terms up to 20 years for destroying or altering documents in federal investigations
- penalties for CEOs who certified false accounts of up to 20 years in prison and fines of up to $5 million.
- a new five-member board to oversee the accounting profession, with disciplinary and subpoena powers
- the restriction of consulting and non-audit services from accounting firms
- the imposition of rules on financial analysts to prevent conflicts of interest.

THE COMBINED CODE

In contrast to SOX was the Combined code (2006 and 2010) of the UK. This grew out of several previous reports of governance, principally Cadbury (1992), Greenbury (1995), Turnbull (1999) and Higgs (2003). It was focused on UK listed companies, but was also offered as an exemplar for other organisations. The emphasis is on responsibility for self-regulation, with the tag-line 'comply or explain'. This is not then a one-size-fits-all model, and each institution should take responsibility for explaining how any alternative approach fulfils core values, such as fairness and transparency. In all this,

- the board should be effective and is collectively responsible
- the chairman/MD's roles and responsibilities should be divided
- there should be a balance of executives and non-executive directors on the board
- the appointment of directors should involve formal, rigorous and transparent procedures
- there should be a formal board performance review annually, with planned training, board refreshment and regular elections
- levels of directors' pay should be sufficient, but not more than necessary
- significant proportions of executive directors' pay should be linked to corporate and individual performance
- there should be formal procedures for determining remuneration, and no director should determine his or her own pay
- companies should be ready to enter into dialogue with major shareholders based on a mutual understanding of objectives
- the board should use the AGM to communicate with investors and encourage their participation.

The board then becomes the transparent environment in which leadership is framed, tested, supported and developed. It would have a strong responsibility for dispersed leadership, and for critical discourse that would make sure that there was no element of leadership that could hide from external gaze. It is within that context, for instance, that the compensation policy can be thoroughly tested and its philosophy developed.

In effect, all this enables dispersed leadership, a sense of shared responsibility and clear negotiation of responsibility. The board would then begin to reflect wider discourse among stakeholders and in the wider community. Ultimately, the chair would be responsible for ensuring the practice of dispersed leadership. In addition to transparent practice it requires the development of board culture that encourages critical dialogue, testing values and practice.

KING III

Alongside and partly influenced by the Combined code is the third King Code (Institute of Directors, 2009), based in South Africa. Some writers suggest that this is a hybrid of the 'comply or else' and 'comply or explain' approaches (Andreasson, 2009). In fact, between King II and King III the Company Act of 2008 established a legal framework to protect stakeholders. King III in some sense is a response to that, recognising the importance of balancing a legal and principled (self-regulating) approach. Both King II and III also move beyond the focus of the combined code, stressing the importance of ethics and core philosophies.

Ethics-centred

In King II and III, ethics is very much the centre of governance. They suggest a six-stage process of governing ethical performance that consists of:

- identifying through stakeholder engagement the perceptions and expectations that stakeholders have of the ethical performance of a company
- determining the ethical values and standards of the company and codifying it in a code of ethics

- institutionalising the values and code of ethics of a company on both the strategic and systems levels
- monitoring and evaluating compliance to the code of ethics
- accounting and auditing ethical performance according to emerging global standards on ethical accounting and auditing
- disclosing ethical performance to relevant stakeholders.

The third stage emphasises the need to take companies beyond implementing the code of ethics to make a significant difference to company culture and performance. Examples of how this can be achieved include regular ethical risk assessment, confidential reporting systems through which unethical or suspicious behaviour could be reported, the integration of ethical performance into existing performance appraisal systems, and integrity assessment as part of selection and promotion procedures. We explore such approaches in the next chapter.

King III goes beyond 'comply' to urge language such as 'apply or adopt'. Comply, King feels, infers a non-thinking use of rules (Institute of Directors, 2009: 3). In contrast, he argues that the board should take responsibility for working through what the ground principles of governance mean in practice. This looks to build ethical thinking into the culture of the board such that members take responsibility in all senses of the word: defining and continually re-evaluating the purpose, aims and values of the organisation, being accountable to stakeholders, and embodying the shared responsibility for the social and physical environment. This includes responsibility for plural stakeholders and also multiple responsibility, such that executive directors are, for instance, both responsible to the CEO and also, with all other board members, to the shareholders, for the direction and operation of the firm.

Philosophy

The philosophy of King III revolves around leadership, sustainability and corporate citizenship.

- *Leadership* is characterised in terms of the core ethical values of *responsibility*, *accountability*, *fairness* and *transparency*. These concepts are not analysed in depth by the report, but reinforce the main meanings of responsibility noted in the last chapter. There is a clear stress on taking responsibility for meaning and practice and on being accountable to all stakeholders. The report goes even further in arguing that these are 'based on moral duties that find expression in the concept of *ubuntu*'. *Ubuntu* is a pan-African communitarian worldview emphasising the interdependent nature of humanity – 'I am because you are'. It stresses empathy, understanding, reciprocity, harmony and co-operation. Moreover, as Andreasson (2009: 14) notes, 'It provides a guiding principle for determining how to organise African societies and measure well-being'. None of this is fanciful given the UK government's attempts to develop shared ideas of happiness that go beyond measuring wealth (http://www.bbc.co.uk/news/uk-11833241-). Remember, happiness or well-being has always been key to ethics. The utilitarians wanted to maximise happiness, and Aristotle thought the aim of ethics was happiness or well-being. For the South African situation this provides an important bridge between business and society. South Africa has a history of civil strife, poverty and capitalism, seen by many as an extension of colonial power (Mbeki, 2007). This demands that business take account of its social environment, with a stakeholder-inclusive approach. This includes awareness of development issues and also of the continuing culture of reconciliation post-*apartheid*. Such a sense of business contributing to the healing of the nation leads King III to stress the use of ADR (alternative dispute resolution) not only as an action of mediation but also as part of ongoing governance. This is developed further in Chapter 7 and Chapter 12.
- The use of *ubuntu* implies that despite the explicit embracing of a stakeholder-inclusive view of governance, King III also contains elements of stewardship theory, with a strong

sense of shared responsibility. This is confirmed with the emphasis on sustainability and corporate citizenship.

- Sustainability is seen by King III as the primary ethical and economic imperative of the twenty-first century. It is at the heart of opportunities and risks for businesses. The interconnections of nature, society and business therefore demand governance that genuinely integrate all of these aspects both in reporting and in development, and King III champions this well beyond the combined code. He even includes the governance of IT. Approaches to integrated reporting are examined in later chapters.

- Inclusivity of stakeholders must also be taken into account in decision-making and strategy. Values such as innovation, fairness and collaboration are therefore key aspects of any transition to sustainability. The integration of sustainability and social transformation in a strategic and coherent manner will, argues King III (page 13), lead to 'greater opportunities, efficiencies, and benefits, for both the company and society'.

- In the light of this, the company is a corporate citizen, from which is required the exercise of responsibility.

In short, then, the King codes bring together all the key elements of responsibility even more explicitly than the combined code, demanding an awareness of meaning, purpose and role in society; clear integrated accounting of practice; and shared response to the needs of the social and physical environment.

A good example of this development of responsibility in leadership comes from Anita Roddick and the Body Shop.

THE BODY SHOP

Launched in 1987 by Anita Roddick, this company is now one of the largest cosmetics brands in the world. It has achieved its reputation through both the excellence of its products and a focus on global citizenship.

Pless (2007) notes several things that characterised Roddick's leadership. First, Roddick constantly used narrative. This provided the base for developing meaning and exemplifying virtues. It also enabled ownership of identity, and good models of developing meaning and practice, taking account of feelings and core ideas and values. Roddick even called upon the philosopher Wittgenstein: ' Wittgenstein said, "Words create the world. You've got to have a language of socially responsible business"' (quoted in Pless, 2007: 456). Second, Roddick focused on the development of networks. At the heart of this was the drive to develop a vision of responsible leadership dispersed through stakeholder management. Management was built around building and sustaining essentially moral relations with stakeholders focused on justice,

accountability, and the broadest view of responsibility, seen in economic, ecological, social, political and human responsibilities. Third, this was sustained by a vision that was essentially focused on taking responsibility for an interconnected world. Roddick reveals what are taken to be essentially feminist values focused in care, creativity and service. Her vision was built around such values, but values that had to be critically tested. The vision was for all franchise holders and stakeholders to experience enterprise in a social context, and thus to take responsibility for ideas, enterprise and change. The first phrase in the formulation of the Body Shop's mission was thus, 'To dedicate our business to the pursuit of social and environmental change' (Body Shop International.com, 2004).

This was the business model that she believed would make her business an experience of worth for all involved, would change the world – and would make a profit. It extended to employees, customers, communities, suppliers and the environment. Some have spoken of

Roddick as both activist and entrepreneur. In fact, both come together in a business identity of steward and change agent. The first had a strong sense of being a custodian of values, and steward of entrusted resources. Part of this was the assertion that business had the power to do good. As she said, 'Political awareness and activism must be woven into the fabric of business. In a global world, there are no value-free or politically disentangled actions. The very act of organising on a global basis is political because of culture, geography and differing value systems' (Roddick, 2000: 168). This meant getting involved in activism but not in a simplistic way. Sometimes it would involve Body Shop franchises in different parts of the globe working with stakeholders, and often working with NGOs such as Greenpeace and Human Rights Watch. The campaigning resulted in legislative action, including a ban on animal testing in the UK.

For Roddick this meant creating a culture of global citizenship, such that this was seen as an integral part of doing business, and such that the stakeholders would in turn take responsibility, and so become leaders. In a sense this approach is a complete form of dispersed leadership, not simply for the followers but for all stakeholders. This in turn led Roddick to assert the need to place such responsibility at the heart of the curriculum and staff development.

None of this is to say that Roddick's leadership has not been critiqued, not least around the chemical colouring of many of the products, and around estimates of what percentage of profit went to social causes (http://www.jonentine.com/the-body-shop.html). Nonetheless, as a leader she successfully set out a form of responsible leadership that held together the different modes of responsibility. This is summed up in the rest of the mission statement, or 'reason for being' (Body Shop International.com, 2004):

- to creatively balance the financial and human needs of our stakeholders: employees, customers, franchisees, suppliers and shareholders

- to courageously ensure that our business is ecologically sustainable: meeting the needs of the present without compromising the future

- to meaningfully contribute to local, national and international communities in which we trade, by adopting a code of conduct which ensures care, honesty, fairness and respect

- to passionately campaign for the protection of the environment, human and civil rights, and against animal testing within the cosmetics and toiletries industries

- to tirelessly work to narrow the gap between principle and practice, while making fun, passion and care part of our daily lives.

CONCLUSION

This chapter argues that leaders are not responsible for making people ethical. Rather, they are responsible for enabling their organisation to be aware of ethical meaning and reflect on it as a core part of practical decision-making.

Those core aspects of responsibility – owning a critical approach to values, purpose and meaning, being accountable and sharing responsibility – should be a natural part of an organisation that learns (Senge, 1990). Key to this has to be an outward-facing organisation, enabling transparency and external critique, avoiding a closed ethics based purely in the defence of the organisation. King III captures much of this in its stress on developing an ethical culture and the board enabling a triple bottom line accountability. In one sense leadership itself can be summed up as 'taking responsibility', practising and enabling others to practise the three modes of responsibility.

This approach takes account of virtue ethics, responsibility ethics and deontological ethics, with a strong sense of stewardship and stakeholder theory.

The next chapter examines how this culture can actually be established, with implications for virtue as well as system and process.

EXPLORE FURTHER

Books

Ciulla, J. (2002) *The Ethics of Leadership*. Independence, MO: Wadsworth.

Fryer, M. (2011) *Ethics and Organizational Leadership: Developing a normative model*. Oxford: Oxford University Press.

Nordberg, D. (2010) *Corporate Governance: Principles and issues*. London: Sage.

DVDs

Enron: the Smartest Guys in the Room (2007, Lionsgate), for an example of closed and defensive leadership, and the ethical implications.

Lord of the Rings (2004, New Line Cinema), for an example of servant leadership, with Frodo leading despite other strong 'leaders' such as Gandalf, Aragorn and Boromir.

REFERENCES

ALIMO-METCALFE, B. and ALBAN-METCALFE, J. (2005) 'Leadership: time for a new direction', *Leadership* 1: 51.

ANDREASSON, S. (2009) 'Understanding corporate governance reform in South Africa, Anglo-American divergence: the King reports, and hybridisation', *Business and Society*, 18 February.

BASS, B. (2005) *Transformational Leadership*. New York: Erlbaum.

BASS, B. and STEIDLMEIER, E. (2004) 'Ethics, character and authentic transformational leadership', in Ciulla, J. (ed.) *Ethics the Heart of Leadership*. Westport, CT: Praeger: 175–96.

BOWIE, N. and FREEMAN, R. (1992) *Ethics and Agency Theory: An introduction*. New York: Oxford University Press.

BURNS, J. (1978) *Leadership*. New York: Harper & Row.

CADBURY, A. (1992) *The Committee on the Financial Aspects of Corporate Governance*. London: Gee.

CALAS, M. and SMIRCICH. L. (1988) 'Reading leadership as a form of cultural analysis', in Hunt, G., Baliga, B., Daschler, H. and Schriesheim, A. *Emerging Leadership Vistas*, Lexington, MA: Lexington Books.

CIULLA, J. B. (ed.) (2004) *Ethics: The heart of leadership*. Westport, CT: Praeger.

COVEY, S. (2002) *Principle-Centred Leadership*. London: Simon & Schuster.

CRUVER, B. (2003) *Enron: Anatomy of Greed*. London: Arrow Books.

ENTEMAN, W. (1993) *Managerialism: The emergence of a new ideology*. Madison, WI: University of Wisconsin Press.

FINANCIAL REPORTING COUNCIL (2005) *Internal Control: Revised guidance for directors on the combined code ('The Turnbull Guidance')*, October. London. Available at: http://www.frc.org.uk/documents/pagemanager/frc/   Revised%20Turnbull%20Guidance%20October%202005.pdf

FINANCIAL REPORTING COUNCIL (2006) *The Combined Code of Governance*. June, London. Available at: http://www.frc.org.uk/documents/pagemanager/frc/ Combined%20code%202006%20OCTOBER.pdf

FUSARO, P. and MILLER, R. (2002) *What Went Wrong at Enron: Everyone's guide to the largest bankruptcy in US history*. Hoboken, NJ: Wiley.

GHOSHAL, S. (2005) 'Bad management theories are destroying good management practices', *Academy of Management, Learning and Education*, 4: 75–91.

GREENBURY REPORT (1995) *On director remuneration*. London: GEC.

GREENLEAF, R. (1977) *The Servant as Leader: A journey into the nature of legitimate power and greatness*. New York: Paulist Press.

HESSE, H. (2003) *Journey to the East*. London: Picador.

HIGGS REPORT (2003) *Review of the role and effectiveness of non-executive directors*. London: Department of Trade and Industry.

HUMAN RIGHTS WATCH (2002) 'Enron in India', 24 January. Available at: http:www.hrw.org/reports/1999/enron/.

INSTITUTE OF DIRECTORS (2002) *King II report on corporate governance*. Johannesburg: Institute of Directors in Southern Africa.

INSTITUTE OF DIRECTORS (2009) *King III report on corporate governance*. Johannesburg: Institute of Directors in Southern Africa.

KEELEY, M. (2004) 'The trouble with transformational leadership: towards a federalist ethic for organisations', in Ciulla, J. B. (ed.) *Ethics: The heart of leadership*. Westport, CT: Praeger, 141–74.

KETS de VRIES, M. (2001) *The Leadership Mystique: An owner's manual*. London: Financial Times/Prentice Hall.

LALICH, J. (2004) *Bounded Choice: True believers and charismatic cults*. Berkeley: University of California Press.

LAUB, J. (2004) *Defining Servant Leadership: A recommended typology for servant leadership studies*. Proceedings of the 2004 Servant Leadership Research Round Table.

MBEKI, T. (2007) Steve Biko Memorial Lecture (Cape Town, 12 September). Available at: http://www.polity.org.za/article/sa-mbeki-steve-biko-memorial-lecture-12092007-2007-09-12.

McGREGOR, D. (1960) *The Human Side of Enterprise*. New York: McGraw-Hill.

PLESS, N. (2007) 'Understanding responsible leadership: Role identity and motivational drivers', *Journal of Business Ethics*, 74: 437–56.

POLLEYS, M. (2002) 'One university's response to the anti-leadership vaccine: developing servant leaders', *Journal of Leadership and Organisational Studies*, 8: 117.

PLESS, N. (2007) 'Understanding responsible leadership: role identity and motivational drivers', *Journal of Business Ethics*, 74: 437–56.

PYE, A. (2005) 'Leadership and organising: sensemaking in action', *Leadership*, 1(1): 31–49.

RAWLS, J. (1971) *Justice as Fairness*. Oxford: Oxford University Press.

ROBINSON, S. (2001) *Agape, Moral Meaning and Pastoral Counselling*. Cardiff: Aureus.

ROBINSON, S. (2008) *Spirituality, Ethics and Care*. London: Jessica Kingsley.

RODDICK, A. (2000) *Business as Usual*. London: Thorsons.

ROST, J. (1991) *Leadership in the Twenty-First Century*. New York: Praeger.

SARTRE, J.-P. (2004) *Les mains sales* (Paris: Éditions Gallimard [1948], 1986) trans. Calhoun; quoted in Laurie Calhoun, *The Independent Review*, VIII, 3, Winter: 363–85.

SCHWARTZ, J. (2002) 'Darth Vader. Machiavelli. Skilling sets intense pace', *New York Times*, 7 February: 1.

SENGE, P. (2000) *The Fifth Discipline: The art and practice of the learning organisation*. London: Transworld.

SHERMAN, S. (2002) 'Enron: uncovering the uncovered story', *Columbia Journalism Review*, 40: 22–8.

TAWNEY, R. H. (1930) *Equality*. London: Allen & Unwin.

TREVINO, L. and BROWN, M. (2004) 'Managing to be ethical: debunking five business ethics myths', *Academy of Management Executive*, 18: 69–81.

TURNBULL REPORT (1999) *Internal Control: Guidance for directors on the Combined Code*. London: The Financial Reporting Council.

TURNER, N., BARLING, J., EPITROPAKI, O., BUTCHER, V. and MILNER, C. (2002) 'Transformational leadership and moral reasoning'. *Journal of Applied Psychology*, 87(2): 304–11.

WESTERN, S. (2008) *Leadership: A critical text*. London: Sage.

YUKL, G. (1999) 'An evaluative essay on current conceptions of effective leadership', *European Journal of Work and Organisational Psychology*, March, 8(1): 215.

CHAPTER 6

Character, Culture and Code – Managing Ethics

When you have completed this chapter you will be able to:

- critically understand the development of personal and organisational virtues
- critically understand the nature and function of ethical codes
- critically understand the idea and practices of culture, and how ethics can be developed as part of that
- critically understand the meaning and practice of conscience in relation to business organisations.

INTRODUCTION

This chapter examines more closely the ethical character and culture pointed to in the previous chapter (on ethical leadership). It is based in virtue ethics and responsibility ethics, and in the first part focuses on the key virtues. The second part focuses on the community of practice and thus the culture of the organisation. Part of that involves a critical examination of the place of ethical codes in business, and how they can be developed. In conclusion we reflect on the nature of conscience in this context.

 ARTHUR ANDERSEN: ARE WE STILL THE GOOD GUYS?

CASE

Early in his career, Arthur Andersen – the founder of the accountancy company of the same name – was faced with a difficult dilemma. An executive from a major railway company had examined the financial audit of the firm's books prepared by Andersen. The executive was not happy with the negative picture painted by the audit and asked Andersen to significantly change the report, or risk losing the railway company's business. Andersen gave the now famous response, 'There's not enough money

in the city of Chicago to induce me to change that report.' The railway company's business was lost, but within the year it went bankrupt.

This incident established the core purpose and values of the Andersen business, summed up in the adage, 'Think straight – talk straight' (inculcated in him by his mother). It established the reputation of a firm that could be trusted. Subsequently, Andersen developed the firm's thinking about corporate and professional social responsibility, which focused on the importance of independent judgement and action. Following Andersen's death in 1947 the firm continued with this strong sense of purpose and prudence.

As late as in 1999, Steve Samek, a managing partner, made the statement, 'The day Arthur Andersen loses the public's trust is the day we are out of business' (quoted in Toffler, 2003). This showed consistency with the early values of the firm.

However, from the mid-1990s things had begun to go wrong. In addition to the audit function the firm had taken on management consultancy. Trevino and Nelson (2008), drawing on the narrative of Toffler (hired as an ethics consultant by the firm), suggest that this set-up functions with two very different values and related virtues. The function of auditing is based on values of truth, honesty and transparency. Consultancy tended to focus on the required needs of the client, and this led to concern for fulfilling their requirements in order to retain their custom. In effect, the Arthur Andersen company began to change its core values. It still retained the ethical framework of the original company, but ethics and the original Andersen values were not talked about. This resulted in a downward spiral. First, the concept of serving the clients became defined as making sure that the clients were happy – something that did not involve challenging them. Second, the focus on the tradition became understood as maintaining loyalty to the partners. This involved unquestioning obedience to the partners, even where this involved irregular practices such as inflating fees and contract estimates. Third, the priority of ethics training – a regular part of the original culture – began to erode. This was exemplified in the practice of hiring experienced practitioners from outside the firm. These new consultants were advised not to attend ethics induction sessions in preference to the development of lucrative new contracts. Fourth, there was a general assumption that recruitment involved ethical screening and that there was no need to reflect further on ethical issues. Fifth, it must be noted that consulting is not *per se* unethical. The key point was that in the light of the developments there was not thought to be a need to focus on the core principles that give ethical meaning to consultancy practice. Sixth, the firm began to develop a form of narrow defensive ethics, aimed at protecting the business, to the extent of instigating 'cover-ups'. Close to the end of the Enron crisis there were even internal emails that asked senior colleagues to be sure that no emails included a 'smoking gun' – ie an imputation of guilt. In light of the recoverability of emails this was not even an effective cover-up attempt.

At one level it is possible to see the way in which the culture of Arthur Andersen changed over time. It began as an intentional culture with clear means of keeping ethics on the agenda and moved across to a narrow, defensive culture, with no attempt to maintain ethical meaning or to work through core vision or purpose. This would seem to confirm the descriptive theories of ethics that without explicit attention to integrating ethical meaning into the firm's ongoing reflective practice there is the danger of falling back into non-responsible or irresponsible practice. It is clear that the firm had crossed the line into such practice without realising what it was doing. For the most part everyone still thought that the firm was 'one of the good guys', a firm of character – and we now begin with the meaning of that character within a firm.

CHARACTER

In Chapter 2 we noted the importance of virtue ethics, and in Chapter 4 we saw how responsibility relates to virtues and can itself be seen as a virtue. It makes sense, then, to regard the development of virtues as a key part of the development of the character of the organisation and of its members. It is the virtues, the strengths of character, that show ethics in operation. As we noted, such virtues, argued Aristotle (2004), are of the 'mean' – that is, the middle – between extremes. Virtues (Aristotle, 2004) are only learned through practice. Conversely, when it is not practised, the virtue is lost – the ethical analogue of muscle strength in relation to physical activity. This was evident in the attitude of the Arthur Andersen workforce who did not feel the need to be involved in the practice of ethical reflection.

At the beginning of the Arthur Andersen narrative several dominant virtues were evident. These were the virtues of practical wisdom, integrity, empathy, justice and courage – and we now examine each of these and others.

PRACTICAL WISDOM

This is Aristotle's virtue of *phronēsis* (2004), the capacity for rational deliberation that enables the wise person to reflect on his or her conception of the good and to embody it in practice. Aristotle sees it not as a moral virtue but as one of the intellectual virtues. This virtue is often the one most tested when targets have to be met, precisely because it is about reflecting on purpose.

Arthur Andersen embodied this virtue, with his stress on the core purpose and moral value of the accounting profession. *Phronēsis* is a virtue that is brought into play whenever there is a value conflict, or an uncertainty about ends, and Andersen was clear about the core values of honesty and transparency, and how they were ultimately more important than any single contract. Indeed, it is precisely those values that led to the development of the unique identity of the firm, and until the end led to its growth and success.

Practical wisdom (Latin *prudentia*) for Aquinas (1981) had at its heart three elements: openness to the past (*memoria*), openness to the present, involving the capacity to be still and listen actively (*docilitas*), openness to the future (*solertia*). This emphasises openness and care before any hasty judgement or decision. In being open to the present and the future it also stresses an appreciation of reality and thus of both constraints and possibilities in any situation. It works against a simple utilitarian view of ethics, and against a primarily target-centred approach to leadership and management. As noted in Chapter 4, this relates closely to responsibility. Its emphasis on awareness of the past is both on the narrative of the community of practice and the wider context of that narrative.

A key point about the later developments of the Andersen firm was that the company had stopped practising this virtue. The induction and other training courses focused on this practice, and the new recruits neither did it nor saw the need to do it. The result was that they did not critically examine the firm's past narrative and the core values, or different competing values and purposes. In business and in other areas of leadership, such as the armed forces, it is not uncommon to hear the argument that the objective is clear and there is no need for *phronēsis*. The leader in wartime thus has the simple objective of defeating the enemy. However, this ignores the context of any situation. As Tawney (1930) observed, the aim of World War II was not simply to defeat the enemy but to fight for core values such as freedom and equality. Those values in turn determine the purpose of action in and after war, focusing not on simply winning the war but on how core democratic values can be achieved. Too great an emphasis on the first could lead then to loss of the second, long-term purpose, as happened in Iraq (Robinson, 2011). There was none of this reflection about future planning at the end of Arthur Andersen.

INTEGRITY

PAUSE FOR THOUGHT

Do you have integrity?

In your learning groups define what it means for you, giving examples.

There is some evidence that business leaders see this as the main virtue. A Council for Industry and Higher Education survey (Archer and Davidson, 2008) showed it to be one of the top three qualities businesses wanted in new recruits from university. The evidence of the Fortune 200 points to it as the most desired quality of the organisation (Kaptein, 2008). As we noted in Chapter 4, Brown (2005) argues that integrity can be developed in the corporation as well as in the individual.

Solomon (1992) suggests that integrity is not one virtue but a collection of several virtues, which come together to help form a coherent character and identity. This theme is taken up by the Institute of Chartered Accountancy in England and Wales (ICAEW), which has focused on integrity in professional practice. In *Reporting with Integrity* (2007) the Institute begin by establishing the usefulness of integrity. Integrity is important because it provides the basis for:

- establishing trust – Trust is critical internally and externally if a business is to operate successfully over a long period. There must be trust between leaders and members of the organisation and trust between the organisation and the stakeholders, including different professions that may be part of the organisation. Trust is partly developed through the maintenance of standards and competency. Solomon (2005) argues that trust also requires the demonstration of relational commitment. Again this is embodied in corporate or individual practice or in the commitment of the wider profession
- giving and receiving reliable information – In one sense this is a subsection of trust. Can the customer or client trust the professional or organisation to present information that is true, relevant and honest? It reminds us that the presentation of any such information is never free from interpersonal dynamics and related values.
- developing markets – By extension, clear and truthful information becomes critical for the wider financial markets. Participants in the markets depend upon accurate information to make choices. In effect, the ICAEW is arguing that the functioning of the whole financial system relies upon the practice of integrity.

In *Reporting with Integrity* the ICAEW acknowledges that promoting integrity is difficult, not least because it seems to be a relative concept. Four different major philosophical approaches to integrity are therefore reviewed:

- self-integration
- identity
- moral purpose
- commitment.

Self-integration

This can also been seen in terms of developing a holistic integration of the self that brings together the cognitive, affective, relational and physical aspects of the person. It leads to holistic thinking that takes account of how these four affect each other. Rowan Williams (1989) notes how emotion can involve feelings which intrude on and control the person. Anxiety or shame, for instance, can be felt so intensely that the person responds to them without understanding how they are influencing him or her. Self-integration involves an awareness of emotion and of how it affects one's thinking and the thinking of others. It involves a positive form of detachment that enables appropriate response to feelings (see also *emotional intelligence* in Goleman, 1996). Integration of physical awareness is equally important, not least because, as Ford (1999) notes, all action involves communication. Indeed, all action embodies in some way attitude and values. Taylor (1989) takes self-integration further, to involve acknowledging the 'plural person', the different cultural aspects of the person (ethnic identity, civic identity, family identity, and so on) and how these can work together.

Identity

Bernard Williams (2005) argues for a view of integrity based on the identity of the person. Faced by a dilemma, such as choosing between causing the death of one person in order to save 20, Williams argues that this is not simply about choosing principle (not to kill) or a utilitarian calculation (saving 20 lives). In the case he offers the man refuses to kill because this involves going against the core moral beliefs that go to make up the identity of the person. Williams argues then that this is the basis of integrity.

Although this is an important part of integrity – one that demands careful reflection on what the basic values are – it is not clear that it is sufficient. Like self-integration it suffers from the problem that the morality at the base of identity may itself be flawed or questionable.

Moral purpose

In the light of that, writers such as Rawls and Halfon argue that integrity must include an acceptable moral purpose at the base. For Rawls this would involve some clear conception of justice (1971), defined in terms of fairness. Halfon is more general. For him the important thing is not which moral purpose is involved but rather that the person sets out an ethical perspective that is conceptually clear, logically consistent and aware of relevant empirical evidence (1989). In effect, Halfon argues that the person of integrity will give a clear account of his or her moral purpose as part of following a rigorous moral decision-making process.

Commitment

As Calhoun (1995) notes, the sense of commitment here is 'standing for something'. Calhoun argues that this involves more than simply standing for an individual moral purpose, and rather for a purpose recognised by the community. The basis for integrity is thus recognised. Integrity here is associated explicitly with something worth striving for, and it assumes a degree of courage and perseverance that will enable the person and group to stand up against internal and societal pressures that impose obstacles to the purpose.

However, much like the other arguments, this has limitations, not least because it could involve standing up for something that means much to one group or community but actually is seen as problematic by communities outside.

None of these approaches is sufficient in itself. The ICAEW report suggests that these partial approaches contain elements that can come together in a more coherent description of integrity, with five core aspects:

- moral values – this demands clear thinking about what they are
- motives – these demand awareness of motives and the capacity to test them in the self and others
- commitments – this involves sustaining commitment to others and to values over a long period
- qualities – these involve the virtues necessary to maintain integrity, and they are considered below
- achievements – the need to integrate moral purpose with practice, walking the talk.

In turn, the Institute argues, these elements lead to key 'behavioural characteristics' of integrity. From moral values emerge the behaviours of being honest and truthful. From motives emerge the behaviours of fairness and compliance with law. Commitment involves the promoting of community interests. Qualities include being open and adaptable, and the capacity to take corrective action. From achievements emerge the behaviour of consistency.

From all this we can sum up integrity as:

- *integration* of the different parts of the person: emotional, psychological and intellectual. This leads to holistic thinking, and an awareness of the self alongside awareness and appreciation of external data
- *consistency* between the self, values and practice; between past, present and future; and between different relationships, situations and contexts. Integrity is tested most of all in the relationship with stakeholders, who may have very different claims and perceived needs. This demands a consistency of approach, with a clarity about core values, and capacity to develop dialogue. The response may not be exactly the same in every context but will remain consistent with the identity and purpose of the person of the organisation. Central to this is the idea of being true to purpose and identity, requiring the practice of *phronēsis*
- *honesty and transparency*, involving an openness to the self and others while remaining focused on the truth of a narrative. Such a truth, of course, is no simple objective truth, found apart from the network of relationships. As David Smail (1984) notes, much of 'truth' about ourselves and others is illusional, built on social myths, and often avoiding genuine reflection on the self or one's group. Honesty is thus very much about how one is able to examine the self and others in a way that both understands and tests such illusions
- *independence*: this is a key element of integrity. It ensures distance, such that the professional can stand apart from competing interests and more effectively focus on the core purpose, enabling professional autonomy
- *responsibility* for values and practice. Without accepting responsibility for ethical values and for response, neither the individual nor the profession can develop a genuine moral identity or agency
- *a learning process*. Given the limitations of human beings it is impossible to have complete integrity in any static sense. Integrity is therefore best viewed in terms of a continual learning process, the person continually discovering more about the different aspects

Figure 6.1 The elements of integrity

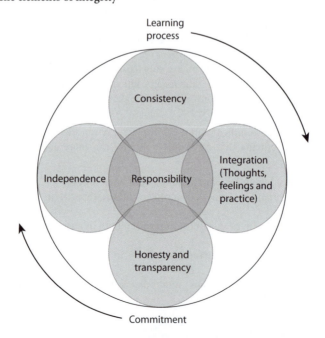

of the self and others and how these connect. Central to this is the capacity to reflect, to evaluate practice, to be able to cope with criticism and to maintain, develop or alter practice appropriately. Integrity is thus focused on relationships, not purely individualist

- *commitment* to purpose, project and people over time, and to the common good. The narrow view of integrity within a closed system has to be tested against fundamental principles such as justice.

All of these aspects of integrity were exemplified in the young Arthur Andersen, and in his firm as it developed. He also saw himself as maintaining the integrity of the accountancy profession as a whole, contrasting sharply with the later firm.

Reinforcing these virtues are others, including temperance, courage and justice.

OTHER VIRTUES

Temperance
This does not involve abstinence, from drink or anything else, but rather moderation, balance and self-control. This is important for effective judgement, self-reliance and the acceptance of responsibility. Plato's *sophrosunē*, temperance or self-control, Reid (2002) suggests, corresponds to discipline. Discipline, for the leader involves continued good practice, such as regular meetings that focus on core values and objectives. Temperance lies between abstinence and incontinence.

Fortitude/courage
This involves courage and resilience and the capacity to withstand a variety of pressures. As noted, courage lies between the extremes of foolhardiness and cowardice. Courage for Plato is quite a complex idea. It includes a capacity to persevere with an aim while also being open to challenge. Andersen showed great courage in sticking to his position.

Justice
Justice can mean several things, from equal distribution to appropriate reward. As a virtue it involves the capacity to treat all people equally and fairly. For Andersen this included all stakeholders, including employees.

For the later Andersen firm there was no sense of such virtues. The narrowing of purpose simply led to focus on technical skills to carry out limited objectives. Three other virtues work against this narrowing in business:

Empathy
Empathy, is closely connected to the virtue of benevolence, and enables the leader to identify with the other. If wisdom is an intellectual virtue, then empathy is an affective (to do with feelings) virtue. It is the capacity to hear and understand the underlying identity and feelings of the other, and respond to them. This involves an awareness of others and their needs, regardless of who they are.

It does not involve total identification (sympathy), but rather enables an appropriate distance between the self and the other. Such a distance is necessary if the other is to be understood, and if the leader is to operate impartially and effectively. A professional cannot do his or her job if too close to a situation; there must, for instance, be some distance between a doctor and a patient.

There was no evidence in the later Andersen firm of this virtue. Any sense of affective understanding was rather a means to get the best price out of clients. Empathy is critical to effective relations with stakeholders.

Humility

Humility is often seen as a nervous doubting of competence, self-deprecation, quite the opposite of the image of successful leaders of businesses. Tangney (2000: 81), however, summarises a very different view of humility, reminding us that all virtues rest between extremes. It involves:

- accurate assessment of one's ability and achievements
- ability to acknowledge one's mistakes, imperfections, gaps in knowledge and limitations, openness to new ideas, contradictory information and advice
- keeping one's abilities and accomplishments in perspective, while recognising that one is but part of a larger universe
- appreciation of the value of all things, as well as the many different ways that people can contribute to our world.

Humility in all this enables the business leader to keep both feet on the ground, not taken off course by secondary perspectives and targets. It allows the leader to stay focused in reality about the self and the situation, and looks to enable critical relationships that promote that. Vera and Rodriguez-Lopez (2004) sum up the importance of humility for leadership as key to organisational learning and resilience, involving openness to new paradigms, eagerness to learn from others, the acknowledgement of limitations, the pragmatic acceptance of failure, and the ability to consult and ask for advice. It is partly the lack of this virtue that led to the downfall of Arthur Andersen (as indeed Enron). In its place was an overwheening pride (*hubris*), causing the leaders to believe that they knew everything and could achieve anything.

Hope

This has often been associated most closely with the so-called theological virtues, faith and love. However, any organisation needs hope if it is to flourish, not least because it is necessary in empowerment for change. It is therefore directly relevant to leading an organisation. Hope is about the capacity to envisage and take responsibility for a significant and meaningful future. As such it is distinct from a generalised attitude of optimism. The experience of hope emerges in and through the growth and development of the organisation. Part of this involves a leader who embodies the virtue, showing a sense of hopefulness. Perhaps even more important, though, is the incidence of hope in the community of practice. The community of practice, then, should embody grounds for hope, ranging from the possibilities for professional promotion to different ways in which individuals might affect the direction of the group. This also involves the development of working practices that creatively enable partnerships with colleagues and external stakeholders. These can in themselves increase possibilities, and thus broaden hope.

Snyder (2000) suggests that the development of hope as a real virtue depends upon three factors: goals, pathways and agency.

- goals – The capacity to hope is generated through a sense of morally significant purpose. Such good hope provides meaning which affirms the worth of the person or group. In the light of such purposes, realistic goals need to be set. Hopefulness develops on goals which can be achieved. Hope may be a major virtue but it needs specific aims for it to be meaningful, aims worked through in dialogue.
- pathways – Hopeful thinking looks to find ways to the goals. It involves a development of the creative imagination to be able to see what ways forward there are. This is enabled through the development of method and through practice, not least the development of multiple possibilities through a negotiation of responsibilities (Snyder, 2000).
- agency – Hope centres in the experience of the person as subject, capable of determining and achieving the goals he or she looks toward. This applies once more to the person and to the organisation. If such hope is to be realistic, it cannot be built on deceit or untruth (both characterised by the later Arthur Andersen and Enron). For leadership to enable hope, then, means developing a culture of respect that values the members of the group or institution, the establishing of shared decision-making, a process and partnership that

enables clarity about goals and maximises pathways. Again this means integrating ethical thinking into the everyday processes of the organisation.

SUMMING UP

Several things should be noted about virtues as a whole.

All the virtues above are focused both in individuals and in organisations. The organisation or community, as MacIntyre (1981) argues, develops its culture through the development of narrative, critical reflection on that, and other means (see below). A culture can enable the development of the virtues at individual and organisational level (Brown, 2005).

Virtues are connected to and deepen the idea of traits. Traits tend to be utility- and skills-centred. Virtues look more to the depth of value and purpose. Skills and virtues enhance each other. The practice of virtues thus both maintains ethical meaning and positively affects core competencies (Robinson, 2005). Empathy, for instance, is central to data-gathering in depth. Several skills – such as listening, teamwork and communication skills – require empathy. Empathy and practical wisdom enable appreciation and care of the other and support imagination, creativity and openness, key to the creative process and making effective decisions. For the importance of creative, entrepreneurial virtues, see Chapter 11. Practical wisdom reinforces the skills of intellectual reflection, analysis and synthesis. Empathy also enables better awareness and appreciation of stakeholders.

The virtues reinforce each other, but it is difficult for one person to embody all the virtues. This would look to the development of virtues through dispersed leadership, so that leadership teams collectively develop the virtues.

Virtues are never 'complete', and indeed might diminish if not practised, as exemplified in the Arthur Andersen case. The so-called 'ethical training' and inductions of the original firm were not simply the rote learning of principles but the opportunity to practise the core virtues, not least practical wisdom, through reflection on the core purpose and the good of the organisation; integrity, through reflection on practice in relation to different situations and stakeholders; and empathy, through critically listening to different ethical perspectives. This means that there has to be an appropriate discipline and culture that enables the practice of virtues. It is to this idea of culture that we now turn.

REFLECTIVE PRACTICE

The UK Government has focused on employability as an important part of education.

In learning groups discuss:

What virtues are the most important ones for work and business?

How are these virtues connected to the skills of employability, such as communication, and teamworking skills?

How you might present your virtues to a prospective employer, through CV or interview?

What virtues are embodied in the institution that you are employed by now or are a part of? Can you provide evidence of them?

CORPORATE CULTURE AND ETHICS

'Culture' in this context is defined as the beliefs, traditions, values and narratives that are shared in an organisation and shape the identity of that organisation (see Trevino and Nelson, 2007: 259). This is exactly the focus of the community of practice in virtue ethics

(MacIntyre, 1981). In the USA there have been strong reasons for developing a corporate ethical culture. In 1991 the Sentencing Commission issued new sentencing guidelines for organisations convicted of federal crimes (see www.ussc.gov for information). These required convicted organisations to pay restitution on top of substantial fines. However, such penalties would be mitigated if the organisation gave itself up and co-operated with the authorities, and if it had developed a legal/ethical compliance process that met due-diligence requirements. This was further reinforced by the Sarbanes-Oxley Act of 2002 (see Chapter 5).

The results have been variable. On the one hand, research suggests that frameworks for compliance have established cultures, not least through the use of explicit ethical language, and have led to an increase in the likelihood that fraud is reported (Trevino and Nelson, 2007). On the other hand, continued ethical crises show how difficult it is to develop and sustain an ethical culture. The danger is a knee-jerk reaction to government regulation such that a firm does not take responsibility for understanding what it is doing. The development of a culture has to engage responsibility and enable the core virtues to be practised.

Codes of ethics or conduct are often perceived as central to the development of culture.

CODES

Not all business persons or philosophers agree with the idea of codes. There have been many arguments against professional codes of ethics in general, one of the most important being put forward by Ladd (1980).

Ladd (1980: 154) argues that codes go against the very nature of ethics. If ethics is about developing thinking around principles, consequences, virtues and the situation, then it cannot be imposed by authority or rule. Genuine ethics demands autonomy. He therefore refers to professional codes as 'an absurdity – moral and intellectual' (*ibid*).

Ladd argues that there is no ethics that is specific to any profession. On the contrary, all ethics espouse concern and respect for clients or patients or customers. All of us understand cheating, lying, deceit or injustice to be wrong. Nothing extra then needs to be said about the context of business or the professions.

A code of ethics runs the danger of doing harm. Specifically, if conduct is summed up solely in terms of the code, anything not explicitly covered in the code might be thought to be acceptable. In cases such as Enron there was a code in place but a very different, unethical, culture.

A related argument suggests that reliance on codes will place the responsibility for ethical response on the code or on the committee which polices the code.

There is no doubt that codes run the danger of being used legalistically. Legalistic thinking, operating to the letter of the law, can obscure the principles or spirit of the code.

However, Ladd's argument does not hold water completely.

- The idea that ethics is purely about autonomy is unrealistic. Descriptive theories (Chapter 3) suggest that autonomy has to develop, and that part of the development has to involve a sense of shared practice focused in community.
- The idea that at least explicit guidelines are not necessary is confounded by the Milgram and related research (see Chapter 3). This suggests that without articulation of ethical ideas a majority of people will opt not to take responsibility for ethical reflection and response.
- Ladd's individualised perspective ignores the virtue ethics perspective. This suggests that the development of the virtues is a social activity.
- There are ethical issues specific to a workplace or profession. In the medical profession, for instance, there is the constant tension between two core principles, the autonomy of the patient and the best interest of the patient, which in medical terms may be best articulated by the doctor. Clearly, both are important, and require the doctor to develop the capacity to hold both together. In business we have already seen core tensions, such as the sustainability of the corporation and the responsibility to and for stakeholders.

The danger of codes is that they become the total focus of ethical thinking and they ossify to an unthinking system. Any code should rather be part of a total culture that precisely aims to enable the members of the organisation to take responsibility for practising the good – in effect practising virtue.

Establishing codes of conduct

Clearly, then, codes can have an important function but must not be used to take away responsibility from the individual or group. To get this right, the purpose of the code must be established. Initially, it will be a function of the board to identify the purpose in consultation with experts and stakeholders. The purpose of a code should be linked to the history, identity and culture of the corporation or institution. A code may be intended either primarily to prevent unethical behaviour (with a prescriptive stress) or primarily to promote and encourage ethical behaviour (focusing on ethical aspirations). Corporations tend to combine elements of both types, providing clear guidelines around common ethical issues and dilemmas, and broader values and principles to frame responsibilities to stakeholders. The first tends to focus on typical ethical issues of dilemmas in that area, such as how to deal with conflicts of interest, the respectful treatment of stakeholders, or the company judgement on receiving gifts. The second focuses on broad responsibilities, encouraging thought about how they will be managed.

The code may have several focuses. It may be intended primarily for leaders, managers and employees, or may include external stakeholders, such as in the supply chain, or in partnerships. The code may also have wider target audiences. Professional codes are core to the identity of professions, tied to foundation values, such as law or health (their administration and distribution), and aim to demonstrate the integrity of the profession. They aim to establish and maintain trust in the profession as whole, and as such are often tied to compliance procedures, not least the withdrawal of the right to practise.

Codes can thus do any or all of the following:

- define accepted standards of behaviour for the group
- promote high standards of practice
- provide benchmarks by which members can measure and develop their personal standards
- define the ethical aspirations and identity of the group both internally and in relation to the public and communities around them
- exhibit a level of maturity and integrity to the outside world.

(See the end of this chapter for two different 'codes' from Barcelona FC and Johnson & Johnson.)

Manley (1992) suggests other more utilitarian functions of codes including:

- pre-empting any calls for government regulation of business practice
- helping managers to deal with external pressure groups
- integrating ethics into the strategic planning of the company
- providing a basis for any ethical training.

Codes are used across a wide spectrum of institutions and professions. They include:

- profession codes, as noted above
- industry codes, as adopted by entire sectors such as insurance, banking, mining corporations, and the alcohol industry (Robinson and Kenyon, 2009)
- issue codes, which may focus on narrow areas of practice, such as the WHO marketing code in the Nestlé case (see Chapter 13), or the codes of governance noted in the last chapter, or codes to do with advertising (see the Advertising Standards Agency website www.asa.org.uk/)
- international codes, such as that of the UN Global Compact (see Chapter 13).

Internal or external stakeholders may well espouse such different codes. Industry and interest codes may well influence the corporation code. Alternatively, the corporation code can become a means of linking into other codes. An engineering company, for instance, may well refer aspects of its practice to one of the many engineering codes (Armstrong *et al*, 1999). The code can also be the centre of integrating ethical thinking about different disciplines. Kaptein (2008) suggests that codes can inform relations with disciplines and stakeholders, including strategy, quality, human resources, security, communication, law, finance, environment and community. A good example of such a code is the outline ethical framework for higher education institutions developed by the CIHE (2005).

The development of codes as part of culture

Kaptein (2008) sees the code as being part of the total culture of the company. If culture is about meaning in practice, it should relate to:

- the mission and vision of the corporation: this should include some sense of how the company relates to the wider environment, so that ethical vision is reflected in the performance vision
- the core values
- the responsibilities to stakeholders and how they are viewed
- any norms, rules or regulations.

The content of codes tends to be located in the bottom two.

Goodpaster (2007) suggests that there are three phases to developing this; orienting, which involves the leadership setting the course of the organisation; institutionalising: making the company's values part of its operating consciousness; sustaining: the transmission of the core values in practice over time.

Orienting

This involves providing the ethical direction, the function of the board. Institute of Directors (2009) argues that this should include:

- developing the vision and values of the organisation
- ensuring the use of ethics expertise, through appointments to the board or consultancy
- ensuring that ethical objectives and benchmarks are an integral part of the firm's central objectives. This should show ethical meaning and values as core to the identity and purpose of the firm
- establishing how things are done – confirming, for instance, that strategic decision-making requires careful consideration of consequences to all stakeholders
- ensuring that ethics is articulated as a normal part of company policies, procedures, practices, conduct and business agendas; and that all decisions should be preceded by deliberation on ethical issues
- communicating a clear message that ethical objectives are critical to the success of the firm, and that failure to address them could affect the success of the firm
- ensuring that a member of the board is responsible for developing the ethical culture, and that resources are in place to operationalise the progammes
- demonstrating the core virtues in the board practice. The leadership has to embody the core values, demonstrating its practice of the key virtues of practical wisdom, empathy, justice, courage and integrity.

All of this sets the tone as one of both seriousness and support in developing ethical meaning.

Institutionalising

Following the direction, structure and processes are put into place. This may involve:

- consultation with stakeholders around core values and how they can be expressed in practice – This ensures that values are owned and developed by the workforce and clearly understood by external stakeholders. The level of consultation might include reflection on the culture as it stands. Ongoing discussion might involve focus groups

PAUSE FOR THOUGHT

Reflect on the ethical culture of the organisation that you work for or are a part of.

Does it express integrity? If so, how?

Does it express a sense of justice? Do you feel that it is concerned with justice and fairness?

Does it express a sense of empathy? If so, how does it model that empathy?

Does it express practical wisdom? Is it open to rigorous reflection on purpose?

- instituting an ethics risk and opportunity profile – The company identifies its ethics risks through a process of engagement with its stakeholders. They can help to clarify the risks and opportunities incurred through ethical and unethical behaviour
- developing a code of ethics – This may be a detailed code (see Barcelona FC below) or one focusing on responsibilities (see the Johnson & Johnson 'credo' below) or have elements of both. Developing a code of conduct is not a one-off exercise but an ongoing process. The code must be the subject of regular reflection. This may require an annual space for revisiting the code to see if still makes sense connecting value to practice. It may be part of an annual review process. It could involve more regular reflection such as the meetings developed by Johnson & Johnson. It might involve setting up an independent group or commission, as in the Nestlé case (see Chapter 13). Such a group would be responsible for mediating the interpretation of the code. The code then becomes part of the development of a learning organisation, exemplifying ongoing critical dialogue and the practice of both practical wisdom and integrity
- integrating ethical standards – This may involve creating a structure such as an ethics office to initiate and co-ordinate operational aspects of the ethics management programme. An ethics officer would act, report to the board and operationalise the ethical programme. This might include developing a good communications strategy, training, structures for action and auditing. The communications strategy is key. Often the very best of values are not communicated well, so that, for instance, employees do not feel that they are being listened to, do not sense the concern for justice, and do not see the way in which the organisation is practising *phronēsis*. Transparency in the organisation involves opening out these practices. Without that, internal and external stakeholders cannot see what the practice of ethics means and cannot participate in it. This requires mutual communication, which also links back to making ethical risk assessments. A good example of this is how the firm rewards ethical behaviour.

Rewarding ethics

Rewarding ethical behaviour and disciplinary actions taken against unethical behaviour makes common sense. We know that reward in general reinforces behaviour (Skinner, 1972), good or bad. In the Arthur Andersen case employees were rewarded for bad behaviour, often persuading clients to pay far more than was necessary. The reward system is, however, more than a means to an end. It is the embodiment of the end, core ethical values, and as such key to demonstrating integrity and justice. This can be part of a long-term commitment, with, for instance, a review of ethical behaviour included in annual evaluations, making it one among other criteria for promotion and compensation decisions. Even at this level there is the danger of employees simply aping what they think the firm wants to hear. The review would therefore have to be part of a critical conversation that reflects on the meaning of the key values and how the virtues can be evidenced, such as the concern for justice.

Some firms look to highlight the most ethical behaviour of certain employees, with nominations received from the management. The person who 'wins' is given an award as part of an annual dinner. This can be part of an ongoing series of 'rituals' that reinforce the ethical culture, with stories of the different nominees (Trevino and Nelson, 2007). The good thing about this approach is that it looks to develop rewards for good behaviour that are not simply financial. It has, however, several problems:

- It rewards exceptional as well as exemplary behaviour. Ethics can thus be associated with the exception and not the everyday practice of ethics. It may be better to associate such rewards with creative approaches to social responsibility – one aspect of ethics.
- It could easily lead to a competition for ethical behaviour.
- Other aspects of an ethical nature, not least the practice of practical wisdom and integrity, evidenced in the planning and questioning of everyday business activity, would have to be given different but equal value in annual evaluations.

Equally important is to show that the structures do not reward unethical behaviour. Unethical conduct should be disciplined swiftly and fairly at all levels. The higher the level of the person disciplined, the stronger the message about integrity becomes. In such cases, in addition to any punishment, there should be a review of the management system to ensure that it has not contributed to the behaviour. Here the responsiveness of the system embodies the virtue of justice. The workforce becomes part of an operation of justice. In the light of that, any system for whistleblowing becomes very important, all members being invited to be part of that practice of justice. (This is examined in more detail in Chapter 7.) The very opposite of this is a system of unquestioning obedience.

The approach to reward would also consider different kinds of reward, not simply financial, and thus with that open up what it means for employees to feel 'rewarded' and happy at work.

Ethics training should also embody the practice of core virtues, and techniques such as alternative dispute resolution, all of which are examined in more detail in the next chapter.

Sustaining

Sustaining the ethical culture involves developing the learning circle (Senge, 1990). Having worked through vision, values, responsibilities and practice, this leads to reflection on the practice and how far practice and purpose are developing. This requires an audit of the triple bottom line noted in the last chapter. It also requires an informal means of sustaining culture. The social and environmental audit is examined in detail in final chapters. Here we note the audit of purpose and meaning.

Ethics audit

An internal ethics audit might involve assessment of the ethical culture of the company, including reporting on:

- the ongoing development of the code, and allied risk assessments
- all ethics-related policies and procedures – eg the gifts and entertainment policy, the declaration of interests policy
- the feedback from training sessions: here, training sessions could be developed as part of the communications system
- steps taken to combat misconduct
- any other ethics interventions or initiatives
- weaknesses in formal and informal systems and processes.

The audit would form the basis for reflecting on and developing the ethical culture.

This is a further level of cognitive reflection: such reflection is often distinguished from informal approaches to the developing and sustaining of culture (see Institute of Directors, 2009).

Informal approaches developing ethical culture
These include the development of symbols, ceremonies and rituals, narratives and heroes:

- Symbols enable the imagination to be engaged around the core values and vision. The badge of Barcelona FC, for instance, brings together the flag of Catalonia and the flag of St George as patron saint. It speaks of an identity that has a long history, and that involves more than simply a football club (see below). Another aspect of the club is the shirt sponsorship of UNICEF, which symbolises the strong sense of social responsibility.
- Ceremonies and rituals that consciously bring groups together signify an important moment for members or the organisation. A good example is the iron ring ceremony instituted by Rudyard Kipling. This envisages engineers receiving the ring to remind them of their responsibility to the profession and to society (http://www.networx.on.ca/~njdevil/mainpage/E_Eng/Academic/jj-ring.htm#4).
- Narrative history, as noted above, is central to virtue ethics. It is the narrative which focuses on the key virtues. This would require space and communication that rehearses such narrative and places it in the ongoing reflection of the organisation. The early stories about Arthur Andersen are good examples of this.
- Conscious use of the idea of the hero also helps to embody core virtues. Whistleblowers, for instance, might thus be celebrated as heroes.

Two things are worthy of mention here. Firstly, the distinction between formal and informal is perhaps not the best. A better distinction is between cognitive and affective. The reward systems, training and so on emphasise the cognitive reflection and cognitive tools needed to develop an ethical culture. Narratives and so on engage emotions, and with that virtues like empathy. These are equally important and can be developed as part of formal reflective events, such as annual reviews. Secondly, although Goodpaster (2007) places these in the phase of institutionalising, we would also emphasise their great importance in sustaining the ethical culture. It is precisely the affective methods that enable motivation essential for sustaining an ethics culture.

LEADERSHIP

Leadership sets the tone as one of both seriousness and support in developing ethical meaning. This in turn should be sustained by leadership example. One instance of this comes (via a personal meeting with the author, which the author gratefully acknowledges) from Phil Watts when CEO of Shell several years ago. Watts determined that health and safety, and later sustainable development, should be core to the ethical practice of Shell. In furtherance of this he ensured that any employee death at work required the leader of the deceased's section going to head office in London and spending an hour with him, working through the circumstances of and response to that death. The very fact that the CEO gave that amount of time to one issue sent the message through to all staff that safety and care were central to any view of purpose in the organisation. The CEO was thus modelling core virtues, and encouraging such virtues to be practised across the organisation.

PAUSE FOR THOUGHT

Conscience

'Conscience' is one of the words that we all use although we don't often consider what it means. Most people view it as a personal thing. It is often also seen as an internal feeling that makes one uneasy at the prospect of doing the wrong thing, or after doing the wrong thing. It is even referred to as having a 'voice'.

So the last place you might think is the home of conscience is a corporation. However, there is no reason to see conscience as simply affective or purely personal. Aquinas, for instance, defines 'conscience' as the 'application of knowledge to activity' (*Summa Theologiae*, I-II, I). This knowledge is partly reason and partly the natural disposition of the human mind to apprehend general principles of behaviour.

Goodpaster (2007) argues that conscience was originally a cultural attribute, not simply personal. It is possible therefore to speak of the cultural development of ethics as the development of corporate conscience.

CASE

MÉS QUE UN CLUB

Barcelona FC is a multi-million-pound co-operative corporation, and it claims to be special – a football club but 'more than a club' (*més que un club*).

Go to the Barcelona FC website and read the statement about the nature of the club there: http://www.fcbarcelona.com/web/english/club/club_avui/mes_que_un_club/ mesqueunclub.html.

In one respect this statement about the identity of the club is simply a piece of good marketing. It sets out a unique selling point – the association with UNICEF (a non-governmental organisation focused on children's rights). It seeks to ensure that people locally, nationally and globally can identify with the club at the level of shared values and not simply of football success. It presents a powerful picture.

However, the statement as presented is not simply about selling a product. It sets the tone of the ethical culture. The culture as set out in the statement involves relationships with multiple stakeholders focused in plural values held together. This locks into the strong national identity of Catalonia, the wider Spanish identity and global identity. The wider the relationships, the more the basis of the relationships is about universal values – most explicitly, human rights. These national and global

values relate to different stakeholders and relate directly to the key stakeholders, the supporters, who are not simply customers but members (as Barcelona is a co-operative which empowers the members). Much of this is focused in the players' strip with the Barcelona badge and the UNICEF logo.

At the time of writing this, Barcelona FC are about to unveil a code of ethics to give greater detail to its ethical identity. The draft begins with core principles (http://www. fcbarcelona.com/web/english/noticies/club/temporada10-11/09/07/n100907112774.html).

This effectively lists the principles of abiding by the law, stewardship of the club, commitment to the club, transparency, democracy, pluralism and the disciplined use of resources.

The draft then set out practices that go against these principles and which are to be avoided.

Finally, it announces the setting up by the board of an independent Control and Transparency Commission. The tasks of this commission include dealing with any complaints, keeping the board abreast of ethical management and developing the code in response to any issues.

REFLECTIVE PRACTICE

Examine the complete draft code and try to answer the following questions:

Does the code relate clearly to the vision and identity of the club?

Is it aspirational or prescriptive?

Do the rules relate directly to the principles?

Does the commission fulfil the same purpose as the ethics committee in King III?

If you were the ethical consultant to Barcelona, how would you critique the code, and what would you recommend they do to improve it?

A very different approach to ethical codes comes from manufacturers Johnson & Johnson.

Johnson & Johnson

Johnson & Johnson is famous for its 'credo'. It forms the basis of their culture and is a different kind of code (www.jnj.com/connect/about-jnj/jnj-credo/). Barcelona focuses on the development of its culture, and begins to focus on details in its code. The Johnson & Johnson credo is much broader.

The credo focuses on:

- responsibilities – It clearly asserts plural responsibilities and carefully shows how these affect practice. So, for instance, the primary responsibility is to the health industry, health professions and patients. This leads to an objective of affordable pricing. The many different responsibilities mean that the firm will aim for a fair return to shareholders (stockholders). This means in turn discussion about what 'fair' means.
- virtues and values – Implicit in the credo are core virtues of integrity, maintaining core values such as respect in all operations, justice (in the concern for fair return and fair treatment) and empathy in the need to be aware of all the aspects of their ethical environment. The very term *credo* ('I believe') expresses something about commitment. This engages feelings in a slightly different way from Barcelona FC.
- ongoing reflection and the practice of responsibility – In the 1980s Johnson & Johnson reacted rapidly and effectively when, through an act of sabotage, poison was found in one of their products, Tylenol. They withdrew all stocks, and faced up to the safety issue, leading the way in developing tamper-proof seals. It was assumed that the company credo was the key to this strong ethical response. In fact, the CEO noted that it was not so much the credo as the regular session held in the firm to reflect on, review and challenge what the meaning of the credo was in practice, that led to that response (Rehak, 2002). In effect, this was the practice of *phronēsis*. The CEO of Johnson & Johnson at the time argued that the values should be kept before executives so that they could be related to their practice, demanding that they either subscribe to the credo or remove it from the wall. He also instituted an annual survey of the credo, inviting employees to say how the company is doing relation to the credal values.

CONCLUSION

In this chapter we have looked at the development of character, culture and codes. It is argued that there is no simple way of developing an ethical culture other than through the practice of virtues, and that this requires critical and affective engagement from stakeholders. The evidence indicates that effective leaders need to do the opposite of imposing ethics, and in particular should 'encourage constructive dissent, rather than destructive consent' (Grint, 2005). Such developments are based in virtue and responsibility ethics, acknowledging the importance of principles and utilitarian calculations.

EXPLORE FURTHER

Books

Bauman, Z. (1991) *Modernity and the Holocaust*. London: Polity, for a classic account of how a culture of instrumental rationalism dominated the Holocaust.

Goodpaster, K. E. (2007) *Conscience and Corporate* Culture. London: Blackwell.

DVDs

Glengarry Glen Ross (2003, ITV Studios), for an intense account of how in a small business the culture can obscure any ethical reflection.

REFERENCES

AQUINAS, T. (2006) *Summa Theologica*. Charleston, SC: Bibliobazaar.

ARCHER, W. and DAVIDSON, J. (2008) *Graduate Employability*. London: CIHE.

ARISTOTLE (2004) *Nicomachean Ethics*. London: Penguin.

ARMSTRONG, J., DIXON, R. and ROBINSON, S. (1999) *The Decision-Makers*. London: Thomas Telford.

BROWN, M. (2005) *Corporate Integrity*. Cambridge: Cambridge University Press.

CALHOUN, C. (1995) 'Standing for something', *Journal of Philosophy*, XCII, No.5, May.

CIHE (2005) *Ethics Matter*. London: Council for Industry and Higher Education.

FORD, D. (1999) *The Self and Salvation*. Cambridge: Cambridge University Press.

GOLEMAN, D (1996) *Emotional Intelligence: Why it can matter more than IQ*. New York: Bantam Books.

GOODPASTER, K. E. (2007) *Conscience and Corporate Culture*. London: Blackwell.

GRINT, K. (2005) *Leadership Limits and Possibilities*. London: Palgrave.

HALFON, M. (1989) *Integrity: A philosophical inquiry*. Philadelphia: Temple University Press.

ICAEW (2007) *Reporting with Integrity*. London: ICAEW. Available at: http://www.icaew.com/~/media/Files/Technical/Ethics/reporting-with-integrity-report.ashx.

INSTITUTE OF DIRECTORS (2009) *King III Report on corporate governance*. Johannesburg: Institute of Directors in Southern Africa.

KAPTEIN, M. (2008) *The Living Code*. Sheffield: Greenleaf.

LADD, J. (1980) 'The quest for a code of professional ethics: an intellectual and moral confusion', in Chalk, R., Frankel, M. and Chafer, S. (eds) AAAS Professional Ethics Project, American Association for the Advancement of Science, Washington, DC: AAAS: 154–9.

MACINTYRE, A. (1981) *After Virtue*. London: Duckworth.

MANLEY, W. (2002) *The Handbook of Good Business Practice*. London: Routledge.

RAWLS, J. (1971) *A Theory of Justice*. Oxford: Clarendon Press.

REHAK, J. (2002) 'Tylenol made a hero of Johnson & Johnson', *New York Times*, 23 March.

REID, H. (2002) 'Taking responsibility of life and death', in Reid, H. *The Philosophical Athlete*. Durham, NC: Carolina Academic Press.

ROBINSON, S. (2005) *Ethics and Employability*. York: HEA.

ROBINSON, S. (2011) *Leadership Responsibility*. Oxford: Peter Lang.

ROBINSON, S. and KENYON, A. (2009) *Ethics and the Alcohol Industry*. Basingstoke: Palgrave.

ROSSOUW, D. and VAN VUUREN, L. (2004) *Business Ethics*, 3rd edition. Cape Town: Oxford University Press.

SENGE, P. (1990) *The Fifth Discipline: The art and practice of the learning organization*. New York: Doubleday.

SKINNER, B. (1972) *Beyond Freedom and Dignity*. New York: Bantam Books.

SMAIL, D. (1984) *Illusion and Reality: The meaning of anxiety*. London: Dent.

SNYDER, C. (2000) 'The past and possible futures of hope', *Journal of Social and Clinical Psychology*, 19(1), Spring: 11–28.

SOLOMON, R. (1992) *Ethics and Excellence*. Oxford: Oxford University Press.

SOLOMON, R. (2005) 'Emotional leadership, emotional integrity', in Ciulla, J., Price, T. and Murphy, S. (eds) *The Quest for Moral Leaders*. Cheltenham: Edward Elgar.

TANGNEY, J. (2000) 'Humility: theoretical perspectives, empirical findings and directions for future research', *Journal of Social and Clinical Psychology*, 19(1), Spring: 70–82.

TAWNEY, R. (1930) *Equality*. London: Allen & Unwin.

TAYLOR, C. (1989) *Sources of the Self*. Cambridge: Cambridge University Press.

TOFFLER, B. (2003) *Final Accounting: Ambition, greed, and the fall of Arthur Andersen*. New York: Broadway.

TREVINO, L. and NELSON, K. (2007) *Managing Business Ethics: Straight talk about how to do it right*. London: John Wiley.

VERA, D. and RODRIGUEZ-LOPEZ, A. (2004) 'Humility as a source of competitive advantage', *Organisational Dynamics*, 33(4): 393–408.

WILLIAMS, B. (2005) 'A critique of utilitarianism', in Warburton, N. (ed.) *Philosophy: Basic Readings*. London: Routledge: 156–69.

WILLIAMS, R. (1989) *Christianity and the Ideal of Detachment*. Oxford: Clinical Theology Association.

CHAPTER 7

The Workplace of the Twenty-First Century

LEARNING OUTCOMES

When you have completed this chapter you will be able to:

- describe, analyse and critique two contrasting approaches to human resource management (HRM)

- analyse underlying ethical concepts and theory, including justice and responsibility at work

- identify a number of ethical issues likely to be present in most organisations, including harassment and bullying

- describe what could be included in ethical training, focusing on the development of virtues and responsibility

- outline and analyse core related concepts including trust and the work ethic.

INTRODUCTION

Human resource management (HRM) professionals, with their concern for people and their welfare, focus on values and responsibility in the workplace. Perhaps it is in the area of human resources that the highs and lows of business life are most keenly felt, ranging from the huge potential present in workforces to build successful and social-facing businesses to the consequences of business failure and business scandals. In all of this HRM is involved in looking at how you reward performance, recruit talent, develop staff, deal with bullying or handle redundancies, each of which aspects has its own obvious ethical significance.

In this chapter we examine the nature of ethics at work through a case study that illustrates both ethics of care and ethics focused on justice and rights. We then analyse a number of ethical issues related to HRM and how they might be addressed. In the light of that we examine the provision and content of ethical training, underlying values of work as expressed in the work ethic, and the relationship of ethics to trust in the workplace. Finally, we present the case of an organisation with a record for some achievement in the area of ethical working in relation to its employees – the John Lewis Partnership.

UNDER PRESSURE

Geoff was referred by his line manager to a counsellor to help with his work-based stress. Geoff was aged 55 and had been under pressure at work for some years as head of his section. New management had led to a change in operations. The new head of department was putting him under further pressure. She increased targets, moved several staff away from his section and introduced more stringent quality control. At the same time, she subjected him to gruelling interviews trying to persuade him to take early retirement. Anyone over 50 was being targeted, but he, as head of section, felt particularly vulnerable. The stress was affecting his family life and now was beginning to affect his work functioning. He was losing his concentration, and having to stay later at work.

In turn, this caused him to lose his temper with colleagues. He also exerted excessive pressure on his office as a whole to meet seasonal deadlines. The response of his department head to this was to put more pressure on. Geoff felt that she was trying to oust him, and that this amounted to harassment. He was anxious and depressed, and felt he was losing his sense of identity and life meaning.

Source: adapted from Robinson 2001; reproduced by permission

At the heart of Geoff's case is an ethical tension. On the one hand the stress would seem to demand an ethics of care, to help him through his stress. On the other hand he is involved in a dynamic of injustice: his actions are causing stress in his office staff. Might his actions be seen as a form of bullying? In all of this, what is the responsibility of the corporation, of his line manager and of human resources management?

HARD VERSUS SOFT MANAGEMENT

HRM 'involves the effective management of people to achieve organisational goals' (Greenwood, 2002). But what constitutes effective management; and what practices, overseen and directed by management, are justified in the pursuit of organisational goals? HRM textbooks often cite two broad and contrasting approaches to HRM, classically labelled either 'hard' (or 'managerialist') or 'soft' (or 'welfarist').

The contrast in the two approaches relates to the fact that they are based on opposing views of human nature and therefore result in two very different managerial control strategies (Truss *et al*, 1997). As its label suggests, the 'hard' model views employees as human resources and from an organisational perspective as a means to a profitable end. In contrast, the 'soft' model puts greater emphasis on employees as having intrinsic value and focuses on their potential to be 'unlocked' if treated accordingly.

The two views of human nature leading to contrasting management styles is reminiscent of McGregor's Theory X/Theory Y (McGregor, 1960). The hard or managerialist approach aligns with McGregor's Theory X, which suggests that employees cannot in essence be trusted and are best managed through tight control systems. On the other hand, the soft or 'welfarist' approach aligns with McGregor's Theory Y, which regards employees as best utilised and motivated through entrusting them with greater freedom to take responsibility. Theory Y therefore allows for greater self-regulation and individual creativity.

The two approaches to HRM are outlined and compared in Table 7.1.

Table 7.1 The 'hard' and 'soft' approaches to HRM

'Hard' (resource-focused) ('Managerialist', 'Mainstream')	'Soft' (people-focused) ('Welfarist', 'Critical')
Employees viewed instrumentally (as a means to an end)	Employees viewed as having their own intrinsic value
Single aim of competitive advantage/ organisational performance	Dual aim of competitive advantage and individual development
Tight (low-trust) strategic control	*Loose* (high-trust) control through commitment
Skills-focused training	Training for development
Individualist and unitarist	Collectivist and pluralist

In the case study, Geoff was supported and counselled through his bad practice – a 'soft' approach which recognised Geoff as a conscientious employee and as a fallible human being – but also put under pressure by his line manager.

Many of his staff felt a strong sense of unfairness at this treatment. Some felt that he was given support whereas they were not. Others felt that the pressure he was under was unfair. Underlying such views were several ethical positions.

First, Duska (2004) argues that the company has no moral status and no responsibility to employees other than to uphold legal obligations, such as health and safety. This simply views the employee–corporation relationship as a contract freely entered into. The employee is responsible for his or her own welfare. It is a view that ignores the fact that health and safety law assumes the moral responsibility of the firm, and that 'health' is capable of wide interpretation. At the least this would have to respond to the health needs of Geoff and all his staff – and the health problems might be caused by the dynamics of the firm.

Second, writers such as Purcell (1987) argue for a more paternalist approach in which care is imposed, or one in which care is a function of inclusion. The issue with this approach is twofold. Where are the boundaries of such care, and how does it take away from the autonomy of the employee?

So, third, a general basis to HRM ethics would be the simple application of Kantian ethics: respect for the person. This would involve working through what respect meant in any particular workplace.

Fourth, Greenwood and De Cieri (2005) argue for stakeholder theory as the basis of an ethical HRM approach, reinforcing the idea of responding to the needs to the employee. This can also focus on the basic rights of the employee, providing a minimum standard (Greenwood, 2002) that would include:

- equality of opportunity, treatment and respect
- the abolition of forced labour
- freedom of association and collective bargaining (International Labour Organisation, 1998: http://www.ilo.org/declaration/thedeclaration/lang--en/index.htm).

These minimum standards are also subject to the interpretation of HRM and organisational managers in relation to the meaning of 'respect' or 'disrespect'. There can therefore be no simplistic application of principles.

Fifth, although the stakeholder model is important, we have noted how responsibility goes beyond the needs to stakeholders to the mutual responsibility of stakeholders.

In Geoff's case this raises questions about justice and responsibility. Both Geoff and his staff felt a strong sense of unfairness, focused on different relationships. However, their perception of unfairness did not lead to a simple assertion or claiming of rights. The sense of unfairness for Geoff was tied to a feeling of powerlessness and frustration. On the one hand he felt oppressed by his manager. On the other hand he felt that he had to maintain the focus on targets, partly because of what he and his workers saw as the value and purpose of the organisation, which in this case was to deliver further education. They all had a strong sense of service to the vision and the clients. Geoff also had strong sense of self-reliance. He would have seen failure to maintain targets as a personal failure. This meant that he never challenged the pressure from his boss, and was never fully aware of his effects on his staff. Indeed, he would have been appalled to think that he was responsible for their stress.

His staff (more than 20) felt that they were being abused, but for different reasons did not feel able to challenge Geoff or go above him. This was partly because of their sense of loyalty to Geoff, some seeing their overwork as a form of support, and partly because of loyalty to clients – they felt responsible for the delivery of the service.

The fact that neither felt able to challenge each other or the management had the effect of sustaining the practice of injustice and irresponsibility – something that could be seen by higher management who also felt powerless, partly because no one had gone through the 'system' of grievance or complaint.

At the heart of the problem, then, was a series of value conflicts that none of the people involved felt able to articulate and work through, leading to a denial of the reality of the situation.

Were there other factors at play? How much were Geoff's ethical perspectives to do with psychological issues, such as a difficulty with dealing with perceived authority? Psychological issues such as these can reinforce the imbalance of ethical values. Counselling would enable him to work through this, how he felt about authority and so on, and begin to identify what the core ethical issues were and how he might respond. Successful counselling helps people to own their ethical views and take responsibility (Robinson, 2001). Questions would still remain. Was his boss prepared for Geoff to come back to the office and begin to challenge the use of targets? Or did she see counselling as a means of making Geoff more compliant, able to better achieve those targets? This would pose an ethical challenge to her leadership.

Greenwood and De Cieri (2005) raise the possibility of a version of unethical human resource management involving the use of the care approach largely to fulfil the needs of shareholders. This is seen as unethical in Kantian terms because the employees are not treated as ends in themselves but simply as the means to an end of business success. Seabright and Schminke (2002) write of using an ethics of care as a means of manipulating employees.

Greenwood (2002) suggests that it is sometimes hard to distinguish the hard and soft approaches in practice. Elements of both may be involved in HRM. Geoff was in this way tightly managed as well as being supported by counselling. Truss *et al* (1997) argue that neither hard nor soft models accurately represents what is happening within organisations; and that it is important to make a distinction between rhetoric and reality – ie what an organisation says it stands for and what it actually does or practises. In none of the firms that Truss *et al* (1997) researched did human resource considerations take precedence over business strategic considerations.

 PAUSE FOR THOUGHT

In the light of the ethical tensions found in cases such as this, Greenwood (2002) poses the question whether HRM ethics ever can be ethical. The human resources manager is caught in the gap between care ethics and the objectives of the organisation.

Is it possible to bridge this gap?

As head of an HRM office, how would you develop the ethical basis to your policy?

In the chapter on responsibility (Chapter 4) we argued that a theory which views stakeholders as simply bearers of rights or needs is inadequate. Stakeholders are also agents with responsibility, and this provides a good way of beginning to resolve the possible ethical conflicts in HRM, and even a way of working through justice.

RESPONSIBILITY IN THE WORKPLACE

There are many different views of justice, as noted above. For most people in the workplace (Cropanzano and Stein, 2010) justice is defined in terms of fairness. Fairness could be seen to be mediated by:

- distributive justice, by which individuals can see that they are treated in the same way. There would have to be good reason for different treatment. This is reinforced by law in areas such as job interviews
- procedural justice – Here the process has to be seen to be fair. Again, differences can be accepted if the process has been conscientiously gone through
- interactional justice – This takes justice down to personal relations. In one sense it is very much about the capacity of the manager to be just. This would ensure, for instance, that there is no mean-spirited approach to assessments and evaluations.

Taken together, these provide the basis for organisational justice. The first two are a key part of any ethical framework, such as set out in Chapter 3. The third begins to move to embedding justice in relationships, taking us down the line of Geoff's problems. Such justice raises issues of how responsibility is shared (the third mode of responsibility). It demands a fair, just, sharing of responsibility. In Geoff's case he had taken on too many responsibilities. In review and evaluation there had been no effective challenge by his boss as to whether together these were actually achievable or not, or what the effect of cutting back on staff would be. For several years during busy seasons, lasting more than a month, this had led him and his staff to work seven days a week, twelve hours a day, to meet the targets.

This raised further ethical issues for his boss. Why did she not address Geoff's behaviour as bullying? It could be thought to be unjust to allow him to oppress his office staff. Was she simply relying on the pool of loyalty in Geoff's office to keep getting things done, without focusing on the reality of the delivery? Why had she in turn not challenged her own management team when it came to planning, or was she more concerned with achieving her own targets?

Geoff's case showed an absence of critical agency and responsibility negotiation. The implicit narrative of loyalty was accepted by his managers, and at no point in review or evaluation was responsibility in any of its modes addressed. There was no critical thinking encouraged to reflect on the underlying view of loyalty, thus allowing this 'ethical' concept of loyalty to dominate thinking, ultimately leading to organisational and individual dysfunction. Nor was there any attempt to work out what accountability meant for Geoff, other than in respect of targets. There was no attempt, for instance, to think through accountability to different stakeholders, from shareholders to those who he managed, and how this might be practised. Perhaps the most important absence was any genuine sense of how responsibility could be shared. All of this reinforced Geoff's feeling that his underlying worth was based on his accepting all the responsibility placed on him, with a dynamic of having to please his manager. This in turn was reinforced by the sense of loyalty to the firm and what it stood for, and meant that he could not easily challenge either the firm's values or his manager.

The role of HRM in all of this would have been more coherent through the ethics of responsibility. Indeed, such an ethics brings together the apparently different views of ethics of care and ethics of justice. The ethics of care does not need to simply answer the 'needs' of the employee. On the contrary, as noted above, effective care focuses on clarification of values, working through conflict between values (often kept in place by psychological issues – see Robinson, 2001), and devising ways of developing agency. Equally, the focus on justice can be effectively answered in such cases through the acceptance of shared responsibility and the effective negotiation of responsibility.

Geoff's case shows how ethical ideas – of justice, fairness, responsibility and respect – pervade relationships at work, with procedural and personal aspects. It demonstrates the need to explicitly clarify and address those ideas, and with them associated feelings, not least through negotiation of responsibility. In the light of that, the conflict between organisational targets and employee needs also becomes less polarised and more focused on critical dialogue.

 PAUSE FOR THOUGHT

Geoff is now returning to work. He is much more confident, and in his return-to-work interview he thanks his boss for providing care – and begins to challenge her about the pervasive stress experienced under her watch. He focuses on the stress, and insists that she address the setting of targets that cannot be sustained. He makes it clear that if this is not thought through, he will go to HRM.

As his boss, how will you respond?

HUMAN RESOURCE DEVELOPMENT

Human resource development (HRD) is concerned with the development of both the individual and the organisation. Its focus is the expansion of human capital, or the personal and professional development of employees, through providing a framework of training and development opportunities both within and outside the organisation. The following elements typically form a part of the framework:

- staff training
- a college course or further qualifications including professional or vocational accreditation
- performance management
- coaching
- mentoring
- career development
- succession planning
- key employee identification.

Garavan and McGuire (2010) helpfully outline the significance of HRD in relation to corporate social responsibility (CSR) and ethical behaviour in business. This, along with their identification of HRD trends, can be summarised as follows:

- There is currently 'little insight' into how HRD practices can be used to support CSR, sustainability and ethical goals. This suggests that the potential of HRD has been underdeveloped as far as these key areas are concerned.
- Sustainability, Garavan and McGuire argue, represents a recent extension of the CSR concept; and the dimension of social sustainability is only a recent addition to the sustainability debate. This means that the consideration of how organisational activities affect people's physical and mental health and well-being lags behind environmentalism and 'green' work practices.
- Nevertheless, HRD has a major role to play in raising the awareness of employees and developing positive attitudes toward sustainability, CSR and the pursuit of ethical goals.
- HRD can help build employee competencies to enable organisations to build sustainability.
- It can also train leaders to become more ethically aware, in a global context to understand human rights, and to be more aware of corporate governance issues.

REFLECTIVE PRACTICE

It is not difficult to identify the types of ethical issues bound up with HRM present in most organisations. Before reading on, reflect on your own experience, or that of colleagues, of ethical issues in the workplace.

In particular, have any involved issues of fairness and responsibility? Were these resolved – and if so, how?

Was the resolution brought about through particular people or through appeal to the HRM system?

HRM-RELATED ETHICAL ISSUES

REMUNERATION

The first example is close to most people's sense of justice – how much employees are paid – and relates, of course, to the remuneration policy of an organisation. As noted in Chapter 2, the finance industry justifies what those in other sectors regard as substantial pay and bonuses on the grounds that the reward is necessary to secure the specialist talent and skill associated with the work. In a competitive environment, organisations will pay what they consider 'necessary'. However, sometimes this may appear inflated, and other times it may correspond to the bare minimum. The ethics of an organisation's remuneration policy consist broadly of:

- how much employees are paid in relation to the precise nature of the work (as, say, 'qualified' accountants or office cleaners)
- what differentials are present in the organisation (between directors, management and non-management positions)
- what employees are paid in relation to what they actually do on a day-to-day basis (a matter which relates to deployment and performance).

Working this through into a 'compensation philosophy' requires a justification of distributive justice (see Chapter 2 for more detailed criteria) that links into the vision and values of the organisation, and to the involvement of members of the workplace, so that all can see not just the procedural justice but also the reasoning behind it and how the process embodies that. This ties such justice development in to the practice of responsibility (in all three modes): clarifying ideas, values and practice; embodying accountability inside and outside the organisation; and showing how responsibility is shared and valued. It moves away from patriarchal and simple therapeutic models of HRM to an intellectual and emotional investment in the culture – such that all members of the organisation can be seen to be responsible for that culture.

HIRING AND FIRING

Beyond pay, there is the important issue of how employees are hired and/or fired. As noted above, this exemplifies all the levels of justice precisely because it demands equal treatment – which means, for example, the same questions being asked of all job candidates. It might be argued that questions should take account of the particular narrative of the candidate. However, the same single question should be carefully framed that requires all candidates to articulate their particular narrative in relation to the prospective job in question.

SCENARIO

You are a black woman who is being interviewed for a post in a Church educational institute. In a very kindly tone of voice the chair asks you, 'How do you think you will you cope in a largely white, male, and upper-middle-class institution?'

How would you respond?

In the actual case behind the *Scenario*, the candidate calmly responded, 'Have you asked that question of all the candidates?' This was an implicit challenge of the ethics of the process. Equal treatment is key to just process in hiring. It was partly because she was able to 'stand up' to the way in which that process was carried out that she got the job.

Equality of opportunity can lead to what may seem on the face of it to be odd practices. If all the candidates for a job had equal scores on character, qualifications, experience, and so on, what would be the fairest way of deciding between them? Ironically, if all the candidates were equal, then random selection – eg through a lottery – would give each an equal chance of success.

THE WORKING ENVIRONMENT

The working environment and working conditions is another ethical focus. Health and safety legislation (see http://www.hse.gov.uk/legislation/index.htm) is there to protect employees from any irresponsible employers and practices. How far does this extend? The principle of non-maleficence would look to ensure that there is nothing harmful involved in the workplace. The principle of benificence would look to maximise well-being. A good example of this in the workplace is respect for the worker in the context of the work environment. This can, for instance, even focus on architecture, neuroscience and well-being. There is increasingly strong evidence that interior design has a significant effect on the brain (Eberhard, 2008). An interesting environment can stimulate brain cells and even lead to the growth of new ones. This can, in turn, lead to a positive effect on productivity. Aside from any assessment of such consequences, at one level this can provide a striking twenty-first-century context for the Kantian view of respect. A stimulating environment embodies respect for the rational person, even leading to an increase in rational capacities, and with that to the development of critical agency and awareness – the first mode of responsibility.

As we noted earlier, such an ethical perspective comes up against the other ethical imperative of stewardship, including cutting back on the space (and the carbon footprint), and developing more shared space. How are the two ethical values to be resolved? How can Human Resources work with Estates to hold both together creatively? Some human resource departments see this as a rights issue, focusing on establishing minimum space requirements. This does not address issues of responsibility for the work environment and the effect it has on employees. It would require critical dialogue between Estates, HR, architects and employees to focus on core values, and how they can be embodied in practice, and in the light of limited resources.

REFLECTIVE PRACTICE

Your line manager has recently watched a television programme on the effects of interior design on the brain (based on Eberhard's book, 2008), and has got the board to agree that space design has to be changed. He wants you to work out how to achieve this and come back with a plan that does not significantly affect the budget.

What would your plan involve? How would it relate to the well-being and rights of the workforce, and the nature and purpose of the enterprise?

RIGHTS AND DISCRIMINATION

Issues of rights at work focus firmly on the justice of the workplace. They aim to enable negative and positive freedom. Positive freedom is found in rights, and ultimately in human rights (http://www.direct.gov.uk/en/Employment/ ResolvingWorkplaceDisputes/ DiscriminationAtWork/DG_10026574), which allow one to practise certain things such as religion at work – under the Employment Equality (Sexual Orientation) and Employment Equality (Religion or Belief) Regulations, 2003.

Rights can vary from the conditions of work, including health and safety, to the right to privacy, and to rights related to roles such as parenting. Negative freedom involves protection against discrimination, including discrimination based on:

- age
- disability
- pregnancy or maternity leave
- race
- religion or belief
- sex
- sexual orientation
- gender identity.

Although rights embody equal respect for the other, there are several ethical caveats:

First, the rights of individuals have to be balanced with the rights of the organisation. The employer has the right, for instance, to monitor communications within the workplace as long as the employees are made aware of the monitoring before it takes place (see Chapter 8).

Second, rights have to be balanced with responsibilities. It is therefore important not to simply leave rights to the law and the process of law. Ethical training that develops the practice of responsibility can provide a good framework within which rights are considered.

Third, there is a danger that rights may become paternalistic, legalistic or in some way abused. This is the territory of 'political correctness'. It involves action against or avoidance of expressions or actions that are perceived as excluding, marginalising or insulting people who are socially disadvantaged or discriminated against.

Although this aims to protect different groups, the ethical dangers of political correctness are twofold:

- In aiming to protect a minority, it can stigmatise the offender. Rather than focusing on the act or words as, for instance, racist, it therefore focuses on the person. *He* is a racist. This can lead to moralising and the use of draconian measures that allow no space for restorative justice. Restorative justice is one aspect of relational justice, seeking to restore relationships, not condemn.
- The focus on protection can easily lead to the uncritical acceptance of offence. Responsibility ethics, however, demands that any assertion of offence, just as any

assertion of conscience (see Chapter 6), should be tested to see what the offence is based on and whether the assertion can be justified. This demands that any assertion of a value statement or judgement should be tested. As noted earlier, any ethical position can be used to negative ends.

Both these points reinforce the argument that ethics in the workplace should be developed around responsibility and virtue ethics, enabling all the workplace to develop key aspects of responsibility, as well as having a framework of rights.

COINS AND CROSSES – NADIA EWEIDA

CASE

British Airways suspended Nadia Eweida in 2006 after she refused to stop wearing her crucifix. Eweida, a devout Christian, claimed that the suspension was discriminatory, especially since BA allows Muslim employees to wear headscarves and Sikh workers to wear traditional iron bangles.

Her case was rejected by the Employment Appeals Tribunal (EAT) in 2008, and in 2010 was again rejected by the Court of Appeal. The Court rejected the appeal because it viewed BA's blanket ban on customer-facing employees' wearing visible jewellery as justified. Furthermore, it judged that Eweida's wearing of the cross was a personal choice and not a religious requirement.

Darren Sherbourne, Head of Employment at business law firm Rickerbys, said, 'It's … a surprising ruling in view of the claims that other religions were permitted to wear religious jewellery, and it may cause something of a backlash.'

Source: *Personnel Today* (2010)

Questions

1 Does Eweida have a right to wear a religious symbol at work?

2 Is wearing a cross in some way contravening the rights of the employer or of the customer? If it is, in what way is it?

3 Where and how should companies draw the line in terms of dress code?

CONFLICT AT WORK

Conflict at work is often not seen as an ethical issue, yet it is usually focused in areas of justice and abuse of power.

HARASSMENT AND BULLYING

Harassment and bullying encompass 'any unwanted behaviour that makes someone feel intimidated or degraded or humiliated or offended' (ACAS, 2011). This definition applies to a range of behaviours commonly found in any social context.

The important distinction between bullying and harassment is that *harassment* is unwanted behaviour related to a specific identity characteristic – such as age, disability, gender, race, religion or sexual orientation. Such harassment is unlawful in the United Kingdom under the Equality Act, 2010. A well-known form of harassment is sexual harassment, by which employees are subject to unwelcome advances or unwanted comments variously motivated. A particularly pernicious form of harassment occurs when the harasser is an employee's manager or is a senior executive. This often leaves harassed employees feeling cornered and not sure about the wisdom of reporting the difficulties for fear of losing their jobs. Here, the ethical issues involve abuse of power.

Bullying has less specificity than harassment and includes any 'unwanted, offensive, humiliating, undermining behaviour towards an individual or groups of employees'

(Rayner, quoted by Vega and Comer, 2005). Below is a list of some of the tell-tale behaviours commonly associated with bullying (Vega and Comer, 2005).

- rude, foul, or abusive language
- repeatedly threatening dismissal
- constant criticism
- assigning meaningless tasks
- humiliating and demanding conduct in front of other workers
- ridiculing taunts
- confusing and contradictory instructions or constantly changing instructions
- undermining work performance
- isolating and excluding persons from various work activities
- leaving offensive messages on email
- blocking an employee's promotion
- overloading of work
- unexplained rages
- unjustified criticism
- withholding of information
- hiding documents or equipment
- setting impossible deadlines
- excluding workers on a regular pattern
- threatening action that could result in loss.

Some facts about bullying begin to cast light on why this is a surprisingly challenging issue for HRM departments:

- Bullies are women nearly as often as men.
- 50% of bullying is done by managers – the power imbalance can create an environment conducive to bullying.
- As much as 89% of bullying is done by someone whose rank in the organisation is higher than the victim's (Namie and Namie, 2000).

Bullying and mismanagement
Bullying is often tacitly accepted or overlooked by the organisational leadership (Vega and Comer, 2005) underlining the complication of senior management's possible complicity in its occurrence. This also applies to situations where bullying is not taken seriously. The kind of response one might look for in this situation is that the individual who complains of being bullied is branded 'hypersensitive', a 'trouble-maker', or unable to take a joke (Vega and Comer, 2005). Occasionally, a lack of response from management is due to the fact that the accused bully is too valuable to the organisation.

Resources and responses
Unlike its response to harassment, the UK (like the USA and Australia) has not enacted legal protections specifically in response to workplace bullying (Yamada, quoted by Vega and Comer, 2005). In some ways this puts added onus on the organisation to take bullying seriously and communicate that bullying will not be tolerated by issuing a policy explicitly stating this. A code of conduct providing concrete examples of desirable and prohibited behaviours further protects against bullying, and has the potential to increase awareness of what constitutes bullying, enabling managers and others to be more conscious of unacceptable categories of behaviour.

Dickson (2005) suggests that a good way of dealing with bullying is to keep a detailed record of incidents to present to the bully's line manager or the HR department. Bullying is a critical test of any ethical process, requiring clarity about the actions involved, and care about how the power dynamic, personal and professional, is addressed. Again at the heart of this are the different modes of responsibility, not least the focus on practice and values and awareness. This includes the bully also. Many bullies are unaware of the effect they have on others, and may even rationalise their behaviour through the assertion of ethical values (Rennie Peyton, 2003). A bully might argue that he or she has the best interests of the workplace at heart by enabling greater productivity or that the victim ought to develop more personal responsibility. Both values and practice should thus be questioned and challenged.

This, and all conflict issues at work, begin to move conventional ethics into the area of conflict resolution involving, for instance, the alternative dispute resolution (ADR) approaches advocated by King III. Lederach (2005) notes how such approaches are fundamentally about ethics. His seminal work on peacebuilding is therefore entitled *The Moral Imagination*. The key to this is enabling all parties to move beyond narrow perspectives of ethics and justice, taking account of all stakeholder perspectives, leading to the empowerment of all parties.

According to Lederach (2005), the essence of peacebuilding is found in four disciplines, each of which develops the moral imagination. These disciplines are relationships, paradoxical curiosity, creativity, and risk.

- *The centrality of relationships* – Relationships form the context in which violence happens, but they also generate the energy that enables people to transcend violence. Core to peacebuilding is the acknowledgement of relational interdependency and recognition that all who are involved may be part of the negative pattern. The moral imagination looks to envisage a wider set of relationships and take personal responsibility for choices and behaviour. In short, peacebuilding requires that people be able to envisage their interconnectedness, mutuality and shared responsibility.
- *The practice of paradoxical curiosity* – Cycles of conflict are often driven by polarities. Choices about how to respond to conflict are forced into either/or categories. Moral imagination involves the capacity to rise above these divisions and reach beyond accepted meanings. Paradoxical curiosity is a matter of respecting complexity. It involves accepting people at face value, and yet looking beyond appearances and suspending

Figure 7.1 Lederach's elements of peacebuilding

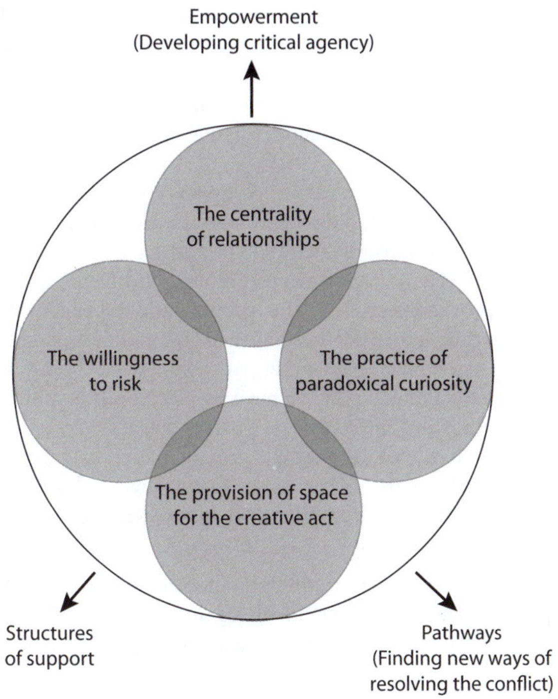

judgement in order to discover untold new angles, opportunities and unexpected potentialities. Lederach advocates then a proper scepticism about any of our perceptions, and the development of the capacity to learn from the unexpected (serendipity).

- *The provision of space for the creative act* – Moral imagination arises through creative human action that emerges out of the everyday and yet moves beyond what exists to something new and unexpected. Because new ways of thinking may pose a threat to the status quo, it is important to provide space for the creative act to emerge. This requires a commitment to creativity and a belief that it is possible to move beyond the parameters of what is commonly accepted. Creativity opens us to avenues of enquiry and provides us with new ways to think about social change.
- *The willingness to risk* – To take a risk is to step into the unknown without any guarantee of success or safety. This is tied to the development of responsibility. For many, conflict at work leads to attempts to avoid responsibility, looking to someone else to take that.

Such peacebuilding is based in virtue ethics, involving the development of virtues such as empathy and creativity. It is also focused in responsibility ethics, aiming to enable employees to develop responsibility for themselves and for their workplace community.

WHISTLEBLOWING

Another aspect of value conflict at work is whistleblowing. This demands an environment that enables members of the workforce to reveal unacceptable practices. Whistleblowing is not easy for the individual concerned. There are core ethical tensions in making such information available either to the public or to superiors, which can make it a real ethical dilemma, including the effects on:

- peer professional relationships: whistleblowing can lead to negative effects on innocent colleagues and firms, not just on those involved in unethical or illegal practice
- relationships with management: in these areas whistleblowers commonly find that they are victimised
- family relations: whistleblowing can affect the family either through subsequent stress or even through loss of employment.

A common argument against whistleblowing is that it is disloyal, and that the employee has a duty of loyalty to the firm. This view of loyalty assumes an unquestioning loyalty demanded of the employee by the employer. However, loyalty cannot preclude the questioning of practice. In any case, it is in the company's interest to learn of unacceptable practice, precisely so that it can avoid major negative consequences to the company and the employees.

The core question then becomes how the company enables whistleblowing so that it recognises the needs of all the stakeholders and appropriately values the whistleblower. In England, the Public Interest Disclosures Act 1998 provides a degree of legal security in that dismissal is forbidden for certain disclosures (see Borrie and Dehn, 2002: 105). Behaviour that falls outside these provisions still remains problematic, especially where standards of ethical behaviour of firms have not been established in a code of practice. The individual whistleblower behaving in a ethical manner remains exposed in these situations.

It is important, then, for the company to have in place both a culture that encourages well-thought-out whistleblowing and a process that enables it.

The oil and petroleum coporation Shell provides one example of provision for whistleblowing, available as part of its campaign to improve its business integrity, in the form of an website helpline: www.compliance-helpine.com/Shell.jsp. The coherence of Shell's whistleblowing policy involves:

- affirming the importance of reporting to the reputation of the company and its brand
- making the helpline available to anyone inside or outside the organisation
- providing a set of criteria with which to measure unacceptable behaviour. This involves

the Shell General Business Principles, which include good practice in competition, business integrity, health and safety, security and the environment, service to local communities, and compliance

- ensuring that the helpline is confidential and professionally managed. This requires that any complaint is given full attention and respect, while also being properly assessed.

Such a system needs to be well managed and may be open to abuse, unless there is some transparency in it to balance the confidentiality. Armstrong *et al* (1999) therefore argue that clear records should be taken and that the reporter should have the right to appeal to an external authority if he or she believes that the issues raised have not been met. It would be in the interests of the group (whistleblower and management) to have independent advisers who could remain part of the circle of confidentiality.

Whistleblowing is a particularly good example of the way in which ethics has moved away from focusing on the individual and on individual responsibility for working out dilemmas. Instead, it sees the responsibility of reporting bad practices as shared by the company and all employees or consultants. Based on the ethical framework of Chapter 3, this ensures that data is effectively gathered. Values then become central to the process as the issue is compared with the stated values and principles of the organisation. The responsibility for taking the situation forward is thereafter shared by the initial whistleblower and the management. Careful attention is paid to how the problem is corrected, and the whistleblower is protected. It is then in the interest of all concerned to get such a process right.

This approach to ethics again has much to do with the culture of the company, and how it develops shared and individual responsibility for addressing ethical problems at work.

Armstrong *et al* (1999: 56) present a useful checklist to back up such a process and one that can focus on maintaining good relationships. This checklist includes:

- confirming that the risk to the public or fellow workers warrants action
- examining the motives for whistleblowing. Here a trusted colleague might be of help in reflection. There is a danger of a heroic motive, suggesting an image of the whistleblower as defeating the 'evil' organisation, or a revenge motive
- ensuring that the evidence is scrutinised, verified and recorded
- stating clearly objections to the practice involved, rather than to the people. Where objections become person-centred there is the danger of losing objectivity
- ensuring that all company procedures are followed by the potential whistleblower, and that only if there is evidence that the company is not responding should external disclosure be considered
- carefully attending to the outcome of the process such that all whistleblowers are treated justly.

SCENARIO

You have noted on several occasions how a senior colleague has severely bullied one of your colleagues in meetings and in one-to-one situations. In meetings he frequently demeans him in front of other colleagues. The colleague is clearly under stress, and does not know how to handle the put-downs. On the one occasion when he tried to fight back, the senior colleague said that it was all really part of banter, and not meant to be serious. As your colleague prepares to go home for the weekend he tells you how depressed he has become. He has contemplated suicide. You suggest that he seeks professional help. He replies that that would show how weak he is, and leaves the office.

Should you blow the whistle? If so, to whom, and at what point?

Should you simply leave your colleague to handle it himself and encourage him to take formal action?

Should you approach the senior colleague to challenge his behaviour?

In what circumstances would you turn externally to a professional body or the press?

ETHICAL TRAINING

A progressive answer to some of the common HRM-related difficulties faced by staff and management in organisations might be staff training or consultancy focused on raising organisational awareness of how to operate more ethically. Such ethical input would deliver the benefits of preventing the costly business disruption and human resource inefficiencies associated with conflict in the workplace and other ethical issues related to HRM as listed above.

Firstly, this would involve developing employees' (including managers') capacities to be ethical. This is focused on developing through practice the capacities needed for the organisation and its members to function well. In effect this focuses on the ethical virtues. Secondly, it would be concerned with training in the ways of responsible behaviour and practices. Here employees could be asked to consider and critically discuss together the ethical meaning that is in all aspects of practice, and particular ethical issues faced in their organisation, on three levels: issues affecting all organisations, issues centred on their specific organisation, and issues present in specific departments and teams. Thirdly, it would focus on the ethical culture and identity of the organisation, so that there was a sense of shared meaning and practice.

EMBODIED ETHICS: THE VIRTUES

We are familiar with a skills-based emphasis on what certain work roles in an organisation demand. Virtues-based training takes this to deeper levels. Key to this is enabling the practice of such virtues and reflection on that practice. The development of core virtues will also be key to the organisation's response to conflict situations. Such virtues include:

- Justice
  Justice as a virtue is the capacity to embody justice in one's work relations (see Chapter 6). To develop that requires employees to own the idea and practice of justice, both understanding what it involves and how it is played out in an organisation. It also requires reflection on individual and group practice to assess how far behaviour embodies justice. This requires both conceptual and practice development, enabling employees to show what justice 'looks like' in practice, and what it feels like. Justice by definition is something that applies to all, and therefore any training would involve critically reflecting on how distributive justice and procedural justice is carried out in the organisation. This might include, for instance, critical reflection on whistleblowing processes, which can be fed back to management.
- Empathy
  Central to the notions of justice or effective care is empathy (see Chapter 6). Key to developing that virtue is critical dialogue. It is such dialogue that enables the kind of moral imagination that can maintain an awareness of and identification with perspectives of different stakeholders inside and outside the organisation.
- Integrity
  As noted in Chapter 6, integrity involves several different virtues. Ethics training would enable clarification of the core values, reflective practice, consistency over time, and ongoing learning at individual and organisational level.
- *Phronēsis*
  The virtue of *phronēsis* (or practical wisdom) is focused in reflective and critical capacities, including:
  - the capacity for rational deliberation that results in effective action
  - the ability to fit the right rule to the appropriate circumstance
  - the result of reflection on a life well-lived
  - the ability to articulate and tell others about how the tasks were undertaken (Halverson, 2001).

Many of these aspects are practised on a day-to-day basis but haphazardly, often without the practice of other virtues, such as empathy. Staff development focused in reflective practice enables these virtues to be practised systematically, and consciously owned and developed.

- Courage
  As we noted in Chapter 6, Aristotle sees courage as a virtue of the mean, between the extremes of cowardice and recklessness. Courage can be practised within staff development precisely through enabling critical conversation that allows the participants to articulate their views and hold them up to the scrutiny of the group. Many participants find that a difficult activity and look to ways of avoiding responsibility for airing or developing their thoughts and reflections on practice. It is therefore important to have managers in the training meetings so that positive dialogue can be modelled. This would take time to develop. As Argyris (1993) notes, even when managers claim to want such mutual dialogue, many employees find it hard to believe.

In effect, through the medium of reflective practice and critical dialogue, virtues can be practised and developed, a mature ethical attitude can be focused, and the ethical culture of the organisation established. Again this focuses on virtue ethics and responsibility ethics. At its centre is the practice of the three modes of responsibility: developing critical agency, accountability, and shared responsibility. Once employees are comfortable with such reflection and gain the confidence to articulate value conversation, then the ideas can become part of any staff reviews. The danger of a paternalist approach to HRM is that it can develop ethical meaning from the top through imposing values – often quite vague ones. In any review this can then easily lead to a parent–child relationship, the employee simply trying to please the employer, without taking genuine responsibility for values, practice and related virtues. Core to any development of critical dialogue would be the recognition of plurality in the workplace, ranging from different perspectives corporately and individually, to different cultural views on the meaning and ethics of work. Engaging such difference precisely enables the development of empathy (and reduction of polarised thinking), openness to critique, and the possibilities of creativity (Erikson, 1964).

Training in ethics would be concerned not only with developing essential capacities whether or not along the lines of those suggested, but also with the recognition that every organisation and every organisational context will throw up multiple opportunities and challenges to develop and practise good or better business ethics. This repositions the study of ethics from being associated exclusively with philosophy or religion as a kind of cerebral pursuit to focusing instead on the ethicality of everyday organisational life with its multiple considerations, contradictions and conflicts.

COACHING

A natural ethical focus can also involve areas such as coaching, a good example of which is Whitmore's work. Whitmore (2009) focuses on key capacities or qualities that the coaching relationship should bring out to enable personal development.

These are:

- values-driven, focused in the values held by the professional and how they relate to the values of the profession or organisation
- vision-centred, seeing how the vision of the organisation connects to the wider world
- authentic, not simply held to please others
- focused in reflectivity and responsibility.

REFLECTIVE PRACTICE

Ethics training: how not to ...

From the US TV series *The Office*, view episode 2 of Season 5, entitled *Business Ethics* (DVD, Universal Pictures), for an example of how not to run an ethics training day.

With a colleague set out how you would approach an ethics training away-day in your workplace.

TRUST

Trust is often seen as a core ethical idea, and is even deemed to be one of the virtues. Caldwell and Dixon (2009), arguing from a care ethics perspective – one close to feminist ethics – suggest that trust is a primary value for leadership alongside love and forgiveness.

Against this it is possible to argue that trust is only an instrumental value, and that it depends upon other values for its ethical content. Trust is thus important only for enabling other ends, and those ends might be good or bad. It is possible to develop and sustain trust in a system which is corrupt, such as the Enron culture, or to trust overtly bad people to achieve a desired end – eg through corrupt practices (see Gambetta, 2008).

In this sense, then, trust is closely related to responsibility (Swift, 2001). It involves the following in relation to the three modes of responsibility:

- clarity about ideas, values and practice – It is very hard to genuinely trust another if these areas are fudged. Again the Enron case, for example, shows a childlike unquestioning trust from the employees, and one that had no basis. The dynamic of trust in this sense would be built through questioning and dialogue, enabling a trust in the thinking, practice and motivations of the other. This works against a simplistic view of trust as uncritical acceptance
- willingness to be accountable – It is precisely those who are not open to giving an account who *prima facie* have something to hide. Trust in this sense requires transparency
- acceptance of shared responsibility – It is difficult to trust another who is not prepared to negotiate appropriate responsibility, or an organisation that attempts to avoid responsibility.

This suggests that trust is tied to the development of ethical maturity, and that such trust is not simply important for the development of relationships *per se* but for healthy, just relationships. This is trust that takes into account change, personal and organisational. Much of the trust argued for in care ethics is built around a familial base, in which the assumption is that certain figures can be trusted because of their role or relationship. However, the psychology of personal development (Bridges, 1980) suggests rather that even key relationships undergo major changes, involving trust developing in different ways. So it is possible, for instance, to still trust one's parents while also being aware of their limitations.

It remains, however, a matter of balance. One of the dangers is of accountability, for instance, leading to what O'Neill (2002) characterises as hyper-accountability. This is where so much time is spent in detailed reporting that trust in the profession becomes eroded. It could be argued, against O'Neill, that the core ethical problem here is not so much the consequence, the erosion of trust, as the limited focus on accountability. Without the other two modes of responsibility, accountability can move the exercise away from the core purpose and value, and away from the sense of shared responsibility. The reports of accountability then become the central target, not the development of good practice.

PAUSE FOR THOUGHT

Who do you trust?

In your workplace, who do you trust?

What is your trust based on – their skills, their role, their character?

Is it possible to trust someone but also question their practice?

Do you trust people who question your behaviour? If you do, why?

WORK ETHIC

Work ethic is distinguished from an ethics of the workplace. The latter is about ethical meaning and practice at work. The former focuses an underlying view of work. In one sense this an important worldview that underlies how we see work and the value of work. It thus often informs ethics of the workplace. In the West the rise of the idea of a work ethic has been associated with the Reformation. The Reformation in sixteenth-century Europe saw the development of Protestant Christianity as a breakaway from the Old (Roman) Catholic Church (Weber, 2002). This led to a stress on individual responsibility, extending from matters of responding to God to everyday life, including work and business. From this the connection was made between individual success and hard work. Since then what has been called the Protestant work ethic has become associated with a view of work ethics that is based in finding personal worth through hard work. Furnham (1990), for instance, notes pathological variants of the ethic that motivate overwork through guilt. There is no need to associate the work ethic exclusively with such extremes, and there is no doubt that any work ethic can reasonably encourage individual responsibility.

Once more, however, such an ethic can best be informed by the concept of responsibility. The different modes would seek to enable a critical attitude that aims to test motivation, and the effect of any work ethic on the individual, on stakeholders, and on the individual's family or community. Critically, it would focus also on shared responsibility and the negotiation of responsibility. It would additionally focus on the culture of the organisation as well as on individual views. Some firms have consciously tied this to life planning and development as work–life balance. Engage Mutual Assurance, for instance, provided staff development sessions on life and career planning, and extended this training also to the public.

REFLECTIVE PRACTICE

The role of HRM revisited

Given the ethically sensitive nature of HRM, with a requirement to enable the development of responsibility, of response to need, and of disinterested procedural justice, and simultaneously to deal with multiple other organisational matters, there is increasingly the sense that HRM should be seen as a profession. As a profession its ethical task is then to hold together these different perspectives.

The CIPD is a good example of this professional focus and, at the time of writing this book, has been developing its professional code. See the draft code for consultation at http://www.cipd.co.uk/NR/rdonlyres/A4E6C04F-BEC3-4E78-B975-8F9731C56277/0/ 5535CPCdraftWEB.pdf.

Analyse the draft code with a fellow student and outline how you might develop it in the light of the professional principles in Chapter 3 and the responsibility ethics of Chapter 4.

CONCLUSION

This chapter suggests that ethical concepts and practice are in the life-blood of HRM. Justice and responsibility, along with work rights and value conflicts, are naturally there in many workplace issues. Working these through demands both training and the development of a culture of responsibility that enables the comfortable use of value language, the ownership of shared values and responsibility, and the capacity to critically reflect on practice.

Even the extreme work ethic is built around a particular idea of justice – 'You get what you deserve', 'You only get out what you put in.' These sentences point to the idea of justice as desert, linking hard work to success.

This chapter has argued for the importance of knowing what we are talking about when it comes to ethics and values at work. Do we want to build the workplace on a narrow view of justice – one that encourages individual responsibility at the expense of wider views of fairness? Or do we want ethical meaning that is more balanced?

The chapter argued that the best is found in an ethics of responsibility which stresses balance, holism and integration. This would seek to balance rights and responsibility, principles, such as respect and justice, with practical questions, virtues and development with ethical frameworks, and ethical awareness of difference both inside and outside the work community.

Many academics argue that this approach will lead to better business results (Valentine and Fleischman, 2008). Regardless of such consequences, this chapter suggests the development of justice and responsibility in work is also the working out of respect, and thus right in itself.

THE JOHN LEWIS PARTNERSHIP

CASE

As our summative case we have selected the John Lewis Partnership (JLP) because in its practice it builds in many of the values and principles that have emerged from our examination of HRM issues in this chapter. The John Lewis Partnership is widely known in the retail and business worlds for its progressive employee ownership structure, and as a company which has sought to reconcile concern for its employees with operating successfully in a highly competitive marketplace. The principles which guide JLP date back to the early part of the twentieth century and the leadership provided by Spedan Lewis, the son of the founder John Lewis. Spedan's three guiding principles were:

- Stemming from a concern for an inequality which he noted between the owners and the employees, Spedan believed that the company should deal fairly with all its employees; and he even sought to extend this principle of fairness to other stakeholders including customers and suppliers.

- Employees should as far as possible

participate in the decision-making process.

- The company should be able to attract the best staff and managers available, thus enabling it to compete successfully in the marketplace. All employees were to carry a keen sense that they were responsible for the success of the business; and that their reward was directly linked to excellent customer service.

Building on these principles led Spedan to three initiatives, all for their time ground-breaking in their high regard for the significance of company staff.

Firstly, *committees for communication*, which were aimed at ensuring good communication between management and workers, and provided a means by which 'rank-and-file' members, who made up the committees, could either air or handle grievances.

Secondly, the in-house weekly journal, the *Gazette*, launched in 1918 which, together with every operating unit also having its own journal, provided the staff with a forum of discussion and a means of anonymously communicating concerns to the management. Like the committees for communication, each relevant manager was charged with responding to every concern expressed within three weeks.

Finally, a staff bonus in the form of managing directors' IOUs was established at the company's *Peter Jones* enterprise. From these beginnings the following principles of the John Lewis Partnership, noted by Robinson (2002), have emerged through time.

Principles of the John Lewis Partnership

Purpose – The Partnership is owned in trust for its members, who share in the rewards of the business as well as the responsibilities of ownership. JLP's ultimate purpose is the happiness of its members, evident in a successful business and worthwhile and satisfying employment.

Power – Power in the Partnership is shared and plural, consisting of three governing authorities: the Central Council, the Central Board and the Chairman. The Central Council is made up of representatives from every branch and meets a number of times a year. Other features of JLP's democracy are the branch councils which convene to discuss the business of the branch. The managers' relationship to the managed is protected by the constitution, which calls for management to be accountable to the federal body of partners (The *Herald*, 1999). The in-house journalism continues to positively encourage anonymous letters from all employees.

Profit – The Partnership aims at good profitability to finance continued developments and ultimately to share among the partners, the staff. Bonuses can equate to substantial shares of each individual's annual pay.

Members – The Partnership's members, the employees of JLP, are selected for their ability and integrity. They are expected to uphold the principles of JLP and exercise mutual respect and courtesy. Individual contributions are recognised and rewarded fairly.

Customers – The Partnership seeks to value its customers and secure their loyalty and trust through providing outstanding service, value and choice.

Business relationships – The Partnership seeks to uphold scrupulous integrity and courtesy in all its business relationships and to honour every business agreement.

The community – Finally, the Partnership aims to contribute to the well-being of every community in which it operates, and to conform to the spirit as well as the letter of the law.

So how might we apply the lessons of the John Lewis Partnership case to human resource management in other organisations? Firstly, the sharing of power (democracy) along with the sharing of responsibility is enabled, sustained and protected through organisational structures. Secondly, success and profitability fit with responsible practice and protecting a happy and interesting life at work for employees. This contrasts markedly from the disempowering working environments that are a feature of some profit-pursuing organisations. Thirdly, JLP has a specific way of making management accountable for its style and practice of management. This even extends to the matter of what managers are paid in relation to those they manage. To avoid all manner of abuses it is essential that management accountability is safeguarded in organisations.

The shared ownership model cannot be replicated across all businesses. The important point is, however, that the example of John Lewis can give an account that is defensible in how it handles power and justice in the workplace, and in how it models respect and the three modes of responsibility.

REFLECTIVE PRACTICE

Examine your own workplace or one that you know, and analyse it in terms of its approach to justice, respect and responsibility. How, for instance, is fairness sustained and the responsibility of employees engaged?

Compare your workplace with that of a student from another place, and together consider how the two might be improved.

EXPLORE FURTHER

Books

Cohen, E. (2010) *CSR for HR: A necessary partnership for advancing responsible business practices*. London: Greenleaf.

DVDs

The Insider (2000, Disney) for an actual case of whistleblowing in the tobacco industry. It looks at the ethics of going against a non-disclosure agreement to reveal questionable practice, and the negative effects this all has on the whistleblower.

Whistleblower (2011, Warner Home Video) for whistleblowing in a global NGO.

Both demonstrate the importance of developing an open culture.

REFERENCES

ACAS (2011) 'Bullying and harassment'. Available at: http://www.acas.org.uk/ index. aspx?articleid=1864.

ARGYRIS, C. (1993) *Knowledge for Action: A guide to overcoming barriers to organisational change*. London: Wiley.

ARMSTRONG, J., DIXON, R. and ROBINSON, S. (1999) *The Decision Makers*. London: Thomas Telford.

BORRIE, G. and DEHN, G. (2002) 'Whistleblowing: The new perspective', in Megone, C. and Robinson, S. (eds) *Case Histories in Business Ethics*. London: Routledge: 96–106.

BRIDGES, W. (1980) *Transitions: Making sense of life changes*. Reading, MA: Addison-Wesley.

CALDWELL, C. and DIXON, R. D. (2009) 'Love, forgiveness and trust', *Journal of Business Ethics*, 93(1): 91–101.

CROPANZANO, R. and STEIN, J. (2010) 'Organisational justice and behavioural ethics: promises and prospects', *Business Ethics Quarterly*, 2(2): 193–233.

DICKSON, D. (2005) 'Bullying in the workplace', *Anaesthesia*, 60: 1159–61.

DUSKA, R. (2004) 'Whistleblowing and employee loyalty', in Beauchamp, T. and Bowie, N. (eds) *Ethical Theory and Business Practice*, 7th edition. Englewood Cliffs, NJ: Prentice Hall.

EBERHARD, J. (ed.) (2008) *Brain Landscape: The coexistence of neuroscience and architecture*. Oxford: Oxford University Press.

ERIKSON, E. H. (1964) *Insight and Responsibility*. London: W. W. Norton & Co.

FURNHAM, A. (1990) *The Protestant Work Ethic: The psychology of work-related beliefs and behaviours*. London: Routledge.

GAMBETTA, D. (2008) 'Can we trust trust?', in Bachmann, R. and Akbar, Z. (eds) *Landmark Papers on Trust*. Cheltenham: Edward Elgar: 133–57.

GARAVAN, T. N. and McGUIRE, D. (2010) 'Human resource development and society: human resource development's role in embedding corporate social responsibility, sustainability, and ethics in organisations', *Advances in Developing Human Resources*, 12(5): 487–507.

GREENWOOD, M. R. (2002) 'Ethics and HRM: a review and conceptual analysis', *Journal of Business Ethics*, 36: 261–78.

GREENWOOD, M. R. and DE CIERI, H. (2005) 'Stakeholder theory and the ethics of human resource management', Monash University Working Paper 47/05, July.

THE *GUARDIAN* (2011) 'Pay gap widening to Victorian levels', 16 May.

HALVERSON, R. (2001) 'Representing *phronēsis*: documenting instructional leadership practice in schools'. Available at: www.distributedleadership.org/DLS/ Dissertations_files/ Halverson%20Dissertation.pdf.

THE *HERALD* (1999) 'Putting great store in a happy workforce', Scottish Media Newspapers, 23 March.

THE *INDEPENDENT ON SUNDAY* (2011) 'Twitter is home to the dull and dysfunctional – I'll never join', 15 May.

LEDERACH, J. P. (2005) *The Moral Imagination: The art and soul of building peace*. Oxford: Oxford University Press.

McGREGOR, D. (1960) *The Human Side of the Enterprise*. New York: McGraw-Hill.

MELLAHI, K. and WOOD, G. (2003) *The Ethical Business: Challenges and controversies*. Basingstoke: Palgrave Macmillan.

NAMIE, G. and NAMIE, R. (2000) *The Bully at Work*. Naperville, IL: Sourcebooks.

O'NEILL, O. (2002) *A Question of Trust*. Cambridge: Cambridge University Press.

PERSONNEL TODAY (2010) 'Christian British Airways "crucifix" worker loses discrimination appeal against airline', 12 February.

PURCELL, J. (1987) 'Mapping management styles in employee relations', *Journal of Management Studies*, 24: 533–48.

RENNIE PEYTON, P. (2003) *Dignity at Work: Eliminate bullying and create a positive working environment*. London: Routledge.

ROBINSON, S. (2001) *Agapē: Moral meaning and pastoral counselling*. Cardiff: Aureus.

ROBINSON, S. (2002) 'John Lewis Partnership: a case history', in Megone, C. and Robinson, S. (eds) *Case Histories in Business Ethics*. London: Routledge.

SEABRIGHT, M. A. and SCHMINKE, M. (2002) 'Immoral imagination and revenge in organisations', *Journal of Business Ethics*, 38(1/2): 19–31.

SWIFT, T. (2001) 'Trust, reputation and corporate accountability to stakeholders', *Business Ethics: A European Review*, 10(1), January.

TRUSS, C., GRATTON, L., HOPE-HAILEY, V., McGOVERN, P. and STILES, P. (1997) 'Soft and hard models of human resource management: a reappraisal', *Journal of Management Studies*, 34(1): 53–73.

VALENTINE, S. and FLEISCHMAN, G. (2008) 'Ethics programs, perceived corporate responsibility and job satisfaction', *Journal of Business Ethics*, 77: 159–72.

VEGA, G. and COMER, D. R. (2005) 'Sticks and stones may break your bones, but words can break your spirit: bullying in the workplace', *Journal of Business Ethics*, 58: 101–9.

WEBER, M. (2002) *The Protestant Ethic and the 'Spirit' of Capitalism*. London: Penguin.

WHITMORE, J. (2009) *Coaching for Performance*. London: Nicholas Brealey.

CHAPTER 8

Business, Management and Professions

LEARNING OUTCOMES

When you have completed this chapter you will be able to:

- critically assess the differences between professions and management in relation to ethics
- critically understand the ethical identity of professions
- critically understand the key factors of conflicts of interest and how they relate to business and the professions, particularly in the context of science
- critically assess the arguments for management as a true profession
- critically assess some of the contributions of professional ethics to business through reflection on aspects of communication ethics.

INTRODUCTION

In Chapter 4 we noted the complexity of the business environment. Such complexity – and such an environment – is to be found in the many different professions to which management has to relate. Some are focused on the practice of any business, such as accountancy or human resources; others are focused in the purpose of the business, such as engineering. Professions like these bring very strong ethical perspectives to the practice of business management – which this chapter explores. First, it examines ethical tensions between professions and management through analysis of the *Challenger* case study. Then it looks at the idea of conflicts of interest, illustrated by the relationship of science to business. It thereafter critically examines in greater detail the argument that management is itself a strong profession, founded on an ethical purpose. Through the example of the IT profession it finally considers how professions can enhance ethical business practice.

 CASE

THE CHALLENGER 51-L STORY

On 28 January 1986, only 73 seconds after launch, the *Challenger* Space Shuttle exploded, creating one of the most public and high-profile disasters of the last century.

At the heart of the case were the central

engineering design problems focusing on the field joints of the external fuel tanks. These were sealed by O-rings. Prior to the launch of the *Challenger* there had been consistent problems with the O-rings, including clear evidence of gas blowing through the seals. The engineers involved continued to work on developing the design of the joint, but by the time of the flight in January 1986 a redesigned joint was not available.

Context

The social, political and economic context of the engineering work was complex.

NASA was under intense pressure both from unexpected external competition and from the US government. It needed to make the strongest case for the Space Shuttle programme and budget, and had scheduled a record number of missions for 1986.

There was additional pressure from Russian competition in space.

Political pressure was added with the desire to have 51-L in orbit during the State of the Union speech. President Reagan was going to make specific reference in this speech to Christa McAuliffe, the first civilian hero in space.

The pressures on the engineers were intense throughout the programme. From the beginning of the programme in 1981 the issue of safety was not addressed with any consistency. Documentation of safety issues was not well maintained, and there was no independent scrutiny of the safety systems. At one point a crew escape system was omitted in order to maximise the fuel payload.

As plans for the launch were made, ongoing problems with O-ring seal erosion were raised by the engineers of Morton-Thiokol Industries (MTI). MTI had been awarded the contract to build the solid fuel rocket boosters for NASA as far back as in 1972.

A task team was set up to address the problems, but did not work well. Far from providing a speedy resolution, there were further delays. Ebeling and Boisjoly, the two main MTI engineers on the team, wrote that management as a whole did not understand the importance of the task and that NASA bureaucracy led to constant delays. At one point, requests for spare parts had to go through eight different offices.

NASA mangement later claimed they knew nothing of these concerns. Throughout the build-up to the launch the MTI engineers operated strictly within the established communications system, reporting to their managers and relying on their managers to communicate the problems to NASA.

Questions

1 What more could the MTI engineers have done at this point?

2 How might the MTI management have best handled the material coming from their engineers?

3 How could NASA have kept itself better informed about this aspect of the project safety?

All involved in the shuttle programme were aware of its high profile and the consequent pressure to achieve targets. The result was a strong incentive to think and plan unrealistically, aiming for a target of 24 launches to be achieved by 1990. This created strain in the system, including:

● a critical shortage of spare parts

● stress on the IT production system, which meant that it was not able to deliver crew training software for scheduled flights by due dates; this in turn meant inadequate time for crew training

● no enforcement of cargo manifest policies, leading to numerous payload changes at the last minute.

The Presidential Commission underlined how this affected attention to safety, because there was not time to address anomalies between flights (Report of the Presidential Commission [RPC], 1986: 14).

The Teleconference

The situation came to a head in a teleconference, organised the night before the launch, aiming to clarify the conditions for launch safety. The conference included MTI engineers and managers and NASA personnel. The teleconference tried to determine whether the launch would be safe if it took place at a low temperature. The engineers had not been able to fully research this, precisely because the necessary time for the research would have resulted in the shuttle programme's being suspended. NASA and MTI therefore did not have the requisite information and were not adequately prepared to evaluate the risks of the launch in conditions more severe than had been experienced before. The MTI engineers argued strongly against launch because of a lack of evidence of safe flights at low temperature.

The response of the NASA and the MTI managers was mutually hostile because of the pressure they were experiencing. The NASA staff questioned the MTI engineers' argument and additionally asserted that the original design specification had involved launch temperatures as low as 31°F/0°C. In fact this statistic referred to storage, not operation, and actually the expected launch temperature was below that. However, the MTI engineers found themselves suddenly having to prove that the *Challenger* was unsafe to fly at low temperatures – with no evidence to prove their case. Without anybody realising it, the criteria for safety had moved from 'Launch only when there is evidence of

safety in these conditions' to 'Launch unless you can prove it is unsafe.'

There was a break in the teleconference before which MTI engineers were urged to come back wearing their 'management hat'. This implied an emphasis on cost-benefit analysis rather than on risk-benefit analysis and a concern 'to accommodate a major customer' (RPC: 11). After further discussions, on reconvening the teleconference the result was a decision to launch.

Questions

1 Once this responsibility divide was crossed, the decision was effectively taken away from the engineers. Whose responsibility then was it to maintain safety?

2 What could the MTI engineers have done differently in this situation? Was their disagreement fully communicated to NASA?

3 Is it morally acceptable for an engineer or other employee to make a case about safety and then pass the responsibility for the outcome to the management involved?

4 How would you have responded in that situation – and how would you have justified your response?

ANALYSIS

The case was problematic at several levels of ethics.

There was a long history of poor communication, giving no space over time for an effective dialogue between engineers and managers. The core values of safety were thus never addressed. There was therefore little concern for the key stakeholders, especially the crew. The management focus remained a focus on 'the customer'.

This meant that the teleconference could not really address an ethical decision-making process since it did not have full awareness of the history or the current issues. The result was a teleconference that was a 'kind of Russian roulette' (RPC: appendix 3) in which standards of safety were gradually lowered (RPC: appendix E3). What emerged later was a massive discrepancy between the engineers' and management's view of safety margins. Engineers estimated a shuttle failure rate of 1 in 100 launches. NASA management had figures of 1 in 100,000. When the NASA figures were questioned by the Commission, the response of their chief engineer was, 'We did not use them as a management tool. We knew that the possibility of failure was always sitting there ...' (cited in Martin and Schinzinger,

1989: 83). These figures were submitted in response to a risk analysis carried out on behalf of the Department of Energy. The context of that safety assessment was the risk involved in the next mission of the *Challenger*, which was scheduled to carry the Galileo probe, carrying 47.6 pounds (21.6 kilograms) of plutonium-238.

Even after the teleconference there was inadequate communication. The conclusion of the meeting was thus communicated as supporting launch. The next levels of management were not aware of the MTI engineers' objections. The Presidential Commission therefore noted 'a propensity of management … to contain potentially serious problems and to attempt to resolve them internally rather communicate them forward' (RPC: 11). In effect, the management system encouraged both narrow thinking – concentrating purely on a limited area of responsibility without seeing the broader connections – and also secretive thinking, not sharing difficulties which might cause problems or require major work for the next level of management.

This led to a focus on solutions rather than to critical reflection on issues. Management therefore did not begin to take seriously the objections of the MTI engineers.

The fragmentation of decision-making led the different parts of the organisation to focus purely on their narrow areas of responsibility, and not to review or feel responsible for the whole operation. The Presidential Commission and subsequent reports stressed that all levels of management should feel responsibility for safety, and not simply leave it to one designated group.

All this led to an absence of integrity (at organisational and individual level), of *phronēsis* (such that even the MTI engineers were not able to critically defend their position on safety), and of responsibility. There was neither a sense of shared responsibility for the whole, nor a clear sense of who the different groups were accountable to – not even clarity about what they were actually doing. The MTI engineers noted that it was only later when they realised that they had crossed the line between one set of criteria and another.

The management system was not conducive to ethical thinking and dialogue, either as professional engineer or as manager. The ethical line was crossed when the key safety principles were eroded, and none of the participants realised it. Part of the dynamic was a successful put-down of the engineering perspective and values, with the assertion that the professional engineering perspective was secondary to the management perspective. The system finally failed to embody the core modes of responsibility when the launch team received only the advice to launch. Those who had final responsibility for launch were not aware of the problematic debate.

The MTI engineers are often seen as whistleblowers, and they did make clear what had happened after the event. However, they did not maintain a strong ethical argument at the time partly because of the limited time for the conference. The uneasiness of the MTI engineers could still have been communicated by them to the launch chief before the launch.

REFLECTIVE PRACTICE

What difference does the management perspective make to the engineer?

What recommendation would you have made to the board of MTI about future practice?

How can a management system be developed to ensure that the modes of responsibility are embodied at all levels?

In particular, how could the management system have shown that critical dialogue was valued and practised?

CONFLICTS OF INTEREST

The case of the *Challenger* showed a strong sense of competing values and of competing interests between management and in this case the engineering profession, with no serious attempt over time to address the different perspectives. In the end the political and financial concerns overrode the scientific and safety concerns. This is an area of ethical concern for any organisation. In terms of governance, for instance, there has to be clarity about interests that may in some way affect good judgement in the area concerned. It could be that a profession's ethical perspective is inherently against commercial interests. The American Medical Association, for instance, therefore states that if a member of the AMA Council should take up a role with the tobacco industry, he or she would have to resign from the AMA (1999). The issue here is that the financial interest of the member might affect how he or she makes a judgement. He or she would no longer have the independence of thinking that marks out a professional – in this case a member of the profession of medicine. It may be argued that it is possible for a professional to bracket these competing interests. However, this raises issues about how we make ethical judgements and whether we are always fully aware of how we are being influenced. Moreover, the board of the AMA has a strong interest in ensuring that external perceptions could not have any reason to doubt the integrity of the board.

A key area of these debates has been the conflict between the freedom of science and the financial interest of business.

At the least this leads to the importance of declaring any other interests. Sometimes it may be possible to hold different interests without their conflicting. Some, however, argue that there are more fundamental conflicts of interest exemplified by the relationship between business and the professions of science and education.

CONFLICT OF INTEREST BETWEEN SCIENCE AND BUSINESS

The debates about scientific freedom, and in particular the freedom of medical science, tends to be focused in the defence of this freedom against commercial interests. The broad argument runs that if commercial interests dominate research, the core elements of scientific freedom will be lost. Much of the thinking around the concept of scientific freedom has been dominated by Weber (1974) and Merton (1942). Merton refined the ideas to four scientific norms:

- *communism*, defined in terms of sharing methods of teaching and research progress and findings (note that this is distinct from the political ideology of Marx) – This is contrasted with the argument that rights over intellectual property should restrict access to such material
- *universalism*, defined in terms of scientific knowledge transcending the interests of politics, commerce or religion – The law of gravity, for instance, cannot be altered by political or commercial interest
- *disinterestedness*, involving a lack of emotional or financial attachments to research – This focuses on the core purpose of research, deemed to be the pursuit of truth
- *organised scepticism*, involving a critical approach to all research – At one level this involves caution about results until they clearly establish facts. At another level this implies a community of practice that can never fully expound the truth. Weber therefore suggests that the profession of science is greater than any individual contribution and will always progress or refute knowledge. The proper attitude of the researcher is thus humility.

These values provide transparent means of testing truth, and are derived from belief about the nature and purpose of scientific enquiry, and so they involve an underlying worldview, a view of knowledge in relation to humanity. They provide a view that science is in essence an ethical activity, with a core aim of pursuing truth. This is an activity that requires science to push at boundaries 'not only of what is technically feasible but also what is intellectually imaginable' (Scott, 2003). Monbiot (2003: 56) takes such a view a step further, from core purpose to overarching moral vision:

> Science tells us who we are and how we can live better. It is the glass through which we perceive the world. If distorted, it twists our understanding of the ways in which we might progress, of the alternatives to existing models of development.

Scientific freedom, he argues, is then important to maintaining 'wider liberties'.

Ranged against this in Monbiot's argument is the essentially self-interested view of business, which, it is argued, negatively affects the purpose of scientific research. This involves:

- skewing the priorities of research away from either the disinterested search for truth or social utility – Monbiot (2003) notes the breadth of this, such that grant-giving bodies, and even scientific advisory bodies, tend to be dominated by business, leading to research in biotechnology and other areas that takes precedence over the key international issues such as global warming
- the assertion of intellectual property rights (IPR) such that profits take precedence over people who are in need (see the pharmaceutical industry case study below)
- the danger that the promotion of goods such as drugs will influence the decisions of scientists or medical practitioners – There is evidence that in the promotion of drugs medical practitioners have been heavily influenced through industry advertising, gift-giving, support for travel, sponsorship for meetings and conferences (Komesaroff and Kerridge, 2002)
- the sponsorship of research and publications, which can also lead to the distortion of research through designing trials to fit business ends, the selective reporting of findings, the suppression of unfavourable outcomes, and delays in the reporting of unfavourable results (Monbiot, 2003).

ANALYSIS

First, the underlying view of science is contested.

- The history of scientific institutions, and particularly universities, has always involved interests that were not 'purely' scientific. In the UK, for instance, Oxford and Cambridge were originally fuelled by core power structures, not least the Church of England, which restricted access to universities until the mid-nineteenth century to Anglicans (Bebbington, 1992). Research has never been free of 'interests'. The key is not simply for research to be disinterested but rather to know how to handle the other interests involved.
- Competing interests are embodied even within universities. There has always been competition among academics for funding, reputation and individual or disciplinary success (Bender, 2005). This suggests another, more fragmented, view of research practice, questioning Mertonian communism. Even when the research is subject to peer scrutiny, this is not value-free. As Scott notes of peer review, 'In all subjects there are prestigious themes, preferred concepts and preferred methodologies' (Scott, 2003: 77). This suggests that Monbiot's view of pure science is idealised.
- Against the Merton norms lies the hard reality of resources. Although these norms are important to maintain, the freedom to research does not bring with it automatically the right to research funding. Over against academic freedom lies a number of competing ethical values, principally sustainability and accountability. The first demands careful reflection about the use of limited resources and how any research can be sustained. This in turn demands criteria about how these resources will be distributed, and these criteria have to be established by wider society. Accountability has perhaps been the biggest challenge to academic and scientific freedom. The scientist is accountable for the resources that he or she uses in practice, in terms of human resources, time and

money. Holding science to account reminds us that historically there have been other views of science, not least the one that science is in fact an amoral activity. This is the 'Frankenstein' view of science, perceiving the scientist as focused purely on innovation and discovery, with no thought of the consequences (Scott, 2003). From nuclear weapons to cloned animals science delights in creating the unthinkable. Although this may have some good consequences, it equally throws up ethical questions requiring regulation from outside science. The key question is how this is to be achieved. At this point business ethics moves away from the narrow perspective of business to the role of government and social ethics.

Second, Streiffer (2006) tests the basic assumptions about the influence of business *per se*. He examines the consequences of the assertion of intellectual property rights (IPR) by business in research. He concludes that there is no evidence to suggest that IPR will automatically lead to bad consequences. On the contrary, in many cases the business funding has led to research that might not have happened otherwise (2006: 139–40). There is no doubt that business funding will lead to different priorities, but this is the case wherever the funding comes from.

Third, there is no doubt that there has been evidence of business using science unethically, through its manipulation of findings. However, what this shows is fraud and deception – aspects of ethical behaviour that it is in the interest of both business and science to guard against. It is thus in the interest of all parties to ensure transparency,

Such arguments would suggest that Mertonian norms have always to be held in tension with other values. Alongside disinterestedness may be interestedness. The scientist has an interest in the sustainability of his or her institution or related centres. Alongside communism there is individual achievement. Alongside organised scepticism there is the value of care and commitment, without which there would not be an academic community. Alongside universalism there is respect for disciplinarity and application. Each of these values relates to plural accountability, requiring that a science holds together managerial values, academic values and social values (Robinson, 2005). In turn this demands that science, business and politics find ways of working together with multiple interests, as well as dealing with direct conflicts.

Scott (2003) helpfully suggests the concept of the *agora* to sum up the context in which such work takes place around the different responsibilities. The *agora* was the marketplace, and more, in ancient Greece. Scott (2003: 80) defines it as a:

> problem-generating and problem-solving environment/arena of contextualisation in which new knowledge is being produced. It is a heterogeneous arena populated by all kinds of organisations as well as the public at large.

It involves both the market and the wider democracy. Here, there is debate about research that is of 'interest' to all.

Much of this debate assumes that in any conflict of interest business provides the negative or ethically bad element. Why should that be the case? Professions have their interests, as do governments or social activist groups. Chapter 11 looks at the pursuit of social interests and how they might negatively affect environmental and enterprise concerns. This suggests the need for a critical analysis of all conflicts of interest such that the values of all stakeholders are ethically tested. It is often argued against this that business tends to have greater resources to exert influence – and this is examined in the section headed *Lobbying* in Chapter 12.

PAUSE FOR THOUGHT

Why should scientists expect freedom of operation if a company is paying them?

Why should any corporation be expected to take responsibility for low-cost distribution of essential goods if it has invested heavily in the research for the goods' development?

Scott's idea of the *agora* is exciting, but where can it be located? Can you think of any place or project where it is realised?

REFLECTIVE PRACTICE

Your CEO has asked you to develop a policy about conflict of interest. Summarise the main issues you would cover.

CASE

HIV/AIDS PATENTS AND THE PHARMACEUTICAL INDUSTRY

The assertion by the pharmaceutical industry of its rights through patenting its drugs was controversial in the context of HIV/AIDS drugs in the developing world. The HIV/AIDS epidemic remains widespread globally, especially in sub-Saharan Africa, with major health, social and economic effects. There are no preventative or prophylactic drugs against HIV/AIDS, but ART (anti-retroviral treatment) does prolong life.

By patenting ART, the drugs companies created, in the view of such as Hagman (2002), 'the major obstacle to increased drug access' in the developing world. Patents can create artificial monopolies and lead to high charging for any group that is given the licence to produce the drugs. Further, it was argued that health, and essential medicine, is a human right that should be available on the basis of need.

The campaign against patents on ART was also linked to arguments against the expansion of intellectual property rights globally.

This expansion was focused in the 1994 Agreement on Trade-Related Intellectual Property Rights (TRIPS). Run by the World Trade Organisation, this agreement aimed to protect the intellectual property of firms globally. TRIPS aimed to balance the needs and rights of the corporation with global needs. So whereas industrial countries were obliged to implement TRIPS immediately, developing countries were allowed transition periods before they had to implement TRIPS through revision of their patent law and enforcing the new rules. Transition periods varied from five years to over 20 in the least developed countries. Arguments for this approach in the drug industry attempted to balance two main ideas:

- Long-term social utility is greater than the economic gain enjoyed by patent-holders.

- The abolition of drug patent rights will not be helpful in the long run because it will inhibit the continuing high cost development of ART, necessary as HIV mutates.

The first was based on the ethics of rights and care. The second was a strong utilitarian argument. It reinforces the view that the development of such drugs needs high investment and creativity, conditions that are best found in corporations operating in the global market.

The issue of ART prices and patents had two climaxes. The first involved AIDS activists generating public support globally. This caused a fall in prices of first-generation ART, after the pharmaceutical industry withdrew its lawsuit against the South African Government's attempts to manufacture generic drugs (Ncayiyana, 2001). The second period of action began in 2004 and is ongoing, involving attempts to keep second-generation developments of ART at prices close to those of the first-generation drugs.

The arguments have focused on human rights and also the need for governments to share responsibility for the distribution of the drugs.

An editorial in *PLoS Medicine* (2010) argues that the key to this ongoing issue is to develop a means of accountability such that the interests of the industry and of society can be balanced. It notes the increasing utility of addressing therapeutic practice with such media as the Access to Medicine Index (http://www.accesstomedicineindex.org/), which provides effective transparency through assessments of most of the major corporations.

Other means of responding to this issue include the development of patent pools, by which major corporations can become part of such pools, leading to a minimising of patent agreements with governments.

One more step along the road?

The underlying debate is ongoing. The President of the Novartis Foundation for Sustainable Development, Klaus Leisinger (2005), one of leading advocates of CSR in the pharmaceutical industry, wrote that 'No private enterprise has the societal mandate or the organisational capabilities to feed the poor or provide health care.' CSR demands care for the health of employees but cannot take more than a limited responsibility for 'overcoming the challenges that we all face on a global level'.

And indeed, major companies in their responses to guidelines established by the UN Commission of Human Rights in relation to human rights in this area (http://www. essex.ac.uk/human_rights_centre/research/rth/docs/Final_pharma_for_website.pdf) argued that their role and human rights responsibilities are not adequately defined (GlaxoSmithKline, 2009).

Questions

1 Critically examine the UN guidelines (see the website address above) in terms of how they work through responsibility .

2 Are they clear?

3 How would you develop them?

4 How far should companies take responsibility for major global issues such as the distribution of drugs?

Three things are clear about the ethical issue of access to drugs:

- It involves balancing several different ethical theories, with deontological concern for equality (of distribution) and human rights (based in needs) on the one hand, and utilitarian concerns about the long-term consequences of avoiding patents on the other. At its heart is a debate about justice (Rosin, 2003). In Chapter 7 we listed three views of justice: distributive, procedural, and interactional or relational. In a sense, all three are very much part of the debate, with distributive justice around access pitted against the justice of recognising the role of the drugs industry and to what its investments entitle it. Procedural justice is still being worked through, via guidelines and patent pools. Interactional justice focuses on the how the different stakeholders come together to weigh the different concerns.
- What some have characterised as a conflict of interest and values between medical

science and business is more complex. First, the debate has far more stakeholders, including governments and global NGOs. This takes the debate away from a simple conflict of interest between science and business. Second, it is in the interest of all parties to make this issue workable.

- This requires commitment to an ongoing dialogue focused in shared responsibility and with that the capacity to negotiate responsibility. Again this demands ongoing dialogue. So, for example, despite the initial response of GlaxoSmithKline (GSK) to the UN guidelines, the debate has moved forward with some speed. Andrew Witty, CEO of GSK, has argued that his industry needs to balance social responsibility more effectively with shareholder reward (Boseley, 2010).

Witty takes this a step further in arguing that public confidence in the industry demands going beyond minimum standards, and in effect leading the ethical dialogue. This has involved the company cutting drug prices by 25% in 50 of the poorest nations, investing 20% of profits from the least developed countries in healthcare infrastructure for those countries, and releasing intellectual property rights for substances and processes relevant to neglected disease into a patent pool to encourage new drug development. It has also led GSK to place in the public domain details of 13,500 chemical compounds related to treatment for malaria. The firm is opening up this data to any scientists (with an $8 million support fund) to develop work in this area.

The response from Médecins Sans Frontières (2009) has been mixed. General support has been combined with scepticism, focusing on two questions:

- Would other companies become involved in this initiative? Ultimately, they are competing with GSK. Even Witty's initiative is seeking to increase his profits.
- Why have the measures not included ART drugs?

 PAUSE FOR THOUGHT

Is Andrew Witty an ethical hero or simply aiming to increase profits in an ethically sensitive area?

Are you convinced by Witty's arguments for excluding HIV/AIDS (see Boseley, 2010)?

Are GSK making a significant contribution to the debate about justice? How would you characterise Witty's view of justice, in contrast to the views of Médecins Sans Frontières?

MANAGEMENT AND PROFESSIONS

The debate about how business relates to science, and underlying issues such as justice, seems to indicate that management has a strong concern for the common good. On the face of it this might indicate that it is wrong to pit management against professions, as if the distinction is that a profession is based in some ethical good and management is value-neutral. Increasingly, there is a call to view management as itself a profession.

The manager's oath
Preamble: As a manager, my purpose is to serve the greater good by bringing people and resources together to create value that no single individual can build alone. I will therefore seek a course that enhances the value my enterprise can create for society over the long term. I recognise my decisions can have far-reaching consequences that affect the well-being of individuals inside and outside my enterprise, today and in the future. As I reconcile the interests of different constituencies, I will face difficult choices.

Therefore, I promise:

- I will act with the utmost integrity and pursue my work in an ethical manner.
- I will safeguard the interests of my shareholders, co-workers, customers, and the society in which we operate.
- I will manage my enterprise in good faith, guarding against decisions and behaviour that advance my own narrow ambitions but harm the enterprise and the societies it serves.
- I will understand and uphold, both in letter and in spirit, the laws and contracts governing my own conduct and that of my enterprise.
- I will take responsibility for my actions, and I will represent the performance and risks of my enterprise accurately and honestly.
- I will develop both myself and other managers under my supervision so that the profession continues to grow and contribute to the well-being of society.
- I will strive to create sustainable economic, social, and environmental prosperity worldwide.
- I will be accountable to my peers and they will be accountable to me for living by this oath.

This oath I make freely, and upon my honour.

Source: quoted in Alles (2009)

The oath above was developed by Harvard Business School graduates, to be taken at their graduation. The oath was undertaken voluntarily and was used by 20% of the students.

PAUSE FOR THOUGHT

What are the main ethical elements of this oath in areas such as responsibility, virtue ethics and justice?

How would you feel about reciting this at your graduation?

What are the main problems for you about this oath?

The oath is based on the idea of the Hippocratic Oath, thought to have been developed by Hippocrates, a Greek physician of the fifth/fourth century BC, and still declared in some medical schools at the end of training. The oath sets out the serious intention of those who profess to be doctors. The word 'profess' at one level simply means 'declare'. It also carries with it the sense of a public declaration about faith in or allegiance to a group, about expertise or knowledge, and about vows or intentions. It aims to show the seriousness and status of the profession – something which, for Hippocrates, was close to a religion.

Such a high view of a profession is reinforced by several things:

- The end or purpose of the profession is focused in the common good. Airaksinen (1994) argues that the sign of a genuine profession is that it has a moral or premoral virtue. In the case of medicine this is health, and the unconditional distribution of health. Where any doctor is faced by illness, he or she should respond to the need, with payment secondary to that.
- The high sense of purpose in turn reinforces a strong sense of responsibility, not least for patients and clients who are disadvantaged or vulnerable. This is tied to a strong sense of the power, and thus potential effect, of the professional for good and bad.
- There is a strong sense of the importance and status of the profession. Precisely because of the high purpose related to caring for a critical need, the profession is held in high esteem by society. Purpose is then related to identity.

- A relationship between the professional and the client or patient requires trust. This reinforces the need for a strong sense of discipline and regulation to be provided by the professional body to reassure society of both competence and care. This involves:
  - clarity that the professional is qualified to do his or her job. The qualifications therefore have to be accredited, with training focused on practice and intellect. In medicine there is stress on the specialised knowledge and skills required to do the job, with a monopoly in training
  - a strong tradition and narrative that demonstrates to society commitment to competence, care and the common good over time
  - a strong framework of ethics. This is most often expressed in a *code* of ethics. The code clarifies in practice core principles such as 'Do no harm', justice and respect (see Chapter 3). It reinforces that ethics are both about guidance that prevents abuse of the power relationship, and the responsibility of the professional to always seek such core principles as part of any relationship with clients or wider stakeholders. Ethics, then, is one the key elements that marks out the identity of the profession
  - a strong sense of independence of judgement and impartiality. The independent judgement involves basing decisions on professional competence, regardless of other purpose or pressures; in the light of the core purpose of the profession (see Chapter 6 for the Arthur Andersen case); and in the light of the wider common good, expressed in responsibilities to client, profession and society. Once again ethical and competency issues are interlinked. Where that judgement is uncertain, consultation is required with other colleagues. Impartiality involves ensuring that there is no conflict of interest that might affect one's judgement.

THE AMBIGUITY OF PROFESSIONS

Professions can, nonetheless, be ambiguous, and their power used to negative effect. Illich (1977), for instance, noted the high number of patients who in the USA died due to iatrogenic illness (illness caused by the doctor). This involved practices such as the over-prescription of drugs or unnecessary operations. Not only did this practice lead to bad consequences but it represented a relationship between doctor and patient that was itself questionable. Illich argued that it set up a power relationship that tended to lead to dependency and passivity in the patient – 'The doctor knows best.' Clearly, the doctor reckoned to know best and in many cases was convinced of his or her own rightness. Since then there has been a strong sense that justice and respect for the autonomy of the patient (Beauchamp and Childress, 1994) should be at the centre of the therapeutic relationship. Just because there is a strong sense of moral purpose does not mean that the ethics of the doctor will be right. The doctor still has to practise *phronēsis*. In this case that means the purpose of the doctor is not simply to tell patients what to do, but to enable patients to become part of, and thus take responsibility with the doctor for, the therapeutic planning and practice. The same *phronēsis* must be exercised in relation to the issues of health distribution, including the questions of how the service is to be sustained. This includes questions such as: is the doctor primarily involved in medicine to distribute health or to make a profit? How might competition be best handled in healthcare distribution? It also includes critical questioning of how the profession defends the interests of the members, and how this purpose should be balanced with the purpose of service. George Bernard Shaw went further, arguing that professions were focused too much on self-interest, and that 'all professions are conspiracies against the laity' (Shaw, 2004). Once more this suggests that it is not adequate to polarise business (self-interest) and professions (service).

MANAGEMENT AS A TRUE PROFESSION

Khurana and Nohria (2008) carefully examine the idea of a true profession, the differences between professions and management, and the arguments for management becoming more professional, in the sense of the above description. They suggest that the development of business schools in the last century was an attempt to bring this about, but that it failed, for several reasons:

- Unlike doctors or lawyers, managers do not need a formal education to practise.
- There is no general or enforceable code to do with management as distinct from the institution. There is thus no shared professional identity for managers.
- Perhaps more fundamentally, MacIntyre (1981) argues that management cannot be a true profession because the manager operates outside ethics. By definition, the manager is not concerned with purpose or value, only with getting things done. He or she treats (MacIntyre, 1981: 30):

  ends as given, as outside his scope; his concern is with technique, with effectiveness in transforming raw materials into final products, unskilled labour into skilled labour, investments into profits.

For MacIntyre, then, the manager's role is perceived in terms of a scientific approach. The aim is to ensure that performance is the most effective and thus measurable, as echoed in many textbooks on management. So the manager simply does not engage in moral debate. Bauman (1989) takes this further in his responsibility ethics. He argues that this emphasis on 'instrumental rationality' (the application of reason to achieving set targets) has neutralised ethics in management. Now the emphasis is on targets, not people or values.

MacIntyre contrasts the genuine community of practice, based in purpose and some idea of a good outside the business, with management that is based on institutional needs. The first is the domain of the professions, and the second involves a secondary set of targets which, if they dominate, threaten to destroy the core purposes.

There are two major problems with MacIntyre's argument:

- He characterises the situation as two extremes: the community focused on the purpose, and the institution focused on survival and secondary targets. A more accurate picture is of several different groupings who make up any business, and how they relate depends on the situation.
- Although there is some evidence that much of business education has focused on the development of quasi-scientific knowledge (Khurana and Nohria, 2008), there is no argument that this should be the case. It could be argued that management is critical in enabling the community of practice to be sustained, and that the very idea of sustainability provides the core purpose of the management profession.

Nonetheless, there is some truth in MacIntyre's argument, mainly around core ethical identity, and the view of the profession in relation to the wider society and itself. A profession such as engineering connects its identity to worldviews, and at different points has seen itself as (Martin and Schinzinger, 1989):

- *saviour*, helping to create a society with material prosperity for all
- *guardian*, ensuring that the structures the keep communities together
- *social servant*, helping to sustain the social and physical environment.

The engineering profession, then, sees itself as holding multiple responsibilities to and for client, institution, profession and the wider society.

There is little of this strong social identity in the manager, and although management can focus on responsibility to client and institution, there is little sense of being responsible for any wider industry, still less any profession or professional body and what that may represent.

To enable managers to become a real part of that ethical dialogue requires – argue Khurana and Nohria (2008) – greater attention to educational qualifications, the development of a professional body and the development of an ethical code for managers. One possible objection to a code of conduct is that the manager is often viewed precisely as the person who avoids rules. Entrepreneurship, for instance, it is argued, is about developing innovation that cannot always play by the rules. However, the fact that entrepreneurship looks to finds new ways of doing things does not imply avoiding ethical reflection. On the contrary, if a new venture has not been thought through in an ethical context, it runs a high risk of failure. Hence King III's emphasis on ethical risk assessment (see Chapter 5).

In a sense, though, these are simply the external signs of a profession. Khurana and Nohria (2008) argue that for the code to be sustained there has to be a stronger sense of the manager as 'an agent of society's interest' (page 76). It involves 'viewing society as [the] ultimate client', which provides managers with a higher-order purpose. This is precisely what a focus on responsibility would provide. At the heart of this they argue for the need to develop such high purpose and value from 'an inward sense of vocation – a conviction that one is doing work that is meaningful' (Khurana and Nohria, 2008: 76).

Khurana and Nohria (2008) favour the identity of the manager as custodian or steward. This is a strong ethical identity, focusing on shared responsibility and sustainability. It also has a strong historical narrative focused in the stewardship of creation (see Chapter 2). The characteristics of a steward are that he or she will sustain an enterprise in the context of the social and physical environment. The future of that environment is therefore as critical as the enterprise. Looking back to the finance industry and the credit crisis, this would mean acting as stewards of:

- clients' finances – remembering that this is not their own money
- the finance system and environment: if this is not sustained, the future well-being of countless people will be threatened
- justice and responsibility in that system. Without a sense of responsibility and justice in the culture of the system, and not just responsibility to and for the shareholder, it is hard to see how awareness of the wider environment, and with that the sustainability of the system, can be maintained. This reminds us of Brown's (2005) point about the importance of culture in developing the ethical environment.

The idea of stewardship relates directly to responsibility ethics, and especially the third mode of responsibility. For this idea to be developed, however, two things would be necessary:

- the recognition that stewardship has to be worked out in relation to a particular situation – This is just the same for any other profession. The doctor brings his or her skills to the practice, and in any situation has to work out how best to use them. This is often not just a matter of simply enabling health. When faced by an alcoholic, the doctor has to work out how best to treat him or her in relation to wider issues of justice. If the patient continues to drink, for example, is it really fair to give him or her a new liver? Equally, a good steward has to work through how the key skills of enabling an enterprise to be sustained are to be practised, for his/her own ends, for his/her clients, for the shareholders and for the wider society. This demands the practice of *phronēsis* and the first mode of responsibility.
- the capacity to work with very different ethical perspectives and narratives – If one is managing an organisation with a public role (such as higher education), a focus is demanded on how the core community of practice can be enabled, and what values stand in its way (see the case study on higher education below). If one is managing a major corporation, attention has to be paid to the different professions and their view and practice and purpose, such as accountancy or human resources. This further demands a regular reflection on the purpose behind the stewardship, a responsibility shared with other stakeholders.

It is tempting to argue that the manager as steward is simply about doing the job of making money (Robinson, 1992). Using the trickle-down theory, the argument that the market will then distribute such wealth to all in society, one might then leave it to that mechanism to distribute. However, the case of the credit crunch clearly shows the importance of sustaining

– being responsible for – a system that embodies justice. The idea that this system can be run without the practice of responsibility is precisely what led to the crisis.

Management, then – far from being value-free, neutral or simply target-centred – can be perceived as a professional narrative focused on the values of sustainability, accountability and purpose. This becomes part of a dialogue with other professions as to how it is practised. In this sense, managing would take its place with other professions in being responsible for articulating and practising ethics. Notably, this would involve elements of two underlying theories – stewardship and stakeholder theory. We examine this argument in more detail in Chapter 11.

What, then, is preventing managers from developing a professional body and a code?

Management codes

In the UK there are several organisations that seek to provide a framework for the profession of management, including the Institute of Directors (IOD) and the Institute of Management Services (IMS). Both have worked hard to develop different forms of code in relation to the profession.

REFLECTIVE PRACTICE

In your learning groups critically examine the codes of conduct/ethics found on the following websites:

- http://www.iod.com/Home/Training-and-Development/Chartered-Director/ Mainwebsite/ Resources/Document/training_Code_of_Professional_Conduct_2011.pdf

- http://www.ims-productivity.com/page.cfm/content/code-of-ethics/

What do they tell you about the profession and its responsibilities?

Are they sufficient to develop a professional identity?

How would you develop the professional identity of management, and how would you link that to an ethical code?

INFORMATION AND COMMUNICATION ETHICS

Thus far we have noted the importance of several different professions to the ethical tone of business, from accountancy to human resource management. In this section we briefly examine the ethical issues and understanding of information and communication technology (ICT). At one level this focuses on issues that any business must take account of, such as the ethics of email use. At another level it shows how a professional perspective can successfully contribute to good business practice. King III added the governance of technology to the responsibilities of the board, stressing the importance of ownership of professional identity in this area. Gotterbarn (1996) argued that what he called 'computer ethics' should be seen as a *professional* ethics devoted to the development and advancement of standards of good practice and codes of conduct for computing professionals.

The US Association for Computing Machinery bases its code on eight general moral imperatives (http://www.acm.org/about/code-of-ethics/#sect1):

- Contribute to society and human well-being.
- Avoid harm to others.
- Be honest and trustworthy.
- Be fair and take action not to discriminate.
- Honour property rights including copyrights and patents.
- Give proper credit for intellectual property.

- Respect the privacy of others.
- Honour confidentiality.

Such broad ethical principles would have to be established within an organisation through clear guidelines about ICT practice. These would include details of how the data protection legislation can be put into practice, including details of how to ensure anonymity and confidentiality in areas such as research and record-keeping, and how access to the Internet should be controlled at work. Two examples of ICT ethics that are frequently in the news are the use of email and the issues of freedom and the Internet.

EMAIL

Email is in many respects still new territory. As a means of communication at work email has few constraints compared with the written letter. The latter was the product of time and thought, leading often to reconsideration of what was written. Email can be sent instantly, and this encourages a lack of reflection either in terms of interpreting or composing, so that broad principles have to be carefully applied. Might what I have written be interpreted in a negative of abusive way? Was the communication clear?

Emails can also be used in a negative or manipulative way. It is easy to copy in a superior to an email sent to a colleague as a way of trying to embarrass or control him or her. The superior may not even read it, but the implicit threat remains for the colleague.

It can also be used to ensure that responsibility for action is focused elsewhere. The email provides 'evidence' that a matter has been passed on to one's colleague and is no longer one's own responsibility.

In that context Simon Rogerson (2000) argues for the importance of a clear email code of practice. It should include the following issues:

- No email should be forged, or in any way attempt to deceive the receiver about authorship.
- No email should be used to menace, threaten, bully or abuse another person.
- No email should be used to harass or discriminate against another person because of their gender, sexuality, ethnicity or religious beliefs.
- The privacy of all emails should be respected. No person may access another's email or pass on another's email communication unless permission has been obtained.

FREEDOM AND JUSTICE

The Internet amplifies freedom of information, enabling views and data to be shared globally with ease. At one extreme this could be argued to be the ultimate in transparency, enabling clarity about truth. This takes us into the territory of Wikileaks (wikileaks. org), the Internet organisation that aims to publish a wide variety of information in the interests of justice. The philosophy behind Wikileaks is freedom of information, with the belief that if global political operations were all transparent, ultimately leaders would act in a more accountable fashion. It would mean that any information could be placed on the web.

The arguments against this include:

- The information involved may belong to a country or a corporation. This would mean that the taking and displaying of that information would constitute theft, requiring legal redress.
- There is no external check of the information. It is not always possible to verify the information displayed. How can such verification be obtained unless there is a code of ethics around this area that specifies how it can be achieved?
- No information is without social context that if made public could lead to intended or unintended negative consequences. Revelation of information about a corporation might, for instance, lead to the demise of the company and the loss of significant numbers of jobs.

These arguments would suggest that any sharing of information ought to be part of a wider framework of justice, in which information can be checked and used by the appropriate arm of justice. One problem with the Internet is that it knows no legal or ethical boundaries. Computer users in the United States, for example, who wish to protect their freedom of speech on the Internet globally cannot appeal to the United States Constitution (which protects freedom of speech).

Ranged against these considerations is the argument that the Internet should resist attempts to control the flow of information. Google faced the attempts of the Chinese government to censor information that questioned its policies. This has led to a continued struggle, and Google has since been losing out in a growing marketplace (http://tech.fortune.cnn.com/2011/04/15/googles-ordeal-in-china/).

It is clear that there is no simple approach to freedom, justice and the Internet. Some communications industry framework of ethics would seem essential, but it would rely on the entire global industry signing up to it.

CONCLUSION

This chapter has examined the relationship between professions and business. We noted areas of ethical conflict and difference. We also noted the view that business management might be perceived as essentially non-ethical, and the view that management could be regarded as a profession based on the principle of stewardship, but also working with other stakeholders. In this sense the different professions in business can be seen as stakeholders (see the case study below). Management may be argued to have central values and purpose, comparable with other professions, but lacks the professional body and sense of shared responsibility and discipline.

Much of this based in responsibility ethics and virtue ethics (with a concern to develop the ethical narrative of the professions and the related virtues). The profession of leadership and management becomes collectively responsible, with other professional stakeholders, for enabling a critical dialogue that embodies the core virtues.

 ### HIGHER EDUCATION

CASE

The enterprise of higher education is focused in several purposes, which reflect the key stakeholders:

- The government, who sees the purpose of the university as to contribute to the economic good of the nation, but also as a means of enabling greater equality and choice.

- The student, who sees the purpose as personal development, thus enabling greater opportunity for himself or herself in the labour market.

- The teaching staff, who may have very different views of purpose, from the development of students for professions, such as nursing, law and medicine, to the provision of critical education. The staff will in turn be based not simply in the teaching profession but in many other different professions, each with its own view of the good.

- The research staff, who will also have different perspectives on values and purpose, from research for its own sake to research in order to achieve aims for the common good.

- Several different stakeholders, who see universities as having a long-term civilising effect on society, not least through embodying freedom of thought (Robinson and Katulushi, 2005).

Sustaining this project involves not simply one narrative of management but several different professional narratives, including:

- accountancy, focusing on the sustainability of the institution

- the estates office, concerned about the

stewardship of space, security and the environment

- the administrators, who aim to maintain appropriate levels of quality, ensuring accountability to the students and to the funders

- the management team, who plan sustainable strategy around possible markets and at the same time aim to sustain a political agenda that will ensure equality of opportunity for students

- academics, who aim to sustain a community of practice based in research and the development and practice of critical thinking and dialogue, focused around personal and professional development.

Each of these narratives embodies core values and enables the different purposes of the university to be fulfilled. Over the long term this demands attention to the different narratives and working through any conflicts of value that may emerge.

Two brief illustrations of narrative critical engagement must suffice.

Sustainability and learning

- *Narrative 1, Estates:* Higher education has been profligate with space. Each academic is allotted an office or study for their work. However, many do not use that space, choosing to work from home. Unused, heated rooms are not sustainable. First, it is unjust because it takes away resources that could be used for other priorities. Second, it negatively affects management of the environment. Third, the university cannot afford to maintain the size of estate.

A more just and sustainable approach to space for academics, then, is to cut space down to a minimum of what is required for the job. At the same time it could involve housing several academics in large rooms. This would improve security, sustainability and teamwork.

- *Narrative 2, the Academics:* The core purpose of higher education is the development of education through

critical dialogue. Critical dialogue is expressed historically through books. Any researcher or teacher brings with him or her a library of books that are important for ongoing dialogue. The right place for those books is the academic study where research and teaching come together and where the dialogic environment, including books, can be shared with students openly (something not possible if academics share rooms). Space for the academic then embodies the core educational purpose of critical dialogue, something that cannot be developed in tightly controlled space.

Both narratives give an account of values that are important. Both run the danger of negatively affecting core values if pursued to the exclusion of the other. In the first narrative there is the danger of squeezing out the space for critical conversation. In the second there is the danger of failing to be responsible for the wider environment.

Questions

1   Ask your Estates Office for its space policy, and critically analyse its values.

2   Invite a member of the estates team to debate in class with an academic about the different narratives.

3   How would you develop a space policy at your university which enables both ethical narratives to be embodied – sustainability of the physical environment and sustainability of the learning culture? (See http://www.academicworkspace.com/content/view/34/151/.)

Consumer or community

- *Narrative 1:* Managers responsible for marketing universities and politicians both now view the student as customers. This ties in with the increase in student fees in the UK. The narrative suggests it is important then to satisfy the students in their time at university. Lord Mandelson, then part of the government, suggested that this would help to make the staff more accountable (Sellgren, 2009). The argument suggests that accountability is important and is properly located in the logic of consumerism.

- *Narrative 2:* Academics argue that accountability does not have to be a function of the consumer model. It is already there in the idea of the academic community (*universitas magistrorum et scholarium* – roughly, a community of scholars and students who think together), something that requires the mutual accountability of staff and students. Ramsden (2009), among others, suggests that focusing on consumerism – often articulated as student-centred learning – runs the danger of developing a culture that is quite the opposite of collegial community. He argues that consumer logic emphasises the satisfaction of individual rights rather than shared learning. It is focused on the passive receipt of goods rather than constituting a critical community that requires active engagement and mutual accountability.

Can these two value narratives be held together? As with the first example, the danger is in polarising the narratives, narrowly defining the good, and developing a limited practice of responsibility. The different narratives of value shape the practice of responsibility, enabling effective critical agency, and a more complex view of accountability and shared practice.

Questions

1 Examine and critically analyse your university's website. Does it show you how the university is managed, making clear the range of values and purposes?

2 Does it show how it relates to the different stakeholders, and to the different professional narratives within the institution?

3 Does it have a code of ethics or conduct that can link in the ethical perspectives of the different professions?

For an example of an ethical framework for higher education, go to *Ethics Matters* (CIHE, 2005).

EXPLORE FURTHER

Books

Oakley, J. and Cocking, D. (2001) *Virtue Ethics and Professional Roles.* Cambridge: Cambridge University Press, for a focus away from professional codes to virtues.

Dare, T. and Wendel, W. (eds) (2010) *Professional Ethics and Personal Integrity.* Cambridge: Cambridge Scholars Publishing, for a view of one profession, the law, and how it relates to personal ethics.

Machan, T. (2010) *The Morality of Business: A profession for human wealthcare.* New York: Springer.

REFERENCES

AIRAKSINEN, T. (1994) 'Service and science in professional life', in Chadwick, R. (ed.) *Ethics and the Professions.* Aldershot: Ashgate: 1–13.

ALLES, M. (2009) Editorial, *International Journal of Disclosure and Governance* 6: 275–6.

AMA (American Medical Association) (1999) Conflict of Interest Policy: www.ama-assn. org/ama1/pub/upload/mm/37/coi-policy.doc.

ARMSTONG, J., DIXON, R. and ROBINSON, S. (1999) *The Decision-Makers*. London: Thomas Telford.

BAUMAN, Z. (1989) *Modernity and the Holocaust*. London: Polity.

BEAUCHAMP, T. and CHILDRESS, T. (1994) *Principles of Biomedical Ethics*, 4th edition. Oxford: Oxford University Press.

BEBBINGTON, D. (1992) 'The secularization of British universities since the mid-nineteenth century', in Longfield, B. and Marsden, G. (eds) *The Secularization of the Academy*. Oxford: Oxford University Press.

BENDER, T. (2005) 'From academic knowledge to democratic knowledge', in Robinson, S. and Katulushi, C. (eds) *Values in Higher Education*. Cardiff: Aureus: 51–64.

BOSELEY, S. (2010) http://www.guardian.co.uk/science/2010/jan/20/glaxo-malaria-drugs-public-domain.

BROWN, M. (2005) *Corporate Integrity*. Cambridge; Cambridge University Press.

CIHE (2005) *Ethics Matters*. London: Council for Industry and Higher Education.

The COMBINED CODE OF GOVERNANCE (2006) London: Financial Reporting Council.

GLAXOSMITHKLINE (2009) Statement in Response to Paul Hunt's Report on GSK (A/HRC/11/12/Add.2) Available: http://www.gsk.com/responsibility/downloads/GlaxoSmith Kline-Statement-in-response-to-the-Paul-Hunt-Report-on-GSK.pdf.

GOTTERBARN, D. (1996) 'Establishing standards of professional practice', in Meyer, C. (ed.) *The Responsible Software Engineer*. Hamburg: Springer Verlag.

HAGMANN, M. (2002) 'World Trade Organization still threatens supply of affordable AIDS drugs', *Bulletin of the World Health Organization*, 80(9): 762.

ILLICH, I. (1977) *Medical Nemesis*. London: Calder & Boyars.

KHURANA, R. and NOHRIA, N. (2008) 'It's time to make management a true profession', *Harvard Business Review*, October: hbr.org.

KOMESAROFF, P. and KERRIDGE, I. (2002) 'Ethical issues concerning the relationships between medical practitioners and the pharmaceutical industry', *Medical Journal of Australia*, 176, 4 February: 118–21.

LEISINGER, K. M. (2005) 'The corporate social responsibility of the pharmaceutical industry: idealism without illusion and realism without resignation', *Business Ethics Quarterly*, 15: 577–94.

MACINTYRE, A. (1981) *After Virtue*. London: Duckworth.

MARTIN, M. and SCHINZINGER, R. (1989) *Ethics in Engineering*. New York: McGraw-Hill.

MÉDECINS SANS FRONTIÈRES (2009) MSF response to GSK patent pool proposal, 2009-2-16.

MERTON, T. K. (1942) 'The normative structure of science', in Storer, N. (ed.) *The Sociology of Science*. Chicago: University of Chicago Press: 267–78.

MONBIOT, G. (2003) 'Guard dogs of perception: the corporate takeover of science', *Science and Engineering Ethics*, 9(1): 49–57.

MORRIS, K. (2009) 'Right-to-health responsibilities of pharmaceutical companies' [editorial], *The Lancet*, 373: 1998. Available: http://www.thelancet.com/journals/lancet/article/PIIS0140-6736%2809%2961090-4/fulltext [accessed 25 August 2010].

NCAYIYANA, D. J. (2001) 'Antiretroviral therapy cannot be South Africa's first priority', *Canadian Medical Association Journal*, 164: 1857–8.

www.plosmedicine.org 2 September 2010 | Volume 7 | Issue 9 | e1000344.

RAMSDEN,P. (2009) *A Better Student Experience*. York: Higher Education Academy.

ROBINSON, S. (1992) *Serving Society*. Nottingham: Grove.

ROBINSON, S. (2005) 'The integrity of the university', in Robinson, S. and Katulushi, C. (eds) *Values in Higher Education*. Cardiff: Aureus: 242–68.

ROBINSON, S and KATULUSHI, C. (2005) *Values in Higher Education*. Cardiff: Aureus.

ROGERSON, S. (2000) ETHIcol, *IMIS Journal*, 10(1), February.

ROSIN, J. (2003) http://pharmalicensing.com/public/articles/view/ 1080562872_406814b87105d.

SAREWITZ, D. (2004) 'How science makes environmental controversies worse', *Environmental Science and Policy*, 7(5), October: 385–403.

SCOTT, P. (2003) 'The ethical implications of the new research paradigm', *Science and Engineering Ethics*, 9(1): 73–84.

SELLGREN. K. (2009) news.bbc.co.uk/2/hi/uk_news/education/8316658.stm Tuesday, 20 October.

SHAW, G. B. (2004) *The Doctor's Dilemma*. London: Literary Society.

STREIFFER, R. (2006) 'Academic freedom and academic–industry relationships in biotechnology', *Kennedy Institute of Ethics Journal*, 16(2): 129–49.

WEBER, M. (1974) 'Science as a vocation', in Shils, E. (ed. and trans.) *Max Weber on Universities: The power of the state and the dignity of the academic calling in Imperial Germany*. Chicago: Chicago University Press.

CHAPTER 9

Consumers

When you have completed this chapter you will be able to:

- understand and critically assess the arguments over the ethics of advertising
- understand and critically assess the ethics of advertising and children
- understand and critically assess the arguments about the ethical consumer
- understand how corporations can work with consumers in developing ethical awareness and response
- understand and critically assess ethics and the PR profession.

INTRODUCTION

This chapter focuses on another stakeholder – the consumer. It considers first the ethics of how business relates to the consumer through marketing. It begins with the hard case of the alcohol industry, asking how far advertising may be responsible for the negative effect of alcohol on society. It then looks at advertising more generally and the arguments that it is ethically problematic. This leads to a focus on vulnerable consumers, especially children. The chapter then examines the ethical identity of the consumer and the argument that, like other stakeholders, the consumer has an ethical responsibility. The arguments for and against ethical consumerism are thereafter addressed. The chapter finally examines the PR profession and the ethical issues around presenting the acceptable face of the corporation.

 THE ALCOHOL INDUSTRY AND SOCIETY

CASE

Alcohol is no ordinary commodity (Babor *et al*, 2003). On the one hand, it is associated with positive values that celebrate community (Robinson and Kenyon, 2009). On the other, alcohol (ethanol) is a social drug that has a depressant effect, lowering awareness, with the potential to lead to addiction. Some religions (such as Islam) argue against any alcohol consumption, largely on the basis that it directly affects the individual's capacity for responsibility. The conspicuously negative effect of

alcohol consumption on society, and the role of the alcohol industry in advertising alcohol, have together led to the argument that alcohol advertising should be banned. There are three parts to this argument.

- UK Government figures (Cabinet Office, 2004), echoed across the world, suggest that the negative effect of alcohol is in four areas:

  - family and social networks. It is estimated that over a million children are affected by parent alcohol problems

- the workplace. Over 15 million working days are lost annually to alcohol-related sickness, and up to 20 million working days are lost due to alcohol-related unemployment

- health. It is estimated that there are annually over 4,000 alcohol-related deaths involving acute incidents, and almost 18,000 alcohol-related deaths due to chronic disease

- crime and public disorder. This in the early 2000s accounted annually for 500 drink-driving deaths, 19,000 alcohol-related sexual assaults, and 360,000 victims of alcohol-related violence.

- The total cost of all these effects in the UK was estimated as over £15 billion in one year.

- It is argued that at least part of these negative effects are due to alcohol advertising and related promotions and sponsorship, which raises awareness of alcohol and relates it to negative or irresponsible behaviour. In particular it is argued that alcohol advertising cannot be controlled, and will always affect the most vulnerable – both children and those with addictive personalities.

- This argument is developed further through the idea of the 'prevention paradox'. Cook (2006) argues that the alcohol industry has an inherent conflict of interest between selling a product, and thus aiming for increased sales, and the aim of harm reduction. The industry looks to espouse both, and he argues that it is impossible to do both. Cook's argument suggests that the alcohol industry must take some responsibility, in the sense of culpability, for the level of harm. Critical to Cook's argument is the evidence, put forward by Babor et al (2003), of the prevention paradox. This suggests that although heavy drinkers are at most risk of harm, they involve the minority of harm cases. Those who

drink less are less subject to harm but more numerous. It is they who account for most of the cases of alcohol-related harm. The conclusion is that the alcohol consumption of the whole population should be addressed. If the alcohol consumption of the whole population ought be reduced, this would certainly suggest that there is a major conflict of interest for the alcohol industry. In light of such a conflict of interest it is easy to view the work of the alcohol industry around social responsibility as, at best, cosmetic. To address this effectively, alcohol marketing would have to be curtailed.

This has led to debate about whether such a curtailment should involve self-regulation or government regulation. Cook (2006) suggested that it also led to the alcohol industry's attempting to influence national governments away from government regulation. The alcohol industry worldwide has set up education and research groups, and it is alleged that these are aimed at 'rubbishing' the findings of the various WHO reports which recommended stringent controls of the marketing of alcohol.

There are several arguments against these views.

- Consumption of the product in question is not illegal, and the industry has a right to market it. The product is not as unusual as Babor et al (2003) or others would suggest. Many products, if used unwisely, can lead to negative effects. The marketing of the food industry and in particular the chocolate industry is in some sense responsible for the increase in obesity and for the development of illnesses such as diabetes. It could be argued in different ways that this is also the case with many other industries, including motor vehicles and computer games. At the very least such industries ought to be aware of the possible effects of their products. In one sense, then, alcohol is not dissimilar from many other products.

- To impose bans on alcohol advertising would have a negative effect on the autonomy of the customer. The individual is part of a marketplace in which many different products seek to gain his or her attention. A robust autonomy should not be protected from such an environment but rather developed so that it can critically challenge the claims of marketers. Here the argument moves away from simple alcohol marketing to the responsibility of families and schools to develop autonomy.

- The alcohol industry has every right to enter into the debate about the effects of alcohol consumption on society. If the data is open to debate, and if the so-called prevention paradox is based on that data, it is not clear that such a paradox has genuinely been established.

- Widespread drinking and related incidents of harm cannot be seen as directly caused by the alcohol industry. The consumption of alcohol may have contributed to that harm, but the harm was ultimately caused by possibly many other factors, including lack of judgement and discipline on the part of the consumers involved, or factors unrelated to the alcohol consumed. This differs from tobacco, the use of which directly causes harm. Sustained responsible drinking, including not drinking and driving, would lessen the figures of harm dramatically. In the light of that, it is in the interest of the alcohol industry as a whole to work with other agencies at effectively reinforcing responsible patterns of drinking. This

would involve a long-term commitment from the alcohol industry. However, ultimately, the trust established with customers and the association of the product with well-being is in the interest of the company.

Such arguments suggest that to simply polarise self-interest of the industry against the interest of wider society is false. There is an area of shared interest that is best expressed in terms of shared responsibility. Responsibility looks to work through the different ways in which this can be fulfilled together. In the light of this, it is clear that self-interest does not necessarily lead to conflict of interest. On the contrary, the work of business is about balancing of different interests. Research about the effects of alcohol advertising is not conclusive (Robinson and Kenyon, 2009). Despite that, it could be argued that the industry has a proactive responsibility to ensure that it does not support or encourage negative drinking cultures. This balances a concern for justice in the marketplace, such that alcohol corporations are nor unfairly penalised. The industry should therefore be working with all stakeholders around these issues.

Questions

1 Where do you stand on the issue of alcohol marketing?

2 Should it be banned? If so, why?

3 Should it be controlled? If so, by whom?

4 Who is responsible for the negative effects of alcohol consumption?

The case of the alcohol industry focuses on some of the key issues in marketing ethics, not least the use of marketing to influence vulnerable people. Some, however, would see marketing as inherently problematic. When does marketing cross the ethical line between selling a product and encouraging ethically questionable practice? It can lead to negative behaviours which business is directly or indirectly responsible for.

MARKETING AS ETHICALLY WRONG

Marketing may be perceived as inherently wrong for several reasons:

- The very aim of marketing is to influence the customer. To do so, the marketers must create in the minds of the customer a need for the product. At its heart, then, the task is to influence or even subvert personal autonomy.

- Marketing manipulates social values and norms. The most effective way of marketing a product is to attach the definition of need to social norms, and thus to bring to bear social and peer pressure as part of the exercise. One example is the mobile phone. First, the need to own a phone is 'established' through advertising, leading to a general use of the product. Once it is established, the key marketing emphasis then becomes the need to have the latest version of the product. This in turn leads to the development of an ideology of consumerism – the creation of a culture that finds meaning and identity in the acquisition of products – 'I shop, therefore I am' (Michaelis, 2000). Galbraith (1958), in one of the great debates about advertising, argued that the creation of consumerist needs as core values were not central to survival; that they set up a 'dependence effect', and that they carry no social utility. Indeed, they set up benefits that are not intrinsic. A good example of this is in food marketing (see below), in which high-calorie foods are in greater demand than essential foods.

- The argument about a consumer ideology is further developed with the view that consumerism leads to the waste of resources and a lack of awareness of an unequal society, especially in global terms. This begins to explore the ethical identity of the consumer and how far the consumer might be deemed responsible for the social and physical environment.

- The virtue ethics variation of these arguments is that marketing focuses not on the virtues of the customer but rather on vices, such as greed and acquisitiveness. Behind this is the argument that there are ethical consequences for any marketing approach. The consequence of an emphasis on such vices is the intentional attack on autonomy, in the sense of self-governance through critical rational reflection. As we noted in Chapter 7, the development of 'vices' such as greed, instant gratification and acquisitiveness have a negative effect on the development of virtues and thus on ethical decision-making, encouraging a lack of awareness of the wider ethical environment (see also Chapter 11).

- This argument raises the question of how one defines autonomy – and it is difficult sometimes to know when a person is autonomous. Autonomy, Erikson (1964) argued, is the capacity to govern oneself, and is a function of maturity, not age. Even old people may therefore not have developed the practice of autonomy. Moreover, if advertising is based on encouraging fear about things such as self-image, sex, ageing and exclusion, it is designed to appeal to the non-rational aspects of the personality. In a sense all advertising is looking to develop some identification with or dependency upon the product or company.

- Considerable stress has been placed on marketing that targets populations which are most vulnerable, such the elderly or children. In the first, the elderly have a disproportionate amount of the world's wealth … and fears about security post-retirement, and about death. In the second, children have a low threshold of gratification deferment, and parents can be prone to feeling guilty if their child does not have what is considered the norm by other children.

Ranged against the view that advertising is wrong in itself are the classical arguments of Hayek (1961). Hayek argues that:

- Regardless of the influence of adverstising, it does not follow that the needs and wants are unimportant.

- Most desires in any case are conditioned in some way. The goods of any great culture – such as poetry or music – are acquired, and not based upon demand. It may be said that the individual is faced by the demands of many different goods offered not simply by business. It is the task of the individual to decide between these goods. Here, Hayek argues that the social environment is filled with different demands and attempts to influence people. He sees Galbraith as essentially paternalist, assuming that people are the victims of advertising.

- Hayek then argues that the autonomy of the consumer should be respected. In this, 'autonomy' is used in a different way: the right to make a choice, rather than the capacity to make a free choice.

Although this ethical debate involves the responsibility of business, and may be seen to have elements of both virtue ethics and deontological ethics (respect for consumers), its main focus is on the underlying value of freedom and on the exercise of autonomy. If autonomy is defined as the capacity to make a free choice, the argument is that this is affected by advertising. If autonomy is about the right to decide for oneself, the issue of advertising is irrelevant.

Underlying these arguments, then, are questions about who is responsible for enabling and maintaining autonomy – the family, the individual, the school, wider civil society, or the government? It could be argued that the different views of freedom are not contradictory. There are two parts to this argument:

- Freedom, and with that, autonomy, is both relational and individual. My freedom is in a social context and might in some way affect the freedom of others. Freedom in this way demands social awareness as much as rational decision-making skills. Freedom and the capacity to govern oneself can thus be seen as based in the practice of responsibility. At one level this is the freedom that comes from knowing one's purpose and how one relates to the wider society, the capacity for critical agency, and thus the first mode of responsibility. This is founded on a view of humanity as interrelational and interdependent. So freedom is also based on shared responsibility and accountability. This is a strong version of positive freedom (Berlin, 1966) – the freedom to take responsibility or do one's duty (Novak, 1990).

- Nonetheless, Hayek is also right in the sense that such freedom cannot be imposed. This is focused in Berlin's (1966) negative freedom – freedom *from*. Faced with this, then, there would have to be significant ethical reasons for regulating advertising. A good example of this is in relation to vulnerable people – something we shortly explore in relation to children. If the issue of autonomy as capacity is to be addressed, we must look to institutions who are responsible for developing this capacity, such as schools or families. The issue of the ideology of consumerism would be the focus on ways in which consumers might develop autotnomy, through awareness of the wider environment, the effects of business on the environment, and shared responsibiity for that environment. This is examined below in the section on the ethical consumer.

The focus on freedom takes the debate away from ethics focused in business to an ethics of business focused in society, with social and business ethics in dialogue. This has even reached the point where some businesses have defended their right to advertise in the way they want as a matter of freedom of speech (Longstaff, 2002).

 PAUSE FOR THOUGHT

Why are freedom and autonomy important?

Why are they important to the management of business?

Which of the different views of autonomy is more important, and why?

How would you resolve the tension between the different views?

The question of autonomy is focused most intensely in the issue of marketing to children, who are assumed to have neither the capacity for nor the right to autonomy. It is most vigorously debated in relation to food.

MARKETING FOOD TO CHILDREN

Childhood obesity has reached a crisis situation in the developed and developing worlds. In the USA over 35% of children are estimated to be overweight, and more than a quarter of them obese (Harris *et al*, 2009). Such is the global prevalence of this phenomenon that over-nutrition is beginning to rival under-nutrition as a major global problem. Associated conditions include type-2 diabetes, caused largely by a calorie-dense diet, inactivity and obesity. It is expected that that type-2 diabetes will rise over the next 20 years by over 36% in the USA, over 75% in China, and more than 124% in India.

Is marketing responsible for these effects? Research suggests that there is a causal connection between the marketing of high-calorie low-nutrient food and the figures noted above. Based on European and US research Harris, Pomeranz *et al* (2009) argue that:

- The food industry allocates enormous sums to advertising these products, largely on television but also via the Internet and increasingly directly to schools. One estimate (Harris, Brownell *et al*, 2009) suggests that several billion dollars is spent in the USA alone in the context of estimates of over $200 billion spent annually on children's food.
- Psychological research has identified ways in which marketing can influence behaviour outside the individual's conscious awareness. The food industry has spent heavily on accessing and developing such research, leading to marketing that associates calorie-dense food with well-being, social acceptance and fun, involving popular cartoon and actual celebrities, free toys given with food, and so on. This in turn is tied to instant gratification, and lack of boundaries in terms of the amount of food eaten. The research suggests that children are targeted at an early age (2 or 3) with attempts to build up a relationship as they grow.
- There are increasing questions about the ethics of psychological techniques used by the food industry (Harris, Brownell *et al*, 2009; Wilcox *et al*, 2004). This argument emphasises the power gap between psychology and the knowledge of the different means of changing behaviour and the vulnerable child who is not aware of this tactic. From a professional ethics angle the psychology profession has a responsibility to wider society as much as to the business/client. This responsibility includes enabling the development of psychological well-being across society. It could be added further, then, that the psychologist is contributing to the deception of the child and parents by associating well-being with a product that might lead to serious illness.
- The vast majority of food marketed to children worldwide constitutes products that will adversely affect their health.

These arguments suggest that the industry is directly responsible for the development of obesity and related conditions, not least through encouraging greed. Against these arguments are:

- High-calorie products are not of themselves responsible for obesity. There is individual and family responsibility for overeating. This was reinforced by politicians in the USA and the UK. Tony Blair (2006: http://www.guardian.co.uk/ society/2006/jul/26/health. politics), for instance, argued that this problem is not a social one but rather to do with individual lifestyle and responsibility. Over 24 US states enacted legislation around common sense consumption, arguing that obesity was the responsibility of the individual.
- The argument about individual responsibility is extended to the family – ie the family is responsible for how the children eat and take exercise.
- Similarly, the argument is extended to school and the government: that they have failed to develop a culture of exercise and responsible eating.

PAUSE FOR THOUGHT

How would you assess the ethical argument of the two sides?

Where would you draw the ethical line in relation to children?

The debate around children's food marketing continues. As it stands, it is difficult to defend simply negative freedom, the freedom of speech or trade, just as it is difficult to argue that the industry is responsible alone for the growth in obesity. This would seem to indicate a need to move to discussions on shared responsibility including all relevant stakeholders:

- *parents*
  Murphy *et al* (2005) suggest that marketing to children alone remains unethical precisely because the child is naïve and cannot usually understand the marketing context. The child is not able to make a rational decision. The parent must therefore assert an overall view of nutrition that demonstrates to the child why the food cannot be eaten or why it cannot be eaten on a regular basis. The parent will additionally have to ensure that any alternative food is associated with positive experiences. It is after all also possible for marketing strategies to include the parents. This can be achieved by stating directly in the advertisement a requirement to consult parents and obtain their permission. It can also be achieved by limiting the appearance of some children's products in parental magazines or by targeting families in general instead of just children (Waymack, 2000; Bakir and Vitell, 2011).

- *the food industry*
  One of the dangers of self-regulation is that it leads across the industry to inconsistent regulation in terms of both developing criteria and enforcing them. The responsibility of the industry is to ensure that a consistent code is developed and that responses to that code are monitored.

- *governments*
  Governments have not been successful in developing guidelines for what is 'better food'. There is therefore little clarity across culture about what should be encouraged. Governments and transnational bodies must help to develop standards.

- *psychologists*
  Psychologists would have to assert their professional view (Wilcox, 2004) and look to ways of enabling the development of autonomy in the child. This also demands careful weighing of professional ethics as to how psychological knowledge is used in relation to children's advertising.

- *children*
  It is difficult to see how children could be effective stakeholders if they are not included in the development of choice – ie if they are not party to thinking about what is good for them and how any marketing fits in with that. Some argue that this may be effectively achieved by informing children about marketing ideas (McGee and Heubusch, 1997). It would mean that children's naivety would not be taken advantage of, and that they would have the power to decide for themselves whether or not products are good for them. The ethical issues that have been brought forward stem from the fact that children are too young to understand the main reasons behind marketing displays. Informing them about it would drastically reduce those ethical concerns, and would at the same time still allow marketers to go about marketing their products (Beder, 1998). There is some evidence that children can understand the effects of commercial marketing after reaching the age of 12 (Beder, 1998), although others have suggested four, and yet others ten. This would underscore the principle of aiming to develop children as critical consumers.

- *education*

  It is precisely in schools that a healthy scepticism about advertising can be developed. Here too, well-being can be explored holistically, including the discipline of physical exercise.

Regulation

On the basis of such research, Sweden decided to ban children's advertising. Other governments have aimed to work together with the different stakeholders through the development of codes. A good example is the UK's Advertising Standards Agency (ASA). Its code relating to broadcast food advertising and children (ASA Broadcast Committee of Advertising Practice: *Food and Soft Drink Product Advertising to Children*) includes regulation against:

- targeting pre-school or primary school children in television advertising
- creating a sense of urgency for purchase or encouraging excessive consumption
- encouraging children to purchase food or drink primarily for a promotional offer such as a toy
- encouraging or advising children to ask parents or other adults to make purchases for them
- advertising that children are inferior to others, or may let others down, if they do not purchase particular products
- advertising that appeals to positive or negative emotions or implies that the product will make the child superior
- advertising that involves high-pressure techniques that may try to cajole the child into purchasing
- the irresponsible use of popular figures or celebrities, fictional or real.

The underlying ethical tone of these regulations involves:

- emphasis on the right reasons for buying something – not appealing to authority or to secondary reasons, such as collecting items
- avoiding excess: for advertising, this would look to avoid the encouragement of greed and gluttony
- the avoidance of any focus on emotions, and of the encouraging of children to express an emotional response to parents.

 PAUSE FOR THOUGHT

Is it possible to have an effective ethics code in a business that relies on emotions and some sense of acquisitiveness to achieve success?

If the code aims to prevent the encouragement of excessive behaviour, could advertising be used to embody appropriate virtues, such as temperance?

How would you argue for and against a ban on advertising focused on children?

The ASA is funded by the advertising industry (through company levy). It can comment on drafts of adverts but is mostly involved in assessing complaints about adverts already published. It has no power to fine, but by publishing its findings it can affect the reputation of a company concerned. If the ASA is faced with repeated offenders, it can refer them to Office of Fair Trading – which does have the power to fine under the Control of Misleading Advertising Regulations, 1988. Broadcast advertisers can also be referred to Ofcom, the licensing authority, which also has powers to fine. There is thus an effective combination of industry regulation and government regulation. The ASA code gives broad guidelines but publishes detailed findings on adverts. Such findings always involve careful judgements.

WIDER ETHICAL ISSUES

Wider ethical issues about advertising, and addressed by the ASA, include:

- *false statements*
  Making a false statement in advertising is unethical and illegal.

- *deception and misleading statements*
  It is accepted that advertising exaggerates aspects of the product. This is part of the 'theatre' of advertising aimed at grabbing attention. Up to a point, then, so-called 'puffery' (a legal term for inflation or exaggeration) is acceptable. The line between that and deception is, however, fine, and deception with the aim of misleading, misrepresenting or omitting key information is the key ethical problem. Deception in pricing, for instance, leads customers to believe that the stated price for a product is lower than it actually is. This may involve false price comparisons, omitting sale conditions, or linking low prices to the purchase of other items. Promotion practices are deceptive when product construction or performance is intentionally wrongly stated, when the context of sale is not declared (such as in pyramid selling, which aims to recruit other people as sellers), or when techniques such as 'bait-and-switch' are used (offering products at lower prices as a bait for more expensive items). Deception might also involve intentionally mislabelled packaging, with respect to contents, size, weight or use, or the sale of hazardous or defective products. Marketing practices are deceptive if customers believe they will get more value from a product or service than they actually receive. Deception, which can take the form of a misrepresentation, omission or misleading practice, can occur when working with any element of marketing.

- *taste and controversy*
  The advertising of certain products may strongly offend some people while yet being in the interests of others. Examples include feminine hygiene products, or haemorrhoid and constipation medication. The advertising of condoms has become acceptable in the interests of AIDS-prevention, but is nevertheless seen by some as promoting promiscuity. Some companies have actually marketed themselves on the basis of controversial advertising – see the sentences on Benetton immediately below. Sony has also frequently attracted criticism for unethical content (portrayals of Jesus which infuriated Christian religious groups, racial innuendo in marketing black and white versions of its PSP product, graffiti adverts in major US cities). Marketers control what they say to customers as well as how and where they say it. When events, television or radio programming, or publications sponsored by a marketer, in addition to products or promotional materials, are perceived as offensive, they often create strong negative reactions. For example, some people find advertising for all products promoting sexual potency to be offensive. Others may be offended when a promotion employs stereotypical images or uses sex as an appeal. This is particularly true when a product is being marketed in other countries, where words and images may carry different meanings from the ones they do in the host country. However, an offensive poster can massively boost a firm's image, even if it has to be taken down. In 1991 Benetton showed several adverts involving striking images, such as a bloody newborn baby with umbilical cord, AIDs sufferers, terrorists, and even a black child depicted as Satan and a white child depicted as an angel. The ASA found against these, but their impact effectively raised the image of Benetton. Benetton further defended the adverts as helping its customers to reflect on major issues. Is it ethical to market a product through helping the potential customer to reflect on major issues? How would that differ from the Co-operative Bank's focus on social responsibility? One answer would be that the Co-op links such advertising to the actual products and

thus directly to the ethical role of the consumer. Benetton's was more generalised, thus causing confusion about intention. The second argument would focus on the offence caused. The difficulty with the idea of offence is how one determines whether the advert is a legitimate cause of offence. The use of harmful stereotypes, for instance, is seen by some as a cause of offence. Sexist adverts, for example, portray women as less intelligent than men, obsessed with their appearance or unable to make decisions. Grace and Cohen (2004: 97) question whether stereotyping is always unethical. Depending on the context, it may involve a level of humour that challenges stereotypes.

Faced by a variety of regulations some firms aim to go beyond the guidelines. One example is Brown-Forman.

CASE

BROWN-FORMAN

The Brown-Forman corporation is one of the largest American companies producing spirits and wine. In its CSR report Brown-Forman (2008) sets out key guidelines, many of which are more rigorous than the ASA guidelines. These include:

- Adverts should not feature children, cartoon figures, or anything that appeals primarily to persons below the legal age limit.

- There should be no suggestion that alcohol use represents a 'rite of passage' to adulthood.

- There should be no suggestion that alcohol is a means to attain success.

- Adverts should not depict situations in which beverage alcohol is consumed excessively or irresponsibly.

- Models and actors must be a minimum of 25 years old.

- There must be prominent responsibility statements in all advertising initiatives.

This sets up the parameters of a community that is quite different from child or youth communities. There is no suggestion of child play (cartoons), the actors are older, and responsible drinking is embodied.

However, with responsibility as a central part of the brand itself, not an afterthought, the company then begins to fill in, through particular advertising, what responsibility might look like. They include some examples of the 'responsibility messages':

'Keep your judgment pure. Drink responsibly' – *Finlandia* Vodkas

'Drink it, love it, know when to stop' – several Brown-Forman brands

'We make our wine responsibly, please enjoy it responsibly' – *Fetzer* Wines

'Celebrate responsibly' – *Korbel* California Champagnes

Some of the messages include clear affirmation of core virtues, including good judgement and maturity. This begins to spell out what responsibility might actually mean. One of the dangers about the simple tag line 'Drink responsibly' is that it does not explain what responsibility looks like. So the more that indications of this can be given – such as tying it in to corporate responsibility – the better. Second, tag lines such as 'Drink responsibly' can easily be seen as 'bolt-on', not central to the marketing message. However, what makes such tag lines most marginal is precisely incongruity with what is communicated in the advert. If the images, narrative or context of the advert emphasise a different message, then that will take precedence over the exhortation to drink responsibly Overt 'messages' must therefore be congruent with the whole presentation. Involving ideas such as celebration, the messages also get across a sense of community ethos. This begins to embrace the positive view of moderate drinking in the context of a community. Alcohol is seen as part of a community of celebration: it is associated with good values and good experiences of the community – not with loss of self-control, hedonism or negative motivations. In effect, Brown-Forman is setting up not simply a positive view of alcohol but a normative view of community in which alcohol is drunk. In terms of autonomy and plurality it sets up an alternative to, for instance, the popular view of student drinking culture or binge-drinking culture. Sketching an alternative community is much more effective than simply saying 'Drink responsibly'. This is at the heart of virtue ethics with its emphasis on the narrative that shows what the community of practice values involve.

Brown-Forman, however (through its Jack Daniels product), goes one step further and also directly sponsors part of a sporting activity, specifically a car in the National Association for Stock Car Auto Racing (NASCAR). On the face it this breaks two cardinal rules of alcohol marketing – the ASA's injunction not to associate alcohol with sport, and the danger of association of drinking with driving. Brown-Forman tackles this head-on and argues that the association of alcohol with sport and driving is not *per se* wrong. It would be wrong to associate uncontrolled drinking with these activities or to imply that success in sport was only possible through drinking alcohol. However, they aim to associate the sport with responsible drinking. Once again this emphasises control and judgement, with the tag line on the cars, 'Pace Yourself, Drink Responsibly'. The message will be

seen by those who are under 18 but it is not one that appeals to a youth culture. On the contrary, it sets out a cultural meaning that they might aspire to. To reinforce this, the Jack Daniels team restricts the sale of team merchandise to 21-year-olds or older. In ethical terms, this is not simply about reduction of harm but more about setting out a positive moral message. It is also, again, a message that stresses the virtues. 'Pace yourself' involves control, maturity and good judgement. The idea is directly against the instant gratification that is associated with excessive drinking. Moreover, virtues such as these are also essential for success in professional driving. This sets up a framework of integrity, using the same virtues in relation to the use of alcohol.

It would be foolish to suggest that such an approach is of itself sufficient. It needs reinforcement in other contexts. It also needs continued reflection on value and practice to enable responsive and effective development in this area, and Brown-Forman sees it as part of its own responsibility to review practice and respond to criticism.

Questions

1 Critically analyse the approach of Brown-Forman.

2 Is it in fact possible to market alcohol in a way that reinforces responsible community values?

The chapter so far has examined ethical problems with advertising, such as deception and offence, the ethics of advertising itself and of advertising to vulnerable people, and issues about the responsibility of the industry and of different stakeholders. Underlying this have been key issues about rights, virtues, freedom, autonomy and integrity (which is examined more closely below).

The debate has increasingly focused on the consumer as responsible stakeholder and how he or she exercises responsibility in the act of purchase, and we now look at how this might be developed.

THE ETHICAL CONSUMER

If stakeholders have responsibilities as much as needs or rights, then that should also apply to consumers. This puts the focus on the ethical decision-making of consumers and on how they might influence or respond to business. Arguments above inferred that consumerism was ethically problematic. This suggests that a culture of simply buying for its own sake is problematic. Underlying these arguments is the assumption that the consumer can actually exercise choice.

McMurtry (1998) goes further to argue that the exercise of choice reflects underlying norms, values and beliefs, and that ultimately all purchasing is ethical in nature. This relates strongly to the stewardship and universal responsibility positions. If stakeholders share responsibility for everything, the corollary is that every decision that we make, including what we choose to buy, has ethical implications. Instead, then, of viewing money as a means of purchasing status, luxury goods or an improved quality of life, we can also view it as the means of making an ethical statement. This encourages consumers to think about:

- the supply chain
- the effect of any purchase (such as of cars on the environment)
- wider issues of justice, such as fair trade
- not just the product being purchased but the wider track record of this and other companies that produce it.

By making informed decisions about these issues, the consumer begins to take responsibility for himself or herself and for his/her environment, looking at the wider cost to the social and physical environment. It might be possible then to speak of the integrity of the consumer.

TYPES OF ETHICAL PURCHASING

These include:

- positive purchasing – favouring particular ethical products, such as energy-saving lightbulbs
- negative purchasing – avoiding products that you disapprove of, such as battery eggs or cars with high fuel consumption
- company-based purchasing, targeting a business as a whole – this might mean positively supporting ethical outlets or negatively boycotting all the products made by one company
- basing decisions on the overall record of the company and the products.

The phenomenon of ethical consumption is on the increase. According to the Co-operative Bank's annual *Ethical Consumerism Report UK* (2010), the overall ethical market in the UK was worth £43.2 billion in 2009, compared with £36.5 billion two years earlier. The growth was despite a 2 per cent fall in overall household expenditure in the previous year. This ran counter to the assumption that ethical consumption would be the first casualty of the recession.

CRITICISMS

Several criticisms of ethical consumerism have emerged:

- It is difficult to see how ethical consumerism can effect real and permanent change. The Co-op Bank's *Report* also notes that despite the increase in ethical spend it remained a small proportion of the total annual consumer spend of some £700 billion. This might reflect the involvement of largely niche markets.
- The basis for choice about any product is limited. Whereas some companies give clear information about the provenance of products, others do not. Yet other companies style themselves as ethical but the consumer has little information to judge whether it is real or cosmetic.
- Mazar and Zhong (2010) examined the evidence about how exposure to green products might affect ethical behaviours. They found a complex picture, distinguishing between exposure to green products and the purchasing of green products. Exposure tended to activate norms of social responsibility and ethical conduct. The purchasing of green

products, however, often led to less altruistic behaviour. They refer to a 'licensing effect' – that having satisfied an altruistic norm, customers felt that this gave them licence to operate unethically in other areas: an unintended consequence of ethical consumerism.

- Monbiot (2007) argues that ethical consumerism has little effect other than to make the consumer feel better. It strengthens motives of status and self-advancement. Although corporations and governments constantly refer to consumer power, consumers are often poorly informed and isolated. Moreover, they have many vested interests in the system, which means that their scrutiny is frequently limited to comparatively superficial issues. In some ways they are complicit with the CSR greenwashing effect, because they would like to believe such a picture.
- There are major questions also about the nature of the consumer's responsibility. Is it really the responsibility of the consumer to drive forward the ethical agenda in business? Should this not be the task of the business, which can then be held to account? In the light of the number of ethical issues around retail, it is not evident that a consumer could grasp them all or that the issues are as clear as some would argue. As we noted in Chapter 5, King III argued that the ultimate agent of compliance for any ethical policy is the stakeholder. This means much more than simply consumers.

The criticisms reflect the lack of clarity around the area of ethical consumerism. Some arguments assert that ethical consumers are driving the demand for the ethical corporation. It is clear that the figures above cannot yet support that argument. Others argue that the corporation should be influencing the consumer to develop ethically. Corporations such as the Co-operative Bank and Interface take the responsibility for engaging consumers and providing information that will enable effective ethical decision-making. There are also great improvements in labelling and standards that can guide the consumer, such as Fairtrade, Social Accountability 8000, organic food, local food, the Organic Trade Association, the Green America Seal of Approval, grass-fed beef, dolphin-safe fish, recycling, and Rainforest Alliance certified.

More generally, organisations such as Ethical Consumer (http://www.ethicalconsumer.org/) provide information about the ethical record of corporations. This involves exhaustive reporting on various areas, including:

- oppressive regimes
- trade union relations
- wages and work conditions
- environmental practices
- marketing
- animal rights
- armaments
- political donations.

This, however, raises a further issue. What are the credentials of NGOs such as Ethical Consumer? Is their ethical perspective ideological? Such organisations can easily style themselves as the voice of ethical consumers, and wield influence that has not been critically established. How, for instance, can the consumer decide about the debate going on between Starbucks and the Ethical Consumer (*Ethical Consumer*, 18 March 2011)? In this, Ethical Consumer aims to rate firms 'holistically', arguing that, despite developments in fair trade, Starbucks' record with its own employees was unacceptable. Because of this, the magazine placed Starbucks at the bottom of the coffee industry ratings.

REFLECTIVE PRACTICE

Starbucks and holistic ethics ratings

Read the debate between Ben Packard and Dan Welch about the ethical rating of Starbucks.

Ben Packard: Starbucks Coffee Company response regarding 'Starbucks bottom of ethical rating despite going Fairtrade', *Ethical Consumer* Magazine, 18 Feb 2011: www.business-humanrights.org/Links/Repository/1004726/jump.

Dan Welch, Co-editor of *Ethical Consumer* Magazine: response to Starbucks Coffee Company comments of 4 March 2011: www.business-humanrights.org/Links/Repository/1005183/ jump.

What criteria would you use to decide between the two arguments?

The example of the Starbucks and Ethical Consumer debate raises several questions. First, what is the power and influence of NGOs such as Ethical Consumer? Second, who determines what the criteria for ethical rating should be? Have these, for instance, been agreed by the industry in question, or is it simply the view of the NGO? Third, in the Starbucks case there have been different views from different consumer organisations, many affirming Starbucks' developments. How do we decide between the different views? The idea of ethical consumption also presupposes that consumers have access to unbiased information, but with millions spent by companies on advertising, much of the available information is heavily biased. The principal purpose of advertising is to make the product seem more essential, more important, more exciting or, in this case, more ethical than it really is. Since few consumers closely scrutinise a company's ethical claims, companies are able to get away with misleading messages even when they are refuted by independent sources. Consumers are therefore not truly empowered. Fourth, is it appropriate to rate an organisation ethically? We look at this more closely in Chapter 11. At this stage it is worth noting several things.

- Ratings can lead to a simplistic view of a corporation, not taking into account the ethical journey and context of the firm.
- Ratings have the danger of seeking ethical perfectionism.
- Ratings assume an accepted set of criteria. This would demand that the criteria be developed by a wide number of stakeholders, not least the industry in question. In any case, as we noted in Chapter 2, although many ethical principles may have general acceptance, they require debate and dialogue to place them into detailed practice. Ratings are not the result of detailed dialogue but rather a particular evaluation.
- The danger of self-proclaimed ratings is that they become judgemental, primarily asserting the moral high ground. Ratings then can encourage ethical thinking that is not mature.

These dangers make it difficult for the consumer to become engaged. The Starbucks case suggests that information and values are not always clear without debate and dialogue. It also raises the issue of the ethical identity of the consumer. In the light of that it is possible to note several different types of ethical consumer:

- the consumer focused on specific shopping decisions – This role requires the appropriate information about products
- the consumer focused on working with others around particular issues of corporate behaviour – A good example of this is the Nestlé boycott (see Chapter 13)
- the consumer focused on social and political change – The example of *apartheid* is telling, and shows how consumers could work with business to address political injustice

- the consumer as activist, concerned to take on big business as a whole to develop his or her approach to CSR.

The first of these focuses on the individual consumer; the other three focus on the consumer working with other organisations in different ways to develop shared responsibility, for criteria and for practice.

INFLUENCING THE ETHICAL CONSUMER

Many firms see it as their responsibility to influence the consumer about ethical choice. A good example of this has been Interface Corps. Interface has a strong sense of the role of business in enabling a sustainable environment and aims to encourage customers to join in with this (Interfaceinc.com). The tone of this approach is about working through a journey about how to develop sustainable practices together with stakeholders. For more details of this, see Chapter 11.

Another corporation shows a different approach to managing ethical consumerism. The Co-operative Group, on the back of doubled revenue, profit and membership over the three years up to 2011, launched an ethical operating plan.

The introduction sets the tone, with a focus on values and responsibility (national and global) and on the role of the business to help navigate ethical consumer choice.

CO-OPERATIVE SOCIETY ETHICAL OPERATING PLAN (2011–2013)

The Co-operative has always had a purpose beyond profit, and recognised that some things are plainly unjust and need to be tackled, with or without a business case. We've learnt that we need to manage and develop our business in a sustainable manner, and will always be transparent and accountable in our pursuit of this (www.co-operative.coop/join-the-revolution/our-plan/).

The introduction goes on to describe the core principles of the Co-operative Society including self-help, self-responsibility and democracy. It also carefully distinguishes the values of equality, equity (fairness) and solidarity (community). It views these as radical and connecting to a history of campaigning for those values. The ethical plan is to be reviewed annually with members through the Values and Principles Committee to ensure the continued congruence of values and practice.

The Co-op's ethical plan includes:

Democratic control and reward
- Dividend scheme to be amended to reward ethical consumerism

Ethical finance
- The introduction of the world's first ethically screened general insurance products
- Double financial support for renewable energy and energy efficiency projects from £400 million to £1 billion by 2013

Protecting the environment
- Increasing its carbon emission reduction target to 35% by 2017
- Adding a further 10% to the 15% packaging weight reductions already achieved
- Increasing the carrier-bag reduction target to 75% by 2013
- The construction by 2012 of a head office that will set new standards in sustainable design, construction and operation in the UK

Building a fairer and better society
- Investing £11 million in co-operative enterprise by 2013
- Boosting existing community investment by £5 million a year
- Investing £30 million in an Apprenticeship Academy and Green Schools programme
- Creating 200 Co-operative Schools by 2013

Tackling global poverty
- The Co-operative will develop a unique range of projects and initiatives that benefit producers and move 'beyond Fairtrade'

Responsible retailing
- Healthier Choice products will be no more expensive than standard equivalent lines and the nutritional content of Simply Value products will be at least as good as standard equivalent lines.

Analysis

This approach to ethical consumerism involves:

- The plan benefits from the careful setting out of principles characterised by balance. Community (solidarity) and equality are balanced with self-help and responsibility for the self. This is an appeal to sustainability, with an underlying worldview based on interaction and interdependence. There is thus support for responsiveness and intervention. This fulfils the first mode of responsibility through clarity about values, purpose, and how the company is aware of and relates to stakeholders. The second and third modes of responsibility – accountability and shared responsibility – are worked out in relation to the workplace and wider society. 'Building a fairer and better society' shows a strong commitment to proactive responsibility.
- There is strong appreciation of justice at several levels, both in terms of the democratic basis of the firm and in the global framework of justice, with an awareness of how firm and customers can respond to that. This begins to address justice as distributive, procedural and interactional.
- The plan shows appreciation of important elements of building an ethical culture, focusing on trust and inclusivity, and providing customers with the data to make informed decisions. It recognises the importance of rewarding ethical purchasing through increased dividends. Core to both of these is the identity of the consumer as a member of the Co-operative Movement, and the plan links this in to major projected increase in membership.
- The plan is built on transparency of principles and practice.

The plan then works through showing what ethical practice looks like. It does not simply provide options for the consumer, but invites the consumer into the community of practice to share in the practice of responsibility. Consumers thus become part of that development, through information, modelling and reward. It also gives members a voice in the critique and development of the plan through annual review. This provides a clear example of integrity through the commitment to principles, the consistency between principles and practice, and an openness to critique and learning.

 REFLECTIVE PRACTICE

Is the Co-op plan simply a means to the end of making money?

Imagine your firm is a competitor of the Co-op. You are in charge of marketing and have been asked by the CEO to develop an ethical plan that can compete with the Co-op's.

Make a critical analysis of the Co-op plan and consider how you might develop a better one. What are the key principles, how do they differ from each other, and how are they worked out in the plan?

Is it possible to develop a plan that includes elements of justice, responsibility and integrity without the Co-op's system of membership?

Selling the corporation

The Co-op is an example of ethical marketing through the development of the ethical identity of the corporation. In a sense they rely upon the corporation 'selling itself', providing an attractive corporate image. This is part and parcel of the public relations (PR) profession. Public relations has been regularly attacked as the lapdog of industry. Corporate Watch went as far as to argue that the PR works against ethical dialogue (http://www.corporatewatch.org.uk/?lid=1570):

> There is a considerable body of evidence emerging to suggest that modern public relations practices are having a very significant deleterious impact on the democratic process ... By giving vested interests the opportunity to deliberately obfuscate, deceive, and derail public debate on key issues, the public relations industry reduces society's capacity to respond effectively to key social, environmental and political challenges.

This negative view of the PR profession is countered by several PR professional bodies who keenly argue for the independence of PR as a profession, with values that transcend simply the interest of clients. The Public Relations Society of America (PRSA, www.prsa.org/AboutPRSA/Ethics) sets out six core values to inform the practice of its members: advocacy, honesty, expertise, independence, loyalty, and fairness. The first of these focuses on the voice of the client and the importance of making it heard in any public debate. Honesty is defined in terms of accuracy and truth in focusing on the interests of the client. Expertise reinforces the idea that competence is in one sense an ethical value. Independence stresses the objectivity of the advice to clients. Loyalty is exercised in relation to the client, but in the context of wider public interest. The final value looks to treat all stakeholders fairly, and also to respect their views.

Such a code attempts to assert a professional identity, stressing honesty, with the PR professional truthfully representing the client but also aware of the need to serve the public interest. This leads to guidelines that include the guidelines:

- Be honest and accurate in all communications.
- Reveal sponsors for represented causes and interests.
- Act in the best interest of clients or employers.
- Disclose any financial interests in a client's organisation.
- Safeguard the confidences and privacy rights of clients and employees.
- Follow ethical hiring practices to respect free and open competition.
- Avoid conflicts between personal and professional interests.
- Decline representation of clients requiring actions contrary to the Code.
- Accurately define what public relations activities can accomplish.
- Report all ethical violations to the appropriate authority.

Such guidelines in many cases lead to further ethical reflection. Who, for instance, determines what the best interests of the client are? In the history of Arthur Andersen it was clear that Andersen felt that the best interests of the client were to face the truth about the finances, and were thus located in value rather than interest. In PR the issue of best interests would lead to dialogue with the client not least about how best to present the client and also how to remain truthful.

Fawkes (2011) argues that in developing the ethics of the PR profession there has to be an awareness of its 'shadow side' – a concept devised by the psychoanalyst Jung. It refers not to the 'dark side' but to the *unexamined* side of behaviours – those that we keep in the shadow. This might include the power that the PR profession has to mould the aims and objectives of the organisation, most famously exemplified in Malcolm Tucker, government spin doctor of BBC TV's *The Thick of It* (2005: http://www. bbc.co.uk/programmes/b006qgrd).

REFLECTIVE PRACTICE

Spinning out of control

You are a PR director charged with making the corporation look ethical following the discovery that several directors have received big bonuses despite the firm's making a loss. What would you recommend the board to do?

Can a PR director ever afford to the tell the whole truth? If not, why not? Can he/she afford *not* to tell the whole truth?

Such an approach to PR tends to focus on the short-term projection of image, and therefore by definition aims to take the spotlight away from the weaknesses of the client corporation. Here PR can tell the truth, but not the whole truth. Again this is something that the PR professional has to determine in context. When does representation of a firm's interest and image become a lie? Any ethics of the PR profession has to take this tension into account. The exercise of integrity and practical wisdom become critical in making such a judgement.

The Stockholm Accords (2010) involve a call to action for the PR profession. Approved by the World Public Relations Forum, this set of principles radically reshapes the purpose and values of the PR profession. It implies that dilemmas to do with presentation and truth can only be addressed in the light of an organisation's attempt to work with good governance and sustainability. This takes the emphasis from image and puts it on integrity. It takes the role of the PR professional away from fire-fighting ethical failures and turns it into one of being a critical part of the development of corporate integrity. In terms of governance, for instance, the accords focus on a stakeholder-inclusive model and advocate (http://www.wprf2010.se/draft-of-the-stockholm-accords/) that PR professionals should be involved in the defining and development of the organisation's values strategies and policies. Sustaining such a culture would then involve the PR profession in helping to develop awareness of its ongoing workings, developing a 'listening culture' that would enable effective anticipation, adaptation and response. The skills of the profession could also be used in relating to, and interpreting, the expectations of stakeholders. In turn, this would enable better governance.

In relation to sustainability, the accords see the PR function as being a key part of enabling good communication with stakeholders. The PR professional would (http:// www.wprf2010.se/draft-of-the-stockholm-accords/):

- ensure stakeholder participation to identify information that should be regularly, transparently and authentically reported
- promote and support efforts to reach an ongoing integrated reporting of financial, social, economic and environmental concerns.

In this view PR would be a part of the development of the ethical identity of the corporation. PR skills would be used to enable good communications with internal and external stakeholders, and the PR professional would contribute to the ongoing dialogue about values and practice.

This model moves away from that of using ethics as a means to an end – that is, to make the company look good. It focuses on the integrity of the corporation precisely because it is hard to sustain merely an image of ethics.

There is no doubt that the ethical identity of any firm can affect its success. It is important both in sustaining trust and in attracting customers. However, making the claim that a corporation is ethical can itself involve risks – as the case study below shows.

NESTLÉ AND THE ASA

In 1998/9 Nestlé continued to try to improve its reputation, following the controversy over the Nestlé company's promotion of soluble breast-milk substitutes in poorer African countries, which provoked strong negative reactions against the company in North America and Europe. The company decided to target university students, reasoning that it is from this population that leaders and opinion-formers would emerge. Because many universities had banned Nestlé products and representatives from their campuses, Nestlé attempted to reach the students at Oxford University through an advert placed in the local free press. One of the claims in the advert was that 'Even before the WHO International Code for Marketing Breast Milk Substitutes was introduced in 1981, Nestlé marketed infant formula ethically and responsibly, and has done so ever since' (quoted in Robinson, 2002: 149). A response came from the UK campaign group Baby Milk Action (a single-issue NGO), who took Nestlé's claims to the Advertising Standards Authority (ASA) to arbitrate on whether Nestlé could be judged to have been ethical in what it sold and how it sold it.

The ASA found against Nestlé on the grounds that the advert made claims that could not easily be substantiated. The response of Baby Milk Action was to claim that this showed the practices of Nestlé to have been unethical (*Marketing Weekly*, 4 February 1999).

In fact, the ASA were making their ruling within the limited terms of the advert. In the light of the case history, any claims about the ethical nature of Nestlé's practice before the WHO code was introduced could not be simply substantiated. The ASA recognised that the ethical practice of Nestlé had greatly developed, but at the time in question there was too much dispute about the marketing practice for the ASA to rule that it was ethical.

The actual findings of the ASA in this case showed a reluctance to get involved. The implication was that it is very difficult to make a claim that any practice is completely ethical. The implications for any ethical claims are that they should be focused:

- on an account of how the organisation views and practices ethics, rather than unsubstantiated claims about the ethical nature of any action. This would base any views on the ongoing ethical reflection of the organisation, evidenced by annual reviews of ethics and responsibility

- on the narrative of how ethical insights and practice have developed over time. There is a strong suggestion that the ASA would have been happy with claims cast in such a context

- on a tone of humility and realism that seeks to engage stakeholders in conversation rather than in trying to win an argument.

Nestlé's approach to this did not have a pragmatic edge to it. If indeed there is no ethical perfection, any attempt to claim an ethical high ground is fraught with danger, and makes it more difficult to deal with any ethical failure. Coming up with an assertion of ethical excellence opens the possibility of polarising the debate and thus increases the danger of this being used against the corporation. More effective would be to bring other stakeholders into the debate, or even to have stakeholders or independent groups give their view of the ethical narrative.

CONCLUSION

In this chapter we have reviewed the relationship between consumer and business, focusing on marketing, the ethical consumer and how the firm develops its image or identity. The conclusion of the Stockholm Accords takes us into the field of integrity, rather than image, which the PR profession enables through its communications skills.

In the next chapter we examine the supply chain in more detail.

EXPLORE FURTHER

Books

Bauman, Z. (2009) *Does Ethics Have a Chance in a World of Consumers?* Institute for Human Sciences, Vienna Lectures Series. Cambridge, MA: Harvard University Press, for an important exploration of the concept of consumerism.

Arnold, C. (2009) *Ethical Marketing and the New Consumer: Marketing in the new ethical economy.* London: John Wiley, for a strong argument on the value of ethical consumerism.

DVDs

Super Size Me (2004, Tartan), for an over-the-top documentary that asks some fundamental questions about consumerism.

REFERENCES

BABOR, T., CAETANO, R., CASSWELL, S., EDWARDS, G., GIESBRECHT, P., GRAHAM, K., GRUBE, J., GRUENEWALD, P., HILL, L., HOLDER, G., HOMEL, R., OSTERBERG, E., REHM, J., ROOM, R. and ROSSOW, I. (2003) *Alcohol: No ordinary commodity. Research and public policy.* Oxford: Oxford University Press.

BAKIR, A. and VITELL, S. (2011) 'The ethics of food advertising targeted toward children: parental viewpoint', *Journal of Business Ethics*, 91(2): 299–311.

BEDER, S. (1998) 'Marketing to children'. Paper given at the conference Caring for Children in the Media Age, New College Institute for Values Research, Sydney, Australia.

BERLIN, I. (1966) 'Two concepts of liberty', in Quinton, A. (ed.) *Political Philosophy*. London: Penguin.

BROWN-FORMAN (2008) *Our Long Term Perspective: Brown-Forman Corporate Social Responsibility*. Louisville, KY: Brown-Forman.

CABINET OFFICE (2004) *Alcohol Harm Reduction Strategy for England*. Prime Minister's Strategy Unit. London: HMSO.

COOK, C. (2006) *Alcohol, Addiction and Christian Ethics*. Cambridge: Cambridge University Press

CO-OPERATIVE BANK (2010) *Annual Ethical Consumerism Report UK*.

ERIKSON, E. H. (1964) *Insight and Responsibility: Lectures on the ethical implications of psychoanalytic insight*. New York: W. W. Norton & Co.

ETHICAL CONSUMER (2011) 'Starbucks bottom of ethical rating despite going Fairtrade': www.ethical consumer.org/Mediainfo/pressreleases/Mediareleasecoffeeshops.aspx (28 February 2011)

FAWKES, J. (2011) 'The shadow of professional ethics', unpublished PhD thesis, Leeds Metropolitan University.

GALBRAITH, J. K. (1958) *The Affluent Society*. London: Penguin.

GRACE, D and COHEN, S. (eds) (2004) *Business Ethics: Problems and cases*, 3rd edition. Oxford: Oxford University Press.

HARRIS, J. L., BROWNELL, K. D. and BARGH, J. A. (2009) 'The food marketing defense model: integrating psychological research to protect youth and inform public policy', *Social Issues and Policy Review*, 3(1): 211–71.

HARRIS, J. L., POMERANZ, L., LOBSTEIN, T. and BROWNELL, K. D. (2009) 'A crisis in the marketplace: how food marketing contributes to childhood obesity and what can be done', (US) *Annual Review of Public Health*, 30: 211–25.

HAYEK, F. (1961) *The Road to Serfdom*. Chicago: Chicago University Press.

LONGSTAFF, S. (2002) 'The ethics of free speech in advertising': http://www.bandt. com. au/news/the-ethics-of-free-speech-in-advertising.

MAZAR, N. and ZHONG, C. (2010) 'Do green products make us better people?', *Psychological Science*, 21: 494.

McGEE, T. and HEUBUSCH, K. (1997) 'Getting inside kids' heads', *American Demographics*, 19(1).

McMURTRY, J. (1998) *Unequal Freedoms: The global market as an ethical system*. Toronto: Garamond Press.

MICHAELIS, L. (2000) *The Ethics of Consumption*. Oxford: Oxford Centre for the Environment, Ethics and Society.

MONBIOT, G. (2007) 'Ethical shopping is just another way of showing how rich you are', *The Guardian*, Tuesday 24 July.

MURPHY, P. E, LACZNIAK, G. R., BOWIE, N. E. and KLEIN, T. A. (2005) *Ethical Marketing*. Upper Saddle River, NJ: Pearson/Prentice Hall.

NOVAK, M. (1990) *Morality, Capitalism and Democracy*. London: IEA.

ROBINSON, S. (2002) 'Nestlé baby milk substitute and international marketing', in Megone, C. and Robinson, S. *Case Histories and Business Ethics*. London: Routledge.

ROBINSON, S. and KENYON, A. (2009) *Ethics in the Alcohol Industry*. Basingstoke: Palgrave.

The STOCKHOLM ACCORDS (2010): www.wprf2010.se/2010/02/22/the-stockholm-accords.

WAYMACK, M. (2000) 'The ethics of selectively marketing the Health Maintenance Organization', *Journal of Theoretical Medicine and Bioethics*, 11(8): 301–9.

WILCOX, B., KUNKEL, D., CANTOR, J., DOWRICK, P., LINN, S. and PALMER, E. (eds) (2004) *Report of the APA Task Force on Advertising and Children*. Washington, DC: American Psychological Association.

Supply Chain and Competition

INTRODUCTION

This chapter examines the ethics of the supply chain and its management by the directing corporation. It starts with a detailed case study of the supermarket store chain Tesco which raises key questions about both the supply chain and competition. Can it be ethically right to prevent competition? In this case Tesco might well appear to be preventing a fair market while also radically affecting the local community. The first has a strong deontological tone to it, about justice, the second, a utilitarian one. We examine the ethics of competition towards the end of this chapter.

CASE

TESCO: THE GIANT GORILLA

It is said that 1 pound in every 8 spent at British shops is spent at Tesco (Smith and Wood, 2008). This suggests that the British public identifies with Tesco.

But what is Tesco's responsibility record; specifically in relation to its treatment of national and international suppliers? And where does it stand in relation to competition? Are its powers monopolistic and therefore in this respect against the interests of the consumer? It is clear that these questions require some investigation.

Adam Leyland, the editor of *The Grocer*,

says that Tesco has 'suffered from being the 800lb gorilla that everyone likes to take a pop at' (Smith and Wood, 2008).

Questions

1 Is size by definition a problem in terms of responsibility practice? Does increased profitability suggest that an organisation is more exploitative?

2 Employing Leyland's gorilla metaphor, is it justified to view corporate giants as being somehow more irresponsible or more monstrous than smaller concerns?

3   Is Tesco a force for good, or not? What evidence could you provide in your answer?

4   Discuss your answers with a fellow student.

Andrew Simms (2007), author of *Tescopoly*, argues that Tesco – Britain's biggest and the world's third largest retailer (*The Independent*, 2011) – is having a negative impact, both locally and globally. In April 2008, following a two-year investigation into the supermarket sector, the Competition Commission – the UK Government's retail regulator – recommended much tougher rules to limit the growth of 'Tesco towns' – communities that are homogenised by the domination of one supermarket and which force many small retailers (including independent butchers and bakers) out of business. Tesco are one among many supermarkets that have a negative effect on the local community, including the phenomenon of landbanking. Landbanking involves buying up space that might be used for the development of stores. Of all the landbank space in the UK it is estimated that Tesco owns up to 55%. If all this were turned into stores it is estimated that it would represent 45% of all selling space in the UK (Townsend, 2006).

Turning attention from local to global, Simms presents a number of case studies that, he argues, show Tesco profiting from global poverty. This is largely through cutting down on global suppliers but making them dependent upon Tesco, and with the threat of loss of business driving down prices. Simms describes Tesco's overseas supply chain as a form of 'neo-colonialism', perpetuating a system of exploitation and injustice (Simms, 2007: 229), instanced by sourcing food from Zimbabwe at a time when the country was facing economic and political meltdown (*The Observer*, 2008). Tesco's trading relationship with a Zimbabwean mangetout farmer showed little concern about the working conditions and welfare of the farm's labour force and more concern for selecting the most 'inch-perfect' beans (Simms, 2007).

The following table summarises some of the arguments for and against the practice at Tesco.

For	Against
Tesco provides thousands of jobs and has an excellent employer record.	Tesco has a record of landbanking – buying up land near its stores to prevent competition.
It provides great choice and value for shoppers who want to buy a full range of goods under one roof and park free.	Tesco's phenomenal growth has driven local shops out of business and created so-called 'Tesco towns'.
Opening hours respond to the Western development of the 24-hour society.	Tesco's buying power pressurises suppliers who can be helpless in the face of late payments.
Price benefits arise from fierce competition between the supermarket giants. These particularly benefit those least able to afford higher prices. (See http://www.guardian.co.uk/business/ 2011/sep/21/tesco-price-war-threatens-supermarkets.)	Tesco's 'aircraft hanger' buildings are like most supermarkets a blot on the local landscape.
	Tesco's colonial exploitation of global southern suppliers adds to global injustice.
New buildings that innovatively meet environmental standards provide a centre for community.	See the DVD *Wal*Mart – The high cost of low price* (Tartan, 2006) for similar arguments about the effect of large corporations. Note its strongly affective tone.

The supply chain that Tesco is at the centre of extends back to the source of the firm's supplies and forward to its customers. How we relate to suppliers becomes a critical issue. It may involve relationships that are directly unethical, with suppliers in some way oppressed by another supplier or by the firm itself. This raises issues about reactive responsibility. Is the firm responsible for trying to address this issue? It also raises the question of proactive responsibility. Should the firm seek to influence the ethical behaviour of suppliers? In the Tesco case in 2007 this led to investors' seeking an external audit of the firm's practice (see http://www.telegraph.co.uk/finance/markets/ 2808987/Investor-puts-ethics-on-Tescos-agenda.html).

It is the supply chain that we examine first.

CHAIN-REACTION

A supply chain is a series of organisations (including suppliers, logistics providers and customers) linked by the flows of products, services, finances and information. Value for the end-customer can be created anywhere within the supply chain, highlighting the significance of strategic partnerships with suppliers, distributors and transporters. Business models often emphasise the importance of and potential for cost-saving throughout the supply chain. However, it is also the case that every link in the chain has the potential for adding broader value, particularly for the end-customer.

Supply chain management encompasses the planning and management of all activities connected to sourcing, procurement, conversion and logistics management. The customer is often not aware of the 'underworld' that exists to supply their demand for goods and services. There is considerable potential in this extended enterprise for responsibility and irresponsibility. Practice in the supply chain was effectively hidden until technological advancement and globalisation made it more accessible to public scrutiny. In consequence, the supply chain system must increasingly be responsive to what the public demands. Increasing significance thus falls on how goods are produced (resisting sweat-shop abuses), how far they are transported (concern with the carbon footprint) and how they can be ecologically consumed, recycled or disposed of (consciousness of landfill and scarce resources). Production, transportation and disposability represent three immediate dimensions for investigation when looking at a trader's supply chain responsibility record and practice. A more detailed approach is provided by the framework proposed by Maloni and Brown (2006) comprising eight dimensions that apply to the food industry:

- animal welfare
- biotechnology
- community
- environment
- fair trade
- health and safety
- procurement
- labour and human rights.

Although different sectors have differing, often unique, supply chains and supply chain issues, the framework can be usefully considered in its application to a range of industries. We introduce each of these dimensions in turn.

ANIMAL WELFARE

Animal welfare seeks to uphold humane approaches to the handling, accommodation, transportation and slaughter of animals, fully recognising that animals are sentient beings. Maloni and Brown (2006) report that animal welfare is increasing in significance, and that practices and regulations are more advanced in Europe, and especially in the UK, than in the USA. They cite the research findings of Schröder and McEachern (2004) to the effect that although consumers are concerned with animal welfare, they will not necessarily change their eating habits as a result. This relates to a disconnection between the consumption of meat and consciousness of the life and death of the animals that accompany that consumption.

CASE

'SUPER-DAIRY' AT NOCTON HEATH

In 2010 the proposal to build a 'super-dairy' at Nocton Heath, Lincolnshire, made the national press. Covering 22 acres/8.9 hectares, the eight buildings would keep 8,100 dairy cows mainly indoors and produce 24 million pints of milk a day (Blacker, 2010). This contrasted markedly with most dairy herds in the UK, which graze outdoors and number on average around 70 cows (*The Week*, 2011). Nocton Dairies said that the new dairy would meet the 'highest' animal welfare standards. Animal welfare groups opposed the proposal and argued that the intensive farming approach would give the cows a short lifespan. The proposal, they said, reflected the 'industrialisation of a traditionally pasture-based system' (BBC News, 2010). For them the 'super-diary' was closer to a factory than a farm. One of the farmers behind the proposal implied that the opposition were seeking to perpetuate a romantic notion of farming. 'Campaigners', he said, 'think cows should be like in the Anchor butter advert, with 50 or 100 cows dancing in a field. It is a lovely idea – but not the reality' (Blacker, 2010).

Campaigners won the day and the idea was shelved. However, the Nocton Heath case highlights a number of critical ethical issues all made clearer by the campaigners (notably The World Society for the Protection of Animals) and journalists. Firstly, Nocton was resisted but it is doubtful whether the industrialisation of agriculture can be halted. Such mega-farms are a response to global developments in livestock farming. *The Week* (2011) highlighted the relentless pressure of cheap imports and competing supermarkets between 1998 and 2008 that caused more than 14,000 dairy farmers (around 45% of the nation's total) to go out of business. Secondly, the industrialisation of agriculture relates to the increased demand for cheap meat, eggs and dairy products. Here the consumer as well as the supermarket and the farmer share responsibility. Thirdly, focusing on the animal welfare dimension of Nocton, from the perspective of the campaigners, the (proposed) lives of the few thousand cows have been protected, but what of the millions of creatures whose lives and welfare are not adequately protected, many being supplied from overseas farms that do not follow the UK's stringent standards?

Questions

1 Nocton Dairies promised that their development would bring money into the local community, not least through new jobs. How does that good balance with the effect on animal welfare on other farms?

2 Many scientists believe that a second agricultural revolution must take place if we are to feed a global population of 9 billion by 2050 (*The Week*, 2011). Can such global responsibility be reconciled with intensification approaches to farming?

3 Whose responsibility is animal welfare; and how can the welfare of farmed animals be better protected?

BIOTECHNOLOGY

Maloni and Brown (2006) report several anxieties about biodiversity practices, including cross-contamination; human safety problems associated with the ingestion of hormone, antibiotic and tranquilliser residuals; and the animal welfare issue of growth hormone effects on animals. The power of the sensitised consumer in this area is beginning to pressurise retailers to raise standards down the supply chain.

COMMUNITY

Community concerns, represented by a broad set of activities providing support for the local community, have for the most part not been applied to the supply chain. Although they include a spectrum of activities such as educational support, employee volunteering and support for culture and the arts, they primarily revolve around financial donations (see Chapter 11).

ENVIRONMENT

This is arguably the highest-profile dimension with respect to the food industry supply chain. The chain has many impacts on the environment. A number of issues have gained increasing consumer and industry attention, including food miles (the distance from farm to customer, and linked with fuel consumption), farming techniques, the application of agricultural chemicals (including pesticides and fertilisers), packaging, and preserving water and soil quality. The demand for organic foods – although a small segment of the overall food market – is growing. The supply of organic foods has presented a number of logistics challenges, including variable availability, higher prices, shorter shelf-life, lower yields and limited supply bases.

FAIR TRADE

Fair trade is focused in the justice of trading relationships, some shoppers opting to pay a little more for certain commodity products so that more money reaches the farmers who grow them. Like organic foods, fair trade products represent a small yet rapidly growing portion of UK grocery sales. Also as with organic foods, a number of challenges to penetration have emerged. These include reluctant and unaware consumers, a limited product range, fragmented supply sources and inadequate retail promotion. Nevertheless, in 2010 sales of fair trade products in the UK broke the £1 billion mark. This compared to £836 million the year before, and favourably compares to $1.2 billion in the United States (*The Independent*, 2011). The same source quotes research that every day (in 2010) Britons consumed 9.3 million cups of fair trade tea, 6.4 million cups of fair trade coffee, 2.3 million bars of fair trade chocolate and 3.1 million fair trade bananas.

A 2010 report by the Institute of Economic Affairs, *Fair Trade Without the Froth* (Mohan, 2010), attempted to assess the progress of fair trade and the difference it was making. Mohan concluded that although fair trade is doing some good, it is still small and accounts for a tiny 0.01 per cent of global food and beverage sales (Hickman, 2010). Smith (2010) indicates considerable variation in approaches to fair trade in terms of both scale and scope of commitment.

The Ethical Trading Initiative (ETI)

A good example of an organisation that audits fair trading is the ETI. This is an alliance of companies, trade unions and voluntary organisations working together to uphold international labour standards. Directed at participating companies, its seven key steps to protecting developing world workers (Blyth, 2007) convey what the organisation stands for:

- Accept that you have a responsibility.
- Sign up to the ETI Code of Conduct.
- Visit your suppliers to find out about existing labour conditions.
- Agree corrective actions with your suppliers and work with them to ensure that they happen.
- If you lack the leverage to persuade suppliers to act, team up with other buyers to present a unified front on the issue.
- Don't squeeze prices and don't always place orders at the last minute.
- Don't treat audits as a pass or fail exercise but as an opportunity for learning and improvement.

A number of points about the audit approach as part of an ethical sourcing programme should be made. First, it is an honourable, if imperfect, way to stem some classical abuses associated with sourcing consumer goods. Monitoring supplier practice through independent auditing safeguards against child labour (ensuring that there are no coerced workers), wage slaves (guarding against excessive working hours) and exploitative wages – insisting instead that suppliers pay a decent living wage.

Second, and related to this point, aside from stemming abuses such an approach is more likely to point suppliers in the direction of paying their workers enough to feed, house and educate their families as well as uphold sound environmental principles. This is the aim of ethical sourcing.

Third, the audit approach is no quick fix for the inadequacies and injustices associated with supply. Arnott (2008) argues that some of these issues are systemic and relate to business models that from an ethical perspective are problematic. She adds that 'Companies can't rely on a once-a-year audit', and that infrequent audits do not (and cannot) go far enough.

Fourth, the most effective approach is to persuade suppliers that responsible practices relating to labour and environmental issues are worthy of pursuit and, from an ethical perspective, desirable. This goes beyond minutely monitoring suppliers to establishing a partnership with the farmer or factory, such that producer and supplier alike look to add value (including ethical value) to the end-product.

The dynamic of this approach to ethical and fair trading increasingly takes a global perspective (see Chapter 13). It also focuses on responsibility rather than simply on human rights, trying to involve the members of the supply chain in the development of shared responsibility. An example of this is the case of Taylors.

TAYLORS OF HARROGATE

CASE

An example of a small to medium-sized company adopting an ethical sourcing policy is provided by Taylors of Harrogate, a tea and coffee merchant perhaps best known for its Yorkshire Tea brand. Founded in 1886, the Yorkshire-based family business has received two awards which recognise Taylors' commitment to trading fairly – the Queen's Award for Enterprise for Sustainable Development, and the Business in the Community Award 'Example of Excellence'. Taylors demonstrates responsible practice in a number of areas including:

- trading fairly and making a difference to the communities it works with overseas
- supporting the local community
- preserving traditional craft skills
- being a good place to work for its staff.

Ethical trading policy

The company's ethical sourcing policy, which Taylors refers to as its ethical trading policy, has two overarching priorities:

- the welfare of workers in the supply chain

- to ensure a sustainable environmental impact.

In relation to social responsibility Taylors states: 'Our business is committed to supporting growers and their communities ... It's only by forging strong trading relationships with our growers, and by paying them premium prices, that we can ensure a continued supply of the best teas and coffees. The price we pay means our farmers get a decent return for their crop and are able to reinvest in their business' (http://www.taylorsofharrogate.co.uk/ TradingFairlyHome.asp).

Taylors works with the Ethical Trading Initiative (see above) and the Ethical Tea Partnership – organisations that align themselves to the International Labour Organisation (ILO) Conventions on Labour and Human Rights, as well as certification schemes such as Fairtade, Rainforest Alliance and Utz Certified.

In respect of environmental responsibility, Taylors ensures sustainable practices on farms by requiring suppliers to develop an environmental management system (EMS). This is aimed at both reducing the environmental impact and managing the environmental aspects of its operations.

Certification schemes

Certification schemes are central to Taylors' strategy of driving sustainability improvements with their tea and coffee suppliers. Farms and estates are free to choose the certification scheme that best suits their business interests. In accordance with the principle of building mutually beneficial long-term relationships with growers, Taylors then assists suppliers in gaining certification and meeting the social and environmental criteria set out in the scheme. In cases where investment is required to improve social and/or environmental standards, suppliers may apply to Taylors for seed funding. Over time, producers that demonstrate commitment to continuous improvements

in such standards become preferred suppliers.

Sustainability projects

In addition to the company's ethical trading structure, a number of sustainability projects add to Taylors' responsibility record.

The Yorkshire Rainforest Project is pledged to save an area of threatened rain forest in Peru the size of Yorkshire (1.5 million hectares/3.7 million acres). Taylors works with the local Asháninka community and the Rainforest Foundation in the area in question.

Associated with Taylors' premium teabags, Yorkshire Gold, the company is also supporting tea farmers in Rwanda, a small Central African nation still recovering from inter-tribal genocide. Working with the British Government in an initiative to improve the lives of more than 10,000 farmers and their families, Taylors will be using a £249,000 grant to improve tea quality, achieve higher prices, lift living standards and protect the local environment.

On a smaller scale, the local project, the Starbeck Cone Exchange, based at Taylors, is designed to assist local schools and community groups to collect items that would otherwise go into landfill. Reading-glasses, mobile phones, inkjet cartridges, stamps, and foreign currency are all collected and donated to Oxfam, which convert these surplus items into money to support its work with some of the poorest communities in the world.

The varied nature of the above projects along with the various aspects of Taylors' practice as an ethical trader illustrate the significance of partnerships and how a business can work with a variety of stakeholders, both locally and further afield, to promote social and environmental sustainability.

The Taylors' programme not only works around developing shared responsibility, it also looks to develop standards – hence its emphasis to suppliers on environmental sustainability certification. But what happens if a supplier does not adhere to the standards which the business sets out? The firm of Hilti argues that this has to be addressed, and that codes of conduct are required.

HILTI: CODES OF CONDUCT FOR SUPPLIERS, FUNDAMENTALS FOR LONG-TERM RELATIONSHIPS

CASE

A variation on an ethical sourcing policy or Taylors' ethical trading policy is a code of conduct for suppliers, like the one formulated by Hilti, a major producer in the field of fastening and demolition systems, as utilised in the construction industry and allied trades. The Hilti code of conduct for suppliers (Hilti, 2008) is not aimed at global supply sources as such, but applies to all its suppliers. The bar for suppliers is a high one, and in certain aspects or for suppliers in certain countries sets standards that are higher than national and international law. What is more, these standards don't just apply to the Hilti supplier in question, but each supplier is required to enforce these standards with all its own suppliers.

As well as setting out high standards, the Hilti code reveals a comprehensive scope covering everything one would expect to find in an ethical sourcing policy targeted at global south farms and factories, and more. The opening and closing sections are noteworthy. The code is headed by a section on *Purpose and Values*. This states Hilti's core purpose as not only to create and enthuse Hilti customers, but also to 'build a better future'. Suppliers are specifically and carefully selected with this core purpose in view, and Hilti will 'support their development' so that they, like Hilti, can embrace responsibility towards the environment and society. The purpose of the code, Hilti (2008) states, is to 'make our position clear and explain what we expect from our suppliers with regard to their environmental and social performance'. The *Purpose and Values* opener also states that 'The way we do things at Hilti is based on living strong

values.' These are integrity, courage, teamwork and commitment. In reference to integrity, for example, Hilti maintains that 'We act with integrity in all we do.' The same is expected from Hilti suppliers.

The final section, *Non-compliance*, also spells out to suppliers how Hilti intends to operate. 'Repeated violations of these requirements will result in the termination of co-operation.' The paragraph continues: 'We are also prepared to take country or cultural differences and other relevant factors into consideration, but we will not compromise on the fundamental requirements described in this Code of Conduct for suppliers.' The section expresses Hilti's commitment to long-term supplier relationships. 'Hilti does not break off relations due to non-compliance only, as long as there is a willingness to improve in the right direction with an agreed plan of action to comply with our requirements within an acceptable time-frame.'

Questions

1 Examine the Hilti Code of Conduct for yourself: http://www.hilti.co.uk/fstore/holuk/LinkFiles/Code%20of%20conduct%20for%20suppliers.pdf.

2 What ethical theory is behind the code?

3 What are its strengths and weaknesses?

4 To improve it, how might you rewrite it on behalf of Hilti?

5 If you were a Hilti supplier, how would you view it?

6 Does size matter? What if you were a small business supplier having to take on such practices?

The two cases we have looked at in relation to their ethical sourcing involved large and small businesses. It is possible to work through these ethical issues, then, no matter what the size of the firm. What is key is a clear ethical sourcing policy that the firm can defend to its owners and to the wider society.

Ethical sourcing policy

A desirable corporate response to sustainability concerns, both environmental and social, is for businesses to follow the route of ethical sourcing. This has a number of dimensions, typically including:

- committing to ensuring that all products are produced ethically
- adopting an ethical sourcing policy
- requiring suppliers to be subject to independent auditing.

An ethical sourcing policy safeguards sustainability practices in a company's supply chain by guarding against suppliers' exploiting, sometimes abusing, their workers and compromising on environmental matters. The content of an ethical sourcing policy varies from company to company but it typically sets out principles on the following issues:

- the employment of appropriate workers
- no child labour
- no coerced workers
- reasonable pay and hours
- decent living wages
- the employment provided is regular
- safe and humane working conditions
- respect of worker rights to freedom of association and collective bargaining
- good environmental standards, involving an ethical sourcing policy that covers such things as:
  - the responsible use of agrochemicals
  - soil protection
  - protection against deforestation
  - the protection of biodiversity
  - water conservation
  - waste management.

To ensure some distance and criticality in monitoring suppliers' factories or farms, audits are best conducted by approved independent third-party auditors.

HEALTH AND SAFETY

In response to a foot-and-mouth scare in 2001 – fear of the dangerous nature of a disease calculated eventually as having infected 2,000 farm animals – to calm public fears, the UK government destroyed literally millions of animals (news.bbc.co.uk/2/hi/ science/ nature/1525066.stm). This highlighted the importance of identifying problems early in the supply chain and underlined the significance of the traceability of food.

An emerging issue is one of 'food security', the food supply presenting a target for biological, chemical or radiological attack by terrorists. This, according to Maloni and Brown (2006), presents a similar challenge to disease.

PROCUREMENT

Cooper *et al* (1997, 2000) have helpfully outlined means and challenges to operationalising ethical procurement practices. Ethical issues permeate the procurement process, particular problems surrounding preferential treatment and favouritism, allowing personalities to influence buying decisions, gifts and bribery, and cases of unlawful and unprofessional conduct.

LABOUR AND HUMAN RIGHTS

The health and safety of food industry workers is also a key issue, reflected in protective practices such as staff training, and regulations and measures when handling dangerous chemicals, during the operation of machinery and for field sanitation. Added to these considerations is upholding international labour standards with respect to collective bargaining, child and forced labour, compensation, grievances and discrimination. Maloni and Brown (2006) note that 75% of even the United States' 2.5 million farmworkers live in poverty and contend with poor working conditions, labour oversupply (due partly to labour migration) and strenuous, often dangerous, working demands. Other noteworthy issues in this area include the call for living wages, especially in the face of the cyclical pattern of temporary and seasonal employment in the sector, and the structural problem that increased prices will not necessarily be passed on to underpaid, overworked and, from a bargaining position, weak and underrepresented workforces.

Blowfield (2007) argues that current approaches to CSR overlook or exclude what is most important for many in the developing world. In practice, he argues, management issues are a result of conflicting cultural values, and a failure on the part of companies to appreciate that what are 'absolute' values for them are not universal and may even contradict the cultural norms or beliefs of supply chain operators (Blowfield, 2005; see also Roberts, 2003). One of the key areas in which this is put to the test is in child labour in developing nations.

Child labour

A case that looks at differences at the heart of global values is that of child labour. On the face of it this would be a good candidate for a universal ethical rule: that child labour is wrong. This is a view that led to vociferous arguments in the case of Nike (Murphy and Matthew, 2001).

The argument against child labour is simply that it is a form of exploitation. Behind this are two factors. Firstly, children should be in the education process. There is a universal right to education (article 26, Declaration of Human Rights). Secondly, children do not have any power and thus are unable to defend themselves against exploitation.

Against this is the view that this is placing a Western perception on childhood which is not shared in a different culture. In a culture of poverty it may be that all members of the family have to earn money for the family to survive. Indeed, it may be that such a culture sees it as a matter of honour and respect for the child to participate in making money for the family. In such a culture the idea of full-time education may not be critical, desirable or even available. Maitland (1997) argues that sweatshops enable families to enter the market. The returns for them may not be equal to Western 'fair wages' but they are significant in their context. He argues that opponents of sweatshop labour are allowing the perfect (Western wage rates) to be the enemy of the good.

It may be argued that the real difference here is not ethical. In both arguments there is a concern to respect the child. The difference is rather in the socio-economic context. But this only gives half the picture. Underlying this is the issue of the relationships between the wealthy developed world and the poor undeveloped world. In this case the developed world sees it as important to give opportunity to the child and has the means of ensuring that the average child in the developed world does have this right – a right that is enshrined in law. Philosophical rights then become legal rights that can be claimed. The non-developed world has neither the resources nor the legal framework necessary for universal education. The developed world also has the wealth and capacity to enable the non-developed world in this area. This raises the basic argument that if they can, they should help.

However, this brings us back to the question of who will do the helping. Business cannot take full responsibility for such issues. It can accept, with governments, a shared responsibility, and then work through the different ways in which such responsibility can be fulfilled. At the basic level it is incumbent upon the firm to be aware of any human rights that may be violated in the supply chain. It is equally important to know if human rights are being violated by stakeholders, including any government that the company is working with. In addition, the aspirational sense of human rights gives any company a framework around which responsibility can be negotiated in context.

In the light of such conflicting values, even if the principle against exploitation is seen as primary, there are real issues about how it might be embodied. So the complex debate involves several questions:

- Should *all* forms of child labour or the *worst* forms be the focus of efforts?
- What is the impact of child labour on adult employment and wages?
- Are work and school incompatible in the lives of children?
- What are the most effective strategies against harmful forms of child work – eg labour legislation, compulsory education, poverty reduction, social mobilisation?
- What are the pros and cons of consumer boycotts of or other sanctions against the products of child labour?
- Should children participate in decision-making processes, and if they should, how?
- What are the key alliances needed for effective policy implementation?
- What are the links between poor health, mortality and child labour, particularly in relation to HIV/AIDS? (For further considerations see the Overseas Development Institute Key Sheet on Child Labour: http://www.odi.org.uk/ resources/download/2307. pdf.)

Such a debate includes a concern for basic principles, such as the autonomy of the children, how different options will affect the different stakeholders, how the issue of child labour links to wider problems such as health and poverty, and how stakeholders, including governments, multinational corporations, non-governmental organisations and intermediate organisations might work together to take account of the different values and constraints. Human rights ideology has to take account of these different, often competing, values. This does not detract from fundamental principles, notably that children should not be exploited. It looks to the practice ethical decision-making (see Chapter 3) that will be able to identify different options, in a complex situation, which will both best embody the principle and enable supply-chain members to take responsibility for that.

SCENARIO

Your board of directors (at Nike) has asked you to draw up a policy and protocol in relation to child labour. This means that you have to work out your ethical position clearly and have ready a convincing form of words that can be used on the website.

Once you have done that, compare your work with arguments against the Nike practice at http://www.sourcewatch.org/index.php?title=Nike, and compare the present position of Nike on working conditions in the supply chain at http:// www. ikebiz.com/crreport/content/workers-and-factories/3-1-o-verview. php?cat=overview.

See below for further reflections on the case of Nike and sweatshops.

ETHICAL AWARENESS

Supply chain ethics inevitably emphasises the importance of developing the widest possible awareness and responsiveness. This puts a proactive stress on the first part of ethical decision-making, and increasingly it means that large firms rely on stakeholders to bring to light practices that are problematic. It therefore becomes important to work with stakeholders in gathering and assessing data. This also emphasises the interconnectedness of the different elements of the data, not least social and environmental issues. Sustainability encompasses both environmental and social issues, the argument being that for the survival or for the stability of future generations responsible action must be taken in both spheres. Environmental and societal matters of course interrelate. Irresponsibility in one of the spheres can cause problems in the other. For example, lack of protection for water resources would soon give rise to public health issues. Here environmental irresponsibility leads to social pressure. But it also works the other way around. The neglect of social issues – for example, obesity, reflecting the larger underlying socio-economic issue of over-consumption – has an environmental impact owing to the inflated demand for cheap food products, to supply the 'habit' of over-consumption. This means that social irresponsibility can lead to environmental pressures.

A number of current trends in ethical working reflect how stakeholder awareness of environmental sustainability concerns leads the way; and how they are connected essentially with social considerations. Firstly, sustainable fishing practices, now decreed by some supermarkets, reflect a wider consumer concern for environment-friendly commodities-sourcing. The gains made in this specific area, however, possibly also reflect an increased emphasis on healthy eating.

Secondly, the public consciousness relating to 'food miles' has at its heart environmental concern. Whereas at one time consumers would probably not have asked questions about how far the commodities they were consuming had travelled or what fossil-fuel resources were expended by the transporting of those commodities, the consumer is increasingly becoming sensitive to the issue of food miles. Can brands of bottled water originating 1,600 kilometres/1,000 miles or more from the consumer be justified from an environmental perspective when there are acceptable alternatives available involving significantly fewer food miles? And when will the same logic be applied to wine, in relation to which the 'new world' is a world of transport miles away? Part of the answer lies with the socio-economic

Figure 10.1 Elkington's stages of developing awareness

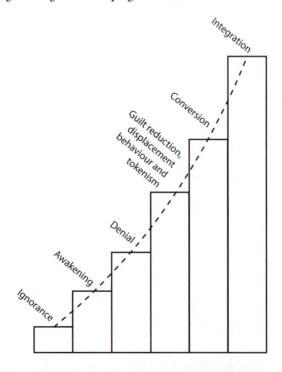

practice of free trade, upheld in a significant and profound way by the world's trading nations and its peoples.

Thirdly, and related, is the growing consumer interest in buying local food. Not only does this eliminate fuel-hungry transportation but it supports local agriculture and the local economy. Hence the resurgence of farmers' markets in village and church halls.

CASE · ITALY'S CO-OP RESISTS BOTTLED WATER

Italians have a taste for bottled water. The 11.4 billion litres/2.5 billion UK gallons/3 billion US gallons that they consume annually equates to 210 litres/46 UK gallons/55 US gallons per person per year. The cost of this over tap water is felt by the environment, which has to contend not only with the pollution caused by the plastic bottles but also with the transporting of the water over long distances. In response, Italy's biggest retailer CO-OP launched an advertising campaign to convince its customers to cut down on bottled water – or at least to buy water sourced more locally. Along with a television advert incorporating the message 'Drinking tap water pollutes less', CO-OP stores displayed maps illustrating the travel distances of bottled brands.

Not everybody welcomed the innovative campaign. Bottled water companies reminded CO-OP that the sector employs 40,000 people in Italy. Other opposition arose from a consumer group complaining that the campaign unfairly favoured CO-OP's own brand over alternative brands.

Source: adapted from PRI's *The World* programme by M. Williams (2010)

Questions

1 Sometimes products and services that have a negative effect on the environment keep many people in employment. How would you critically respond to that dilemma?

2 Despite the CO-OP's ethical stance, it evidently also stocks its own brand of bottled water. If this is true, does it matter so long as food miles are reduced?

3 Lynas (2007) writes in the *Guardian*, 'Once upon a time, cherries came from Kent, and apples from the Vale of Evesham. Now cherries come from Turkey, and apples from New Zealand or Chile. Supermarkets may talk about localism, but their entire business model precludes them from adopting it.' In the light of consumer demands, what would a different business model look like?

EXTENDING ETHICAL AWARENESS

The Taylors case study (above) illustrates what can be achieved when a business operates out of some measure of ethical awareness. The degree of ethical awareness – that is, the level of conscious appreciation by an organisation of ethical concerns – can be detected in three areas. Firstly, it is seen in whether and to what degree the organisation knows what it stands for and knows what is its purpose, particularly from an ethical perspective. Secondly, it is demonstrated in an awareness of the social and physical environment, central to which is the firm's supply chain. This demands clarity about both the social and environmental values of the different parts of the chain. Without an awareness of the different, often conflicting, values it is difficult to achieve real focus on the chain. The values reveal the significance of the chain. In other words, there is no value-neutral way to perceive this complex web of relationships – something that became clear to Nike, as we note below. Thirdly, without this deeper awareness of the supply chain it is difficult to know how to respond to the ethical environment. This awareness has a utilitarian element, enabling a firm to work through the implications and consequences of values and value conflicts (see Chapter 3), and to work through the responsibility of the firm in that situation.

Proactive responsibility takes it upon itself to set up mechanisms to maintain the highest level of awareness, such as working closely with stakeholders, including NGOs. It is precisely because of its awareness of the value issues that ensures that the responsibility response of any firm is not cosmetic. This reinforces and develops King III's argument for all stakeholders as the ultimate regulators (Chapter 5) to the idea of the stakeholders as those who share responsibility, in this case, for awareness. Key to the involvement of the supply chain in the development of responsibility is involving them in decision-making, from decisions about what to buy to decisions about partnerships and collaboration. All this suggests that responsibility is directly connected to awareness. Further, effective negotiation of responsibility cannot be achieved without such levels of awareness.

 PAUSE FOR THOUGHT

The growth of awareness

Elkington (1994) provides a vocabulary and some useful scales that can be applied to the idea of ethical awareness and its development. He suggests first that Western industrial societies have undergone a growth of awareness – consisting of a number of stages and stretching over several decades – as the scale of the environmental and natural resource problems has become increasingly clear. These have involved stages of: ignorance; awakening; denial; guilt reduction, displacement behaviour and tokenism; conversion; and integration of this awareness into practice (see Figure 10.1).

At another level, Elkington refers to the gradual 'greening' of the average citizen, produced from a longitudinal survey tracking public opinion on environmental attitudes in 22 countries. Between the early 1980s and the early 1990s the journey of key trends included 'a green minority', 'a green concern', 'the green bandwagon' to 'the ethical consumer'.

In a final scale he argues that there is has been a development from involuntary forms of environmental disclosure (eg whistleblowing, press and media exposé), through mandatory forms (eg annual reports and accounts, disclosure of environmental information) to voluntary forms (eg eco-audits, advertised availability of eco-information).

Such an evolution can only be developed and sustained through the conscious practice of responsibility.

What is the evidence for Elkington's view?

Lucy Siegle on the 'fashion mountain' and supply chain

A good example of the gradual development of awareness of the ethical nature of the supply chain is provided by the fashion industry. On 25 May 2011 BBC Radio 4's *Women's Hour* (http://www.bbc.co.uk/programmes/b011c220) profiled a new book by journalist Lucy Siegle, *To Die For*, and invited both Siegle and the fashion mogul Jeff Banks to discuss the issues of ethics and fashion. *To Die For* investigates the environmental and social footprint of the enormous and increasing demand for 'fast' fashion, and concludes that it has become ethically unsustainable. The human cost is exemplified by the harsh exploitation and physical exhaustion of female garment workers in factories across Bangladesh and Cambodia. The cost to the environment is borne by such things as waterways polluted by the fabric dye and leather-tanning fluids. The issue is heightened by the disposable attitude Western buyers adopt toward fashion items. Siegle argues that fashion has become so expendable it can be likened to litter.

Siegle made the point that 'Fashion is very good at distancing itself from the origins' (BBC Radio 4, 2011; see also http://www.bbc.co.uk/search/tvandradiosites/lucy_siegle for a recording of another discussion on green fashion).

This suggests that the fashion industry as a whole and the consumer have colluded in avoiding awareness of the 'value chain'.

REFLECTIVE PRACTICE

Listen to the 25 May debate.

What evidence is there to back up Siegle's argument?

Assess the response from Banks. How does he perceive the value chain and the responsibility of the fashion industry?

Banks at one point argues that the fashion industry is like any other global industry and has to make a profit through trade. Is this an effective ethical argument? If not, why not?

What causes a lack of awareness of the supply chain and related values issues?

The fashion debate raises the question of what prevents awareness of the supply chain. At this point we offer a brief summary of factors raised in the book so far:

- an intentionally positivist view of the social environment that focuses on a scientific understanding of relationships (see Chapter 4) and simply does not take account of values
- a narrowing of purpose that focuses only on successful business enterprise (see Freidman). Both of these radically affect what the firm sees as significant. It could be argued that in neither of these is the firm intending to harm groups in the supply chain. Nonetheless, such stances can lead to the denial of responsibility, both reactive and proactive
- a lack of resources to respond, and the priority of having an organisation (with all the connected personnel and families) to maintain
- the intentional pursuit of greed (see Chapter 4). This is characterised by viewing the supply chain as a means to the end of wealth accumulation. In Kantian terms all respect for the chain and for the people in it is lost.

Elkington's developmental view of awareness involves working through different degrees of these obstructions. In the light of that it is easy to see why some industries struggle, working from denial of reality, to denial of responsibility, to attempts to deal with value conflicts and the related sense of dissonance.

DISSONANCE

Increased awareness leads to value dissonance. The second stage of the ethical decision-making framework (in Chapter 3) involved working with value conflicts. Such conflicts cause the person or the firm to question data and values, and often lead to a sense of dissonance or disharmony. The process is not a simply intellectual one, and can be strongly emotional, not least because it might question values felt to be associated with the identity of the organisation. It is this which can lead to attempts to distance the self or organisation from the clash, as suggested by Siegle, amounting to a form of denial. Festinger's theory of cognitive dissonance suggests that an individual strives toward consistency within himself or herself. His basic hypothesis (Festinger, 1957) is twofold:

- The existence of dissonance (or inconsistency) creates felt discomfort and will motivate an individual to try to reduce the dissonance and achieve consonance (consistency).
- When dissonance occurs, in addition to trying to reduce it, an individual will actively avoid situations and information that is likely to increase the dissonance.

In other words, when faced with dissonance, something has to give. The individual either reconsiders his or her former practice or thinking or by some device denies or blocks out the new information.

NIKE: 'VICTORY' DEIFIED

A good example of dissonance is the Nike sweatshop case. Nike Inc. is a worldwide producer of sports footwear, clothing and equipment. Most of its products are manufactured by independent contractors. Much of its footwear is produced in developing countries. In the 1990s NGOs noted that 85% of the workforce in Indonesia was female, and that over 30% of the workforce had suffered verbal or physical abuse. More broadly, there were accusations of low wages and poor working conditions. One commentator also accused Nike of abandoning countries who were developing improved conditions and pay in favour of countries such as China, where production costs were low.

Nike put remedial action into effect. This included attempts to develop increased transparency through working with NGOs. The debate with other NGOs is ongoing (see above for websites), with the claim of ongoing value conflict.

The strength of this can be seen simply by looking at the ideas, values and feelings associated with the case. Nike and its products are associated with:

- sport and health – By extension these are associated with personal and collective well-being and happiness. This reaches its ultimate values in Nike's long association with the Olympic Games. The Olympics have their own set of global values, focused in peacebuilding and equality (Parry, 2007). This stands in profound dissonance with working conditions across the globe that contribute to chronic ill-health, low age of mortality and massive inequality across gender, age and culture.

- individual success – Sports apparel is partly aimed at increasing the chances of success. This success is costly. A pair of running shoes can cost over £100. Individual success as a value

contrasts sharply with the global scale of collective poverty and oppression in sweatshops. The value of success in terms of winning in sport even resonates with the name of the firm Nike – an ancient Greek goddess symbolising victory.

- individual success and associated glory, as focused in the marketing images of Nike – The financial success of the firm is thus tied to such images and related values. Moreover, the customer becomes associated with such values – and by extension with the dissonance that comes from the conflict between the values.

Four things are key to this analysis. Firstly, until the 1990s Nike was not simply unaware of the conditions in their supply chain, it was unaware of the values, and especially the conflicting values. As noted in Chapter 4, the company's perspective was purely about shareholder value and the related values that would maintain it. Secondly, although the initial response was focused in the effect on shares, an effective response required an awareness of values which characterised the situation. Indeed, Nike only became fully aware of its supply-chain data when it experienced the dissonance of value conflict shown to them by the NGOs.

Thirdly, there was genuine emotional depth to the value conflict and the associated dissonance. Partly, this was associated with issues of justice and fairness. Partly, it involved the strong sense of incongruity aroused by the realisation that high values such as peace and health could be based on means that were exactly contrary. Partly, the conflict was associated with identity – the identity of the corporation and of the customer, neither of whom wished to be associated with such a conflict. Dissonance can be felt most strongly when associated with self- or organisational image, understanding and worth.

Fourthly, these dynamics begin to account for why Nike and debates about similar cases find it hard to achieve closure, even after a long period of time. It is partly about the long process of regaining trust, but also in some cases about the unresolved emotional element of the ethical reflection.

SCENARIO

You are the new head of marketing at Nike, and are co-leading the team bidding to sponsor the 2016 Olympics. You have been asked to work with the head of corporate responsibility (a student colleague) to make sure that any ethical issues are worked through in the bid, so that the Olympic Committee can be clear that the event will not be overshadowed by any other ethical crises. You begin with an analysis of the Nike CSR report http://www.nikebiz.com/crreport/content/pdf/documents/en-US/full-report.pdf.

In the light of the above discussion, what criteria would you use to analyse this? Would you modify it in any way? If so, how? With your corporate responsibility colleague write a commentary (one side of A4) that sums up the core message of the policy (values, purpose, history and response) that you would communicate to the Olympic Committee.

At the same time, the chair of the board has asked for advice about presenting the image of the firm in the 2012 Olympics. Should the main web page and any adverts try to present an image of integrity? If so, how? What strategy would you recommend for responding to any crises that may come up during the 2012 Olympics?

Refer to the ethical tools in the first four chapters.

THE ETHICS OF COMPETITION

In any map of stakeholders, competing firms are important. In many cases, how competitors work together can affect broader social responsibility and particular supply-chain issues. Thus, if the industry as a whole was to work to respond to supply-chain problems, it would be more effective (Robinson and Kenyon, 2009). We begin this reflection on competition, however, by examining the ethical nature of the concept itself.

At the outset it is important to make the distinction (Pharo, 2005) between producer competition and consumer competition, which together form the basis of economic life. Producer competition is directly linked to the development of trade, and the best profit possible. Consumer competition, on the other hand, is focused around access to goods that are necessary for a decent and full human life which, as Pharo highlights, includes not only survival goods such as food, shelter and medical care, but also basic freedoms and education. We shall be focusing here on producer competition, although it is worth highlighting that both forms of competition, which together lie at the heart of capitalism, are essentially about enrichment as an end in itself.

The profit motive behind producer competition is clear. However, there is, in fact, no agreed and accepted understanding of the concept of profit (Child, 1998). For supporters of capitalism 'profit' has strongly positive connotations, whereas to its critics it is a strongly pejorative term (Gaus, 2010). Capitalism's most famous critic, Karl Marx (1818–1893), argued that it was built on injustice. What Marx called his theory of surplus is the gap between the amount the worker (termed 'the labourer') gets paid and the value of the worker's work. This is brought out very vividly by Ian Markham, who writes (Markham, 2007: 106):

> So when a person starts work at a factory at 9am in the morning, he/she has probably earned his/her day's salary by 10am. For the next few hours, he/she might be covering the cost of the materials and infrastructure that enables him/her to work. However, for the last five hours, he/she isn't getting paid for his/her labour. This is the surplus value ... The capitalist will be claiming this as 'profit'.

It could be argued, therefore, that producer competition and the quest for profit drives the producer to minimise costs and leads to injustice.

However, as Markham notes, capitalism has its roots in an ethical worldview and actually depends on ethics (Markham, 2007). Max Weber (1864–1920) famously made the case that capitalism was a child of Calvinism. This supported the industrious 'Protestant work ethic' and the emergent notion that work was a legitimate sphere by and in which to glorify God.

This positive view of capitalism moves to the arguments that competition leads to more employment and greater wealth that may be well distributed. It also produces progress in the form of technological advancement and innovation. Competition drives producers to make improvements in production processes and the end-product presented to consumers, all fuelled by the profit motive. Allied to this argument is the viewpoint that competition produces efficiency, and certainly greater efficiency than publicly provided goods and services (Gaus, 2010; Wolff, 1994). There is thus the debate in the UK about whether more competition in healthcare will lead to better stewardship of healthcare resources and improved standards of care (see below). At the heart of this is the underlying worldview that competition enables greater choice and that greater freedom of choice is a basic value.

REFLECTIVE PRACTICE

Go to the NHS Future Forum Report on Choice and Competition: http://www.dh.gov.uk/ prod_consum_dh/groups/dh_digitalassets/documents/digitalasset/dh_127541.pdf.

Does this provide a convincing view of choice and competition in the health services?

Why is choice so important for the ordinary consumer?

Why is choice important for a patient?

SCENARIO

As the chair of the local Chamber of Commerce you have been invited to speak to local politicians about the importance of choice and competition. What would be your three main arguments, and what evidence would you provide for them?

COUNTER-COMPETITION

Counter-arguments are made by Shleifer (2004), who suggests that a number of high-profile unethical phenomena are a direct consequence of competition. These include child labour, corruption, excessive executive pay, corporate earnings manipulation, and the involvement of universities in commercial activities.

Shleifer (2004) argues that in all but the last of his examples that censured behaviour reduces producer costs. This is true of child labour where the pressures of competition bring children into the labour force. As long as hiring children is cheaper than hiring adults, and therefore promises reduced costs, it will be attractive to producers, particularly in nations that do not adequately protect against child employment. Corruption comes in two forms – with theft, and without theft. In both cases the keener the competition, Shleifer (2004) argues, the higher is the pressure to reduce costs, and the more pervasive is corruption. An illustration of this is the intense competition in certain countries for government jobs, which makes for the bribery and corruption associated with senior officials' effectively auctioning off sought-after government posts. A final example from Shleifer (2004) is the increasing commercialisation of universities expressed in their pursuit of research purely for commercial reasons and the emerging commercial competition for students. This commercialisation has the danger of undermining the core missions of research and teaching in universities.

Most of these arguments are utilitarian in nature in that they focus on the consequences of producer competition. However, as we noted in Chapter 2, utilitarian arguments do not provide the answer to what actually is the good. The core of this ethical debate therefore comes down to the question of choice and of purpose.

THE ETHICS OF CHOICE

The ethics of choice brings us back to the issue of freedom and whether freedom of choice is sufficient. The simple proffering of more than one option does not of itself provide an ethical value. It offers self-governance, but not necessarily the capacity to choose wisely – that is, to understand the context, value and reason for making the choice. The argument that has been developed through this book is that although choice is a necessary freedom (partly involving respect for the other and partly giving power to the other – so it can be seen as involving negative freedom: freedom from attempts to make choices for us), it is not sufficient. The exercise of choice also requires the three modes of responsibility outlined in Chapter 4, without which the significance of the choice and how it affects one's environment cannot be really determined. In this respect choice involves a capacity as much as a right, and significant choice requires critical dialogue.

This suggests that competition and choice require a framework which enables the practice of responsibility, organisationally and individually.

Importantly, a key part of the exercise of responsible judgement (which is precisely what many groups argue should be encouraged in consumer behaviour – see Chapter 9) is reflection on purpose and the underlying good. This brings the debate about choice back to the virtues and especially the virtue of *phronēsis* (practical wisdom – see Chapter 2). In the debate about competition in the NHS there is a strong view that the focus on competence excludes the core practice of care. It is argued that recent negative reports on care of the elderly (http://www.dh.gov.uk/en/MediaCentre/Statements/ DH_127233; http://www.telegraph.co.uk/health/healthnews/8824539/Hospital-staff-should-have-respect-for-the-elderly.html0) reveal a lack of practical wisdom, such that staff are focusing not on care but on targets and how they can measure efficiency. It is therefore argued that an unrestrained focus on competition would make that worse.

CONCLUSION

In our investigation into supply chain management and competition and its accompanying issues a number of key themes have emerged.

First, ethical supply-chain management for large corporations is complex simply because of its extent. It relates closely to the wider issues of social responsibility and global ethics – as we shall see in the next chapters.

Second, there are several categories of supply chain issues, and these involve at least three different perspectives:

- immediate issues of how a firm relates to a group or person in the supply chain. This might involve decisions as simple as paying supplier bills on time (see the Tesco case)
- wider issues that might be either common to the industry sector as a whole or relate to whole sectors down the supply chain (see the Nike case)
- global issues in which there is a concern to develop justice and sustainability. These are examined more closely in the final chapters.

Third, the chapter has shown that this is an important ethical area for small (see the Taylors case) and large firms, involving at different times reactive and proactive responsibility.

Fourth, the chapter has shown that key to managing the supply chain is the development of the ethical decision-making framework, focusing on the development of awareness, the analysis of conflicting values, the establishing of fundamental values (see the paragraphs on child labour) and the negotiating of shared responsibility.

Fifth, the chapter suggests that this more than a cognitive exercise, demanding attention to the underlying emotional response to values, value conflict and the resulting dissonance.

Finally, the chapter examined the ethical nature of competition and the importance of holding this together with shared responsibility.

EXPLORE FURTHER

Books

Jamison, L. and Murdoch, H. (2004) *Taking the Temperature: Ethical supply chain management*. London: Institute of Business Ethics.

Maloni, M. J. and Brown, M. E. (2006) 'Corporate social responsibility in the supply chain: an application in the food industry', *Journal of Business Ethics*, 68: 35–52.

DVDs

Food Inc (2009, Dogwoof), for a searching view of the US food industry and supply chains.

REFERENCES

ANDERSON, H. (2011) 'An ethics girl goes on the warpath: *To Die For* – is fashion wearing out the world?', *The Observer*, 12 June: 36.

ARNOTT, S. (2008) 'Primark drops three Indian suppliers for using child workers', *The Independent*, 17 June: 34.

BBC NEWS (2010) 'Super-dairy' cow welfare fears. Available at: http://newsvote.bbc. co.uk/mpapps/pagetools/print/news.bbc.co.uk/1/hi/england/lincol.

BBC RADIO 4 (2011) 'The ethics of fashion', *Women's Hour*, 25 May.

BLACKER, T. (2010) 'Factory farms, welfare and a load of bull', *The Independent*, 3 March.

BLOWFIELD, M. E. (2005) 'Operations and supply chain management going global: how to identify and manage societal expectations in supply chains (and the consequences of failure)', *Corporate Governance*, 5(3): 119–28.

BLOWFIELD, M. E. (2007) 'Reasons to be cheerful? What we know about CSR's impact', *Third World Quarterly*, 28(4): 683–95.

BLYTH, A. (2007) 'Ethical trading', *Retail Week*, 2 March.

CHILD, J. W. (1998) 'Profit: the concept and its moral features', *Social Philosophy and Policy*, 15: 243ff.

COOPER, R. W., FRANK, G. L. and KEMP, R. A. (1997) 'The ethical environment facing the profession of purchasing and materials management', *International Journal of Purchasing and Materials Management*, 33(2): 2–11.

COOPER, R. W., FRANK, G. L. and KEMP, R. A. (2000) 'A multinational comparison of key ethical issues, helps and challenges in the purchasing and supply management profession: the key implications for business and the professions', *Journal of Business Ethics*, 23(1): 83–100.

ELKINGTON, J. (1994) 'Towards the sustainable corporation: win-win-win business strategies for sustainable development', *California Management Review*, Autumn.

FESTINGER, L. (1957) *A Theory of Cognitive Dissonance*. Palo Alto, CA: Stanford University Press.

GAUS, G. (2010) 'The idea and ideal of capitalism', in Brenkert, G. G. and Beauchamp, T. L., *The Oxford Handbook of Business Ethics*. Oxford: Oxford University Press.

HICKMAN, M. (2010) 'Let's be fair to Fairtrade: it can reduce poverty', *The Independent*, 6 November: 68.

HILDEBRANDT, A. (2008) 'Good is cool: the new green movement is changing the economy', *ChangeXPartnerforum*, 28 March.

HILTI (2008) Code of conduct for suppliers: Overview: http://www.hilti.co.uk/fstore/holuk/LinkFiles/Code%20of%20conduct%20for%20suppliers.pdf [accessed 14 May 2011].

HOWKER, E. (2009) 'Is Tesco now too powerful in Britain, and can its growth ever be checked?', *The Independent*, 5 March: 34.

THE INDEPENDENT (2011) 'Fairtrade market experiencing explosive growth in UK and US', 16 June.

IN-STORE MARKETING (2007) 'Market report: shift to neutral', 8 October.

KLEIN, N. (2000) *No Logo*. London, Flamingo.

LYNAS, M. (2007) 'Can shopping save the planet?' *The Guardian*, G2, 17 September: 4.

MAITLAND, I. (1997) 'The great non-debate over international sweatshops', British Academy of Management Annual Conference Proceedings: 240–65.

MALONI, M. J. and BROWN, M. E. (2006) 'Corporate social responsibility in the supply chain: an application in the food industry', *Journal of Business Ethics*, 68: 35–52.

MARKHAM, I. S. (2007) *Do morals matter? A guide to contemporary religious ethics*. Oxford: Blackwell.

MOHAN, S. (2010) 'Fair trade without the froth', London, Institute of Economic Affairs; available at: http://www.iea.org.uk/sites/default/files/publications/files/ upldbooks524pdf.pdf [accessed 24 September 2011].

MURPHY, D. and MATHEW, D. (2001) 'Nike and global labour practices', a case study prepared for the New Academy of Business Innovation Network for Socially Responsible Business.

PARRY, J. (2007) 'The "religio athletae", Olympism and peace', in Parry, J., Robinson, S., Nesti, M. and Watson, N. (eds) *Spirituality and Sport*. London: Routledge: 201–14.

PHARO, P. (2005) 'The ethics of competition', *International Social Science Journal*, 57(185): 445–55. Oxford: Blackwell.

QUINN, D. (2007) 'The Leahy defence', *Estates Gazette*, 31 March.

RISH, G. (2011) 'Wardrobes of mass destruction', *Hobart Mercury*, 15 July: 24.

ROBERTS, S. (2003) 'Supply chain specific? Understanding the patchy success of ethical sourcing initiatives', *Journal of Business Ethics*, 44: 159–70.

ROBINSON, S. and KENYON, A. (2009) *Ethics and the Alcohol Industry*. Basingstoke: Palgrave.

ROEHRIG, L. (2011) 'The rise of the locavore', *Library Journal*, 1 April: 53.

SAWCHUK, K. (2000) 'No logo: taking aim at the brand bullies', *Canadian Journal of Communication*, September: 25.

SCHLOSSER, E. (2002) *Fast Food Nation: What the all-American meal is doing to the world*. London: Penguin.

SCHRÖDER, M. J. A. and McEACHERN, M. G.(2004) 'Consumer value conflicts surrounding ethical food purchase decisions: a focus on animal welfare', *International Journal of Consumer Studies*, 28(2): 168–77.

SHLEIFER, A. (2004) 'Does competition destroy ethical behavior?', *American Economic Review*, 94(2): 414–18.

SIEGLE, L. (2011) *To Die For: Is fashion wearing out the world?* London: Fourth Estate.

SIMMS, A. (2007) *Tescopoly: How one shop came out on top and why it matters*. London: Constable & Robinson.

SMITH, D. AND WOOD, Z. (2008) 'Are we falling out of love with Tesco?' *The Observer*, 29 June: 24.

SMITH, S. (2010) 'For love or money? Fairtrade business models in the UK supermarket sector', *Journal of Business Ethics*, 92: 257–66.

THOMPSON, J. (2011) 'The unassuming empire-builder', *The Independent*, 26 February: 48.

TOWNSEND, A. (2006) 'Tesco owns more than half the unbuilt UK supermarket sites', *The Observer*, 12 March.

THE WEEK (2011) 'Mega-farms of the future', 16 July.

WILLIAMS, M. (2010) 'Italy's campaign against bottled water', PRI's *The World*, available at: http://www.theworld.org/2010/12/italys-campaign-against-bottled-water.

WOLFF, C. (1994) *Markets or Governments: The choice between imperfect alternatives*. Cambridge, MA: MIT Press.

CHAPTER 11

Social Responsibility

LEARNING OUTCOMES

When you have completed this chapter you will be able to:

- understand some key ideas, including corporate social responsibility (CSR) and corporate citizenship

- benefit from an overview of CSR policy and practice through an examination of the practice of Aviva

- understand and critically analyse the responsibility of stakeholders, focusing on shareholders and NGOs

- understand and critically analyse CSR in small and medium-sized enterprises (SMEs).

INTRODUCTION

Corporate social responsibility is not a new concept. For instance, Rowntree – now owned by Nestlé – have been makers of confectionery and cakes since 1725, and have a long history of care for employees and for the wider community.

ROWNTREE IN THE EARLY TWENTIETH CENTURY

CASE

1904 The company appoints a dentist and a doctor.

1904 A model village for the workers is developed.

1906 A pension scheme is made available to all employees.

1909 Yearsley Swimming Bath is given by the company to the City of York.

1913 Dining facilities for 3,000 employees are built.

1916 One of the first Widows' Benefits Funds is established.

1916–18 Works Councils are created,

developing democracy at work. Profit-sharing is introduced at about the same time.

1921 An unemployment scheme is introduced.

Throughout this time community involvement with schools, the local mental hospital and other local institutions was seen as a key part of the senior manager's role.

Rowntree had a strong sense of identity, and pride, as part of the local community. Accordingly, they wanted the community to understand the role, purpose and values of the business. They did not have to develop a corporate social responsibility policy because it was not regarded as a separate aspect of management. Rowntree were also part of a Quaker tradition that involved social activism.

The first decades of the twentieth century were a time when there was limited concern for social care on the part of the government. Not until the 1940s, and the Welfare State, did the UK government begin to take a fuller responsibility for health and social care. In the 1960s and 1970s business came under increased scrutiny in the areas of equal opportunities and health and safety at work. This led to the establishing of legal standards (Reed, 1999), which have been a continuing feature of the defining of corporate social responsibility. Public concern for how business relates to society emerged strongly at the end of the twentieth and the beginning of the twenty-first centuries following the various business scandals such as Enron and pressure from increasingly vociferous NGOs (Moeller and Erdal, 2003: 3–4; Zadek, 2001).

This chapter explores the meaning and practice of corporate social responsibility. It first examines the meaning of social responsibility, giving an example of the policy of Aviva. Then it scrutinises the arguments against the wider view of corporate responsibility, and views based in stakeholder theory, before looking at shareholder and NGO responsibility, and responsibility in SMEs. It ends with the hard case of the tobacco industry and CSR.

CORPORATE SOCIAL RESPONSIBILITY

A simple definition of corporate social responsibility is (European Commission 2001: 366):

> Companies' integrating social and environmental concerns in their daily business operations and in their interactions with their stakeholders on a daily basis.

This takes CSR away from simply a concern with philanthropy (charitable giving) to an integrated view that includes responsibility for the social and physical environment, and stakeholders inside and outside the business. Carroll (1991) therefore suggests that there are several interconnected layers of corporate responsibility: economic, legal, ethical and philanthropic.

- An economic responsibility towards shareholders is to provide reasonable returns on shareholders' investments. Economic and financial gain is the primary objective of a corporation in a business sense and is the foundation upon which all the other responsibilities rest.
- At the same time businesses are expected to comply with the laws and regulations as the ground rules and legal framework under and within which they must operate. A company's legal responsibilities are seen as coexisting with economic responsibilities as fundamental precepts of the free enterprise system. Such regulation focuses on issues such as health and safety and environmental care.
- Ethical responsibilities within a corporation ensure that the organisation performs in a manner consistent with expectations of ethics in society. Good corporate citizenship is defined as doing what is expected ethically, and it is important to recognise and respect new or evolving ethical trends adopted by society. It must be noted that the corporate integrity and ethical behaviour of a company go beyond mere compliance with laws and regulations, entailing the obligation to do what is right and fair, and to avoid harm.
- Philanthropic responsibilities include corporate actions that are in response to society's expectation that businesses be good corporate citizens involved in activities or programmes to promote human welfare or goodwill. Philanthropy – literally 'love of fellow humans' – is highly desired by society, although it is not ultimately necessary.

Carroll's view is comprehensive and usefully brings together different views of corporate responsibility. However, we are still left with some difficult questions. Firstly, although the primary aim of a business may not be to promote human welfare, it is responsible for the effects it has on the social and physical environment. Accordingly, as we examine more closely in Chapters 12 and 13, it has to be aware of any actions that lead, for instance, to the abuse of human rights.

Secondly, citizenship is not the same as philanthropy. Andriof and McIntosh define corporate citizenship as 'understanding and managing a company's wider influences on society for the benefit of the company and society as a whole' (2001). Indeed, the very term 'citizenship' refers to the civic or social responsibility of the person or corporation. It involves both fulfilling legal obligations, including paying taxes and complying with health and safety legislation (Carroll, 1991), and working reactively and proactively in the community. Civic responsibility in this is less a matter of doing things out of kindness and more a matter of recognising responsibilities to society. Reactive responsibility involves dealing with negative effects on society. Proactive responsibility involves planning for positive effects in the community. At the heart of social responsibility are thus the simple principles of non-maleficence (first do no harm) and beneficence (seek to do good). These are the basics of how any corporation relates to society and can hardly be considered optional.

Thirdly, Carroll's view places too much weight on 'corporate' and not enough on 'responsibility'. He does not develop the full meaning of responsibility in the way we detailed in Chapter 4. He therefore does not show how critical agency, awareness of the social and physical environment, accountability and liability relate to each other or to practice. So the different levels of responsibility are not connected.

Figure 11.1 Carroll's levels of corporate social responsibility

PHILANTHROPIC
Desirable – a response to society's expectations

ETHICAL
Expected – to do what is regarded as 'ethical'

LEGAL
Fundamental – to comply

ECONOMIC
Foundational and necessary – primary objective of a company

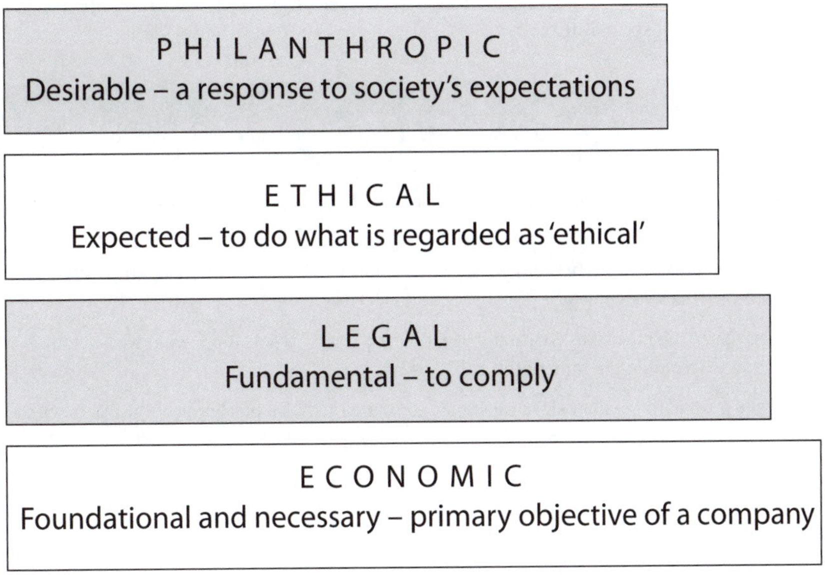

A more integrated and responsive view of CSR is summed up in the CSR policy of Aviva, the world's fifth-largest insurance group. The policy (see http://www.aviva.com/corporate-responsibility/) aims to develop a proactive response to the social and physical environment. It begins with some core values:

> At Aviva we believe that corporate responsibility means taking positive action, treating our colleagues, customers and suppliers with respect, applying consistently high standards in everything we do and having a constructive role in the communities in which we operate. Our vision and strategy for CR is aligned to the company strategy and informed by stakeholder analysis, to make sure that we meet their needs, from our employees and customers to our shareholders and investors.

These values generate a policy that covers standards of business conduct, customers, human rights, the workforce, health and safety, the suppliers, the community and the environment.

ANALYSIS

Aviva's approach involves several elements:

- a holistic and integrated viewpoint that sees CSR as encompassing all stakeholders, including employees, thus not confining the response to a narrowly defined 'society'
- the inclusion of stakeholders, and in particular, customers, in dialogue and planning
- a transparent framework that includes monitoring and regular reporting
- staff development that seeks to communicate core standards across the group – this is particularly important in the light of the multinational nature of the group
- a policy that is grounded in reflection on purpose and values and in certain standards of conduct. It further involves measures to embed the standards throughout the career of employees.

It is not surprising that social responsibility is increasingly seen in the more integrated terms of corporate responsibility.

 REFLECTIVE PRACTICE

If you are in work, find out if your corporation has a CSR policy. If it has, what are the differences from and similarities to Aviva's policy?

If you are a full-time student, find out what the CSR policy of your education institution is and compare it with the Aviva policy.

If you were given the chance to create the CSR policy of your organisation, what would you include, and what would the tone of the policy be?

If you are in a small to medium-sized business, compare the Aviva policy to your firm's practice and see how much of it applies to you.

THE BASIS OF CSR

If CSR is so much on the agenda, the next question is what the basis of it is. We look first at the underlying arguments about the nature and justification of CSR, and then sum up the reasons for being involved in it.

The limits of CSR

For Milton Friedman (1983) the answer was simple. The role of business is the creation of wealth, and thus the prime responsibility of business is to make a profit. The exclusive duty of the company is to its owners, usually the shareholders. In this, the executive acts as an agent serving the interests of his or her principal. The interest of the principal is profit maximisation, and involvement in any activities in the community outside this sphere would be a violation of trust and thus morally wrong. Friedman does not argue against the social involvement of the company as such, rather simply that the company, and the owners especially, can decide to do what they think is fit. There can be no ethical or legal constraint on the company to be more socially aware so long as it is pursuing legal ends.

Four things follow on from this:

- If the company executive does decide to get involved in a community project, Friedman argues that this should not be an obligation but rather a means of achieving company aims, such as improving the image and reputation of the company and thus contributing to improving profits.
- For Friedman, pursuing social responsibility would involve costs that would have to be passed on to the customer, possibly to the shareholder in reduced dividends, and to the employee in reduced wages. This is unfair.
- It also constitutes a form of taxation without representation and is therefore undemocratic. Moreover, it is both unwise, because it invests too much power in the company executives, and futile, because it is likely that the costs imposed by this approach will lead to a reduction in economic efficiency.
- Finally, he argues that the executive is not the best person to be involved in making decisions about social involvement. He or she is neither qualified nor mandated to pursue social goals. It is social administrators who understand the needs of the local area and who can determine local priorities. Such a task is better suited to local government and social concern groups, whose roles and accountability are directly related to these tasks. For business to enter this field would lead to a confusion of roles and a raising of false expectations.

 PAUSE FOR THOUGHT

Is there one core purpose of business? If so, how does that relate to any other role of business?

Is there one purpose generic to all business, or do different businesses have different purposes?

Make a list of all the possible purposes of your business or university. How might a public organisation, such as a university, differ from a business? Is it possible that your core purpose is also the focus of your responsibility to society?

Friedman's argument focuses, then, on the primacy of the purpose of profit-making (written into the contracts of the executive), the obligations of the executive within such a contract, the freedom of the executive to pursue company goals, and the local government as the proper focus for social activity. This approach is a good example of contract ethics, in that responsibility is determined by the freely entered contract.

There are a number of criticisms of this view of the responsibility of business:

- Seeing profit maximisation as the exclusive purpose of business is simplistic. Managers may have several different purposes each of equal importance: care for shareholders, clients, the physical environment, and so on. Shareholders may want profits but they could additionally be concerned for the environment or for the community in which they live. This can only be tested in dialogue with each group of shareholders, and in the light of the nature of the business and its effects on society.
- There is an assumption that the ethical worlds of social concern and business are quite separate. In fact the two are interconnected. The actions of a company affect the social

and physical environment in different ways, demanding an awareness of those effects and a capacity to plan for positive effects (beneficence) and respond to negative effects (non-maleficence).

- It is difficult to predetermine what the exact responsibility of the business person or the business should be, just as it is not possible to be precise about the responsibility of, for instance, local or national government. In practice there are broad responsibilities, but these are continuously being debated and negotiated.
- As we noted, there is no single business perspective on responsibility. Within business there are several different professional perspectives, from human resources to accountancy to management. Each emphasises a different aspect of responsibility that will question a simplistic view. Moreover, the focus of different firms may add to this diversity of purpose. An engineering firm, for instance, may have a strong focus on a proactive purpose in relation to the infrastructure of society (Armstrong *et al*, 1999).
- The increased emphasis on responsibility for the environment (see Chapter 14) has led to an emphasis on shared responsibility (see Chapter 4) that takes this beyond Friedman's corporate-centred view of responsibility – the idea that any responsibility has to be simply in the company's interest.
- Friedman simply assumes that the state should take responsibility for social concerns. There is, however, neither historical nor ethical ground for this argument. Historically, there has never been a simple state responsibility for social concern, only for legal justice. The boundaries of responsibility have shifted over time and continue to shift. Thus, in the UK after World War II there was a dramatic shift to the Welfare State. At the time of writing this is being modified to include competition from business organisations (www. http://healthandcare.dh.gov.uk/vision-for-a-new-public-health-system).
- Underlying Friedman's argument is a stress on freedom. In this case it is the freedom of the business person to pursue the purpose of making profits. His view of freedom involves largely negative freedom (Berlin, 1969) – that is, freedom *from* attempts to take the executive away from his or her core task. Friedman simply asserts this view of freedom with no attempt to justify it. Berlin (1969) notes other views of freedom, including positive freedom – freedoms that enable groups and individuals to do things, such as rights. In any case all freedoms take place within a social context where any assertion of freedom may affect the freedom of others (Tawney, 1930). Behind that there is for Friedman a worldview of a fragmented society which is neither interconnected nor interdependent. Against this it can be argued that freedom has to take account of the interconnected social environment, and thus that freedom is best embodied in the practice of the responsibility noted in Chapter 4. Such freedom is based on an awareness of the social environment and the capacity to respond to its challenges (see Fischer and Ravizza, 2000).
- The contractual basis of Friedman's argument also makes unjustified assumptions, not least the view that shareholders have only one goal: to make money. Shareholders, however, may balance that goal with others (see *Shareholders and the stewardship code* below).

In general it can be argued that Friedman's focus on the particularity of 'corporate' has taken away from any development of the concept of responsibility, and his focus on 'social' has led to him not to be aware of the integrated nature of responsibility. In Chapter 4 we noted the more complex view of responsibility, focused on the practice of responsible moral judgement, leading to a wider view of shared responsibility.

STAKEHOLDER THEORY AND SOCIAL RESPONSIBILITY

One of the most important responses to Friedman's argument has been stakeholder theory. It is possible to identify different versions of stakeholder theory (SHT), as argued by Heath and Norman (2004). These include:

- strategic SHT – a theory that attention to the needs of stakeholders will lead to better outcomes for the business
- SHT of governance – a theory about how stakeholder groups should be involved in overseeing management – eg placing stakeholders on the board
- deontic SHT – a theory that analyses the legitimate rights and needs of the different stakeholders and uses this data to develop company policies.

It is possible to see all these theories as simply aspects of a larger stakeholder view that sees any organisation as accountable to its stakeholders. Most organisations are in a position of having to handle quite complex multiple and mutual accountability. A commissioning firm is, for example, a stakeholder to the tendering firms as much as the tendering firms are stakeholders to the commissioning firm. Equally, each company would have some very different stakeholders, with different and sometimes conflicting values. The company is accountable to its shareholders, but also to its customers. By extension the government and wider industry might hold them to account for professional standards, and even some non-governmental organisations and consumer associations might call them to account for the effect of their products.

Sternberg (2000: 49ff) argues against stakeholder accountability on the following grounds:

- It is not clear to which stakeholders a company is accountable or what this might involve. Simply to say that a company has to be accountable to its stakeholders does not begin to differentiate what accountability might mean in any particular relationship. Being accountable to clients or customers, for instance, is very different from being accountable to local government.
- The argument that firms are accountable to the stakeholders assumes that the firm should respond to the demands of the stakeholder by fulfilling its needs. The idea of accountability thus involves some idea of stakeholder entitlement. It is not clear that stakeholders are entitled to have their needs met, or even if their view of needs is acceptable.
- It is likely that the interests of stakeholders will conflict at times. How does the firm resolve this? There are no clear criteria for saying which claims should be prioritised.

Responses to Sternberg's arguments include:

- The idea of accountability does not require that all stakeholders are entitled to have their needs, as defined by them, fulfilled. This is an example of setting up a straw man argument (see Chapter 3). This is a fallacy involving setting up your opponent's position in such a way that it can be easily knocked down.
- The logic of giving an account depends upon the relationship, and this will be different across the stakeholders. The relationship of the firm with the client or customer, for instance, involves concern for both standards and care. Accountability here is about working through continual improvement. The criteria of account around standards may be set by the industry. At one level it may involve core safety standards. It may also involve an industrial code, such as set out for the alcohol industry (Robinson and Kenyon, 2009) for marketing practice. Such a code will specify responsibilities for wider stakeholders. Again, in the case of the alcohol industry this involves issues such as how to avoid negatively affecting the behaviour of young people. The firm is also accountable to the law. In this case this involves relationship with the institution of the law and or the government, and accountability is expressed through fulfilling rules and laws. The laws themselves may embody a sense of the civic identity of the firm which sees it as accountable to the wider community for the social and physical environment. See the Nestlé case of Chapter 13 for a good example of complex accountability focused on the nature of the product. Sternberg's argument fails to grasp the interconnectedness of relationships and purpose.

In Chapter 4 we also noted that responsibility involved shared responsibility for the social and physical environment. This, along with the complex nature of accountability, suggests stakeholder theory based on fulfilling the need of the stakeholder is inadequate. From the perspective of shared responsibility, business is simply one among many that have a stake in the wider environment, and that share responsibility for it. This is also stronger than simply shared interest, demanding the negotiation of that responsibility. As we noted in Chapters 4 and 5, this is focused more on stewardship than on stakeholding.

CITIZENSHIP

The theme of stewardship also takes responsibility into the related idea of corporate citizenship (Andriof and McIntosh, 2001). Citizenship can be viewed as narrow legal obligation, with a focus on fulfilling legal obligations such as taxes. It can also be viewed as proactive responsibility to civil society and the common good. This is essentially about working through what the corporation's contribution to society might be in relation to its particular context. It places business in the wider arena of civil society, and as a contributor to social capital (Maak, 2007). This term refers broadly to networks and social relations that have productive benefits (http://www. socialcapitalresearch.com/definition.html).

In the light of this we examine two stakeholders and their responsibilities: shareholders, and then NGOs.

Shareholders and the Stewardship Code

Shareholders have a particular interest in keeping share values high. This can lead to what Longstaff (2004) refers to as structural irresponsibility. Longstaff offers the case of a CEO who regrets under-resourcing the fund set up to assist asbestos victims, but tries to justify it in the following statement (quoted in Longstaff, 2004: 2):

> The fact of the matter is we can't wish away our legal and fiduciary duties. As much as we would like to, in many respects, at the end of the day we're custodians on behalf of the shareholders. We have obligations to our shareholders. I think that perhaps that's been forgotten in all of this.

In effect the CEO was using a legal contract to avoid fully examining the responsibilities to employees. This is an ethical argument because it attempts to argue that the obligation to shareholders has priority over other responsibilities. It also avoids any attempt to engage the responsibility of the shareholders themselves, to include them in the ethical reflection.

 PAUSE FOR THOUGHT

Does the obligation to shareholders prevent any organisation from fulfilling other responsibilities?

What are the responsibilities of shareholders in this situation?

The Financial Reporting Council (FRC) argues that shareholders are not mono-dimensional and that shareholders themselves have responsibilities. It has published the UK Stewardship Code (2010), based on the work of the Institutional Shareholders' Committee.

The principles of the UK Stewardship Code are that institutional investors should:

- publicly disclose their policy on how they will discharge their stewardship responsibilities
- have a robust policy on managing conflicts of interest in relation to stewardship, and this policy should be publicly disclosed

- monitor their investee companies
- establish clear guidelines on when and how they will escalate their activities as a method of protecting and enhancing shareholder value
- be willing to act collectively with other investors where appropriate
- have a clear policy on voting and on the disclosure of voting activity
- report periodically on their stewardship and voting activities.

The code is notable for several reasons. First, the stress on stewardship takes the code away from a simple stakeholder approach to ethics and responsibility to one based on shared responsibility. It thus requires the development of mutual responsibility in shareholders rather than a one-way relationship of fulfilling shareholder needs. This is also an assertion of the autonomy of shareholders.

Second, although it is set out in the form of a code, it is not simply prescriptive, aiming rather to enhance the quality of engagement between institutional investors and companies, to help improve long-term returns to shareholders and the efficient exercise of governance responsibilities. It stresses the importance of, and gives examples of, good practice built on mutual dialogue between companies and institutional shareholders. Monitoring this is key to practice.

Third, it aims to sit alongside the UK's 2010 reworking of the Combined Code (www http://www.frc.org.uk/corporate/ukcgcode.cfm). It is all thus part of an integrated approach to responsible governance. The UK Stewardship Code is 'addressed in the first instance to firms who manage assets on behalf of institutional shareholders such as pension funds, insurance companies, investment trusts, and other collective vehicles'. Like the Combined Code, the Stewardship Code is based on a 'comply or explain' model.

Ethical investment

The responsibilities of shareholders are further engaged in the ethical investment movement. The aim of this is to enable the investor to make ethically informed decisions, weighing up the sustainability of the corporation with other issues. Such decision-making is helped by relevant data about major firms. The FTSE4Good series of indices (www.ftse.com/Indices/FTSE4Good_Index_Series/index.jsp) provide both a benchmark, so you can see how well any investments are doing comparatively, and a listing of companies that an ethical investor might wish to put money into. It is independently defined and researched, and covers most major markets. The five key areas that the series reports on are:

- environmental sustainability
- human rights
- countering bribery
- supply chain and labour standards
- climate change.

This is a broad approach to socially responsible investment (SRI). The indices exclude companies involved in armaments, nuclear power and tobacco, but this will be lifted once appropriate ethical assessment criteria have been developed for these industries (see the case study at the end of this chapter).

Responsibility and NGOs

A key part of 'value creation' and reflection on responsibility has been the work of NGOs. Their advocacy work has enabled them either to represent vulnerable stakeholders or to be direct stakeholders (both exemplified in the Nestlé case of Chapter 13). Their activism has also led to ethical criticisms of their practice.

These have focused on the lack of clarity about their responsibility (Fassin et al, 2009). NGOs are accountable to donors who are different from the beneficiaries of their work. This can lead to many different problems, not least around purpose. The two main purposes of NGOs are service provision and advocacy. In the first, NGOs may work closely with governments in providing services in areas such as famine relief. In advocacy, the NGOs look to stand up for the cause of minorities, which may involve critiquing the governments or big business. This in turn leads to criticisms from developmental agencies about working too closely with service provision (to satisfy donors) and not enough on advocacy, and from business about the emphasis on advocacy skewing the service provision role (Fassin *et al*, 2009). In some developing countries the service provision is further skewed when MNCs subcontract to NGOs CSR policy and practice. The problems with purpose are exacerbated by the fact of increasing competition among NGOs. The NGOs in turn rely on publicity and this can lead to the exaggeration of crises in order to develop and maintain an image (see the Brent Spar case study below). This can result in the polarisation of ethical debate, in which it is in the interest of the NGO to be perceived as occupying the moral high ground and the business to be seen as 'the enemy'.

Questions of accountability are also raised about the relationship of NGOs to their beneficiaries. It is not clear how NGOs can speak for their beneficiaries, leading to a potentially paternalistic approach to the service provision.

A good example of the ethical debate within NGOs about purpose is the recent issue of Amnesty International's support for Moazzam Begg. Amnesty wanted to develop a campaign around the prisoners at Guantánamo Bay, and Begg had been associated with this. However, he has also been associated with the Taliban and other Islamist extremist views. The comments from donors on http://livewire.amnesty.org/2010/02/14/amnesty-international-response-to-the-sunday-times/ show that even within NGOs there are major ethical differences that have to be addressed.

A case that raises several of these issues is that of Brent Spar.

BRENT SPAR

CASE

Brent Spar was an offshore oil storage facility owned by Shell and based in the North Sea. In 1992 this huge facility, with six large storage tanks beneath the water, was due to be decommissioned. Because of its size Shell argued against the usual practice of towing the structure to shore to have it broken up on land. Sinking in deep water, they argued, was in this case the cheapest way of dealing with the problem, but also, some claimed, the best method environmentally. In discussing it with the government, agreement was reached with a date in 1995 established for the sinking of the facility. Shell had not consulted Greenpeace in this process.

On 30 April 1995 Greenpeace occupied Brent Spar, accompanied by German and UK journalists. Greenpeace reported that they had not been consulted and that Brent Spar was a 'toxic time bomb', with oil residues and radioactive waste that could seriously damage the marine environment. Dismantling would have to be undertaken on shore.

During the subsequent battle Greenpeace managed the publicity in such a way that when the Spar buoy was first towed out towards the deeper sea it appeared that what was happening was a war of integrity between a profit-hungry multinational and the NGO who represented the environment.

The result was that that Shell backed down under the pressure of intense publicity.

It was only later that the Greenpeace action and the data that they based it on were questioned. Shell argued that there was only 53 tonnes of toxic sludge or oil on the Spar. Greenpeace argued that there was over 14,500 tonnes of toxic rubbish and over 100 tonnes of toxic sludge. An independent study later noted that there was in fact between 74 and 100 tonnes of oil on board the Spar, and that the greater part of this could have been removed easily. In addition subsequent expert testimony proved that sinking the Spar in deep water would indeed have been the least bad environmental option. This led Greenpeace finally to offer a public apology.

For more details, see Entine (2002).

Several critical issues emerged from this case, summed up by Jon Entine (2002):

- the contested use of science – risk-benefit analysis/cost-benefit analysis, 'junk science', environmental politics
- the role of the media
- stakeholder reputation management and 'greenwashing' by corporations and activist groups
- the problematic role of dialogue in stakeholder conflict resolution.

In the first of these issues, the very fact that Greenpeace was not consulted led to different perceptions of the situation. In turn, this led to contested scientific judgement and lack of clarity about the actual facts. It would have been in Shell's interests to open up the conversation at the earliest stages so that data-collection could have been agreed. This in turn depends upon the development of dialogue between NGOs and major industry. However, because of the often adversarial role of the NGOs, dialogue itself can become difficult. Some NGOs claim that if they are even seen in sustained conversation with global business, it will be perceived by their supporters as 'selling out'. Some means of ensuring the development of trust is therefore vital, not least in allowing NGOs to develop purpose which is not primarily adversarial.

If the relationship with NGOs is poor, it can become even worse through media involvement. The impetus to sensationalise tends to promote polarisation and partiality, and in this case there was the assumption in most of the press that big corporations lie and that activist groups pursue the truth. So despite the more complex nature of the case, Greenpeace won the battle for public support by some margin (Entine, 2002: 73). However, the long-term reputations of Shell, Greenpeace and the UK government were all tarnished. Perhaps the most striking aspect of this case was the awareness that activist and industry alike were using spin doctors in the attempt to win the battle.

Kaldor (2003; see also Elkington, 2001) suggests that three things are required to develop NGOs' work:

- NGOs should not be privileged in the debate, but should be held to the same account as other stakeholders.
- Regulation of NGOs should be better developed, in part by bringing donors and beneficiaries more closely together, including both in discussion about role, purpose and targets, thus developing the exercise of responsibility.
- Spaces for dialogue in civil society have to be created. A good example of this is the Nestlé case study, in which all the actors engaged as part of civil society and developed a framework of ethical meaning and practice.

GOOD REASONS FOR RESPONSIBLE PRACTICE

If poor practice, irrespective of company size, can negatively impact on the reputation of businesses, then conversely, good responsible practice can produce a number of benefits for the business organisation. These include:

- competitive advantage
- the stimulation of customer confidence and loyalty
- the enhancement of stakeholder relationships
- the improvement of staff retention and recruitment
- the reduction of waste or wasteful practice.

Competitive advantage

The notion of making responsible practice a source of competitive advantage has become associated with Porter and Kramer (2011). Porter describes this concept of shared value as (Porter, 2011):

policies and operating practices that enhance the competitiveness of a company while simultaneously advancing the economic and social conditions in the communities in which it operates. Shared value creation focuses on identifying and expanding the connections between societal and economic progress.

This accords also with the idea that CSR should be treated as integral to business strategy and not 'bolted on'. Even the goods and services an organisation provides might be bound up with responsibility, including, for example, a health-giving drink, or a medicine, or a product that protects ecology, like an industrial air filter (see the interview with Michael Porter at www http://blogs.hbr.org/video/2011/01/rethinking-capitalism.html).

The kinds of questions that might be part of any decision-making then might include:

- Are we serving all the communities that would benefit from our products?
- Do our processes and logistical approaches maximise efficiencies in energy and water use?
- Could our new plant be constructed in a way that achieves greater community impact?
- How are gaps in our cluster holding back our efficiency and speed of innovation?
- How could we enhance our community as a business location?
- If sites are comparable economically, at which one will the local community benefit the most?
- Could our product design incorporate greater social benefits?

Porter's concept of shared value is related to shared responsibility but distinct. Shared value recognises the values' interest and that it is therefore in the interest of all parties to respond to these. Shared responsibility looks to empower fellow citizens in the exercise of responsibility for the common good and negotiate how it can be shared.

The stimulation of customer confidence and loyalty

Related to competitive advantage is the consideration of engendering customer satisfaction and identification with one's product or brand. This raises the issue of how businesses make and keep customers happy, and how purchases contribute to the managed identities of buyers (whether conscious or subconscious).

The enhancement of stakeholder relationships

For organisations to be successful, there are many parties other than one's customers to keep happy and to satisfy. The view of investors, one's owners and the financial community are critical. Added to these every business has suppliers and every business operates in a community. Even the smallest organisation has some interface with local and national government. Responsible practice can and will positively influence all these relationships.

The improvement of staff retention and recruitment

A major contemporary driver for responsible practice has become the need for organisations to attract and retain staff. Employees do not wish to be identified with ethically weak organisations (Brown, 2005).

The reduction of waste or wasteful practice

Irresponsibility is bound up with not counteracting waste in all its forms, from wasting energy to demeaning human resources. Conversely, responsible practice results in the reduction of waste and the elimination of wasteful practices. In a business environment becoming more conscious of sustainability and sustainable practices, responsible practice is increasingly significant. This is examined more closely in Chapter 14.

ETHICS AND ENTERPRISE

As we noted in the first chapter, it is easy to polarise ethics, seeing self-interest as wrong and concern for the other as right. In this light it is possible to argue that ethics and enterprise are polar opposites – the one focusing on the interests of the firm and the owners, the other focusing on wider concerns.

The arguments immediately above look to the balance of self-interest with the interest of others, and this takes the underlying ethical debate away from simple deontological and utilitarian approaches. As noted in Chapter 4, ethics of responsibility include responsibility for and to the self and the organisation, along with wider responsibilities.

The very idea of enterprise, in the sense of the capacity for creativity and innovation, has strong ethical support, balanced with the shared values and responsibility of others.

TRIPLE BOTTOM LINE

If a firm wishes to badge itself as ethical, it must demonstrate its practice in a transparent manner, and this has led to a proliferation of different styles of reporting – in effect tools for ethical accounting. This is focused in the triple bottom line (Elkington, 2001), reporting on the financial, social and environmental performance of the firm. Two of the strongest tools are BIRG (Business Impact Review Group) indicators and ISO26000.

Developed by Business in the Community (BITC), the Business Impact Review Group devised a series of 'indicators that count' (www.bitc.org.uk/document.rm?id=2089).

This framework sets out to define key indicators for measuring an organisation's environmental and social performance in four impact areas, particularly in relation to the task of reporting that performance:

- the environment
- the community
- the marketplace
- the workplace.

There is an implicit understanding with the BIRG model that an organisation cannot be expected to perform across all the areas, but rather that it should focus on the most important topics for the business in question. Not only would the significant items differ from company to company, but also from industry to industry. The selection of indicators is also assisted by consultation and dialogue with key stakeholders.

A small selection of indicators for each of the impact areas is listed below:

Environment	Community
Overall energy consumption	Individual value of staff time, gifts in kind and management costs
Water usage	
Solid waste produced by weight	Impact evaluations carried out on community programmes
Environmental impact over the supply chain	
	Perception measures of the company as a good neighbour

Marketplace	Workplace
Customer complaints about products and services	Staff absenteeism
	Staff turnover
Customer satisfaction levels	Value of the training and development provided for staff
Upheld cases of anti-competitive behaviour	
	Number of staff grievances

The BIRG framework would obviously assist organisations of all sizes in defining their spheres of influences, but its great value is providing a listing of key indicators for each of the impact areas.

Another framework to assist organisations in defining their sphere of influence and in seeking to operate in a socially responsible manner across a range of areas is the international ISO 26000 standard. This has been developed by the International Standardisation Organisation, and aims (http://www.iso.org/iso/iso_catalogue/ management_and_leadership_standards/social_responsibility/sr_iso26000_ overview.htm) to:

- develop an international consensus on what social responsibility means and the related issues that organisations have to address
- provide guidance on translating principles into effective actions
- refine best practices that have already evolved and disseminate the information worldwide for the good of the international community.

It addresses seven core areas of social responsibility, listed below along with selected issues included in the standard.

Organisational governance
Integrating social responsibility with company strategy and operations
Internal competency for social responsibility
Internal and external communications on social responsibility
Regular reviewing of actions and practices

Human rights
Upholding economic, social, political and cultural rights
Adhering to fundamental principles and rights at work
Avoidance of complicity

The environment
Pollution prevention
Sustainable resource use
Climate change and business
Protection of the environment

Labour practices
Work conditions
Health and safety at work
Training and development

Fair operating practices
Fair competition
Anti-corruption
Social responsibility in the value chain

Consumer issues
Fair marketing
Consumer data protection
Sustainable consumption

Community involvement and development
Community action and involvement
Employment creation and skills development

An examination of ISO26000's core subjects and a number of its listed issues reveals that the content of the standard applies to all organisations, irrespective of size. It provides the most comprehensive overview presented so far of the scope of social responsibility practices. Again, it is somewhat more applicable to larger organisations in that it is more likely that a larger concern would seek to implement the standard itself.

DOES SIZE MATTER? SMALL AND MEDIUM-SIZED ENTERPRISES AND ETHICS

The perspective of small businesses on responsibility seems different from that of the major corporations. Many different agencies – including governments, sectors (through sector-specific tools), eco-label and certification schemes, and specialist networks – have attempted to introduce triple-bottom-line thinking to SMEs (Perera, 2009). Research increasingly also suggests that SMEs tend not to strategise social responsibility in the same way that bigger firms do (Perera, 2009). Responsibility is worked through more informal processes, often dependent on the values of the leaders.

Little and large
There are five factors which differentiate responsible practice between 'little and large' organisations.

- Governance

  Large organisations are often very structured or multi-layered, consisting of a board, a senior management team, and a number of departments or functions each with its own management. Here corporate responsibility, in terms of leadership and management alone, is vested in many hands. This contrasts with organisations led by one person (the owner-manager) or consisting of one person. In many large organisations one member of the board may be expected to act as a guardian or champion of CSR issues. The organisation may have its own CSR department and a senior executive responsible for CSR, who may report to the board. Here the contrast of resource is significant, but also perhaps most significant in terms of time available to attend to or service the responsibility issues and practices.

- Ownership

  In PLCs the presence of shareholders and the wishes of these shareholders are significant. A central purpose of producing an annual CSR report is to communicate the status of responsibility activities and operations to shareholders, presumably to inspire their confidence in the business, to ensure their identification with the business, and perhaps even to create a feel-good factor about owning a share of an organisation that they can be proud of being identified with. In a smaller concern the ownership is hugely significant too in relation to responsibility practice. However, it might be owned by one person, or family-owned, or owned by a small number of business partners. The outlook of these small business owners and the nature of their convictions in relation to responsible business practices will determine the direction of their businesses. Research also suggests that the motives of SME leaders tend to be less instrumental, using CSR strategically, and more focused on motives such as giving back to the community, or feeling part of the community (Perera, 2009).

- Specialisation

  The prospect for specialisation of CSR in a larger concern is obviously much greater than in a smaller one. What we might refer to as the 'CSR architecture' differs significantly between little and large companies, in that codes of conduct, vision statements, standards and reports are associated with larger organisations (Spence, 2007). Many small businesses find the term 'corporate social responsibility' in itself off-putting (Roberts *et al*, 2006), irrespective of whether or not their practices are responsible. In practice this has led to SMEs prioritising areas of CSR. Perera (2009) notes that 30% of SMEs focused mainly on community contributions and 23% on social benefits provision. Importantly, then, there is evidence of SME leaders' taking responsibility for determining key areas of responsibility and not simply trying to keep up with CSR orthodoxy.

- Reporting

  Corporate responsibility reporting (increasingly referred to as sustainability reporting) is fast approaching becoming standard practice in large companies. However, it has still largely not been assimilated by the SME community. Nonetheless, although SMEs find little time to develop the same level of reporting, they are increasingly being drawn in to the reporting of larger companies as part of the supply chain, which in itself demands the practice of accountability and even shared responsibility. In this sense the SMEs are increasingly becoming part of the larger CSR enterprise.

- Brand management/protection

  Looking after the customer and producing products and services to meet customer needs are fundamental to business success, irrespective of size. However, with increasing scale comes a corresponding sophistication to brand management and protection, and the largest organisations are able to direct significant and specialised resources towards this activity. The largest brands are subject to the greatest scrutiny – and again, this explains why organisations devote considerable attention to ensuring that brands are not harmfully associated with irresponsibility, and are conversely identified with responsible practice. In contrast, SMEs operate in communities where there are more direct relationships and thus more immediate transparency.

Ethical drivers and blindspots

The drivers for SMEs to work through responsibility are in some respects more immediate and intense than for large corporations. SMEs by nature are closer to and more dependent on their customers, employees, neighbours and other key stakeholders than larger, more impersonal enterprises, and so need to be more directly and immediately responsive to them. In terms of sustaining business, for instance, SMEs rely on staff continuity, creating an incentive for responsible labour practices.

Many SMEs also have a stronger sense of rootedness within a particular community or geographical location, sometimes framed around family identity. This often means that owners manage the firm, bringing together another core relationship in one person. The result of this is frequently that the personal ethics of the mangers become more directly embodied in the firm. The integration of ethics then is often not labelled as ethics. Formal CSR strategies can therefore seem alien.

The problem with such integration is that it can lead to the development of blindspots, a lack of awareness of the bigger picture. With an emphasis on a well-known local community, it is possible not to be open to wider issues. A small company may make 'widgets' for bigger companies that have a poor record of responsibility, for instance. This means that more attention might be needed around the supply chain (see Chapter 10). Equally, for many SMEs economic survival is so pressing that ethical issues can seem to be secondary (Luetkenhorst, 2004).

In some cases the standards of supply chain management may work against SMEs. For example, pollution prevention measures stipulated by environmental standards may require investment in technology that is not possible for SMEs. The process of reporting compliance with these standards may also set up barriers. SMEs are less likely to have the structure for formal measurement and recording. Even FairTrade SMEs do not have the frameworks to include things such as ethics committees (Moore *et al*, 2009). Fassin *et al* (2011) also argue that the small business leaders rarely find their understanding of social responsibility from the different academic concepts. They develop their ideas in relation to professional groups and their community context.

Addressing CSR in SMEs

SMEs differ in nature and scope, then, but share the need to develop socially responsible practice – something encouraged by government. The blocks to CSR practice in SMEs noted above are partly a matter of the lack of resources, and partly the continuously developing material about CSR, which is hard to keep up with. One SME manager quoted in Perera (2009: 14) said, 'When you don't know what to do, and if you are not sure what you are doing is needed, it is best to do nothing.' Over 68% of those surveyed in the report said that SMEs were not engaging in CSR because they were afraid of performing poorly and thus exposing themselves to additional risk. SMEs also reported a lack of power to effectively influence the social environment.

These points raise two questions: one for corporations in general and one for SMEs in particular. For corporations in general:

Has the development of CSR, with its stress on standards, reporting, CSR tools and strategic focus, lost its ethical centre?

The International Institute for Sustainable Development (Perera, 2009: 9) suggests that the emphasis on developing CSR tools has focused more on unthinking compliance than on a genuine appreciation of the meaning and value of responsible practice in the particular social and physical environment. In effect, the emphasis on tools and standards can prevent the development of the three core capacities of responsibility noted in Chapter 4: the critical understanding of ideas, value and practice, and how these affect and might affect society; an understanding of who the firm is accountable to and how best to give that account; and an understanding of what the firm is responsible for and shares responsibility for. In terms of ethical theory, then, there is a danger that CSR will focus on prescriptive ethics (deontological ethics) and utilitarian ethics (through emphasis on the strategic use of CSR), and ignore virtue ethics (emphasising the capacity for responsibility) and responsibility ethics (emphasising the need to work through the three modes of responsibility in the practice of the firm). This can also lead to a form of 'teleopathy', by which fulfilling standards becomes the main purpose and not the underlying appropriate and creative engagement with society and the environment. It can be distinguished from greenwashing (see Chapter 14). Greenwashing refers to an intentional lack of integrity – developing CSR policies that that are in effect hiding a lack of concern about working responsibility out. The teleopathy above might believe in the importance of CSR targets but not have thought through the underlying practice of responsibility.

PAUSE FOR THOUGHT

What is your view of CSR? Can it actually lead to negative and even unethical results?

Think back to the ethical disconnect expressed in the major ethical disasters, such as Enron, where the corporations had apparently strong ethical codes and CSR policies but no 'lived' responsibility. How would you prevent that in a small or big business? (See Chapters 4 and 5.)

None of this is to argue that standards and tools are wrong – only that they should be practised within an ethical framework that focuses on the underlying purpose. This takes us back to virtue ethics, with Aristotle's emphasis on getting the balance right, and responsibility ethics.

This leads to the specific question for SMEs:

How can SMEs develop responsible practice in business?

There are several ways in which the CSR problems of SMEs might be addressed. First, SMEs might focus on underlying ethical capacities rather than on standards. An important finding in the Perera report (2009) is that the biggest hurdle to developing responsibility is not the lack of time but the lack of expertise, not least about how to integrate ethics into everyday decision-making. It is therefore argued that the development of ethical skills, and indeed the capacities involved in the three modes of responsibility, is critical to enable the growth of confidence in ethical decision-making.

Second, an SME, like any organisation, must practise the main elements of ethical decision-making, including developing an awareness of its environment and of its influence upon that environment, the core values of the organisation and wider communities, and the capacity to deal with and prioritise different values (see Chapter 3). Every business has a decision to make about defining its sphere of influence in terms of both its environmental and its social responsibilities. Theoretically, the larger the company, the larger its sphere of influence can and perhaps should be in terms of exercising corporate responsibility. However, in practice there is a discretionary dimension to the decision about which responsibilities an organisation will concern itself with, or certainly the way in which it will choose to approach each area of responsibility.

Third, SMEs are themselves part of supply chains, and often stakeholders in bigger businesses. Being part of that network it may be possible to link into the larger businesses' CSR capacity (Luetkenhorst 2004), perhaps at least in terms of training, advice and support, and assistance in meeting reporting requirements. This would be a good example of larger corporations' empowering smaller ones in developing and sustaining responsibility practice.

Fourth, in addition to business links there can be more comprehensive business support services developed on CSR for SMEs. Organisations such as Business in the Community (BITC) can establish mutual support networks (Grayson, 2007). Wherever there is a support system, such as chambers of commerce, or professional bodies, such as the Institute of Directors, these can make CSR part of their everyday support. Core to these relationships is the development of dialogue that is central to ethical reflection and responsibility negotiation. In this way they begin to form, externally, the ethical culture that bigger firms aim to establish internally (see Chapter 6).

Fifth, SMEs can also usefully work together around the reporting mechanisms that most fit them and that can be worked through together. Again this looks to reflection of responsibility as the starting point for what is possible for an SME individually and in partnership.

Sixth, CSR collaboration can often be focused in response to shared crises.

 ALCOHOL AND THE COMMUNITY

CASE

Many social responsibility initiatives emerge from local need or crises. In 2007, Haringay was plagued by public alcohol abuse and conflict. The response was a public meeting that brought together the alcohol industry, wider businesses, the police and other groups in the community.

The meeting began to negotiate responsibility and develop moral imagination leading to simple but effective changes in practice. This included the local pubs making a contract with taxi firms to take customers directly from the pubs, cutting down on the taxi queues that were the centre of considerable conflict. The pubs also instituted a dress code and refused to admit customers under 21, thus focusing on the responsible behaviour of

the customers. With core flash points cut out, this allowed the police to target their limited resources more effectively.

It was not apparent at first that the practice of this shared responsibility would be in the interest of all parties. The pub landlords, especially, thought that this might cut their custom. In the event the plan led to an increase of custom, with improvement in the community leading to an atmosphere that encouraged customers who had previously avoided the town centre at the weekends. This therefore represented more than a simple coincidence of interests.

Source: summarised from a case study in Robinson and Kenyon, 2009: 179

A good example of where the ethical perspective has been integrated into a developing medium-sized business is in Innocent Smoothies. Ethics is focused in the identity of the company from the declaration of ethical humility to sustainability practice and sharing of profits (see http://www.innocentdrinks.co.uk/us/ethics/).

 REFLECTIVE PRACTICE

As manager of a small business with ten employees, describe how you would give an account of your business ethics.

CONCLUSION

This chapter has looked at some of the different views of CSR, and how it is practised. The arguments about the meaning of the term have caused some to suggest that it should either be reworded as simply 'corporate responsibility' or as 'corporate citizenship'. Both terms attempt to capture the broader, more integrated, view of responsibility, moving into the monitoring that involves the triple bottom line, accounting for the corporation's responsibility for finance, society and the environment. It also moves the stakeholder debate away from simplistic response to need and into the view that responsibility is shared with stakeholders. Even shareholders must therefore take responsibility. In effect this involves, as Porter suggests, a rethinking of capitalism. This is not on the basis of an ideological argument, from, for instance a Marxist perspective. That would take the form of arguing against capitalism on principle. This rather is about how responsible capitalism can be practised. All this takes us beyond the triple bottom line, with a focus on meaning and purpose, and partnership.

As we noted in Chapter 4, this once again moves to a more genuinely stewardship-oriented view of responsibility. This takes responsibility into relationships to the state, the global context and the environment, as covered in the next three chapters.

We end this chapter with a case study that tests corporate social responsibility.

CASE

THE SOCIAL RESPONSIBILITY OF THE TOBACCO INDUSTRY

If business and ethics are seen by some to be an oxymoron (a contradiction in terms), then the social responsibility of the tobacco industry would seem to be the ultimate oxymoron. Arguments for this include:

- The industry's product is itself physically addictive and causes death. Scientific research confirms that over 50% of regular smokers will suffer premature death. It could be said, then, that the tobacco industry is directly responsible for the death of almost 5 million people per annum globally (Ezzati and Lopez, 2003).

- The second argument relates to the cynical way in which the tobacco industry has attempted, from the 1950s onwards, to influence scientific and public thinking about tobacco, questioning the scientific data about addiction and the carcinogenic nature of tobacco smoke. This has involved both the denial of risk and manipulation of information. The integrity of the industry has therefore been questioned. This questioning of the industry now extends to its global operation, both in production – including the effects of this on the social and physical environment

in places such as Malawi (Geist, Otañez and Kapito, 2008) – and in attempts to generate new markets in places where there is little regulation.

- Tobacco as a product is unambiguously against the common good. In this respect it could be argued that other 'difficult products' have a degree of ambiguity. Alcohol, for instance, is strongly related to the celebration of community (Robinson and Kenyon, 2009). The arms industry can point to the legitimate use of arms, small or large, for the defence of life or property. Tobacco leads directly to suffering for the majority of smokers and has a negative affect on healthcare resources. If, as Drucker (1973: 368) suggests, the first principle of CSR is 'First do no harm', then the tobacco industry cannot even get past that.

Several arguments have been made against these:

- The responsibility for the suffering caused by tobacco is not purely that of the tobacco industry. The individual smoker is responsible for the practice of smoking. He or she buys the product and uses it. Moreover, the customer is aware of the lethal nature of tobacco, precisely because warnings such as 'Smoking kills' are on the packet. The responsibility is therefore shared.

- The freedom of the consumer to choose to take tobacco should be respected.

- Tobacco is not an illegal substance, has been used for centuries, and generates tax which can be focused on social policy. In this respect, tobacco is as ambiguous as alcohol.

Ranged against these arguments are the following:

- The argument for freedom of choice focuses purely on individual freedom and responsibility. The sale and consumption of tobacco, however, is matter for much wider, social and political, responsibility. At one level this is confirmed by the issue of passive smoking, in that smokers negatively affect the wider environment, both social (providing models for younger people) and physical (affecting the long-term health of others).

- The cost of tobacco-related illness, in states that contribute to healthcare, is not borne by the individual but by taxpayers who may never have smoked. The debate quickly moves then from freedom to responsibility and then to justice.

- One of the major problems about the freedom argument is to do with children and young adults. It is not clear that they have autonomy in the sense of good decision-making skills. Despite attempts to cut advertising there are signs that smoking by children is still very common (http://info.cancerresearchuk.org/cancerstats/types/ lung/smoking/#children).

Ethical theory does not give an easy way through this argument. Deontological theory does not provide a simple principle to follow. On the contrary, principles such as respect for freedom are ranged against care for health. Similar tensions are there in healthcare (Kendrick and Robinson, 2002). Utilitarian arguments are used by both sides, and it is clear that these depend on an underlying view of the good. Virtue and feminist ethics do not have a strong input into this debate.

This would suggest that there is no simple ethical 'knock-down' argument for or against. The ethics of responsibility, working through responsibility with stakeholders, would therefore seem to be the most effective approach. This inevitably takes the case into a global context. As we shall see in the chapter on global ethics, the history of the tobacco industry is complex.

Palazzo and Richter (2005) suggest that it is possible to develop a CSR policy in the tobacco industry, but that it has to be different from usual approaches. They argue that there are three levels of CSR:

- the instrumental – the responsibility to produce products of the quality expected by the customer
- the transactional – referring to the integrity of the corporation. The authors define this as complying with the legal and moral rules of the society. It also involves transparent, fair and consistent behaviour
- the transformational – going beyond self-interest to contributing to the common good.

Palazzo and Richter argue that is possible to have a 'thinner' sense of CSR. This would involve focusing on the transactional level. The transformational level is so contrary to the tobacco industry that they argue it cannot be part of CSR policy. At the transactional level, they argue that this would involve pulling out of lobbying groups and focusing on transparency that shows them facing the key dilemmas in the industry. It would thus involve, for instance, the corporation honestly looking at how the habit is developing in children and looking to working against it. It would involve more industry-wide attempts to change the patterns of the behaviour. In effect this would involve accepting the negatives of the product and working together with others to mitigate these effects. This might involve working with an NGO. The terms of such a partnership would have to be worked through carefully. In the case of BAT's partnership with Earthwatch Europe, this caused difficulties because the partnership was not transparent (see McDaniel and Malone, 2011).

REFLECTIVE PRACTICE

Read Palazzo and Richter's paper.

Does it convince you? If it does, why does it? If it doesn't, why not?

Analyse the tobacco industry in terms of the three modes of responsibility.

Share your view with your learning group.

SCENARIO

Up for the job

The job of new CSR director has come up at World Tobacco Corp. and you have got an interview. They want you to give a presentation to several board members about developing a new CSR policy. In groups of four work out how you would develop that presentation on three PowerPoint slides, involving an analysis of all the stakeholders involved in the tobacco industry and their responsibility.

See the DVD film *Thank You for Smoking* (2007, Twentieth Century Fox).

Does this help you to develop a CSR policy, or does it simply reinforce the cynicism about the industry?

How do you feel about the anti-hero?

Is it possible for him and the industry to retain integrity?

EXPLORE FURTHER

Books

Brown, M. (2005) *Corporate Integrity*. Cambridge: Cambridge University Press.

DVDs

The Corporation (2006, In 2 Film). This documentary film has a negative view of the corporation and its relation to society, but does encourage critical dialogue. If you were asked about the film as the member of a board, how would you respond?

REFERENCES

ANDRIOF, J. and McINTOSH, M. (eds) (2001) *Perspectives on Corporate Citizenship.* London: Greenleaf Publishing.

ARMSTRONG, J., DIXON, R. and ROBINSON, S. (1999) *The Decision-Makers.* London: Thomas Telford.

BERLIN, I. (1969) *Four Essays on Liberty.* Oxford: Oxford University Press.

BROWN, M. (2005) *Corporate Integrity.* Cambridge: Cambridge University Press.

BUSINESS IN THE COMMUNITY (2011) *Indicators That Count* (Internet). Available at http://www.bitc.org.uk/resources/publications/indicators_that.html [accessed 14 June 2011].

CARROLL, A. B. (1991) 'The pyramid of corporate social responsibility: towards the moral management of organizational stakeholders', *Business Horizons*, July–Aug: 39–48.

DRUCKER, P. (1973) *Management: Tasks, responsibilities, practices.* New York: Harper & Row.

ELKINGTON, J. (2001) 'The "triple bottom line" for 21st-century business', in Starkey, R. and Welford, R. (eds) *Business and Sustainable Development.* London: Earthscan.

ENTINE, J. (2002) 'Shell, Greenpeace and Brent Spar; the politics of dialogue', in Megone, C. and Robinson, S. *Case Histories in Business Ethics.* London: Routledge.

EUROPEAN COMMISSION (2001) Green Paper: *Promoting a European Framework for Corporate Social Responsibility*, Com (2001) 366 final, Brussels.

EZZATI, M. and LOPEZ, A. (2003) 'Estimates of global mortality attributable to smoking in 2000', *The Lancet*, 13 September, Vol.362, Issue 9387: 847–52.

FASSIN, Y., VAN ROSSEM, A. and BUELENS, M. (2011) 'Small-business owner-managers' perceptions of business ethics and CSR-related concepts', *Journal of Business Ethics* 98: 425–53.

FISCHER, J. and RAVIZZA, M. (2000) *Responsibility and Control.* Cambridge: Cambridge University Press.

FRIEDMAN, M. (1983) 'The social responsibility of business is to increase its profits', in Donaldson, T. and Werhane, P. *Ethical Issues in Business.* New York: Prentice Hall.

GEIST, H., OTAÑEZ, M. AND KAPITO, J. (2008) 'The tobacco industry in Malawi: a globalized driver of local land change', in Millington, A. and Jepson, W. (eds) *Land-Change Science in the Tropics: Changing agricultural landscapes.* New York: Springer.

GRAYSON, D. (2007) *Business-Led Corporate Responsibility Coalitions.* London: BITC.

HEATH, J. and NORMAN, W. (2004) 'Stakeholder theory, corporate governance and public management: what can the history of state-run enterprises teach us in the post-Enron era?', *Journal of Business Ethics*, 53(3): 247–65.

INTERNATIONAL ORGANISATION FOR STANDARDISATION (2011) ISO26000 – Social responsibility. Available at http://www.iso/iso/social_responsibility.

KALDOR, M. (2003) 'Civil society and accountability', *Journal of Human Development*, 4(1): 5–27.

KENDRICK, K. and ROBINSON, S. (2002) *Their Rights: Advance directives and living wills explored.* London: Age Concern.

LONGSTAFF, S. (2004) 'A hard place', *Sydney Morning Herald*, 28 August.

LUETKENHORST, W. (2004) 'Corporate social responsibility and the development agenda: the case for actively involving small and medium enterprises', *Intereconomics*, May/June.

MAAK, T. (2007). 'Responsible leadership, stakeholder engagement, and the emergence of social capital', *Journal of Business Ethics*, 74: 329–43.

McDANIEL, P. A. and MALONE, R. E. (2011) *British American Tobacco's partnership with Earthwatch, Europe and its implications for public health.* http://www.ncbi.nlm.nih.gov/pubmed/21347934.

MOELLER, K. and ERDAL, T. (2003) *Corporate Responsibility towards Society: A local perspective.* Brussels: European Foundation for the Improvement of Living and Working Conditions.

MOORE, G., SLACK, R. and GIBBON, J. (2009) 'Criteria for responsible business practice in SMEs: an exploratory case of UK Fair Trade organisations', *Journal of Business Ethics*, 89: 173–88.

PALAZZO, G. and RICHTER, U. (2005) 'CSR business as usual? The case of the tobacco industry', *Journal of Business Ethics*, 6(4): 387–401.

PERERA, O. (2009) *How material is ISO26000 social responsibility to small and medium-sized enterprises (SMEs)?* Winnipeg: MB International Institute for Sustainable Development.

PORTER, M. (2011) *Harvard Business Review,* http://hbr.org/2011/01/the-big-idea-creating-shared-value/sb1.

PORTER, M. and KRAMER, M. R. (2011) 'Creating shared value: how to reinvent capitalism – and unleash a wave of innovation and growth', *Harvard Business Review*, Jan–Feb: 62–77.

REED, D. (1999) 'Three realms of corporate responsibility: distinguishing legitimacy, morality and ethics', *Journal of Business Ethics*, 21(1): 23–36.

ROBERTS, S., LAWSON, R. and NICHOLLS, J. (2006) 'Generating regional-scale improvements in SME corporate responsibility performance: lessons from Responsibility Northwest', *Journal of Business Ethics*, 67: 275–86.

ROBINSON, S. (2009) 'The nature of responsibility in a professional setting', *Journal of Business Ethics*, 88: 11–19.

ROBINSON, S. and KENYON, A. (2009) *Ethics in the Alcohol Industry.* Basingstoke: Palgrave Macmillan.

SPENCE, L. J. (2007) 'CSR and small business in a European policy context: the five "c's" of CSR and small business research agenda', *Business and Society Review*, 112(4): 533–52.

STERNBERG, E. (2000) *Just Business.* Oxford: Oxford University Press.

TAWNEY, R. H. (1930) *Equality.* London: Allen & Unwin.

UK STEWARDSHIP CODE (2010) London: Financial Reporting Council.

ZADEK, S. (2001) *The Civil Corporation: The new economy of corporate citizenship.* London: Earthscan.

Business and Government

INTRODUCTION

This chapter begins with the case history of how businesses related to the South African government at the time of *apartheid*. This is an extreme case that tests the ways in which business should relate to the government, from simple obligations such as the payment of taxes through to the challenge of how to respond to the abuse of human rights. The issue of human rights and the question of the responsibility of business is then further developed in relation to the case of Caterpillar and the use of its earth-clearing machines by the Israeli army in Palestine. This explores different views of responsibility – proactive, reactive, shared and limited.

The chapter then critically examines how the UN in 2011 attempted to develop guidelines for the relationships between government and business, particularly in terms of human rights. It then explores the everyday relationship between government and business, looking particularly at issues surrounding lobbying and conflicts of interest. The chapter concludes with the case study of Shell in Nigeria, raising questions about shared responsibility even for social concerns such as peace and conflict resolution.

CASE

APARTHEID AND THE SULLIVAN PRINCIPLES

The Sullivan Principles evolved in the 1970s. Faced by the South African government's institutionalised racial discrimination there was growing international pressure to apply economic sanctions. Alongside this was an increasing more general concern for ethical investment and greater corporate accountability, expressed in increased activism and public protests.

In the 1960s, however, the general view from corporations was that business should not use its power to influence political reform of any kind. The argument was shaped in broadly Friedmanite terms (see Chapter 11). The task of a business was to make profits in the free market. The chair of Chase Manhattan Bank in 1965 therefore responded to a student demonstration with these words: 'We can't be responsible for the social affairs of a country. Where there's commerce and trade, we feel we should be part of it' (quoted in Massie, 1997: 193). In effect, the chairman was arguing that the morality of the market was prior to any ethical issues in the country which hosted the bank's operations or of which the government was a client of the bank. This was an essentially liberal argument about the freedom of business in a global capitalist society to operate in that market. Moreover, it was argued that the free market was essential for the developing world. Chase Manhattan, for example, argued that 'It would endanger the free world if every large American bank deprived developing countries of the opportunity for economic growth' (Chase Manhattan Bank spokesperson, quoted in Sampson, 1987: 87).

Thus, by the early by 1970s over 300 American corporations were established in South Africa, involving over $900 million in investments (Blashill, 1972: 49). The public debate, however, did not go away, and three events challenged the liberal position. First, in 1970 it was discovered by some Polaroid employees that the firm provided the film for photographs used in the black South African identity passes, a key part of the *apartheid* law. Their drawing attention to this both within and outside the company led to a change in company policy, and Polaroid pulled out of the contract.

Second, there were increased protests, including student takeovers of university buildings. These in turn led to focusing on the investment practices of both higher education institutions and the Church, and debates at the UN. Such public analysis eventually led to a General Motors Annual General Meeting (May, 1971) at which a bishop from the American Episcopalian Church presented a shareholder resolution urging the company to withdraw its presence from South Africa.

The resolution failed but led directly to the third event: the development by the Revd Leon Sullivan of the Sullivan Principles. Sullivan had been appointed to the GM board as a result of Ralph Nader's campaign for racial equality within US business. Faced by the shareholder resolution on South Africa in his first meeting, he developed – despite opposition from the board – his series of principles aiming to achieve change in South Africa through the work of business over time.

There are three stages in the work of Sullivan.

- After an early call for complete withdrawal, he argued for changes in US business operations in South Africa that would be within the law. This would include desegregating eating, comfort and work areas; ensuring equal pay policy and practice; full training for black employees; and developing attempts to improve the quality of life for employees outside the workplace.

- For much of the next decade the Sullivan Principles faced major criticisms from anti-*apartheid* groups in South Africa and the USA. The Principles did not, for instance, question South Africa's job reservation rules (reserving the best jobs for whites) or *apartheid*'s migrant pass laws. This led to a further development of the Principles including attempts to encourage corporations to support freedom of association for workers and to increase employee participation in contributions to black communities.

- By 1985, the Principles were further beefed up to include a requirement for companies to take a public stance against *apartheid* and to work positively for the breaking down of racial exclusion.

(For a series of interviews around the work of Sullivan, visit http://muweb.marshall. edu/revleonsullivan/indexf.htm.)

The gradual advances in the Sullivan Principles represented very different ethical positions. The first was broadly utilitarian, looking to balance the needs of a business with the needs of its workforce. All of this was in the context of the legal framework of South Africa. It was assumed that this framework could not be questioned. This was reinforced by some firms' arguments that if business were to contribute to social change, it would lead to negative effects on their workforce and on the wider society.

The second development involved business in supporting positive freedom. Positive freedom (Berlin, 1966) is one step beyond negative (freedom *from*). In this case it was support for the right of the workforce to develop unions and so begin to develop power in negotiations with the companies. This still did not address the central issues of the loss of basic human rights of the black population. The third phase began to move towards a more deontological position, with the firms being asked to face up to the social context that they were operating in, and take a stand on the principle of supporting change in that society.

The activists tended to focus squarely on human rights, and their case was reinforced by the riots in the black township of Soweto, when student protestors were fired on by police. The businesses tended to focus on more complex areas of workplace practice and felt very nervous about the possibility that they might fall foul of the law. Behind it also was the concern about what appropriate responsibility might be, echoing Friedman: 'We cannot transform the nature of South African society, and we will have serious problems … if we try' (Sal Marzullo, minutes of a Conference board meeting on South Africa, 15 March 1978, quoted in Sethi and Williams, 2000: 12).

These very different ethical perceptions made it difficult to successfully monitor the record of the companies in South Africa. The activist concerns focused on the change of a political system. Under that thinking, even the payment of taxes that support a system which abuses human rights is questionable. The companies for the most part aimed to do what they could within the limits of shareholder concerns and the legal framework of South Africa. Importantly, the debate continued throughout this time and certainly accounted for the tightening up of the Principles. The debate, in effect, was forcing companies to give an account of their practices to the different stakeholders. The debate moved the thinking away from questions about the limitations of responsibility into more stark issues of shared responsibility and how far, by supporting the South African government, the business was actually supporting and therefore in some way sharing in the responsibility for *apartheid*.

Arguments against direct political involvement

Companies gave several reasons why direct action of any kind was wrong:

- There was a primary need to respect the rule of law in South Africa.

- The responsibility for issues such as human rights cannot be taken by business. This is the responsibility of the state and for the wider global organisations such as the United Nations.

- Any action that challenges a government raises the possibility of placing the company and its employees in direct danger, not least involving the possible loss of contracts and jobs.

- Direct action could lead to a failure of the business with a negative effect on shareholder value.

- Direct action might have a negative effect on the surrounding community, either through government forces targeting that community or through encouraging local resistance that might cause an escalation of violence.

The first argument is a straight deontological view that all laws should be respected, including the obligation to pay taxes. The second looks to draw clear lines of responsibility around how companies relate to human rights issues. The other arguments have different aspects of utilitarian thinking. It is not clear just what the outcome of direct action would be. In the light of the uncertainty about consequences and the potential danger to different stakeholders involved there is a strong ethical argument for use of the precautionary principle. Accordingly, the businesses in effect argued that they would do what they could.

Arguments for direct action

Against the cautious responses of business in general was the action of Polaroid. This was the result of a lengthy decision-making process. The firm began by gathering data, sending out black and white employees to South Africa. The resulting strategy involved:

- continuing a business relationship in South Africa, but not directly with the government

- improving the salaries and services of non-white employees in the South African operation

- committing a percentage of profits to non-white education in South Africa

- initiating training programmes in relation to higher posts for non-whites.

Only when Polaroid discovered that its equipment was being used for the passbook ID programme did it withdraw from South Africa in 1977. The argument here is that there was a direct causal link between the product sold by Polaroid to the South African government and its oppressive actions. The direct connection was perhaps even more powerful, in that the reproduction of an individual's image was in a sense more critically personal. Levinas's (1991) dictum that ethics begins with the face of the other is exemplified here, leading to a response that was more than simply rational, and tending towards identifying with the experience of the other.

Seidman (2003) argues that the general response of business in South Africa was to avoid this direct focus on responsibility. Instead, Seidman argues, these companies focused on narrower targets of responsibility in the workplace, attempting to demonstrate good intentions without working through the issue of responsibility. When companies finally did withdraw from South Africa, it is argued (Seidman, 2003) that it was largely for economic reasons – by which time the battle against *apartheid* had been won.

You are the CEO of a corporation that is operating in a country where the government is systematically abusing human rights. How would you relate to that government?

Give an account of how you would justify your position. How would you present that to the board?

Is it possible to both operate in such a country and argue that attention to some aspects of labour relations should embody social responsibility?

Does the support of companies for work in that country mean that they are giving support to the political system?

One of the striking things about the Sullivan case history is the way in which it takes in so many ethical issues. It could be centred on governance, with Sullivan challenging the board. It is also focused in local social responsibility and in relationships with the government. This takes it beyond simply accepting the legal framework of the law, because racial equality was still contentious in the USA. It also takes ethics into a more global context – something that is part of the supply chain (see Chapter 10). What binds all of these aspects together is responsibility ethics, focusing on what part any business could or should play in relation to the government, and leading to several questions:

- Should business become involved in what are, in effect, attempts to change the policy of a government or even to change the government itself? The case of the Sullivan Principles reveals a continuing dialogue in which business was using influence both within its own enterprise and beyond, but rarely if ever moving beyond the law.
- Should business become involved with other stakeholders or the wider industry to develop its influence? Guidelines on this are noted below.
- Should there be limitations in the use of a business's power to influence government policy in ordinary contexts? This is examined more closely in respect of lobbying below.
- How far can a company be held responsible for the use that its products are put to by governments? This issue came to head more recently in the case of the use of Caterpillar earth-clearing machinery by the Israeli army in Palestine.

CASE

CATERPILLAR

According to United Nations reports, a total of 4,170 Palestinian homes were destroyed by the Israeli army between September 2000 and December 2004 (War on Want, 2004: 4). Other sources suggest that the effect of such demolition since 1967 has been to make 70,000 people homeless (ibid: 5) The Caterpillar D9 is the main bulldozer used by the Israeli army to demolish homes and destroy farmland in occupied Palestine. The justification for this sustained action was that it involved punitive action against the family homes of Palestinians engaged or suspected of engagement in armed activities against Israel. It remains unclear that sufficient

evidence for these actions has always been given (ibid: 6). Even with such evidence the practice is a breach of Article 53 of the Fourth Geneva Convention (to which Israel is a signatory). This states (http://www.icrc.org/ihl.nsf/385ec082b509e76c412567 39003e636d/ 6756482d86146898c125641 e004aa3c5 [accessed 29 June 2011]):

Any destruction by the Occupying Power of real or personal property belonging individually or collectively to private persons, or to the State, or to other public authorities, or to social or cooperative organizations, is prohibited, except where such destruction is rendered absolutely necessary by military operations.

One of the most widely reported episodes in the intensified Israeli assault on the Palestinians over the previous four years was the Battle of Jenin in April 2002. Caterpillar bulldozers were a key to this action. Jenin was a densely populated refugee camp containing over 14,000 people. Based on eyewitness accounts, it is claimed that house demolitions continued after the end of the action (War on Want, 2004: 13), leading to the flattening of an entire district with the camp. Some people were unable to escape from houses because of the crossfire, and many were buried alive under the ruins, including some who were ill and disabled.

Following the death of the activist Rachel Corrie at one of the Palestinian sites being cleared (www. rachelcorriefoundation. org/), the argument has increasingly focused on legal issues, involving lawsuits filed by the Corrie family in the USA and in Israel. The thrust of the lawsuits is to hold the different parties accountable for their actions. US companies that aid and profit from violations of human rights can be held responsible under US law (www. guardian.co.uk/ world/2010/mar/10/ rachel-corrie-civil-case-israel).

Questions

1 If you were on the board of Caterpillar, how would you respond to the request of the Corrie family for a meeting and the continuing campaign for investors to withdraw their money?

2 Up to this point CEO James Owen has refused to see the family, and has advised investors to withdraw if they do not like what Caterpillar is doing. What might act as a constraint to such a meeting, and what might enable it?

RESPONSIBILITY: THE ARGUMENTS

Moral responsibility

The key ethical issue emerging from this is whether Caterpillar can be held to be responsible in some way for the use to which the Israeli government puts its product. The first argument from Caterpillar indicates that no company can be held responsible for how a government uses its product. An individual analogy might be the sale of a kitchen knife. No company who sells knives can be held responsible for individuals who decide to kill members of their family with such knives or use them to dig the garden. This argument is, in one sense, self-evident. The second argument is that the product itself is not designed to be used as an instrument of aggression. If it were classified as an armament, its sale would have to be licensed by the home government, with a clear indication of the use accepted. Despite accusations that Caterpillar had modified the D9 and D10, it is clear that the Israeli government effected modifications for their use in the combat zone.

The conclusion from these arguments would be that the primary area of responsibility for any acts that violated human rights or conventions would be with the government of Israel or possibly with the US government if it was involved in the supply of the products. Importantly, responsibility in this context is about direct moral or legal liability, such that the party in question can be said to be to blame, partly or wholly, for any offences that may have been caused. Caterpillar's defence has been based on this narrow view of responsibility. Supporting this stance would be a further pragmatically ethical argument that Caterpillar could be subject to serious penalties if they did admit any sense of liability. The danger here is of admission of moral responsibility moving into legal responsibility, along with potential financial loss. From the perspective of sustaining Caterpillar it could therefore be argued that the most ethical response is not to accept responsibility for the use of the product.

This approach tends to focus on reactive responsibility – being responsible for reacting to a corporate crisis, and defending the corporation.

Proactive responsibility

Against these arguments is a different view of responsibility: proactive responsibility. This goes directly back to Chapter 4 and the idea of shared responsibility, and the argument that responsibility has to be worked carefully through with others who share it. If we return to the analogy of the sale of a knife, the argument would be that although it is true that the seller cannot be held responsible for what the person does with the knife, a different sense of responsibility emerges if the buyer has made it clear that he or she intends to use the product for an unethical or illegal purpose, or if there has been a record of this happening before. In this sense, knowledge of the use and outcome of that use poses the issue for proactive responsibility. If you know what use is being or will be made of the product, and the use has a negative end, do you not share in the responsibility? This raises the question, could the seller do anything to affect the use of the product or to prevent the illegal or unethical use of the product? For this responsibility to be exercised, the seller would have to be clear that the use of the product is essentially unethical or illegal. It may be a straightforward matter in the use of a knife, but in the Caterpillar case this leads to further debate.

On the one hand, the Israeli government defends the use of the D9s on punitive grounds and the basis that terrorists intentionally make use of the houses to defend themselves. Israel argues that it has to clear away such a defence. In that argument moral responsibility moves across to the terrorists who have intentionally involved families and their houses. They are to blame for any consequences to innocent people, it is argued.

On the other hand, the evidence of War on Want and others suggests that Israel had further options open to them in pursuing their end than simply flattening the houses with people still inside them. This side of the argument also questions why families should be punished for the fact that terrorists have made use of their homes.

At this stage the debate is moving beyond a simple issue of human rights and into matters of justice. Israel wants to argue that their action is just. Could Caterpillar have the temerity to argue against that? As we have seen in Chapter 7, justice is not something alien to decision-making in business. We will look more closely at underlying definitions of justice in the next chapter. In this case we simply want to look at the options the firm might have.

In October 2010 Caterpillar reported that they would delay delivery of the D9 and D10 while the lawsuit in Israeli courts was ongoing. This would seem to indicate that Caterpillar might change its stance if the action of Israeli government was deemed to be unethical or illegal. Clear proof of this would raise directly with Caterpillar the need to respond to the challenge of proactive responsibility.

However, another argument asks, does exercising proactive responsibility have to depend on waiting for proof of human rights abuses? The exercise of proactive responsibility would seem to focus on how the company might take responsibility for responding to the actions of a government that have been questioned, and for working through how they might contribute responsibly to the situation. In that light there are several options that fit proactive responsibility:

- Work with the appropriate international agency, such as the United Nations or other NGOs, to determine the exact nature of the actions in question. Until this is clear in terms of international law, a combination of proactive responsibility and the precautionary principle leads to an argument for suspending supply. This is where Caterpillar now seem to be.

- Withdraw from dealing with the government, like Polaroid. Responsible work in this demands that, as in the Polaroid case, there should be extensive data-gathering and the development of strategy. Polaroid's final decision was based on a direct connection between its equipment and an action that denied human rights to an entire ethnic group. By continuing to supply the equipment, once the use was clear, Polaroid would have been supporting, if not liable for, a systematic abuse of human rights. This does not take responsibility to be inclusive, but rather shared. The problem with the Israeli government's argument was that in placing responsibility solely at the door of the terrorists it did not address the possibility of shared responsibility. This led to a narrowing of options.

- If it is difficult to be clear about the first two options, another would be to state clearly the action and behaviour that the firm would not wish to be associated with, and to agree on a process for monitoring that action in the future, possibly involving external bodies, such as the UN, to judge. At the least this would demand agreement between the wider industry and the different stakeholders involved about the criteria of judgement and a means of monitoring the practice.

None of this demands that the corporation makes a stand against the government, or even that it makes a stand about justice in general. In a sense, making a stand about justice is precisely the task of the NGOs involved, such as War on Want. The ethical task of proactive responsibility is rather to share responsibility for working through the issues.

All of this demands constructive dialogue between board and shareholders and all the stakeholders in order to develop the most effective response.

The Caterpillar case is characterised by a lack of proactive engagement and the fear of being held to a narrow sense of responsibility. There is therefore little by way of developed dialogue with the stakeholders.

Caterpillar's code of practice (see www.cat.com/Code-of-Conduct), in contrast, stresses a commitment to proactive responsibility. It notes the power of responsibility and a commitment to health and safety in the supply chain and in end-users.

As proactive members of its communities, Caterpillar aims to promote their health, welfare and stability, encouraging employees to contribute to the common good. This proactive stance is summed up in the words:

> We believe that our success should also contribute to the quality of life in, and the prosperity and sustainability of, communities where we work and live. As a company and as individuals, we hold ourselves to the highest standard of integrity and ethical behaviour … If we do any less, we put Caterpillar's name and our reputation for integrity at risk.

SCENARIO

As the head of CSR in the Caterpillar corporation, how would you show the company's actions as fitting with this code?

As a non-executive director, how would you set out the ethical issues in this case before the board?

Would you stress the importance of defending the company, or would you seek to work with stakeholders to find the most just position? What are the risks of taking either of these positions?

As the CSR director, how would you pursue your relationship with the NGOs who are attaching the case against Caterpillar to the Rachel Corrie incident? How would you respond to the many videos (see http://video.google.com/videoplay?docid=-66458108575955294097#docid=-1010455058971006040 for an example of one video)? Would you ignore them, enter a dialogue, or attempt to portray such treatment as ideological propaganda?

THE REGULATION OF BUSINESS AND GOVERNMENT RELATIONS

As we have already noted in the chapter on governance (Chapter 5), a great deal of the relationship between business and government involves legislation and issues of regulation. In every area of business practice there is a raft of legislation that expresses core ethical imperatives, from health and safety to equality and diversity, to financial probity.

The issue of who should regulate is a source of constant debate. King III, for instance, grew out of the debate between the South African government and business about how far governance itself should be developed through government regulation or informal codes.

In March 2011 the United Nations attempted to bring this debate together in respect of human rights, providing guidelines of how business and state should relate. By providing guidelines they came firmly down in favour of self-regulation with the acceptance of a global framework entitled *Protect, Respect and Remedy* (http:// 198.170.85.29/Ruggie-protect-respect-remedy-framework.pdf).

The guiding principles grew out of an early United Nations-based initiative called the *Norms on Transnational Corporations and Other Business Enterprises* (Ruggie, 2008). This attempted to establish directly under international law the same range of human rights duties that states have accepted for themselves under treaties they have ratified: 'to promote, secure the fulfilment of, respect, ensure respect of and protect human rights'.

The resulting debate led to several years of research with business, NGOs and governments to establish core understandings of this issue.

The framework was developed under the three headings Protect, Respect and Remedy.

The first involves the duty of the state to protect against human rights abuses by third parties, including business enterprises, through appropriate policies, regulation and adjudication. The second focuses on the corporate responsibility to respect human rights, which means that business enterprises should act with due diligence to avoid infringing the rights of others and to address adverse impacts with which they are involved. The third centres on responding to the need for greater access by victims to effective remedy.

The report aims to clarify responsibilities, and sees the three areas as fundamentally interconnected. The normative contribution lies not in the creation of new international law obligations but in elaborating the implications of existing standards and practices for states and businesses, integrating them within a single, logically coherent and comprehensive template, and identifying where a current regime falls short and how it should be improved. Each principle is accompanied by a commentary, further clarifying its meaning and implications.

These guiding principles are grounded in a recognition of:

- a state's existing obligations to respect, protect and fulfil human rights and fundamental freedoms
- the role of business enterprises as specialised organs of society performing specialised functions, required to comply with all applicable laws and to respect human rights
- the need for rights and obligations to be matched to appropriate and effective remedies when breached.

It is claimed that the principles apply to all states and to all business enterprises, regardless of their size, context, ownership or structure.

In the first part it is argued that a key role of the state is to ensure that businesses have properly addressed human rights issues, including the exercise of due diligence in assessing the dangers of human rights abuse. The guidelines note the particular importance of this in relation to businesses operating in conflict areas. The commentary works through how this can be effected, including the provision of training and support. States should encourage fellow members of international institutions to work together with business in the protection of human rights.

At the heart of this is the assertion that business, of whatever size, has a responsibility to respect human rights. Section 15 spells out what is required.

15. In order to meet their responsibility to respect human rights, business enterprises should have in place policies and processes appropriate to their size and circumstances, including:

(a) a policy commitment to meet their responsibility to respect human rights

(b) a human rights due-diligence process to identify, prevent, mitigate and account for how they address their impacts on human rights

(c) Processes to enable the remediation of any adverse human rights impacts they cause or to which they contribute.

Several aspects are worth underlining.

The responsibility of the company to respect human rights exists regardless of any state's lack of capacity or unwillingness to fulfil human rights obligations. So even if the state ignores human rights, the company is responsible for respecting human rights.

The guiding principles understand a business enterprise's 'activities' as including both actions and omissions. Its 'business relationships' include those with business partners, groups or entities in the value chain, and any other non-state or state entity directly linked to its business operations, products or services. Responsibility is thus not limited to a narrow view of liability but includes proactive responsibility.

If a business is in some way involved with human rights abuses, it should take the necessary steps to either end the involvement or use what the guidance terms 'leverage' to ensure that the impact on human rights is lessened. Leverage involves the use of the corporation's power to influence government actions. Leverage is possible where the enterprise has the ability to effect change in the wrongful practices of an entity that causes harm.

The commentary on the principles then goes through more complex scenarios, in effect setting up an ethical decision-making process. Within that the enterprise will have to assess how best to use the leverage it has, how important the relationship is to the enterprise, the severity of the abuse, and whether ending the relationship with the entity would itself have adverse human rights consequences. Greater complexity increases the case for involving independent expert advice on the response. The guidelines are clear that if the business enterprise does have leverage to prevent or mitigate the adverse impact, it should use it. If it lacks leverage, it should explore ways to increase it, not least through working with other stakeholders in the area. There are situations in which the enterprise lacks the leverage to prevent or mitigate adverse impacts, in particular when dealing with governments, and is unable to increase its leverage. At this point the commentary suggests ending the relationship, once the human rights impact of that is properly assessed. None of this decision-making is easy and the relationships may be critical to the survival of the business, in which case the business should at the very least demonstrate its ongoing efforts to mitigate the impact on human rights. The company then will have to estimate the consequences of continuing the relationship, in terms of reputation, finance and legal issues.

All this requires policies and procedures that integrate the means of developing awareness of the social environment and human rights impacts; the firm's effect on that environment, and the government's role; an ongoing monitoring of the relevant events; and responsiveness to the events that will include remedial action through proper channels (sections 19–22).

The basis of these guidelines is a framework that aims to empower all the stakeholders. The guidelines thus aim to be clear both about the basic responsibility of the key players and also about the means by which the detailed responsibility can be worked through. This works against simple regulation that tells the actors what to do. The working through of responsibility includes the examination of the power of the different organisations. Proactive responsibility also means that there is no simple division of responsibilities. If human rights are being abused at any point in the value chain, there is a responsibility to deal with this and to find ways of dealing with it. It requires an ongoing review of the relationship with the government. The guidelines also argue that business should prioritise, seeking first to respond to abuses 'that are most severe or where delayed response would make them irremediable' (section 24).

THE DEBATE OVER THE UN GUIDELINES

The debate is ongoing. Human Rights Watch, among others, argues that the guidelines are too weak and that there should be global regulation. 'In effect, the [UN] Council endorsed the status quo – a world where companies are encouraged, but not obliged, to respect human rights,' Arvind Ganesan, Business and Human Rights Director at Human Rights Watch, has said. 'Guidance isn't enough – we need a mechanism to scrutinise how companies and governments apply these principles' (Human Rights Watch, 16 June 2011: http://www.hrw.org/node/99908).

The argument is that governments should provide legal frameworks for business practice. There are two problems with this. First, the very idea of human rights can be challenged, both as a concept and in practice. This is examined more closely in the next chapter, on global ethics. Second, to effect this would require a global focus for and a means of policing such rights, and it is not clear that one exists.

The issues about regulation are there in ongoing relationships with government, as we have noted, for instance, with the alcohol industry. Of particular concern are the issues surrounding the attempts of business to influence the government for its own interests, most obviously seen in lobbying.

LOBBYING

Lobbying involves deliberate attempts to influence political decision-making in the interest of a particular group. It is often perceived as focused on big business, partly because serious business resources have been put into lobbying. However, lobbying is carried out by many groups from NGOs to religious organisations. Industry inevitably wants to influence governments in many different ways, from levels and types of taxation to levels and types of regulation.

Lobbying can take place through formal or informal groups or through professional lobbyists. The ethics of lobbying focuses on how the lobbying is carried out. In one sense lobbying is simply part of political debate. Political debate takes place most effectively if advocates for different groups make their arguments known with absolute clarity. The motivation may well be based on ethical thinking. Brown-Forman, for instance, have therefore argued that they have to be involved in lobbying the US government on the basis of justice, establishing a fair alcohol market (Robinson and Kenyon, 2009) and appropriate systems of regulation. Lobbying in that situation is not simply about creating and using influence. It means getting involved in the whole debate about what constitutes a fair market, consumer autonomy and the nature and function of regulation. This requires a clear account of how the company regulates itself and how the industry works together to that end. It is clearly in the interest of any industry not to have heavy regulation imposed by government, but it also involves the company and the wider industry in debate about ethical values and how they can be addressed in practice. So for a company such as Brown-Forman it may even involve giving an account of how they go further than present regulation in their practice (Robinson and Kenyon, 2009).

In the best of all possible worlds, then, lobbying involves debate about ethical standards and the demonstration of responsible practice. The context of this is the kind of rigorous public debate required for informed decision-making. Ethical problems with lobbying centre on the attempts of lobbyists or law-makers to undermine the openness and fairness of that debate process in such a way that the interest of the groups only is addressed, and not the common good.

BUSINESS INFLUENCE

The most obviously questionable lobbying practice is payment in some kind – such as contribution to campaign funds – for votes or favourable consideration in legislation. This is both illegal and unethical. If it were allowed, it would always skew decisions and fatally affect any public debate. There are, however, more subtle ways of influencing members of the government, from hospitality to invitations to sponsored events, to what are known as 'revolving doors contacts'. The latter involves former public officials who now serve as lobbyists and aim to influence former colleagues. This may extend to present friendships. The key issue here is that the nature of the relationships is in danger of circumventing open debate, leading to an unfair advantage. The whole issue is under further scrutiny following the resignation of Liam Fox MP (http://www.bbc.co.uk/news/uk-politics-15333707) and the UK government's planning for the regulation of the lobbying industry.

Ways in which business can influence a government and what this leads to can be much more subtle and, Monbiot (2003) argues, much more insidious. He argues, for instance, that business has become involved in government research councils, and thus finds itself directly influencing how public money is spent on research. In effect, this leads to business determining the agenda of research and subtly moving away from independent academic research and debate. Monbiot gives two examples. First, the Biotechnology and Biological Sciences Research Council in the early 2000s had as its chair an executive director of the biotechnology company Zeneca. The council included a chief executive of a pharmaceutical firm, a former director of Nestlé, the President of the Food and Drink Federation, a consultant to the biochemical industry and the general manager of Britain's biggest farming business. The BBSRC's strategy board included executives from SmithKline Beecham, Merck Sharp & Dohme, and AgrEvo UK, the company hoping to be the first to commercialise genetically engineered crops in Britain (http://www.bbsrc.ac.uk [accessed 21 January 2000]). Monbiot argues that this has led to a skewing of the debate, and that the chair of the BBSRC was using what is a government research body 'as a platform for contentious and in some cases misleading political statements, which appear to favour the interests of the biotechnology companies' (2003: 54). He notes that on one occasion the chairman used his position to argue against a report from Friends of the Earth about the risk of cross-pollination from GM crops. Monbiot further argues that the scientists who were involved in the relevant research projects were formally gagged from becoming involved in political controversy.

Monbiot's second case involved the work of the Office of Science and Technology's Foresight Panels. These were official sources of scientific advice to both central government and to the research councils, and were heavily influenced by business. The Food and Drink Foresight Panel, for example, was made up of eight representatives of food companies and trade bodies, three university representatives, and members of the BBSRC and the Medical Research Council (both of whom advised on research priorities). The report of one subcommittee, drawn up in consultation with five trade associations and three industry-sponsored research institutes, called for research that would help break down 'unnecessary barriers', caused by regulation, to innovation and growth in the industry.

The recommendations of the Food and Drink Foresight Panel showed evidence of influence, both in terms of policy and the agenda, of research councils. The BBSRC had 'a much more explicit emphasis on consumer science, a priority topic identified by the panel' (Department of Trade and Industry, *Winning through Foresight: Action for food and drink*; http://193.82.159.123/documents/fsze00002/ fsze000023.html).

The Retail and Consumer Services Foresight Panel, chaired by Sir John Banham, the then head of Tarmac, warned of the 'potentially dire' impact of public anxieties about the environment (Monbiot, 2003: 47). It argued that this would lead to problems in greenfield development and the restriction of traffic, resulting in a collapse in living standards, including cuts in state pensions.

Monbiot's argument relies heavily on a view of the independence of science that in Chapter 8 we argued is problematic. This leads easily to a polarisation of the debate with science as good and business as bad. Nonetheless, his cases show how easily business can cross a line, and the importance of transparency. In fact, there have always been issues about conflicts of interest both between higher education and business and between business and the government. Indeed, given the different stakeholders, it is difficult to see how conflicts of interest would *not* arise in some way at some point. This raises the importance of maintaining clear practice about how to handle such conflict, potential and actual.

CONFLICTS OF INTEREST, POLICY AND PRACTICE

Conflict of interest occurs across several different areas of business. It is business that so often causes this issue to emerge precisely because of its power and capacity to influence the decision-making process. Where government is making decisions, a potential conflict of interest has to be clearly set out. None of this is to say that business should not be involved in the debate. It is the terms and nature of the debate that must be clarified. This leads to three areas that have to be addressed: transparency, critical dialogue and the nature of advocacy.

Transparency

Improving the fairness of the lobbying process requires that possible sources of influence are visible to the public. With over 15,000 lobbyist organisations involved in the EU, this becomes increasingly important. Transparency International argues for several actions with regard to the EU (http://blog.transparency.org/2011/03/24/mind-the-gap-meps-must-tighten-up-their-act/ [accessed 28 June 2011]), including:

- a fully fledged, cohesive code of conduct, showing how alleged breaches of the code are to be handled
- rules on the disclosure of financial interests in a standardised format and in a searchable electronic database. This would enable all stakeholders to monitor business and politicians' activities
- a 'legislative footprint'. This would enable tracking the influence of external advice on amendments and legislation
- clear whistleblowing channels
- stringent rules related to MEPs holding a second job
- strong guidance on gifts and hospitality.

Critical dialogue

Critical dialogue has to be at the heart of the political context of lobbying. Ultimately, decisions made by governments must be based on clear criteria that are agreed by all the parties involved. This demands that all involved give a clear account of the basis of their thinking and how it relates to evidence. It means that the government has to ensure that the debate is public, and that all who have an interest give an account of their position. Similarly, any interest group must also give an account of how its views fit in with any sense of the common good.

Advocacy and the common good

Lobbyists are often seen as advocates for an interest, moving the argument to the analogy of the court of law in which lawyers defend someone's interest. The lobbyist provides one among several different views that enable the politician to make a decision. They contribute, in this sense, to the common good.

The problem with this model is that it does not reflect the public sphere. The courtroom analogy assumes two equally powerful legal advocates, with legal rules and laws that the judge interprets and upholds. In the political arena there may be no opposite voice or even an arena in which the different interests are examined and tested. There must therefore be a framework to ensure that all views that pertain to the common good are examined. Politicians thus have an obligation to solicit the views of those who are not represented by powerful business lobbying groups.

For business in this area, the ethical imperative is that non-transparent use of influence should be avoided at all points. For the government the establishment of codes and frameworks that enable this openness is important. This brings the debate back to the more subtle influence that Monbiot detects in the research agendas. Here too the government has to establish appropriate governance to enable the critical dialogue to take place in the governing bodies of the councils and panels. Parallel to the work on corporate governance this would demand that beside business and academics there also sit other interest groups that have a concern for the common good.

One of the most complex and difficult case histories concerning the relationship of business and government in the past half-century has centred on the oil company Shell's presence in the Niger Delta.

CASE

SHELL IN THE NIGER DELTA

Shell has operated in the Niger Delta since the discovery of the first oilfield there in 1956. After Nigeria's independence in 1960, the Shell Petroleum Development Company (SPDC) – a joint venture of Shell and the Nigerian Government – was formed. This includes the Nigerian National Petroleum Corporation (NNPC), holding 55%, Shell (30%) and the French company Total (formally Elf) with 10% (Ite, 2004: 3).

Poverty and the resource curse

Poverty has been a persistent problem in the Niger Delta, despite the fact that the region accounts for over 90% of national export earnings from oil production and exportation. The majority of Nigeria's oil wealth benefits a mere 1% of the population (Ite, 2004: 3).

Many of Nigeria's problems surrounding conflict and development can be attributed equally to wealth, as much to the existence of poverty. Resource-rich African countries have been among the poorest and most violent on the continent. Underdeveloped countries become dependent upon natural wealth, failing to diversify into and develop other industries or invest in human resources (Frynas, 2009: 135). This is often referred to as the 'resource curse'.

Business, conflict and peace

Although Nigeria is formally a democracy, it has a long history of corrupt and unstable government. The wealth from natural resources has therefore been focused in the hands of corrupt political elites, the vast majority of the country living in poverty, denied basic infrastructure, education and health services (Frynas, 2009). This has led to ongoing conflict (www.guardian.co.uk/environment/.../ shell-oil-spill-niger-delta). Much of this has been centred on Ogoniland in the southern part of the Niger Delta. The community there voiced grievances against Shell and the government through the formation of the Movement for the Survival of the Ogoni People (MOSOP) in 1990. Following further violent protests (unrelated to MOSOP), Shell withdrew from the Ogoni area in 1993. Following this (Kline, 2000: 383) the military government sought to eradicate the Ogoni threat. In November 1995, the Nigerian Government executed Ken Saro-Wiwa, leader of MOSOP, and eight others following accusations of inciting the murder of Ogoni chiefs in opposition to MOSOP. During the trial, the 'Ogoni Nine' were tortured, and denied access to their families, legal aid and the opportunity to appeal against the decision.

Shell's response

The response of Shell initially focused on the different approaches to relating to governments. It involved three phases.

In the first, Shell tried to draw a clear line between business and government. Moody-Stuart, chairman of Royal Dutch Shell from 1998 to 2001, argued at the UN Conference on Human Rights and the

Extractive Industries, 10 November 2005, that:

> We should remember that governments bear the prime responsibility for ensuring the human rights of their people. They have subscribed to that great foundation document, the Universal Declaration of Human Rights.

Shell argued that their major contribution to communities in the Niger Delta was through the taxes and royalties paid to the federal government. The revenues to the government from SPDC were disclosed as amounting to $36 billion from 2005 to 2006 – a degree of wealth that holds potential for community development in Nigeria. Nonetheless, this potential was lost due to corruption within the government.

The second response, developing over time, accepted the need to revise practice and statements of value. The revised Statement of General Business Principles, first drafted in 1976 (Shell International http://www-static.shell.com/static/public/downloads/corporate_pkg/sgbp_english.pdf), promoted the company's values in support of human rights and sustainable development, leading to increased work with stakeholders. SPDC in Nigeria hired consultants and development specialists in order to strengthen its contribution to the Niger Delta, while also working with partners such as USAID, UNDP and Africare. Idemudia and Uwem (2006) note how this differed from the original, philanthropic, approach in the 1960s. It involved 'gifts' to the local groups, more focused on 'securing local right of way'. This was perceived as securing Shell's licence to operate, leading to a local 'dependence culture' (Ite, 2004: 5). In 2006 SPDC signed the Global Memorandum of Understanding (GMoU) with local communities near to the company's operations. The overall objective was to build the capacity of the local communities to negotiate with the oil companies for development funding, and then manage the process of implementing the development projects in their own communities.

The GMoU had the potential to create independent rather than dependent communities – a vital aspect in creating ownership of projects and increasing sustainability. Shell has invested over $20 million in over 80 projects, including the construction of roads, health centres, schools, markets, water schemes and the introduction of micro-credit schemes for small businesses. Key to all of this has been transparency, and increased autonomy and shared responsibility of stakeholders, with a committee including representatives from communities, government, NGOs and SPDC overseeing how the money is spent. At one level this focuses on proactive responsibility. It also recognises the importance of responding to the local social environment in which the firm operates.

The issue of responsibility comes to a head with Shell's third response, to the Saro-Wiwa case. At one level the company has remained distanced, preferring not to respond publicly, or to publicly use any leverage to question the then government's actions. Shell deny complicity with the arrests and executions. Ruggie (2008: 20) defines complicity as 'knowingly providing practical assistance or engagement that has a substantial effect on the commission of a crime'. To accept such an idea of complicity might make Shell legally responsible, and this in turn could lead to major company losses. It might be argued that although the firm was not legally responsible, it was morally responsible. The argument runs that by financing security forces controlled by the Nigerian government, the company by action or omission was at least partly responsible for what happened.

Following a court case over allegations of human rights abuses in the Niger Delta, Shell agreed to pay a settlement of $15.5 million in June 2009 (www.guardian.co.uk/environment/cif.../09/saro-wiwa-shell). The company continued to dismiss all claims made against them, maintaining that they played no part in the violence

(Pilkington, 2009). It argued that the settlement was a 'humanitarian gesture', intended to compensate the plaintiffs' legal costs and benefit the Ogoni people.

The debate is ongoing, with four NGOs now arguing for better ways of engaging the political situation in the Niger Delta. According to the Ecumenical Council for Corporate Responsibility (ECCR, 2010), Shell's response has not been sufficient owing to failure to grasp the issues of government and local relationships. The result, it argues, is a loss of trust in Shell in Nigeria. To regain such trust it claims that there is a need to increase transparency in working at local and national level, and to develop the use of more international principles and standards, and independent groups. Its recommendations (ECCR, 2010: 78: http://www.eccr.org.uk/module-htmlpages-display-pid-78.html) are listed below.

ECCR recommendations and Shell's response

In view of Shell's loss of social licence in Ogoni, these recommendations can help the company avoid a similar future occurrence elsewhere.

1 Disengage from community development programmes and establish neutral mechanisms comprising community members of the highest reputation, in collaboration with communities at the appropriate level, to implement programmes according to community priorities.

2 Work with the federal government in setting aside a proportion of oil revenue to address community priorities.

3 Establish a mechanism for direct dialogue with communities where the company operates based on principle of respect, inclusion and informed consent; ensure that communities have good access to information relating to activities that affect them.

4 Overhaul SPDC's Community Relations Department, establish a culturally sensitive and conflict-sensitive approach to community relations, and elevate the department to a higher and more substantive role within the company, with more qualified and professional staff who are knowledgeable in managing community expectations and fears.

5 Stop using community development projects as channels of patronage, recruitment and appeasement of violent youths, thugs and community elites.

6 End the double standards employed in oil pollution clean-up exercises and apply international standards.

7 Voluntarily stop gas flaring in the Niger Delta.

Shell's response closed with the following (198.170.85.29/Shell-response-re-Niger-Delta-report-17-Feb-2010.doc):

SPDC and Shell have always maintained that the problems in the Delta can only be solved through collaborative solutions. The first step is to identify areas of shared interest involving industry, communities, government and NGOs. SPDC looks forward to continuing to play its part and hopes that others will take the opportunity to engage in constructive dialogue. SPDC alone cannot provide the answers to the problems of the Delta, but it has to be part of the solution.

Questions

1 Has Shell gone far enough in developing a transparent practice that enables good stakeholder relations which avoid the negative influence of business or government?

2 Has Shell worked sufficiently with international standards and bodies in developing its response?

3 Has Shell effectively addressed its relationships with successive Nigerian governments? Has it, for instance, addressed any of the issues in the UN Guidelines above, such as the need to develop leverage that might influence the government or call it to account?

SCENARIO

Following Shell's initial response to the ECCR, and as the Number Two in Shell's CSR department, you have been tasked to open up dialogue with the ECCR. To prepare yourself for this, you and your colleague have been asked to critically analyse the ECCR recommendations. What are your conclusions, and how will you put those conclusions to the executive committee of the ECCR?

BUSINESS: DEVELOPMENT AND CONFLICT

The Shell case shows the development of shared responsibility in relation to the government over time. This further tests assumptions about the responsibility of the government, even in the area of peace and conflict. Shell's increasing work with the immediate community has begun to address economic issues which are critical to post-conflict development. This is building up a virtuous circle. Economic stability and wealth distribution provide a secure basis for peace, and such security provides markets for business. In this sense, although peacebuilding is ultimately the responsibility of the state, business plays a key part. This may be one of direct influence on government policy, as in South Africa, or through building the economic infrastructure that enables peace. The different approaches are summed up in the UN Global Compact's *Doing Business Whilst Advancing Peace and Development* (2011).

Key to developing such an approach is the use of the moral imagination (Lederach, 2005), involving the capacity to see the connections and possibilities (see Chapter 7). It is the use of this imagination that makes it possible for SMEs to be involved in this area, in different ways from larger firms. A good example of this is the Turkish Muslim firms who work together to finance the development of secular schools in post-conflict situations (see Mohamed, 2007).

Of course, business can also take self-interested advantage of conflict situations. War can generate economic opportunities (Ferguson, 2009; http://news.bbc.co.uk/1/hi/business/3006149.stm).

A good example of business involved in development is that of Grameenphone. Part of the company's focus is in the enabling role of mobile phones and computers across Bangladesh (see http://www.grameenphone.com/about-us/corporate-information/corporate-responsibility/cr-initiatives).

CONCLUSION

The Shell case revealed something of the complexity in the relationship between business and the government. The company's relationship with the Nigerian government showed how in the context of the developing world it is insufficient to work simply with the state. The ethics of shared responsibility demands that business work with all the other stakeholders in addressing the core problems. In some situations that means working with stakeholders to address the role of the government; in others it means working with stakeholders directly; and in yet others it might involve working with the government directly, exerting whatever leverage can be used. Government and business relations always occur within a complex web of relationships. Recognising that is part of the reason why transparency is so important in that relationship. The primary importance is that business focus on the common good in relation to the government and not simply on its own interests.

The relationship of business to government further develops issues of responsibility, testing the awareness of business on its effect on the government, business's responsibility in matters of human rights, issues of transparency and how responsibility can be shared. In the Niger Delta case this even raises questions about how business relates to poverty and to conflict. That in turn raises questions of how business relates to governments in areas of war or post-conflict development. This takes the debate about business ethics firmly into a global context.

EXPLORE FURTHER

Books

Haley, U. (2001) *Multinational Corporations in Political Environments: Ethics, values and strategies*. London: World Scientific Publishing.

Williams, O. (2008) *Peace through Commerce: Responsible corporate citizenship and the ideals of the United Nations Global Compact*. Notre Dame: University of Notre Dame Press.

REFERENCES

BERLIN, I. (1966) 'Two concepts of liberty', in Quinton, A. (ed.) *Political Philosophy*. London: Penguin.

BLASHILL, J. (1972) 'The proper role of U.S. corporations in South Africa', *Fortune Magazine*, July: 49.

DTI (2000) *Winning through Foresight: Action for food and drink*: http://193.82.159.123/documents/fsze00002/fsze000023.html

ECCR (2010) *Shell in the Niger Delta: A framework for change*. Ecumenical Council on Corporate Responsibility (ECCR), Feb: http://www.eccr.org.uk/module-Downloads-prep_hand_out-lid-20.html [accessed 19 May 2011].

FERGUSON, N. (2009) *The Ascent of Money*. London: Penguin.

FRYNAS, G. (2009) *Beyond Corporate Social Responsibility*. Cambridge: Cambridge University Press.

HUMAN RIGHTS WATCH (2011) 'UN Human Rights Council: Weak stance on business standards': http://www.hrw.org/news/2011/06/16/un-human-rights-council-weak-stance-business-standards.

IDEMUDIA, U. and UWEM, E. (2006) 'Demystifying the Niger Delta conflict: towards an integrated explanation', *Review of African Political Economy*, 33(109), September: 391–406.

ITE, U. (2007) 'Changing times and strategies: Shell's contribution to sustainable community development in the Niger Delta, Nigeria', *Sustainable Development*, 15(1), Jan/Feb: 1–14.

KLINE, J. (2000) *Ethics for International Business*. London: Routledge.

LEDERACH, J. P. (2005) *The Moral Imagination: The art and soul of building peace*. Oxford, Oxford University Press.

LEVINAS, E. (1991) *Entre Nous: On thinking of the other*. New York: Columbia University.

MASSIE, R. (1997) *Loosing the Bonds: The United States and South Africa in the apartheid years*. New York: Doubleday.

MOHAMED, Y. (2007) 'The ethical theory of Fethullah Gülen and its practice in South Africa', in Yilmaz, I. (ed.) *Muslim World in Transition*. Leeds: Leeds Metropolitan University Press: 552–71.

MONBIOT, G. (2003) 'Guard dogs of perception: the corporate takeover of science', *Science and Engineering Ethics*, 9(1): 49–57.

PILKINGTON, E. (2009) 'Shell pays out $15.5m over Saro-Wiwa killing', *The Guardian* (London): http://www.guardian.co.uk/world/2009/jun/08/nigeria-usa.

ROBINSON, S. and KENYON, A. (2009) *Ethics in the Alcohol Industry*. Basingstoke: Palgrave.

RUGGIE, J. (2008) http://www.reports-and-materials.org/Ruggie-protect-respect-remedy-framework.pdf [accessed 24 July 2011].

SAMPSON, A. (1987) *Black and Gold: Tycoons, revolutions and apartheid*. London: Hodder & Stoughton.

SEIDMAN, G. (2003) 'Monitoring multinationals: lessons from the anti-apartheid era', *Politics and Society*, 31: 381–406.

SETHI, S. and WILLIAMS, O. (2000) *Economic Imperatives and Ethical Values*. Boston, MA: Kluwer Academic.

TRANSPARENCY INTERNATIONAL (2011) 'Mind the Gap! MEPs must tighten up their act': http://blog.transparency.org/2011/03/24/mind-the-gap-meps-must-tighten-up-their-act/.

UN (2003) *Norms and Responsibilities of Transnational Corporations and Other Business Enterprises with regard to Human Rights*: http://www1.umn/edu/humanrts/links/norms-Aug2003.html.

UN (2011) *UN Protect, Respect and Remedy Framework: Guiding Principles*: http://www.ohchr.org/documents/issues/business/A.HRC.17.31.pdf.

UN GLOBAL COMPACT (2011) *Doing Business whilst Advancing Peace and Development*. New York: UN Global Compact.

WAR ON WANT (2004) *The Alternative Report*. London: War on Want.

Global Ethics

INTRODUCTION: 1493 AND THE AFTERMATH

In his book *1493: How Europe's discovery of the Americas revolutionized trade, ecology and life on Earth*, Charles Mann shows how globalisation is not a twentieth-century phenomenon but part of history. A key moment in that history was when Christopher Columbus founded the first colony in the Americas. Within a short time trade links were established across the world, often enabled by abuses such as slavery. African slaves were used to develop the silver mines in the Andes, the products of which were sent to China. Tobacco from the Caribbean was exported to the Philippines, India and Arabia, while shells from the Maldives were exchanged for slaves. The global links were enabled by business working hand in hand with government, and had the effect of changing the world, socially and in terms of the ecosystem. Some tribes in the Americas, such as the Taino, were all but wiped out through the 'importation' of smallpox and malaria. Later trade would lead to massive ecological and wealth redistributions. A good example of this was the nineteenth-century collection of rubber plant seeds sent from Brazil to Malaysia via Kew Gardens, in London, and to Ceylon (now Sri Lanka). By the early twentieth century there were over 650,000 rubber plantations in these British colonies. Asian production of rubber overtook that from the Americas, leading to the destruction of the Brazilian rubber industry. There was little sense of any ethical niceties in all this, partly because trade was tied to the development of political power. This reached its heights in examples such as the East India Company, which was an arm in the development of the British Empire. The company even traded in opium, supplying it covertly to China, although its consumption was illegal there.

The devastating consequences of early globalisation were far beyond the awareness of any government or business. The tobacco industry entirely changed Virginia in the USA, for instance. Along with the increase in horses and pigs, tobacco plantations had the effect of drying out the soil, making it harder for the Native American Indians to produce the tubers that were part of their staple diet. The introduction of horses also led to communication that was much quicker than Indians could manage, making it easier for the Europeans to gain the upper hand. The tobacco industry in Jamestown, Virginia, almost collapsed due to the malaria brought by the Puritans from the fens of East Anglia – until, that is, it was realised that West and Central Africans had greater natural resistance to malaria. It was thus determined that African slaves would be the best answer, despite the fact that the cost of transporting them made them more expensive than indentured servants.

It is difficult to make ethical sense of the history of globalisation when we can see the extraordinary effect that business and trade has had upon the world since 1493. Mann's history shows clearly how culture, economics and ecology were interconnected. There was, however, no sense of responsibility for societies or environments across the world. Twentieth- and twenty-first-century business witnessed both an extension of globalisation and a questioning of its ethical nature and the meaning of global responsibility. This chapter begins, then, by critically examining the phenomenon of globalisation in the twenty-first century. This leads to a consideration of what a global ethics and global justice might look like, including the justification for human rights. How all this affects the operation of multinational corporations is then examined, including how they relate to the ethics of NGOs. Global justice is then worked through into the practice of ethical and fair trading. The chapter ends with a consideration of how firms handle ethical difference, across different cultures.

GLOBALISATION

Globalisation is a contested concept in social, economic and ethical terms. Steger (2003) suggests this all-encompassing definition:

> Globalisation refers to a multidimensional set of social processes that create, multiply, stretch and intensify worldwide social interdependencies and exchanges while at the same time fostering in people a growing awareness of deepening connections between the local and the distant.

At the core of this process has been the expansion of capitalism across political boundaries. This has not simply been the intensification of worldwide trade, something evident since the fifteenth century. It also involves the organising of production across national boundaries. This may be the result of critical natural resources or because of lower labour costs. It has led to the development of huge multinational corporations (MNCs), some of which have annual financial turnovers larger than the gross national product of nations. Over 53% of the world's largest economies are MNCs (de Bettiginies and Lepineux, 2009). In 2006 the total sales of the top 200 transnational corporations were bigger than the combined GDP of 187 countries – more than 30 per cent of world GDP. In addition:

- Distance has been 'shortened' through rapid technological change, leading to significant increases in the speed of communication and transport. The Internet relays information in seconds and news-gathering technology can enable the real-time reporting of major events.
- All this has led to what Steger calls the 'expansions and stretching of social relations, activities and interdependencies' (Steger, 2003: 11). In retail, for instance, Western supermarkets are now stacked with produce from across the world. The justice of some of these relationships is questioned, and this has led in turn to the development and proliferation of global non-governmental organisations (NGOs) such as Oxfam, Fair Trade and Amnesty International.
- The opening up of the world has led to increases both in migrations, with the workforce moving across national boundaries, and in cultural interaction. Business has had to learn how to operate in very different cultures. These changes have led, some would argue, to changes in national identity, accelerating the process of the breakdown of local communities (Steger, 2003: 12).

Making ethical sense of this tends to divide into two broad views: globalisation as good, and globalisation as bad.

GLOBALISATION AS GOOD

Several arguments see globalisation as having very good effects:

- Globalisation involves freeing and integrating markets across the world. This suggests that the global market is the best way of distributing goods between the nations, while at the same time ensuring that nations remain free.
- Globalisation is now inevitable. Given the developments of the last three decades it is also irreversible. This is partly due to the increased recognition that the different parts of the world are interdependent. This argument gives the impression of globalisation as an unstoppable force. If that is so, then no single organisation is in control, and the key to handling it is working together.
- In the light of the above it is argued that globalisation benefits everyone, leading to greater efficiency, an increase in jobs, and equalising of incomes between countries.
- Allied to an economic growth, it is argued that there is global development of shared values, not least through the development across the world of democracy, and human rights.

GLOBALISATION AS BAD

The major criticisms of globalisation focus on the problems of the market approach and the need to develop ways of addressing global inequalities. These include:

- The global market is of itself inequitable and needs political control. The idea that the market distributes equitably assumes that all in the market have similar power and similar opportunities, whereas in reality there are massive differences in power. The worldwide market, with monetary and trade systems, often disables the developing countries, not least through massive interest on debts they have incurred (Munck, 2006).
- The global market is in fact dominated by the MNCs who are concerned primarily with their own profits. The practice of MNCs is often contrary to any idea of equal distribution, frequently characterised as the 'race to the bottom'. This is where companies and countries try to compete with each other by cutting wages and living standards for workers, and the production of goods is moved to the place where there is poor regulation of business practice, with the wages low and workers having few rights.
- The idea that globalisation can or should spread democracy is questionable. It is not clear that Western democracy is appropriate for other parts of the world, or that even if it is a universal good it should be prescribed for other nations. These issues have been played out most recently in Libya (http://www.guardian.co.uk/commentisfree/2011/mar/12/conversation-libya-intervention-george-galloway).
- Globalisation does not respect the uniqueness of the different global cultures. Indeed, it leads to what has come to be known as 'McDonaldisation' – the domination of a uniform and often consumer-led culture.

Not only, then, is the concept contested, but the effects of globalisation and its ethical base are contested. One way of trying to deal with this is to develop a global ethics which can set universal standards by which the practice of all parties in the global economy can be judged.

GLOBAL BUSINESS ETHICS

There have been several attempts to develop an approach for business based on globally accepted principles. Some groups, such as the Caux Round Table (www.cauxroundtable.org), have focused on basic principles which apply across cultures. They see this as practising 'moral capitalism'. The group is made up of academics and companies, including Canon and Philips, and builds on two basic guiding principles:

- human dignity (the quality or state of being worthy, honoured or esteemed). This is a core ethical principle of the equal value or worth of all human beings, sometimes expressed as the principle of equal respect
- *kyosei* (working together for the common good, or harmony – see Chapter 2).

The Round Table has charted these principles through four basic levels: economic survival, co-operation with the workforce, co-operating with stakeholders, and global activism. The last of these argues for the responsibility of MNCs to help governments redress core global imbalances, in the areas of trade, technology, wealth and the environment.

THE UN GLOBAL COMPACT

Another example of a global business ethics institution is the United Nations Global Compact, involving several thousand companies worldwide which have signed up to ten basic principles focused on human rights, labour standards, the environment and the elimination of corruption (http://www.unglobalcompact.org/AboutTheGC/TheTenPrinciples/index.html.).

Human rights
Principle 1   Businesses should support and respect the protection of internationally proclaimed human rights, and
Principle 2   Ensure that they are not complicit in human rights abuses.

Labour standards
Principle 3   Businesses should uphold the freedom of association and the effective recognition of the right to collective bargaining,
Principle 4   The elimination of all forms of forced and compulsory labour,
Principle 5   The effective abolition of child labour, and
Principle 6   The elimination of discrimination in respect of employment and occupation.

Environment
Principle 7   Businesses should support a precautionary approach to environmental challenges,
Principle 8   Undertake initiatives to promote greater environmental responsibility,
Principle 9   Encourage the development and diffusion of environmentally-friendly technologies.

Anti-corruption
Principle 10   Businesses should work against all forms of corruption, including extortion and bribery.

The UN Global Compact pursues two complementary objectives:

- to establish the ten principles in business practice worldwide
- to bring together actions in support of broader United Nations goals, including the Millennium Development Goals (MDGs).

THE MILLENNIUM DEVELOPMENT GOALS AND BUSINESS

The Millennium Development Goals (MDGs) were developed out of the eight chapters of the United Nations Millennium Declaration, signed in September 2000. There are eight goals with 21 targets, and a series of measurable indicators for each target, with a deadline of 2015 for achieving the targets.

The first six goals are not business-specific, although they may involve business, for instance, in the supply of antiretroviral drugs for HIV/AIDs. The last two have a strong emphasis on partnership between business, NGOs and government.

Goal 1: Eradicate extreme poverty and hunger

Goal 2: Achieve universal primary education

Goal 3: Promote gender equality and empower women

Goal 4: Reduce child mortality rate

Goal 5: Improve maternal health

Goal 6: Combat HIV/AIDS, malaria, and other diseases

Goal 7: Ensure environmental sustainability

Targets include:

- Reduce biodiversity loss, achieving, by 2010, a significant reduction in the rate of loss
- Halve, by 2015, the proportion of the population without sustainable access to safe drinking water and basic sanitation.

Goal 8: Develop a global partnership for development

Targets include:

- Develop further an open, rule-based, predictable, non-discriminatory trading and financial system
- In co-operation with pharmaceutical companies, provide access to affordable, essential drugs in developing countries
- In co-operation with the private sector, make available the benefits of new technologies, especially information and communications

GLOBAL JUSTICE

The Millennium Development Goals are built around the idea of global justice and the developing world. The debate around global justice mirrors the earlier ethical debates about responsibility.

There are broadly four different approaches to global justice:

- particularism
- nationalism
- a society of states
- cosmopolitanism.

PARTICULARISM

This argues that ethical standards are formed from shared meanings and practices in particular societies (Walzer, 1983). They are created and sustained by cultures. Any view of justice, such as equal distribution, may be accepted within a community, but does not apply beyond it. This means that there can be no criticism of other nations' ethics. In effect, this is ethical relativism – each country can 'do its own thing'.

NATIONALISM

Nationalists (Miller, 2007) argue that justice in the nation and in the wider world are both important, but that the first is more pressing than the second. The needs of the first therefore have to be answered before those of the second, in the same way that the needs of a family will take priority over the needs of the community. Distributive justice is an issue within nations but not necessarily between them.

A SOCIETY OF STATES

In this approach, states are seen as individual entities that can form mutual agreements on common interests and rules of interaction, including moral rules. It is often perceived as a social contract approach, perhaps best set out by Rawls (1971). Rawls's first work on justice was built around the idea of an imagined 'original postion' in which none of the people involved knew what wealth or postion they held. In that situation the people would tend to opt for justice as fairness such that no one had too much or too little. Rawls extends this in his later work to global justice, using the same thought experiment by which no leaders would know who they represent. In international terms this would lead not to egalitarian justice but agreed contracts, involving accepted treaties and strict limits on creating conflict.

COSMOPOLITANISM

This argues for a moral universalism that goes beyond national boundaries. Justice in this view is owed to everyone, not simply fellow citizens. The underlying argument begins with the nature of humanity, with ethically significant characteristics shared by *all* humans, not least basic psychological and physical needs (Nussbaum, 1999). This is close to universal responsibility. Based on the moral status of all humanity, it looks to global justice.

There are two broad approaches to the justification of cosmopolitanism:

- consequentialist cosmopolitanism
- human rights cosmopolitanism.

Consequentialist cosmopolitanism

Peter Singer (2002) argues that the proper standard of moral judgement for actions, practices or institutions is found in their consequences. We measure these actions in terms of the consequences to the welfare of humans. Singer extends this to the welfare of all sentient creatures. In the light of the moral status of sentient beings, suffering – such as poverty or famine – creates a moral demand for help.

The argument is set out as follows (Singer, 2002):

- Suffering and death from lack of food and medical care are bad.
- We ought to prevent something bad happening, provided that we do not sacrifice something of comparable moral importance in doing so. So, for instance, we ought to rescue the small child drowning in the canal, provided that it will not cause one's own death and adversely affect others.
- It is in our power to prevent suffering and death in the developing world, without involving sacrifice.
- Therefore we ought to contribute to the famine relief at least up to the amount that we spend on other more trivial things.

This is a utilitarian argument, weighing up the different consequences of actions. It can also be seen as an argument based in global justice and the ethics of responsibility. In particular, it stresses the same sense of shared and proactive responsibility found in the MDGs.

One of the main arguments against this comes from another utilitarian. Hardin (1972) argues that to give to the starving would not actually improve their lot and would radically and negatively affect the wealthy. The analogy is with the lifeboat: if the lifeboat took all the drowning people on board, it would capsise, risking the lives of all. Hardin's perspective, however, shows up the limitations of utilitarianism in a global context. It does not reflect on the nature of suffering and death in the developing world. Famine and response to famine, for instance, may be connected to a widespread network of cause, from lack of resources at national level to corruption. In other words, the wealthy may be part of the cause, contributing to the poverty in the first place. Sen (2009) therefore states that any argument for cosmopolitanism should be based on rights. Human beings have a right to life and well-being.

Human rights cosmopolitanism

In this approach, Pogge (2008) argues that human beings have rights, such as those set out in the UN's Universal Declaration of Human Rights. Those with the power then have a positive or negative duty. The first is the duty to uphold and even guarantee these rights. The second is a duty not to impose actions or order that violates human rights.

Quite how this is worked out is another thing. The recent NATO defence of Libyan civilians is based on the use of force to protect human rights. As we saw in Chapter 12, working through how a business responds to abuses of human rights can be difficult and protracted, requiring close working with other stakeholders. Behind that, the case for accepting the value of universal human rights has still to be argued for.

PAUSE FOR THOUGHT

Which of these views of global justice do you find most convincing, and why?

Which of these views would best fit the practice of your business or your university?

As we saw in Chapter 7, issues of justice pervade business ethics, not least in the workplace. But how can business get involved in global justice? If there is such a thing as global justice, does it not need a global system of justice, not just a number of non-governmental bodies such as the Global Compact?

Some would argue that such organisations do not in fact help at all. See the case study below.

CASE

A TOOTHLESS COMPACT?

There have been several criticisms of the UN Global Compact. Critics accept that the compact has put global responsibility on the agenda. However, they argue that it is fundamentally cosmetic, largely because there is no mechanism for dealing publicly with members that contravene or do not fulfil the principles. Entine (2010) raises the case of PetroChina, a division of CNPC, the world's largest oil company. This company is building a major pipeline in the Sudanese region of Darfur to transport gas to China. Entine suggests that convincing evidence has emerged that PetroChina was complicit in the displacement of thousands of people, and the disappearance of many others, in Darfur, violating Global Compact's principles and international law. He also notes that the response of the Global Compact to the accusations was to argue that PetroChina was one of few companies working in conflict areas to have joined the compact, and that it was unfair to target them.

This highlights that the model of the Global Compact is both self-regulatory and developmental, and that the compact plays a supportive role. It may be a useful role with respect to the SMEs who are newly developing their practice. However, the majority of large corporations who are part of the compact already have well developed CSR policies and departments. Sethi (2011) argues, firstly, that even a development model cannot be sustained if there is no independent way of assessing allegations. Without that, it is not clear that any genuine learning can occur, and it runs the danger of covering up major abuses. The compact would therefore have to have more transparency and some means of regulating members. Sethi, secondly, argues that without such transparency, the compact can be seen largely as a means of cushioning business from stronger national or international regulation. The Global Compact response to the PetroChina situation is perhaps insufficient. The fact that PetroChina is operating in a conflict zone does not make any critique unfair. Indeed, such a critique might be important for a learning response from PetroChina and other firms.

Those who support the Global Compact have argued that it has shaped an initiative that provides collaborative solutions to the most fundamental challenges facing both business and society. The initiative seeks to combine the best properties of the UN, such as moral authority and convening power, with the private sector's solution-finding strengths, and the expertise and capacities of a range of key stakeholders. The Global Compact is global and local; private and public; voluntary yet accountable.

The benefits of engagement include the following:

- establishing a globally recognised policy framework for the development, implementation and disclosure of environmental, social and governance policies and practices

- enabling best and emerging practices to be shared and thus advancing practical solutions and strategies to common challenges

- enabling sustainability solutions in partnership with a range of stakeholders, including UN agencies, governments, civil society, labour and other non-business interests

- working with the UN and being able to access its extensive knowledge of and experience with sustainability and development issues (Rasche and Kell, 2010).

A more detailed analysis of the benefits of participation in the Global Compact can be found in the compact's *The Importance of Voluntarism* – which also focuses on the importance of the Global Compact as a complement to rather than a substitute for regulatory regimes.

Finally, the Global Compact incorporates a transparency and accountability policy known as the Communication on Progress (COP). The annual posting of a COP is an important demonstration of a participant's commitment to the UN Global Compact and its principles. Participating companies are required to follow this policy as a commitment to transparency, and disclosure is critical to the success of the initiative. Failure to communicate may result in a change in participant status and possible delisting.

GLOBAL ETHICS AND HUMAN RIGHTS

Behind efforts to globalise business ethics remains the question of whether it is possible to have a global ethics in which certain principles are accepted universally. Kung (1991) argues strongly for this, based on necessity. Globalisation raises many issues of injustice and conflict, from financial and labour markets to ecology and organised crime. From this, he argues, a global ethics is necessary if the global order is to be managed. He goes further to suggest that many global conflicts have been based in religion, not least from the interrelation of different religious groups with politics. Therefore, argues Kung, such an ethics has to be genuinely inclusive, reaching across religions, cultures and civilisations.

Kung argues that global ethics is not a uniform system of prescriptions but rather 'a necessary minimum of shared ethical values' to which different regions, cultural groups, religions, nations and other interest groups can commit themselves. This involves an ongoing process of dialogue which uncovers the shared values already implicit – what are characterised as universal ethical principles. The commandment 'Thou shalt not kill,' for instance, becomes, in positive terms, 'Have respect for life,' calling for the safety of all minorities, social and political justice, a culture of non-violence, respect for the environment and universal disarmament. The commandment 'Thou shalt not steal' becomes 'Deal honestly and fairly,' standing out against poverty and the cyclical violence which occurs in a society of wealth extremes. Just economic institutions must be created and sanctioned at the highest levels, suggests Kung, and limitless consumption curbed in the developed countries while the market economy is made socially and ecologically conscious.

Principles and responsibilities that arise from this can be affirmed by all persons with ethical convictions, and who oppose all forms of inhumanity. Such an ethics is aspirational rather than prescriptive, forming the basis of the Declaration of Human Responsibilities (Kung and Schmidt, 1998), intended as a complement to the key foundation of global ethics, the UN Declaration of Human Rights.

But what *is* the basis of human rights?

THE BASIS OF HUMAN RIGHTS

The preamble to the UN Declaration of Human Rights sees such rights as derived from the 'inherent dignity of the human person' (http://www.un.org/en/documents/udhr/). This points to a pre-legal and pre-political moral belief in some key human characteristics that require universally specifiable ways of responding to human beings. However, if business is to be involved in respecting these rights (as we noted in the last chapter), it has to be aware of why human rights are important. Many would argue that human rights are problematic.

Arguments against the concept of human rights

The concept of human rights has been criticised on philosophical and social grounds.

- The more specific the rule or right, the more difficult it is to find universal support for it (Forrester, 2005; O'Donovan, 2000). C. S. Lewis (1978) argued for a universal ethic, based around a general acceptance of the various versions of the Golden Rule, 'Do unto others what you would have them do onto you.' This is such a general principle that it seems unexceptionable. More detail is needed to understand the ethical meaning in context, and the Human Rights Declaration soon becomes contested.
  Human Rights article 18, for example, suggests a right to change religion, but in some countries religion is tightly bound up with national identity, and there are religious and legal constraints against this. Equally, rights surrounding freedom of speech or asylum-seekers are subject to major questions in practice. What are the limits to freedom of speech, and how is it possible to deal equitably with all who claim asylum? General moral principles, then, seem unexceptionable, but when faced by the particular context come up against the difficulty of how they may be embodied in practice. Underlying that difficulty is the phenomenon of ethical pluralism, the vast array of different ethical beliefs apparent in the world. Even within one nation, such as Britain, there has been a gradual breakdown of any meta-narrative, an overarching 'story' that gives shared spiritual or moral meaning (Connor, 1989).
- Philosophers such as Rorty (1993) argue that the concept of human rights attempts to provide a rational basis for ethical practice, and that ethics cannot be founded purely on that. Ethics demands an affective as much as a cognitive base, and this involves some degree of subjectivity. Bauman (1993) goes further to suggest that shared responsibility is the base of ethics and that this is pre-rational.
- Rights and even responsibilities assume the basis of a democratic nation which can regulate them. Many developing nations do not have such resources. In any case, there are very different views of democracy (Chenyang, 1999). By extension, there is no global governance that can easily police human rights or global justice. As we saw in the last chapter, there is therefore reliance on codes developed by organisations such as the UN.
- It is argued that the Declaration of Human Rights is Eurocentric, focused in a particular Western view of what is good. This contrasts sharply with other cultural views. The very term 'right' is legalistic and prescriptive, contrasting with the Buddhist philosophy, for instance, which values mutuality, based on a view of interdependence and underlying

empathy. Such a philosophy does not have place for rights, looking rather to develop spiritual meaning as the base of ethics and responsive virtues. Rights are based around individualistic views of equality and freedom. This contrasts, for instance, with the values of Confucianism. Although Confucianism is not totally averse to the idea of human rights (Twiss, 1998), it emphasises communitarian values, including paternalism and respect for authority, over freedom and equality. Other cultures, such as the Dinka in Sudan, have a strong sense of rights but only as far as the members of the community. These therefore form the basis of conditional, not universal, rights (Drydyk, 1999). Once again, then, the major debates about what is good come down to disagreements about values, especially how freedom, equality, community and justice relate.

- The dynamic of human rights is criticised as paternalistic. Mutua (2002), for instance, notes how the West characterises the developing world as unable to develop ethical values without the help of the West, who are seen as 'saviours'.

Arguments for human rights

Against these critiques are several arguments.

- Development of the Human Rights Declaration was not simply Western; there was global consultation (Twiss, 1995). Some would therefore argue that it is possible to have a global ethic which is not Eurocentric.
- The examples of the Holocaust and subsequent genocides do point to the need to have some sense of justice and right that transcends national boundaries. This provides a negative rational argument for the development of a shared ethic. As Nussbaum (1999) notes, without such a view, respect for different cultures can lead to support for oppression, sexism and racism.
- Behind Kung's argument is an increasing sense of the world as interconnected, with nations mutually responsible for the shared physical and social environment, and for the long-term effects, such as global warming. Much of the argument is thus based on both rights and utilitarian terms.

These arguments suggest that alongside respect for ethical plurality there should be the balance of a shared ethic that transcends the particular interest of nations and major corporations. This leads inevitably to an ethics that is not easily or simplistically applied, requiring careful dialogue around the many different principles, cultural and religious perspectives, ideologies and social expectations that give meaning to any particular situation. Sandel (2010) argues that a just society or world cannot be achieved simply by maximising utility or securing freedom of choice. To achieve justice it is necessary to reason together about the meaning of the good life, and to create a public culture that allows the disagreements that will inevitably arise (visit http://www.justiceharvard.org/ to see Sandel's lecture series on justice).

This suggests that human rights are the starting point for critical dialogue and that business is a key part of this. King III's (Institute of Directors, 2009) chapter on developing ethics (see Chapter 5) in the corporation thus emphasises the importance of developing ethical awareness, including assessments of the ethical risk – ie what might happen if major ethical issues are not addressed.

Building around a Kantian view of ethics, O'Neill (2000) argues that global responsibility is not a matter of consequences or rights but rather of a broad sense of obligation. This is quite close to Singer's argument. The problems of the developing world are interconnected. They are not blocks of problems that we simply have to find technical solutions for. On the contrary, they involve many different stakeholders. Some may contribute to the problems negatively; many may be able to contribute positively. This reinforces the argument of a shared responsibility. The argument in global terms is reinforced precisely because there is no transnational governance that could be given responsibility for regulation. Rather does it stress the idea of global citizenship, and business as a global citizen, with rights that have to be recognised and responsibility exercised in collaboration with other stakeholders (Dunning, 2003).

PAUSE FOR THOUGHT

Read through the Declaration of Human Rights (http://www.un.org/en/documents/udhr/).

How many of these rights would apply across all nations?

What are the core human rights?

Whose responsibility is it to uphold human rights?

How would you convince a board of directors that the firm has a responsibility to uphold human rights, and what would that mean in practice?

MULTINATIONAL CORPORATIONS AND THE BALANCE OF POWER

The issue of business involvement in the dialogue on global justice is most evident in the work of MNCs. The argument of Friedman that the role of social responsibility is properly that of the state has even less force in a world in which many MNCs have more power than some states. The annual turnover of the largest corporations in the world exceeds the GDP of many countries, not only the poorest. Accepting that these comparisons are crude, they nonetheless indicate influence and economic strength in relation to states, as noted above. One comparison illustrates this well in relation to the Niger Delta case study. In 2003 the net sales of Shell were $268.9 billion and the gross domestic product of Nigeria $2.7 billion.

De Bettignies and Lepineux (2009) argue that three things are changing the way in which MNCs operate globally:

- the imperative of the preservation of the biosphere
- the rise of anti-globalisation sentiment
- the necessity to design a global social contract and sovereignty.

For the multinational corporation all three are interconnected, taking business ethics into a responsibility model that is the continual negotiation of responsibility between the different players.

The first of these factors is examined in our final chapter.

The second focuses on attacks on MNCs. These involve:

- concern with the influence of MNCs on political decision-making. It is argued that this threatens ultimately to affect democracy
- the influence of MNCs in determining even what well-being and core values might be, focused on material wealth. This includes the purveying of the core market philosophy to all aspects of life (Gorringe, 1999). In this respect there are parallels between MNCs and the influence of the great world religions
- the fact that the MNCs directly reinforce global inequalities, in collaboration with international finance institutions such as the World Bank (Stiglitz, 2002; de Bettignies and Lepineux, 2009). One illustration of this is that out of over 6 billion people worldwide, 2.3 billion live on less than $2 per day, whereas the richest 20 per cent have more than 80 per cent of the world's wealth.

In effect, such arguments pull MNCs further into the debate about global justice. They are part of, and make the most use of, a system that perpetuates inequality. This leads to two further arguments against the Friedman liberal position, noted in Chapter 11.

First, Friedman wants to argue that social concerns, and thus issues of justice, are exclusively the responsibility of the state. However, the power of MNCs is such that they directly affect global justice, whatever they do.

Second, the ethics of the MNCs are further questioned in practices that although not illegal work against any sense of global justice. A good example of this, and part of the 'race to the bottom', is tax practice.

Taxing justice

Taxation can be crippling to business. Nonetheless, the principle of taxation is ethically important. Taxation is a critical part of the development of democracy and justice (Owens and Perry, 2009). In effect, it is an expression of citizenship and stewardship, providing an appropriate contribution to the state, to be used on behalf of society. Taxation strengthens the citizen's right to hold governments to account, especially in developing nations that have relied so much on donations.

Where tax is not paid, for whatever reason, the result is a reduction of potential state funds. In developing countries it is estimated that unpaid tax from MNCs in some cases is more than national debts owed. Estimates of total unpaid tax go up to £160 billion (Christian Aid, 2009), along with illicit flows of cash estimated between $500 and $800 billion.

The pressure is now on MNCs to report on their tax practice country by country (Christian Aid, 2009). The Wall Street Reform and Consumer Protection Act, July 2010, also requires energy and mining companies to disclose how much they pay foreign countries and the US Government for access to oil, gas and minerals.

In effect, this is arguing for transparency and thus clearer accountability from MNCs in their finances.

In addition, the tax structures in developing nations would have to be strengthened. African tax commissioners from 30 countries, backed by the African Development Bank and the OECD, are therefore seeking to create an African Tax Administration Forum (Owens and Perry: http://www.oecdobserver.org/news/fullstory.php/aid/2943/).

Attention to these levels of operational justice would radically affect wider issues of global justice.

The third factor in de Bettignies and Lepineux's thesis argues explicitly that in the global context nation states can no longer be assumed to be the guarantors of the common good. Other economic and social actors progressively understand that they have a role in solving global problems too, and that they have to contribute their share to the common good. Corporations, NGOs and international organisations are increasingly expected to act on behalf of the public interest. In a sense this is part of the logic of globalisation. In a global context there is no single organisation that has the power or jurisdiction to take responsibility for everything. Globalisation demands that all parties work together to share responsibility and ensure that it is worked through. This is also the logical conclusion of the King III (2009) argument that regulation cannot be vested purely in the state but has to involve all stakeholders. It requires strong active participation, including a strong civil society. Summing up, de Bettignies and Lepineux (2009: 176) argue that 'Corporations have become leading players in contemporary society; indeed, they can legitimately be considered the central value-creation institutions of our time.' This involves a shared focus on justice, including issues such as fair trade.

PAUSE FOR THOUGHT

De Bettiginies and Lepineux's view places even greater responsibility on the multinational corporations, to contribute to the creation of value.

Is that unrealistic, or is it necessary in a globalised world that places MNCs under intense ethical scrutiny ?

ETHICAL TRADE AND FAIR TRADE

It is possible to distinguish between ethical and fair trading.

- Ethical trade – This focuses on areas such as effective governance, efforts against corruption, working conditions and environmental issues (see also Chapter 10 on supply-chain management).
- Fair trade – This focuses on setting up just relationships, and is accordingly characterised by:
  - direct relationships between producers and consumers, cutting out intermediaries as much as possible
  - clear negotiation of a fair price so that the producer and his or her family can live with dignity. This may involve a premium for development
  - maximum transparency in product pricing (the part that corresponds to each operator is publicly known)
  - where producers are salaried, respect for the minimum working conditions subject to the provisions of the international norms of the International Labour Organisation, or the individual countries where these conditions are higher (minimum wage, right of association, prohibition of forced labour, etc)
  - the possibility for producers to obtain pre-financing when needed
  - setting up long-term relationships and contracts, based on mutual respect and ethical values. These relationships not only aim to achieve a fair price, they also seek sustainable development for groups of producers or salaried workers
  - in some fair trade organisations, established criteria for assessing improvements are made, ensuring advances for the groups of producers or salaried workers beyond the minimum condition (Kestemont and Fraselle, 2006).

In practice the two approaches are often combined. Justice, after all, involves a social dimension of ethics.

This has involved the development of advocacy networks, including:

- the International Federation of Alternative Trade (IFAT)
- the European Fair Trade Association (EFTA)
- the Fairtrade Labelling Organisation (FLO). The labels inform consumer choice.

In turn, many of these have developed codes of practice which combine ethical and fair trade elements. The code of Co-operation for Fair Trade in Africa (COFTA), an organisation very closely linked with IFAT (http://www.cofta.org/en/forms/Code.of.Practice.English.pdf), includes aims to

trade with concern for the social, economic and environmental well-being of marginalised producers in developing countries. This means equitable commercial terms, fair wages and fair prices. Unfair trade structures, mechanisms, practices and attitudes will be identified and avoided.

IFAT/COFTA code headings include:

- Transparency
- Ethical issues
- Working conditions
- Equal employment opportunities
- Concern for people
- Concern for the environment
- Respect for producers' cultural identity
- Education and advocacy.

These initiatives contribute to sustainable development in three ways:

- by taking into account the environmental and social costs of production. The organisation opposes social dumping – the practice involving the export of goods from a country with weak or poorly enforced labour standards, where the exporter's costs are artificially lower than its competitors' in countries with higher standards, so corresponding to an unfair advantage in international trade
- by developing stable relationships based in integrity, involving authentic co-operation between producers and consumers
- through the regulation of trading partnerships. This contributes to sustained co-operation.

INTERCULTURAL ETHICS

The involvement in working through global justice also means that business is faced by some very different cultural views of ethics. As Xu (2006) notes, the economic growth of China, for instance, makes it a key region of global business and raises major questions about different ethical views. China's own philosophical traditions, especially Confucian and Taoist, would seem, in areas such as the ethics of corruption, to favour family and friends, in contrast to the Western emphasis on transparency and justice (Rothlin, 2004). However, Rothlin notes that, despite differences, such cultures – including religion in general (Farrar *et al*, 2012) – are not monolithic, referring to one Chinese philosopher, Mozi (formerly spelled Mo Tzu), who argued against the Confucian emphasis on clan obligations and for an ethics of universal caring. (For a good discussion of this in relation to religious issues such as the wearing of the veil (*niqab*) at work, see Jackson 2011; see also http://www.campusalam.org/resources/ situations-sorted---staff/religious-needs/ban-the-niqab/.)

This means that different cultural views can reasonably be questioned, enabling debate that occurs within the culture itself. Such questioning should be mutual, and involve a careful application of the ethical decision-making process described in Chapter 3:

- Listen carefully for and discuss the very different values that may be embodied in practice.
- Focus on areas of shared practice-centred concern. This can both build up trust and also tease out both shared and possibly conflicting values. Any value conflict, between cultures and within cultures, will emerge and can be discussed openly.
- Remain focused on the critical assessment of values and actions, while respecting underlying belief systems.
- Work on possible partnerships and the sharing of responsibility. Again, this can build up trust, not least through a demonstration of commitment. If there is a religious issue, it is good to work with a formal representative of the religion.
- Focus on the key ethical issues, ranging from respect for the other culture to health and safety, or customer care.

This suggests that intercultural ethics is not simply about applying ethical ideas but also getting to know the other. Rothlin (2004) argues that this demands an inclusion of the other in working through the right practice, and not the assertion of a Western perspective.

BRIBERY AND CORRUPTION

A good example of different cultural approaches centres on bribery and corruption. Most firms have a statement forbidding taking bribes. Bribery is defined as any situation in which there is an attempt to procure services outside the normal contract negotiations or any attempt to use public money for private gain. This is reinforced by la Fédération Internationale des Ingénieurs Conseil (FIDIC), whose statement on this (http://www1. fidic.org/resources/integrity/oecd_policy_bribery_nov04.pdf) argues that bribery and corruption are both morally and economically damaging and therefore should be banned globally. If this was taken seriously, however, it would be hard to see how business could be done at all in some countries.

There are in fact three traditional approaches to this issue:

- ethical conventionalism – This argues that the conventions of the country should be followed. In some countries bribery is seen as a type of fee for work done: 'When in Rome, do as the Romans do'. This accepts ethical relativity without question
- ethical fundamentalism – This argues that the same high ethical standards be applied across different cultures
- ethical case work, in which each case is examined separately – There is broad acceptance of the importance of global justice, but also of the need to carefully examine how it is developed in particular cases.

The most effective way to operate would seem to be to have a clear statement in the firm's code of ethics to avoid bribery and corruption and then discuss how this applied on a case-by-case basis. Such a policy would require the firm to be clear about what is defined as bribery, and about accepted company reactions to any attempted bribe. It is relatively easy, for instance, to have the rule that no employee should accept a gift of more than £25. As Weiss (2003: 295) notes, this would be all the more effective if the ethical perspective is shared by several different companies, groups and nations.

Clarifying the situation may, of course, involve careful work with stakeholders, including government departments. In this case it is important to know the national policy on bribery, so that any attempts at bribery can be challenged in the light of that. The UK's Anti-Corruption Forum (http://www.anticorruptionforum.org.uk/acf/pages/acf.php) emphasises the importance of building up and becoming part of networks of governments, banks, professional associations and companies who work together to respond to this problem. Their newsletter No.2 (May 2006) provides a summary of many different initiatives.

However, this is a long-term response to bribery and corruption. There will always be cases where it is not clear if a bribe has been offered or accepted – the ski trip offered as part of hospitality, and so on. In all cases the definition of bribery has to be returned to, such as 'undisclosed payments that are intended to influence the judgement of someone who has the power to decide in favour of the person offering the bribe'. The ski trip may or may not be an explicit bribe, but when in doubt it should be disclosed, again taking the ethical issue away from simply an individual ethical dilemma to one that is responded to in the light of a transparent ethical culture.

Weiss (2003: 330) sums up an attempt to work across cultures with the idea of 'ethical navigation'. It includes:

- articulating basic choices in the light of company and stakeholders' values
- being aware of the limits of responsible corporate power
- maintaining responsibility in 'flexible business relationships' – This includes developing a reflective company such that the experiences of fellow professionals can be shared, allowing the development of a 'repertoire' of different approaches that embody responsibility
- negotiating among the different cultural values, while retaining one's own

● listening to and asserting the different interests of the parties involved.

Weiss stresses the importance of getting the dynamic right, suggesting that conflict resolution techniques are important in working through any cross-cultural issues (see Chapter 8).

You are in charge of an overseas office of a UK company. In the UK the company operates a strict policy of not accepting bribes. However, in the international environment in which you work, bribery is commonplace and accepted. Part of a major project is being delayed by equipment held by local customs officers, who are waiting for their usual 'emolument' to release it. What would your policy be for this?

Suppose that on seeking advice from your UK office you are told to use your own initiative to expedite the situation – but that if you decide to make the payments, you should 'hide' them somehow in the accounts submitted for the UK company audit. How would you feel about this advice, and what action would you take? What ethical principle would you base that action on?

CONCLUSION

In the context of globalisation, firms have to work harder at being ethical and being seen to be ethical. They are faced by:

● NGOs who demand transparency
● media who regularly monitor business practice
● global organisations who are looking to develop broader ethical perspectives
● different cultures and religions which if not respected can cause major problems
● governments that may have very different and varied agendas
● major environmental issues shared across the globe.

In the light of all this, the global perspective demands that companies have in place carefully considered ethical principles and policy. Such policy has to centre on how the ethical meaning can be developed through working closely with the other stakeholders involved.

This dialogue has to take seriously both a global ethical perspective, as summed up by human rights, and also the particular and possibly different values of different communities. If either is given too much precedence, the result may be injustice. So the focus of practice is in shared responsibility, with an ongoing dialogue around justice and responsibility (Sandel, 2010).

REFLECTIVE PRACTICE

Working with other students, sketch out a policy for CSR for a company working in Iraq.

Find a statement about bribery from three different MNCs on the Internet. Do they show any differences in values or practice? Which one would you choose, and why?

Working with other students, work out government guidelines on the ethics of companies working in a war zone.

CASE

NESTLÉ AND INFANT FORMULA

In the 1960s, infant formula ('baby milk') companies began to search for markets in the developing countries where the birth rate was soaring. In moving into this market, the companies began to cross the divide between commercial and pharmaceutical industries that existed in the developed world. There, food companies tended to advertise directly to the consumer, whereas pharmaceutical companies promoted their goods primarily to the health professionals. The formula companies marketing in the developing nations targeted both health professionals and consumers.

Jeliffe (1971) and others later argued that advertising implied that infant formula was the best for the baby, and that the use of nurses, employed by the companies to advise on how to use infant formula, was 'endorsement by association' and 'manipulation by assistance'.

Promotional techniques ignored three critical factors in the Third World: poverty, poor hygiene and illiteracy. The mother left hospital with a limited amount of free formula and continued to use it, leading to her own breast milk drying up. The formula was often not mixed correctly, leading to the use of unsterilised water and the baby suffering diarrhoea. The diarrhoea meant that the baby was unable to absorb the nutrients in the formula. The free sample began to run out and the formula was thinned out to make it last, often with contaminated water. This resulted in the death of the baby from malnutrition and dehydration. Milk banks were not a solution to the problem because the poor could not afford even those prices. Based on such arguments, Jeliffe suggested that the increase in the infant mortality rate in the Third World and the decrease in breast-feeding were directly connected.

In response to this the United Nations Protein Advisory Group recommended that:

- the formula industry encourage breast-feeding in new mothers, avoid promotion in hospitals and ensure

that the directions for use on the cans were clear, not least about the need for hygiene

- paediatricians should stay in discussion with the formula industry, particularly about the needs of those on low incomes, and should keep up to date with developments in research on breast-feeding and the use of processed foods

- governments, especially in the Third World, be encouraged to make use of the media for education on breast-feeding and on the responsible use of formula products, and consider financial help for the most vulnerable groups for infant and weaning foods.

The global debate

In March 1974 the debate became global through Mike Muller's pamphlet *The Baby Killer*. This was a broad, more sensationalist, restatement of previous arguments, accusing Nestlé of being responsible for the death of massive numbers of babies in the developing world. Nestlé sued, leading to a two-year court case – which it won. However, Nestlé lost the publicity battle. It gave the impression of a global giant trying to stamp out the protests of ordinary decent people.

Instead of damping down the global concern, there was increased collaboration between international health organisations and concerned groups, including the churches and NGOs, which led directly to a worldwide boycott of Nestlé goods in June 1977.

Nestlé responded by:

- characterising those responsible for the boycott as 'a worldwide organisation with the stated purpose of undermining the free enterprise system'

- targeting key professionals, including 300,000 clergy and community leaders, trying to directly refute the allegations

- developing, with the World Health

Organisation, UNICEF and the other formula companies some initial guidelines on practice. These were with the declared intention of developing a full code of practice for marketing. This signalled a change in approach, urged by new PR consultants, aiming to avoid confrontation

- aligning itself with and funding 'independent' research into child nutrition.

The WHO code

The WHO code on formula marketing took until May 1981 to be ratified, due partly to disagreements between and within the formula industry, not least about the validity of Jeliffe's arguments. The code directives included:

- All direct advertising and sampling to consumers should be stopped.

- Labels should carry the advice that 'breast is best', and there should be no text or picture that idealised the formula.

- Marketing should continue – but only if it did not undermine breast-feeding.

At this time Nestlé began to widen its non-adversarial approach. It entered into dialogue with the Methodist Task Force, which the American Methodist Church had charged to take a detailed look at the issue. It set up the Nestlé Coordination Center for Nutrition (NCCN), which served as an information centre for key issues in nutrition, and to act as receiver of information that might help Nestlé in meeting new demands and achieving organisational change.

By May 1982 the continuing dialogue led to the development of the Nestlé Infant Formula Audit Commission, an independent monitoring agency chaired by Senator Edmund Muskie, former US Secretary of State. Nestlé's practice was seen as increasingly transparent and in line with the code. Support for the boycott of Nestlé products therefore began to wane. The boycott was officially suspended in October 1984.

The second front

On the face of it, the issues had been sorted out through the code and the various forums set up to develop the dialogue. This led to the gradual scaling down of the NCCN, and the eventual ending of the Muskie Commission.

However, opposition still remained in certain quarters. Some NGOs were concerned that Nestlé was trying to find ways of getting round the code, especially in the supply of free formula to hospitals. Although this practice was neither banned by the code nor illegal, Nestlé remained committed to end all such supplies in developing countries, except for the limited number of babies who needed it. Nonetheless, conflict continued over the interpretation of the code in several areas, including the matter of which language should be used for the packaging of formula.

The early 1990s also saw important moves towards a goal of universal breast-feeding, driven by WHO and UNICEF, including the Baby-Friendly Hospital Initiative. This led to further pressure on Nestlé, especially from UNICEF. In July 1993, UNICEF issued the document *An End to Ambiguities*.

This reflected further frustration with the difficulties in the interpretation of the code. In an attempt to end those ambiguities UNICEF expanded the code, without consulting either WHO or the industry. The first response from Nestlé was to argue that this by itself went against the code. Thus, far from resolving ambiguities it led to further wrangles.

Subsequent reports from NGOs alleged practices which broke the WHO code, all of which were hotly disputed by Nestlé, both in terms of content and data-gathering methodology.

Disputes have continued since then, often in local legal contexts, often discussing minutiae of how to interpret the code. There has been no return to the boycott ... or any sign that the different parties might agree on ways forward.

The Nestlé case study is long and complex. It presents a heady mixture of issues – questionable marketing practices, injustice, and poverty, as well as matters concerning health. The whole issue of breast-feeding in the developed and non-developed world is part of that.

The initial response from Nestlé was divisive and fragmentary, and this could be seen to correspond to the Friedman position, involving a market perceived as a neutral environment in which the company should be allowed to do its business. The change in Nestlé's position began as a PR exercise and then moved into the development of genuine dialogue. Key to this dialogue was:

- the development of a code of practice – This provided key criteria for the ongoing assessment of practice. However, although this was a part of the solution, it could not be used in a simplistic or prescriptive way. The code was the basis for ongoing dialogue and the negotiation of responsibility. So, for instance, in some cases determining what might be the local language for marketing might have to be referred to the local legal system to choose between several possible languages. In effect, the code was helping to focus on the first mode of responsibility, enabling clarity about what the issues were, the effects of bad practice, and the means of addressing the issues (see Sethi, 2011)
- a focus of dialogue and reflection, in this case the Muskie Commission – This was key to developing trust and ensuring that the terms of the code were applied critically
- stakeholder involvement at every stage, so that the central issues could be represented and worked through – Once more this involved the sharing and negotiating of responsibility and not simply addressing the interests or needs of the stakeholders, with, for instance, NGOs such as the World Health Organisation developing the code in consultation with the baby milk industries. It is this level of involvement that enables the King III emphasis on stakeholders as regulators to be achieved (see Chapter 5).

In short, this case, at a global level, shows the development of responsibility, from a denial of responsibility (with Nestlé accusing the *New Internationalist* of trying to destroy global capitalism, and thus ignoring the issues) to responsibility developed as part of a PR exercise, to global responsibility work in developing accountability and shared responsibility, to ultimately enabling all stakeholders to be involved in the practice of responsibility and dialogue about justice. It gives an example of how a firm can share in the 'value creation' activity, and rests on ongoing dialogue.

 ## REFLECTIVE PRACTICE

Make a list of the different stakeholders in this case. Can you suggest what their values might be?

How did the stakeholder values affect their view of the data?

Is there any evidence of effective negotiation of responsibility in this case? How would you suggest responsibility might be negotiated in the present phase of the case?

What constraints were there to developing a solution?

How were these constraints addressed?

EXPLORE FURTHER

Books

Arnold, D. (2012) *Ethics of Global Business*. Oxford: Blackwell.

Donaldson, T. (1992) *The Ethics of International Business*. New York: Oxford University Press.

Hutchings, K. (2010) *Global Ethics: An introduction*. London: Polity Press.

REFERENCES

BAUMAN, Z. (1993) *Postmodern Ethics*. Oxford: Blackwell.

CHENYANG, L. (1999) 'Confucian value and democratic value', in Koggel, C. (ed.) *Moral Issues in Global Perspective*. Peterborough, Ontario: Broadview.

CHRISTIAN AID (2009) http://www.christianaid.org.uk/images/accounting-for-change-shifting-sands.pdf [accessed 17 March 2011].

CONNOR, S. (1989) *The Post-Modern Culture*. Oxford: Blackwell.

DE BETTIGNIES, H.-C. and LEPINEUX, F. (2009) 'Can multinational corporations afford to ignore the global common good?', *Business and Society Review*, 114: 153–82.

DRYDYK, J. (1999) 'Globalization and human rights', in Koggel, C. (ed.) *Moral Issues in Global Perspective*. Peterborough, Ontario: Broadview.

DUNNING, J (ed.) (2003) *Making Globalization Good: The moral challenges of global capitalism*. Oxford: Oxford University Press.

ENTINE, J. (2010) 'The last word', *Ethical Corporation*, November.

FARRAR, M., ROBINSON, S., WETHERLY, P. and VALLI, Y. (2012) *Islam and the West*. Basingstoke: Palgrave.

FORRESTER, D. (2005) *Apocalypse Now?* Aldershot: Ashgate.

GORRINGE, T. (1999) *Fair Shares: Ethics and the global economy*. London: Thames & Hudson.

HARDIN, G. (1974) 'Lifeboat ethics: the case against helping the poor', Garrett Hardin Society: http://www.garretthardinsociety.org/articles/art_lifeboat_ethics_case_against_ helping_poor. html.

INSTITUTE OF DIRECTORS (2009) *King Report on Governance for South Africa* (King III). Institute of Directors in South Africa.

JACKSON, T. (2011) *International Management Ethics*. Cambridge: Cambridge University Press.

JELLIFFE, D. (1971/2) 'Commerciogenic malnutrition? Time for a dialogue', *Food Technology*, 15: 55–6.

KESTEMONT, M. and FRASELLE, N. (2006) 'Fair trade and ethical trade: new forms of trading partnerships', *Puent@Europa*, 4(2), June.

KUNG, H. (1991) *Global Responsibility: In search of a new world ethics*. London: SCM.

KUNG, H. and SCHMIDT, H. (1998) *A Global Ethic and Global Responsibilities*. London: SCM.

LEWIS, C. S. (1978) *The Abolition of Man*. New York: Prentice Hall.

MANN, C. (2011) *1493: How Europe's discovery of the Americas revolutionized trade, ecology and life on Earth*. London: Granta.

MILLENNIUM DEVELOPMENT GOALS (2000) http://www.un.org/millenniumgoals/.

MILLER, D. (2007) *National Responsibility and Global Justice*. Oxford: Oxford University Press.

MUNCK, R. (2006) *Globalization and Contestation: The new great counter-movement*. London: Routledge.

MUTUA, M. (2002) *Human Rights: A political and cultural critique*. Philadelphia: University of Philadelphia Press.

NUSSBAUM, M. (1999) 'Human functioning and social justice in defence of Aristotelian essentialism', in Koggel, C. (ed.) *Moral Issues in Global Perspective*. Peterborough, Ontario: Broadview.

O'DONOVAN, O. (2000). 'Review of *A global ethic and global responsibilities*', *Studies in Christian Ethics*, 13(1): 122–8.

O'NEILL, O. (2000) *Bounds of Justice*. Cambridge: Cambridge University Press.

OWENS, J. and PARRY, R. (2009) 'Stronger and cleaner tax systems would help development, but there is much work to be done', *OECD Observer*, OECD Centre for Tax Policy and Administration.

POGGE, T. (2008) *World Poverty and Human Rights*, 2nd edition. Cambridge: Polity Press.

RAWLS, J. (1971) *Justice as Fairness*. Oxford: Clarendon.

RASCHE, A. and KELL, G. (2010) *The United Nations Global Compact: Achievements, trends and challenges*. Cambridge: Cambridge University Press.

RORTY, R. (1993) 'Human rights, rationality and sentimentality', in Shute, S. and Hurley, S. (eds) *On Human Rights*. New York: Basic Books.

ROTHLIN, S. (2004) *Eighteen Rules of International Business Ethics*. Beijing: Renmon University Press.

SANDEL, M. (2010) *Justice: What's the right thing to do?* London: Penguin.

SEN, A. (2009) *The Idea of Justice*. London: Allen Lane.

SETHI, P. (ed.) (2011) *Globalization and Self-Regulation: The crucial role that corporate codes of conduct play in global business*. London: Macmillan.

SINGER, P. (2002) *One World: The ethics of globalisation*. Melbourne: Text Publishing.

STEGER, M. (2003) *Globalization*. Oxford: Oxford University Press.

STIGLITZ, J. (2002) *Globalization and its Discontents*. New York: W. W. Norton & Co.

TWISS, S. (1998) 'Religion and human rights: a comparative perspective', in Twiss, S. and Grelle, B. (eds) *Exploration in Global Ethics*. Oxford: Westview.

UN (1948) *Declaration of Human Rights*: http://www.un.org/en/documents/udhr.

UN (2000) *United Nations Global Compact*: http://www.unglobalcompact.org/AboutTheGC/ The Ten Principles/index.html.

UN (2010) *The Importance of Voluntarism*: http://www.unglobalcompact.org/docs/about_ the_gc/Voluntarism_Importance.pdf.

WALZER, M. (1983) *Spheres of Justice*. New York: Basic Books.

WEISS, J. (2003). *Business Ethics*. Mason, OH: South-Western College.

XU, K. (2006) 'The implications of Confucian and Daoist values for multinationals in intercultural business communcation'. Proceedings of the 71st Association for Business Communication Annual Conference, 25–28 October. San Antonio, Texas.

CHAPTER 14

Environmental Sustainability

LEARNING OUTCOMES

When you have completed this chapter you will be able to:

- understand and critically assess underlying views about the environment and ecosystem
- understand and critically assess the concept of sustainability and how it relates to responsibility
- understand and critically assess the arguments around obligations to future generations
- understand and critically assess the arguments around global warming and business
- understand the main approaches to integrating sustainable practice and reporting.

INTRODUCTION

This chapter begins by looking at awareness of and responsibility for the environment, and at what the philosophical basis for that might be. It goes on to examine more closely the core understanding of sustainability and sustainable development, and how that relates to responsibility and corporate social responsibility. It then examines the continuing case of BP and its venture in the Gulf of Mexico, and the arguments about greenwashing and corporate integrity. It explores ways of integrating sustainable practice and reporting.

BEYOND PETROLEUM

CASE

In the 1990s British Petroleum (BP) decided it was important to respond to the issues surrounding global warming and climate change. A significant initial step was for BP to withdraw from the Global Climate Coalition. This had been set up by firms from the energy industry to challenge what was increasingly becoming the accepted scientific view of major industry as contributing to climate change.

By 2002 BP had also withdrawn from the US lobbying group that was seeking to drill for oil in the Arctic National Wildlife Refuge. The withdrawal coincided with a change in image. The name British Petroleum was

formally changed to BP. This now stood for 'Beyond Petroleum', and was accompanied by a new logo involving a green, yellow and white sunburst. The accompanying narrative was that BP was the first oil company to recognise the risks of global climate change. This did not necessarily involve uncritical acceptance of climate change science. It did accept that potential risks had to be taken into account. It thus focused on both the development of alternative fuels and the reduction of its own carbon emissions. This led to a 10 per cent cut in emissions of greenhouse gases several years ahead of its target date, and to increased investment in solar energy equipment. Emissions reduction even saved over $600 million through increased energy efficiency and the sale of natural gas that was no longer being vented and flared.

The developments met with some scepticism both internally and externally. Internally, there was increasing concern that this approach did not take into account opportunity costs and potential business lost through time spent on the green agenda.

Externally, the media began to question the very basis of the firm's approach. Frey (2002) put it bluntly:

How can an oil company be 'Beyond Petroleum' without actively distancing itself from its core product, and how can a company that digs big holes in the ground possibly advertise itself as a sensitive steward of the environment?

Murphy (2002) inferred that BP was in fact not really taking the issue of environmental ethics seriously. In the six years before 2002 BP had spent $200 million on the development of solar power. In 2001 it had spent $8.5 billion on the exploration and production of fossil fuels. Murphy (2002: 44) adds that there is nothing in the BP advertising campaign to indicate that it would be spending $15 billion developing oil rigs in the Gulf of Mexico in the following decade.

To be continued …

REFLECTIVE PRACTICE

This snapshot of the developing environmental strategy of BP raises several questions.

Why should any corporate organisation be concerned about the environment? This focuses on the nature of corporate responsibility and sustainability.

How can any organisation properly fulfil its obligations to the environment? The concern of BP about its carbon footprint is shared by all organisations. It focuses on the running of the plant(s), the production process, the final product and external issues.

There is the problem of environmental effects associated with the purpose of a particular industry. In BP's case this involves extracting resources from the physical environment, which seems to work directly against the idea of caring for it.

ENVIRONMENTAL ETHICS

The Earth's natural resources – air, water and land – are increasingly polluted and abused, much of which is related to human activities. The expansion of human settlements and intensification of agriculture has led to the destruction on a global scale of natural habitats and ecosystems.

The rise in green thinking and sustainability concerns since the early 1970s has been accompanied by the development of environmental ethics. This focuses on the ethical relationship between human beings and the natural environment, in an attempt for both to co-exist without compromising the futures of either (Des Jardins, 2006).

PHILOSOPHY OF THE ENVIRONMENT

There are three main schools of thought with respect to environmental philosophy – instrumental, axiological and anthropological – each placing different priorities on human activities and the natural world (Carson, 1962).

Instrumental

The instrumental approach is human-centred. At one level this simply means that nature's resources should be used for the good of humanity – a basic argument for the extractive industries, corresponding to the claim that the extraction of oil, gas, coal and the like improves the well-being of society. The problem with this argument is that it is not always clear that such extraction aims for or achieves anything more than fulfilling partial needs. In the case of oil it may be argued that it is primarily involved in fuelling cars, the use of which is questioned:

- Cars are part of an economic system premised on the idea that growth is good. It is no longer clear that unlimited growth is either necessary or good (Jackson, 2011).
- Car emissions have a negative effect on the environment.

The instrumental view, then – like utilitarianism in general – depends on the underlying view of well-being or what is good.

Behind the instrumental approach is also a view of humankind as dominating and exploiting the environment. This has a long history of debate. White (2006), for instance, argues that it is based in the Judaeo-Christian tradition, involving dominant humanity subduing the Earth for its own well-being. White has been criticised as misunderstanding Creation theology (Gill, 2006). Gill argues that this involves God's placing humankind as vice-gerent, manager or steward of creation. Although this elevates humanity above creation, it also places responsibility on humankind for the care of the Earth, and recognises the equal value of the whole of creation.

Axiological

Sometimes known as the biocentric argument, the axiological approach argues that nature and all life has intrinsic value, and that we should protect it because of this value, and for no other reason. The view seeks to establish what this intrinsic value consists of and where it comes from. In this approach, the environment has intrinsic value independent of human beings. This is hard to maintain because it considerably diminishes humankind's significance and importance in taking responsibility for the environment. Mele (2009) accordingly argues that not all life is of the same value.

A development of this view is eco-centricism. This places the interactive ecosystem at the centre of value. The task of humanity is then to ensure that the interdependent environment is sustained. Critics argue that this provides a romantic view of nature, and that although there may be interaction and interdependence in the physical environment, it is not precise and is constantly changing in ways that make simple maintenance impossible (Mele, 2009: 350).

Not surprisingly, underlying these environmental ethics are worldviews and specific beliefs about the environment. One of the more prominent is the Gaia hypothesis devised by biologist James Lovelock (1979). He suggests that the Earth should be seen as a single organism. Like any organism it continues to attempt to maintain a healthy balance and fight disease. Some take this literally, seeing the human race as a part of this organism, and therefore profoundly interconnected. In this light there is no sense in humanity's trying to destroy or degrade the environment because it is the equivalent of destroying one's own body. The problem with this hypothesis is that if we view the human race as literally part of an organism, it takes away any real sense of moral autonomy, and thus responsibility. Another view, that of deep ecology, focuses on the values of self-realisation and biocentric equality (Vesilind and Gunn, 1998).

Neither of these views is based in rational justification but both are intuitively felt. Deep ecology thus falls under the heading of existential awareness or even spirituality. Self-realisation is an awareness of the self in relation to the wider universe. Given this awareness, humanity cannot think of itself as greater than any aspect of the universe – hence the belief in biocentric equality: all parts of the universe are equally valuable. The emphasis in deep ecology is on proper respect for nature – hence the importance in this view of maintaining the wilderness. It is argued that even the idea of stewardship is questionable in this light, because it implies intervention, if not domination, rather than respect for what is.

Deep ecology requires a fundamental change in humanity's relationship with the environment. Ultimately, it would require massive depopulation. This would require a complete change in terms of technology, and some critics suggest that it would necessitate a return to a hunter-gatherer society. In turn this raises major questions of how it is to be achieved and who, other than the elite, might remain. So although the underlying values of this view are important, the practical implications are less clear.

Anthropological

The approach most widely used in environmental ethics today is the anthropological, which aims to balance respect for nature and human involvement in nature. This is summed up in the work of Jonas (1984). As we noted in Chapter 4, Jonas focused on the responsibility of humankind. The rise of technology, he argues, changed the nature of human action. It so extends human power that we are directly responsible for what happens in the future. With responsibility comes an obligation to get the balance right.

Jonas argues then that:

- living nature is good in itself, attested to by matter's capacity to organise itself for life
- the creation/evolution of humankind is an event of the highest importance, establishing a reflective stewardship responsibility for nature
- the imperative to be responsible is answered by the capacity of humankind to feel responsible for the whole. Responsibility in this is based on an identification with the environment and an acute awareness of humankind's role in relation to the environment.

The anthropological approach, then, focuses on stewardship, building up a primary concern with human nature, how it relates the wider environment, and how both are sustained and enhanced in creative interaction.

When environmental ethics emerged as a new sub-discipline of philosophy and ethics in the early 1960s, it did so by posing a challenge to traditional anthropocentrism. First, it questioned the assumed moral superiority of human beings to members of other species on earth. Second, it investigated the possibility of rational arguments for assigning intrinsic value to the natural environment in its non-human elements (Carson, 1962). All this is reinforced by a positive utilitarian argument about the importance of the environment to humanity. Humanity needs a healthy environment if it is to survive. It is therefore in the interests of humankind to sustain it.

Animal welfare

Concern for the ecosystem includes animals. Arguments here emphasise the need to maintain species as part of that system. Business, however, also accepts that some animals are used as resources for humanity, from food to the use of animals in the testing of products. Underlying ethical discussions consider whether animals are of equal value to humans (Singer, 1975), whether they have rights, or whether they simply have needs and interests that should be respected. The general argument (Mele, 2009) is that even where animals are used as human resources, they should have the best possible quality of life (Oxford Centre of Animal Ethics: www.oxfordanimalethics.com).

REFLECTIVE PRACTICE

How do you view the environment?

What part should business play in sustaining the environment?

Your board has asked you to develop an environmental sustainability policy, and you have been asked to provide the justification for it in the first page. How would you argue this?

SUSTAINABILITY AND ETHICS

'Sustainability' is a broad term. In some firms it has become a buzzword and a marketing tool through which projects are promoted. Where sustainability is part of this green marketing strategy, it is open to abuse. The term 'sustainability' must therefore be critically defined.

SUSTAINABILITY

The concept of sustainability is not simple. There are, Judge (2011) suggests, over 70 definitions. Judge (2011) argues that there are two broad aspects of sustainability and sustainable development:

- IRGE – intergenerational equity: fairness between generations. This counts the future as of equal importance to the present generation.
- IAGE – intra-generational equity: fairness between different groups within the same generation.

Both these positions can be developed in different ways, often characterised as 'weak' and 'strong'.

- Weak sustainability – IRGE involves ensuring maintenance of living standards. IAGE looks to compensatory action for the poor through support programmes.
- Strong sustainability – In IRGE this looks to go beyond the standards of living and endeavours to 'replace losses in environmental capital' (Judge, 2011) as well. In IAGE compensation remains but is extended to sustaining the environment.

PAUSE FOR THOUGHT

The relationship of sustainability to responsibility

The distinction between responsibility and sustainability continues to be debated (van Marrewijk, 2003). Broadly, the distinctions are these:

- Sustainability is the same as responsibility. Here, commonly, one divides sustainability up in much the same way as responsibility. This refers thus to institutional, economic, social and environmental sustainability.

- Corporate sustainability and responsibility are two sides of the same coin. This offers the view of responsibility and sustainability as having different emphases, both of which are necessary.

- Corporate sustainability is seen as the primary concept. This is the view set out by van Marrewijk (2003). It is strongly supported by King III, arguing that it is the primary concept. Marrewijk argues that corporate responsibility, with its stress on the triple bottom line, with financial, social and environmental accountability, is the way of achieving corporate sustainability.

- Responsibility is the primary concept from which sustainability flows. See below.

One way of testing the meaning and status of the two different ideas is by asking which of the ideas is logically primary – that is, which of the two ideas does not rely on the other for its understanding or justification.

In this light, the two different views of sustainability above depend on another moral idea – that is, our obligation to future generations and the environment. In other words, both ideas depend on working out what our responsibility is to future generations. Logically, therefore, the idea of responsibility, as discussed in Chapter 4, is prior to sustainability and sustainable development. Here, responsibility is broader than simple corporate responsibility, involving the three interrelated modes set out in Chapter 4. This forms the primary ethical category within which sustainability is discussed. Sustainability is part of the third mode: responsibility or liability for. This brings us back to a further consideration of the responsibility for future generations.

RESPONSIBILITY FOR FUTURE GENERATIONS

The greatly increasing pressure on technology-based human activity has given rise to the environmental insecurity and depletion of natural resources. This raises the question of how we can continue to operate what we see as civilisation (Ferguson, 2011) as we have been doing without negatively affecting the future for ourselves and our descendants.

Sustainable development is an attempt to balance two moral demands that requires serious ethical consideration. The first demand is for development, including economic development and growth. It arises mainly from the needs or desires of present generations, especially those groups who have a low quality of life and urgently seek steps to improve it. The second demand is for sustainability, for ensuring that we do not sacrifice the future for the sake of gains in the present (Hurka, 1992).

There are three main arguments against the present generation's having responsibilities for the future generations:

- The present generation is inevitably ignorant of what will be required for the conservation of the ecosystem for future generations. They cannot know how the future will develop.
- We have no obligation to bring future generations into existence because there are no particular people to whom responsibility is directed.
- We cannot impose responsibilities on people who will not exist for many years to come.

Although such arguments have some elements of truth, they do not take away responsibilities for our actions and their consequences, even if those consequences are to occur at some point in the future. It is not the timing of the actions that humans should take that is critical in determining the human responsibility and accountability, therefore, but the course of detrimental action itself. Barring an unforeseen disaster it is safe enough to assume that people will exist in the future and that they will be similar enough to us that we can develop a good idea of their future requirements to sustain their existence. Taking this into account and knowing that the actions of the present generation can seriously influence the future generations' well-being, it is reasonable to assume that the future generations must be given some form of ethical consideration. Jonas's (1984) stress on the effects of technological advance reinforces this argument.

What do we owe future generations?

It is reasonable to argue for a general responsibility towards future generations to sustain the environment and the Earth's ecosystem so that the existence of future generations is not compromised. But what do we owe future generations in particular, and how do we decide where these responsibilities lie? The ethical basis of these responsibilities and their designations must also be established (Warren, 1980).

First, it can be argued that those responsibilities can sometimes be overridden by the interests and needs of the present generation. Behind this is the view that each generation has the responsibility for its own time. The present generation has to face very difficult decisions that have to be focused in the present, and these cannot be based solely on a concern for the future of the environment. So, for instance, faced by the possibility of a war, the decision will involve not simply sustainability in present or future senses but also concern for immediate effects on survival and culture.

Conversely, the interest of future generations might be jeopardised by the less important interests of the present. It is thought by some that the interests of the present population always overrides future interest because of the uncertainties in the needs and interest of future generations, and therefore that the interests of future generations can be 'discounted' on the grounds that uncertain and remote pleasure counts for less than certain immediate ones. The discounting of the interests of future generations is done on the same principle as the notion that one unit of monetary value is worth more today than in some point in the future, so the future value of money must be discounted in order to be equivalent to the present value (Arndt, 1993). As a result the practice of discounting future interests is common practice in economic analysis of environmental issues.

Second, against this is the egalitarian view. This can take several forms, but all centre on the basic principle that considers each generation to have a duty to pass on to its successors a total range of resources and opportunities that is at least as good as the one it inherited. A generation that enjoys favourable conditions of life must pass on similar circumstances of life to its successors. Generations that are less fortunate have no such stringent obligation. One egalitarian approach characterises our duty concerning future generations not in terms of their well-being or quality of life but in terms of their range of opportunities. Future generations, then, have the responsibility to use these well. This view fits the Bruntland Commission's view that 'Development that is sustained is not quality of life as such, but the economic and other activity that permits quality of life' (Bruntland, 1987).

The problem with equality as determining responsibility is that it has too many possible meanings, from equality of outcome, treatment or access, to equality of respect. It is not clear which of these would be used (Hurka, 1992).

Such objections lead to a third view about responsibility for future generations. Contrary to the utilitarian and egalitarian views, the duty of the present generation is not to make the condition of future generations as good as possible or as good as our own, but only to make the condition of future generations reasonably good. This view argues that each generation has a duty to pass on to its successor a range of opportunities that allows for a reasonable quality of life. If a generation can pass on a better range of opportunities, one that allows for a more than reasonable quality of life, that may be a fine or even good thing to do, but it is not its duty to guarantee this. This view rests on an idea for which economists have coined the term 'satisficing', which is a behaviour that attempts to achieve at least some minimum level of a particular variable but that does not strive to achieve its maximum possible value. Such an approach therefore suggests that the present generation does not have to obsessively strive for the best possible outcome but can be content when it finds one that is reasonably good. If their own lives are not reasonably good, they may weigh a concern for their own interests against their duty to their descendants – a view that helps regulate and moderate its demands on later generations. This is illustrated if we imagine that our present range of opportunities allows us a quality of life that is more than reasonably good. We do not violate a satisficing duty if we pass on a marginally smaller range of opportunities to our successors, so long as this range is reasonably large, and that the future generations can live above a certain threshold standard of living. The defining concepts of the Bruntland Commission on the environment and development (1987) are: meeting the needs of the present, and enabling future generations to meet their own needs. Needs are not all that matter for a good life, but they come first, before luxuries, and have a certain priority.

REFLECTIVE PRACTICE

How would you personally justify concern for future generations?

How would you justify concern for future generations as an accountant?

How would you justify concern for future generations as a managing director?

How would the board begin to justify its concerns?

Would there be any difference in the justifications?

GLOBAL WARMING: THE DEBATE

One might ask why the debate about global warming is in a book on business ethics. The answer is partly that business has ensured that it is part of this debate. In Chapter 8 we noted the issues around conflicts of interest, and the argument that business was actually skewing research agendas away from global warming. This is largely due to the perception that focus on environmental issues might have negative effects on some areas of business.

In fact, the debate is much more complex than environmentalists versus business interests, as the response to the Stern Review shows.

The Stern Review (2006)

The Stern Review (2006: http://www.direct.gov.uk/en/Nl1/Newsroom/DG_064854) into the economics of climate change was given strong support by the UK Government. The dangers of climate change it pointed to included that:

- all countries will be affected, but the poorest countries will suffer earliest and most
- average temperatures could rise by 5 degrees Celsius from pre-industrial levels if climate change goes unchecked
- warming of 3 or 4 degrees (Celsius) will result in many millions more people being flooded. By the middle of the century, 200 million may be permanently displaced due to rising sea levels, heavier floods and drought
- warming of 4 degrees (Celsius) or more is likely to seriously affect global food production
- warming of 2 degrees (Celsius) could leave 15–40% of present species facing extinction
- unabated climate change could cost the world at least 5 per cent of GDP each year; if more dramatic predictions come to pass, the cost could be more than 20 per cent of GDP.

According to the Stern Review, action in three areas is required: carbon pricing, technology policy and energy efficiency.

- Carbon pricing, through taxation, emissions trading or regulation, would demonstrate to all stakeholders the full social costs of their actions. A global carbon price across countries and sectors is recommended.
- Emissions trading schemes should be expanded and linked.
- Technology policy should drive the large-scale development and use of a range of low-carbon and high-efficiency products.
- There should be at least a doubling of global support for energy research. Support for low-carbon technologies should be increased fivefold.
- International funding should go into researching new crop varieties that address global food needs.

The review concluded that climate change is at least partly anthropogenic (caused by humans), and that the benefits of decisive and early action would outweigh the costs.

The Stern Review has been criticised, not least by scientists and economists. They argue that the review overstates the severity of global warming and underestimates the cost of acting now to deal with it. More cautious approaches have emerged from groups such as the Intergovernmental Panel on Climate Change (IPCC 2007 Working Group II Report, *Impacts, Adaptation and Vulnerability*: http://www.ipcc.ch/publications_and_data/publications_and_data_reports.shtml), who argued at one point, for instance, that a temperature increase of 2–3 degrees Celsius would not take place until the end of the century.

Despite the differences even within those who argue for climate change, there are still clear grounds for supporting the case (Judge, 2011). In any event, the argument cannot be based solely on science. The danger of focusing on scientific evidence is, as Sarewitz (2004) argues, that we place too much weight on science to solve the issue of global warming. No predictive science can be certain. He argues that this demands a clearer debate about the core values of both of the different stakeholders and of leadership, rather than imagining that science alone will break the decision-making log-jam. Politicians still have to take the decision even if the science is not absolutely clear. In the light of this, and the general thrust of the scientific data, it is reasonable to base a response on the precautionary principle. Gibson (2007) compares this to Pascal's wager. Pascal argued that it is prudent for us to believe in God. If God does not exist, we lose nothing. If he does exist, we may have infinite future rewards. Gibson adapts this principle to argue that the worst possible option is if climate change is a real problem and we ignore it.

Such arguments do not make the issue of how governments and business respond any easier. Attempts to develop possible responses from the development of the Kyoto Protocol (http://unfccc.int/kyoto_protocol/items/2830.php) to the Copenhagen Conference (Judge, 2011) have had to face many problems around global justice and national self-interest. Global warming is generated mostly by a small number of Western nations, while many – including the poorest nations – suffer from it. Moreover, cutting back on industrial emissions will negatively affect fast-growing economies, such as China and India, and thus hinder wider development.

 REFLECTIVE PRACTICE

Review the argument of Al Gore's film *An Inconvenient Truth* (2006, DVD Paramount).

Review the response from the Competitive Enterprise Institute in Washington (http://cei.org/pdf/5539.pdf).

As the CEO of a car manufacturing business, how would you resolve this debate for a forthcoming Annual General Meeting at which some shareholders, including one of Al Gore's family, intend to raise the poor sustainability record of the firm?

Remember: dealing with ethical issues at this level is not simply about knocking down arguments but also about managing the values of the different stakeholders (see Chapter 13).

BUSINESS ETHICS, SUSTAINABILITY ETHICS AND CORPORATE SOCIAL RESPONSIBILITY

The World Business Council for Sustainable Development states (Lehni, 1992) that:

> For the business enterprise, sustainable development means adopting business strategies and activities that meet the needs of the enterprise and its stakeholders today while protecting, sustaining and enhancing the human and natural resources that will be needed in the future.

Becoming sustainable makes business sense, and moves towards the '3-Ps' approach of focusing on people, planet and profits.

Business's involvement in sustainability is based in:

- business as global citizen, with the same responsibility as individuals or groups to respond to environmental needs
- business as sharing responsibility with other stakeholders of the environment. This looks to building effective partnerships
- business as directly responsible for its particular effects on the environment. Once more, the extractive industry is a good example.

Green companies

Popularly businesses that are committed to sustainability are referred to as 'green' companies. According to the UK Government's website (Directgov), companies do three things to be green:

- They have a corporate social responsibility policy, many consulting their customers in drawing them up. Larger companies typically have information about the policies on their websites and commit to reporting their progress to customers and investors.
- They provide green products, which usually consists of sourcing raw materials from sustainable sources and letting customers know what other companies they work with. Sometimes providing a green product is about offering products with a green element to them – for example, donating money to a green cause.
- They make their business greener. This may amount to a 'leaner is greener' approach reflected in reducing packaging, cutting transportation costs and removing chemicals from the manufacturing process or products that may harm the environment.

According to this definition, Swarovski – a world leader in cut crystal – is a green company.

 SWAROVSKI

CASE

Daniel Swarovski (1862–1956), the founder of the major crystal jewellery company bearing his name, said that 'supporting social and environmental projects is the obligation of a responsible company'.

Founded in 1895, in Wattens, Austria, and remaining independently owned, Swarovski now employs 20,000 people in 120 countries. The core natural resource needed for crystal manufacture is water, a supply of which is available in the Tyrolean Alps of Austria. Water is used in the grinding and cleaning of crystals as well as in the recycling of metal, all processes they have now exported into numerous countries.

Continuing in the founder's principle, the Swarovski Water School was conceived in 1998, the central idea being to educate schoolchildren – the future custodians of the world's water resources – in the importance of sustainably maintaining this most vital natural resource.

Through residential trips, workshops and a mobile educational programme, children actively participate in experiments, games and other forms of learning which raise their environmental awareness.

The Living Yangtze Project has extended the work of the Swarovski Water School to local youth in the vast area of the Yangtze River basin in China. The Yangtze River is 6,300 kilometres/3,940 miles long and is the life source for much of China's population, flora and fauna.

Source: based on http://www.swarovski.com/Web_AA/en/crystal_society?contentid=10007.119277

Going green, however, may not be authentic.

Greenwashing

It is all too easy, especially for large companies with marketing resources, for companies to get on the bandwagon of sustainability in order to offset any harm that might be done to their reputation and thus to the bottom line of profit. This has become known as 'greenwashing', defined as 'disinformation disseminated by an organisation so as to present an environmentally responsible public image' (*Concise Oxford English Dictionary*).

Below, adapted from a feature included in the *Guardian* (2008), is a summary of some of the signs to look out for when trying to distinguish between greenwashing and the real thing in company advertising.

How to spot a fake It's greenwash if it ...	How to spot the real thing It might be true if...
• is ludicrously general *Making claims without support* • is overspecific *Check out the numbers or 'facts' included* • relies on nature pictures *Attempting to green products by association* • is backed up by a 'tame' academic *Research credentials are important* • is simply absurd *If a claim sounds absurd, it probably is*	• what the company says matches what it actually does • the company is in partnership with an independent ethical organisation • the company takes that extra, obsessive step • the company introduces green innovations • the company sets itself targets • the company takes action even if it may harm business • the company has been audited • the company makes it easy for you to find all this out

The 'Don't Be Fooled' Awards (alternet.org/wiretap/15699) point to several major corporations who, the originators argue, are greenwashing. Exxon Mobil, for example, has contributed $100 million to the Global Climate and Energy Project. However, at the same time it has invested $100 billion in oil exploration.

It is of course very easy to take aim at any major company, find problems, and from them conclude that its environmental concern is a cynical front. Several things make this issue very hard to deal with:

- Many companies, particularly in oil and mining, are involved in businesses which could be said by definition to be environmentally harmful.
- Such companies are each only one of several stakeholders, including governments, who have some responsibility for the effects of their industry.
- The size of such companies makes it very difficult to know the truth about any accusations of greenwashing. It may, for instance, be that bad practices occur in parts of the operation of which the central management is unaware.
- The dynamics surrounding attempts to develop sustainability in large companies can easily become polarised. It is easy to assume that multinational corporations' concern for profits excludes genuine attempts to develop sustainability, and thus not recognise any progress that may in fact have been made. Behind this is the ethics as perfection argument – ie that a company cannot be deemed ethical if it does not get *everything* right. Given the impossibility of getting everything right, companies can become easy targets. One such target has been BP.

This brings us to the second part of the BP narrative.

CASE

BEYOND PETROLEUM II: DEEPWATER

Ten years after BP's development of corporate sustainability, the company's exploration of the Gulf of Mexico was reaching fruition.

The *Deepwater* Horizon

On 20 April 2010 BP's *Deepwater Horizon* oil rig, drilling at the Macondo well, exploded due to methane gas forcing its way through the drill column. The resulting fire burned for 36 hours, leading to the loss of 11 human lives. Subsequently, the oil leak was estimated at 4.9 million barrels, the largest leak in US waters. The leak took some time to plug, and went on to affect hundreds of miles of coastline, coastal industries, and a great deal of wildlife, including thousands of seabirds.

The incident was complex, not least because lines of responsibility did not always seem clear. The drilling unit itself was owned by Transocean, leased to BP, and the unit was working with Halliburton Energy Services in setting a concrete base for the operation.

The National Commission on the *Deepwater Horizon* disaster (2011: http://www. oilspillcommission.gov/final-report) reported that systemic failures across all the organisations involved were likely to recur. The commission and other reports further noted that:

- There had been inadequate oversight by government bodies. A flawed safety plan was signed off by the government environmental agency. Even more serious was the fact that the Minerals Management Service (MMS) granted a 'categorical exclusion' from the National Environmental Policy Act to BP's oil and gas activities in the Gulf of Mexico. The effect of this was that the MMS would not thoroughly review the environmental impacts of the exploration phase for the *Deepwater Horizon* site. It was argued that this was wrong because the exploration was in deep water and was using

relatively new technology – both criteria for not granting an exclusion.

- Engineering planning and decision-making was not effective in the light of deep-water drilling practice that was not well established. This included flawed designs and inadequate judgements about the signs of blowout.

- Several decisions saved time and money, whether this was the primary intent or not.

- There were a series of key decisions which although they did not of themselves lead to the disaster, when taken together, caused it. This pointed to a lack of awareness about the internal work environment, and a lack of overview. This was therefore not characterised as an individual aberration but as a systemic failure.

- The evidence suggests that BP's engineering team did not conduct a formal, disciplined analysis of the combined impact of risk factors on the prospects for a successful cement job.

In all this there was little sense of a culture of responsibility (see Chapters 3, 4 and 6). On the contrary, there was evidence of a lack of awareness of the environment, internally and externally; a lack of sustained risk assessments at every point and in terms of the overall project; a lack of systematic concern for safety; and little effective negotiation of responsibility with stakeholders or partners.

Safety plans

Much of the precautionary safety material was summed in BP's 582-page regional spill plan for the Gulf, and its 52-page site-specific plan for the *Deepwater Horizon* rig. Many fundamental errors were later found in both of these documents. For instance:

- There were major understatements of the dangers posed by an uncontrolled leak and major overstatements of the capacity of the company to deal with one, The *Deepwater Horizon* plan notes that 'BP Exploration and Production Inc. has the capability to respond, to the maximum extent practicable, to a worst-case discharge, or a substantial threat of such a discharge, resulting from the activities proposed in our Exploration Plan' (quoted in http://www.timesonline.co.uk/tol/news/world/us_and_americas/ article7146713.ece).

- Under the heading 'Sensitive biological resources', the safety plan listed marine mammals including walruses, sea otters, sea lions and seals, none of which lives in the Gulf of Mexico. It is thought that this was probably a cut-and-paste from another plan altogether.

- The names and phone numbers of several Texas A&M University marine life specialists were wrong. One professor had died four years before the plan was published. The numbers for marine mammal stranding network offices in Louisiana and Florida were no longer in service.

- There was no information about tracking sub-surface oil plumes from deepwater blowouts, although more oil might be spreading below the surface than at the top.

- The plan included no oceanic or meteorological data, despite the ocean-floor site in a hurricane-prone region.

Although a disaster of the size of this major oil spill would of course create problems that are unforeseen, it raises major questions of governance and of the approach to sustainability. Two seem critical for any corporation of the size of BP.

First, there is little evidence of the kind of integrated thinking and practice that King III argues for. This would involve a clear sense of sharing responsibility with different agencies, not least the government and NGOs. Such governance thinking also demands perspectives that would challenge ideas and practice. There was little evidence of such challenge

at any stage of the boards dealing with the disaster. On the contrary, the initial response gave the impression of believing all the estimates in the safety plans, leading to continual changes in the response as the data was perceived to be flawed.

Second, and in turn, the evidence suggests internal contradiction between the sustainability policy and the practice of responsibility on the ground in everyday decisions. The former is well developed and thought through, as noted above, and the latter reveals little sense of agency (knowing what was being done and what effect it had or might have on the environment), no clarity about accountability, and no worked-through shared responsibility. In that sense there is no evidence of a culture of responsibility or of the individual or corporate capacities of responsibility. King III would suggest that dissonance between values and practice is an issue for the board.

All of this takes business back to the precautionary principle set out by the Rio Declaration of 1992, which states (quoted in Grace and Cohen, 2005: 150) that:

> In order to protect the environment, the precautionary approach shall be widely applied by States according to their capabilities. Where there are threats of serious or irreversible damage, lack of full scientific certainty shall not be used as a reason for postponing cost-effective measures to prevent environmental degradation.

This means that governments and businesses should anticipate unintended consequences, and also the potential effect of any major disaster in making any major decision with respect to the environment. This is a higher standard than the law, placing the proactive responsibility on those who engage in a potentially harmful activity.

Questions

1   Compare this chapter's first case study *Beyond petroleum I*, and its strong commitment to sustainability, with *Beyond petroleum II*. What accounts for apparent differences?

2   You have applied for the job of CSR director at BP and have been asked to bring to the interview an outline of how you would ensure integrity of principles, policy and practice in BP. Analyse the practice of BP in terms of the three modes of responsibility.

3   What would be your major learning points, and what would be the implication for practice at board level and at operational level? How would you set about convincing the interview panel of your case?

(For ongoing debate around the issues see http://news.nationalgeographic.com/ news/ energy/2011/04/110420-gulf-oil-spill-anniversary/.)

BUSINESS PRACTICE

Business practice must begin with principles – and a good example of an attempt to bring together principles and practice is the list of CERES principles. The Coalition of Environmentally Responsible Economies (CERES) initiated the Global Reporting Initiative in 1997 and set out these basic principles in response to the *Exxon Valdez* disaster of 1989.

The CERES principles are (Grace and Cohen, 2005: 154):

1   Protection of the biosphere: provides for the elimination of pollution, the protection of habitats and the ozone layer, and the minimisation of smog, acid rain and greenhouse gases

2   Sustainable use of natural resources: commits signatories to the conservation of non-renewable resources, and the protection of the wilderness and biodiversity

3   Reduction and disposal of waste: obliges signatories to minimise waste, to dispose of it responsibility and to recycle wherever possible

4   Energy conservation: commits signatories to conserve energy and use it more efficiently

5   Risk reduction: provides for minimising health and safety risks to employees and the public by using safe practices and being prepared for emergencies

6   Safe products and services: seeks protection of consumers and the environment by making products safe and providing information about their effect on the environment

7   Environmental restoration: accepts responsibility for the repair of environmental damage and compensation for those affected

8   Informing the public: obliges management to disclose to employees and the public information about environmentally harmful incidents; also protects employees who blow the whistle about environmental or health and safety hazards in their employment

9   Management commitment: commits signatories to provide resources to implement and monitor the principles; also means that the CEO and the company board must be kept abreast of all environmental aspects of the company's operations; this principle also has implications for the initial selection of board directors

10   Audits and reports: commits signatories to an annual assessment of compliance with the principles that they will make public.

Firms might also work through the underlying vision of sustainability – a good example of which is Interface.

INTERFACE INC.

Interface deals with commercial and institutional interiors, including carpeting. It is a good example of a firm that has developed with sustainability at its centre. Go to http://www. interfaceglobal.com/ Sustainability/Interface-Story.aspx for the full story.

Ray Anderson, the CEO, has even spoken of an epiphany (the revelation of a truth) leading him to focus not simply on values like justice and fairness but on values such as restoration. The final part of their mission is thus summed up in these words:

> We will honour the places where we do business by endeavouring to become the first name in industrial ecology, a corporation that cherishes nature and restores the environment. Interface will lead by example and validate by results, including profits, leaving the world a better place than when we began, and we will be restorative through the power of our influence in the world.

For Interface this requires an integrated practice focusing on people, process, product, place and profits. At the heart of this, Interface suggests that there has to be a developing awareness of how the world works and how society and business in particular can respond. This awareness involves the realisation that 'everything we do, everything we take, everything we make and everything we waste affects nature's balance, and how our actions will ultimately affect our children and the children of all species'.

For Anderson this has included an awareness of how business has abused the physical environment in the past. This level of awareness guides the particular actions they take and the continual critical reflection on these.

The objectives include (http://www. interfacesustainability.com/elim.html):

- eliminating waste in every area of business

- ensuring that emissions from products, vehicles and facilities are benign

- operating facilities with renewable energy sources, including solar, wind, landfill gas, geothermal, tidal and low-impact/small-scale hydroelectric or non-petroleum-based hydrogen

- transporting people and products efficiently to reduce waste and emissions

- creating a culture that integrates sustainability principles and improves people's lives and livelihoods, and which involves stakeholders

- creating a new business model that shows the importance of sustainability-based commerce.

Underlying this are several core values, including:

- respect for the members of the firm – this is based around a view of humanity as continuously learning and developing

- responsibility for the state of the environment along with other stakeholders

- commitment to find ways of responding to the environmental crisis

- concern to enable all stakeholders to develop an environmental awareness, and to give them opportunities for responding to environmental needs

- concern to play a part in restoring the environment. In this Interface lock in, consciously or not, cultural values such as *kyosei* and *shalom*. The first is the concept of 'harmony' used by the Caux Round Table (see Chapter 13). The second is a Hebrew term meaning peace. It stresses the need to restore relationships.

Interface sets out a holistic approach to environmental concern and sustainability – one that seeks to involve all stakeholders.

These values sum up the three modes of responsibility. First, there is a concern to fully understand what the business is doing in relation to the environment. This agency includes a valuing of the environment, without which it is not possible to be fully aware of the environment (see Chapter 4). Second, there is a concern to give an account of thought, value and practice to the widest possible audience. Third, responsibility is consciously shared with stakeholders – something that requires a statement of values as much as the negotiation of responsibility.

MONITORING SUSTAINABILITY

Monitoring sustainable activity is clearly a part of developing a culture of responsibility.

Anglo American provides an effective example of responding to environmental challenges. The multinational mining and natural resources corporation has signed up to the Global Reporting Initiative (GRI) reporting mechanism, the website of which (www.globalreporting.org) describes the GRI as:

a network-based organisation that pioneered the world's most widely-used sustainability reporting framework. GRI is committed to the framework's continuous improvement and application worldwide. GRI's core goals include the mainstreaming of disclosure on environmental, social and governance performance.

The network involves stakeholders from global business, non-governmental organisations, labour organisations and professional bodies.

As a reporting initiative the GRI involves triple-bottom-line reporting on the economic, environmental and societal dimensions of the corporation, underlining the point that all three are interconnected.

The environmental section of their reports includes information on:

- total material use
- direct energy use
- indirect energy use
- total water use
- impacts on biodiversity
- greenhouse gas emissions
- ozone-depleting emissions
- the total amount of waste
- the environmental impact of products.

Anglo American accept that such reporting has been relatively recent for them and that there is a long way to go for their whole corporation. Their report includes fines and legal actions taken against them (73% down from 2004), and environmental incidents (level-2 incidents up by 5%), alongside reference to awards and effective partnerships. On energy efficiency, the 2005 report gives a summary of work across the different companies in the group. This includes an aim of 10% reduction in carbon intensity over 10 years. On air quality, sulphur dioxide emissions decreased by 43% in one company. On water, there is sustained attempt to preserve fresh water and neutralise acidic waste water. The section on biodiversity lists work in which companies have been involved in land stewardship and reclamation projects.

Reporting of this nature serves to establish benchmarks for performance but also seeks to engage the imaginations of the different companies. Imagination is often best engaged through narrative, not simply data. A good example of this is the case study noted in the 2005 report on turning waste water from mines into drinking water.

CASE

DRINKING WATER FOR THE EMALAHLENI MUNICIPALITY

Years of mining in the area around Witbank in Mpumalanga, South Africa, disrupted natural water cycles. Water that would otherwise flow into rivers was leaking into mines, where coal deposits turned it acidic. This hampered mining activity and might in time have led to the pollution of local water supplies. At the same time, growing demand from local communities and industry was draining supplies from local reservoirs.

'We saw an exciting opportunity to solve this problem by converting a mining environmental liability into a sustainable public/private partnership asset by addressing the water shortage challenge facing the local municipalities in the district,' said hydrologist Peter Gunther (Anglo American, 2005).

Anglo American and project partner Ingwe began exploratory work in 2002 on the feasibility of a plant that would convert waste water from the mines to drinking water standards. Local communities and water regulators were closely involved in

the plans and the project was given the go-ahead in 2005.

The plant and storage dams for the project were constructed at Anglo Coals Greenside colliery. The water treatment plant aimed to neutralise acidic water from mines, remove metals and salt, and chlorinate the water. Water quality was to be monitored regularly, with waste products from the treatment process disposed of alongside other waste from Greenside mine. Ways of recycling – and possibly selling – waste minerals such as limestone, magnesite and sulphur were explored.

The plant aimed to provide about 20 per cent of the Emalahleni Municipality's daily water requirements. Local communities would also benefit from about 25 permanent positions at the plant and between 100 and 150 temporary jobs during construction.

Source: Anglo American *Report to Society* (2005: 32)

The extent of environmental audits is taken further by the British Safety Council (www. Britishsafetycouncil.co.uk) in its Five-Stage Environmental Sustainability Audit. Its five levels relate to:

- environmental compliance – This looks to develop standard organisational compliance
- environmental management – This involves the development of core principles and benchmarks
- environmental management systems – This includes supply-chain management
- environmental performance evaluation – This looks to develop environmental reporting, including the GRI, as part of an environmental risk strategy
- environmental sustainability – This includes developing a greenhouse gas reduction policy, a biodiversity action plan and ecological footprinting (monitoring the effects of the business on the environment).

Clearly, such an approach takes time to develop, culminating in the kind of proactive response of Interface in the case study above. The different levels resonate with Hunt and Aster's (1990) suggestion of the five stages of environmental commitment of any business. These involve:

- beginner – There is little resource commitment, and no management strategy
- fire-fighter – Environmental issues are addressed when necessary, often only in response to legal requirements

- concerned citizen – With a minimal budget, environmental issues are part of the management strategy
- pragmatist – Environmental management is an accepted business function, and has a sufficient budget
- proactivist – Environmental issues are a priority, with top management actively leading.

Developing the integration that King III recommends (see Chapter 5) demands attention to several aspects of the firm's circumstances (Judge, 2011):

- the site history, involving an environmental impact assessment (EIA)
- the production process – it has been estimated that firms lose 30% of their energy in this
- product and communications, which might include product design, packaging and labelling
- the external environment, including transport and relations with the supply chain.

In light of the potential savings from this attention, the British Safety Council can argue (www.britsafe.org) that by focusing on the process there are clear benefits to the company, including:

- improved corporate reputation
- increased sales to greener clients
- improved productivity
- increased profitability
- improved staff morale
- improved quality
- more control over organisational issues
- better corporate risk management
- improved relations with key stakeholders
- more environmentally sustainable ways of doing business.

SUSTAINABILITY AND SMES

What of SME engagement with sustainability issues? A useful study is provided by a group of researchers from Kingston University (Taylor et al, 2009) in their case study of sustainability in Surrey SMEs. Their findings were that that the profile of the sustainability agenda remains low across all sectors in the Surrey SME business community, and that few SMEs have developed formal environmental policies or hold accredited environmental standards. Related research confirms that SMEs produce significant environmental impacts (Williamson and Lynch-Wood, 2001), accounting for an estimated 60% of commercial waste and 80% of pollution incidents in England and Wales (NetRegs, 2005).

Other results from the research by Taylor et al (2009) suggest that climate change and biodiversity were thought to have little immediate relevance to SME practice. However, transport, energy and waste were regarded as significant. These findings are similar to those of Perera (2009; see Chapter 11), and seem to indicate that too much stress on complex tools takes away from the focus of reflecting on responsibility in the local context and working with others to develop sustainability plans.

CONCLUSION

The ethics of sustainable development suggest that a concerted effort must be made to promote the principles of sustainability at a local and community level. Sustainable development is connected with ideas from community development to produce an integrated process for securing sustainable communities (Didham, 2002). This takes business ethics out of the narrow concerns that were evident in the 1960s and 1970s into a concern for the common good. That concern, focused in shared responsibility for our shared environment, demands the negotiation of responsibility. This in turn demands stakeholders working together to respond proactively to the needs of the social and physical environment. The question, then, for business is not whether it is responsible, but how it should fulfil its responsibilities alongside other stakeholders.

A unified approach to these issues is complicated by the lack of a standard definition, different practices domestically and overseas, and a mixed bag of regulations from various levels and professionals across industries. In response, business first has to be aware of the environmental legal frameworks in whatever country it is operating. Secondly, it must work with stakeholders in achieving a shared view of sustainability, and of what is possible through creative partnerships.

All of this has shown that business ethics cannot be arbitrarily confined to the boundaries of business. Business ethics inevitably has to addressed and work with broader professional ethics, from professions that make up business, such as accountancy, to professions that form industries, such as engineering. It also has to work with wider social and environmental ethics, because it is a part of that. This means integrating and testing ethical thinking and practice, placing key responsibility on leaders and boards to enable ongoing reflection on ethical meaning and practice.

REFLECTIVE PRACTICE

With two other students write an environmental policy for your company, imaginary or real, bringing together underlying values concerning the environment, the role of your business in relation to the environment, details of how awareness of good practice could be raised with employees and stakeholders, and details of how practice is monitored.

EXPLORE FURTHER

Books

Jamieson, D. (2008) *Ethics and the Environment: An introduction*. Cambridge: Cambridge University Press.

Eweje, G. and Perry, M. (2011) *Business and Sustainability: Concepts, strategies and changes*. Bingley: Emerald.

DVD

The Truth About Climate Change (2008, BBC), for a thoughtful documentary from David Attenborough.

REFERENCES

ANGLO AMERICAN (2005) *Report to Society*. London: Anglo American.

ARNDT, H. W. (1993) 'Review article: Sustainable development and the discount rate', *Economic Development and Cultural Change*, 41: 3.

BRITISH SAFETY COUNCIL (n.d.) *Five Star Environmental Audit*: https://www.britsafe.org/audit-and-advisory/audits/five-star-environmental-audit.

BRUNTLAND, G. H. (1987) *Our Common Future – The World Commission on Environment and Development*. Oxford: Oxford University Press.

CARSON, R. (1962) *Silent Spring*. Boston, MA: Houghton Mifflin.

DES JARDINS, J. (2006) *Environmental Ethics: An introduction to environmental philosophy*. Belmont: Thomson Wadsworth.

DIDHAM, R. (2002) *The Case of Eco-Citizenship: Shaping the future through sustainable development and community development*. University of Edinburgh: The Centre for the study of Environmental Change and Sustainability.

DIRECTGOV. 'Choosing "green" companies'; available at: http://www.direct.gov.uk/en/Environmentandgreenerliving/Greenerhomeandgarden [accessed 8 November 2011].

FERGUSON, N. (2011) *Civilization: The West and the rest*. London: Allen Lane.

FREEMAN, R. E., PIERCE, J. and DODD, R. (2000) *Environmentalism and the new logic of business*. New York: Oxford University Press.

FREY, D. (2002) 'How green is BP?', *New York Times*, 8 December.

GIBSON, K. (2007) *Ethics and Business*. Cambridge: Cambridge University Press.

GILL, R. (2006) *A Textbook of Christian Ethics*. Edinburgh: T. & T. Clark.

GRACE, D. and COHEN, S. (2005) *Business Ethics*. Oxford: Oxford University Press.

GUARDIAN (2008) 'The great green swindle', 23 October, g2: 5–7.

HUNT, C. and ASTER, R. (1990) 'Proactive environmental management', *Sloan Managament Review*, Winter: 9.

HURKA, T. (1992) 'Sustainable development: What do we owe to future generations?'. Paper given at the Environmental Ethics Conference, University of British Columbia, October.

INTERGOVERNMENTAL PANEL ON CLIMATE CHANGE (2007): *Impacts, Adaptation and Vulnerability*: http://www/ipcc.ch/publications_and_data/publications_and_data_reports.shtml.

JACKSON T. (2011) *Prosperity Without Growth: Economics for a finite planet*. London: Routledge.

JONAS, H. (1984) *The Imperative of Responsibility: In search of ethics for the technological age*. Chicago: University of Chicago Press.

JUDGE, E. (2011) 'Global warming, resource depletion, and sustainable development', in Wetherly, P. and Otter, D. (2011) *Business Environment*. Oxford: Oxford University Press, 257–85.

LEHNI, M. (1992) *World Business Council for Sustainable Development: Business strategies for sustainable development*. London: Deloitte & Touche.

LOVELOCK, J. (1979) *Gaia: A new look at life on Earth*. New York: Oxford University Press.

MELE, D. (2009) *Business Ethics in Action*. Basingstoke: Palgrave.

MURPHY, C. (2002) 'Is BP beyond petroleum? Hardly: BP's ads are all over Manhattan, but green energy makes up a tiny portion of its revenues', *Fortune*, 16 September.

NATIONAL COMMISSION ON THE BP DEEPWATER HORIZON OIL SPILL AND OFFSHORE DRILLING (2011) *Final Report*: http://www.oilspillcommission.gov/final-report

NETREGS (2005) 'SME-nvironment 2005: England'; available at: http://www. netregs. gov.uk/static/documents/utility/2005_eng_summary_1197354.pdf [accessed 22 September 2011].

SAREWITZ, D. (2004) 'How science makes environmental controversies worse', *Environmental Science and Policy*, 7(5), October: 385–403.

SINGER, P. (1975) *Animal Liberation: A new ethics for our treatment of animals*. New York: New York Review/Random House.

STERN REVIEW (2006) *Stern Review on the Economics of Climate Change*: http://www. direct.gov.uk/en/NI1/Newsroom/DG_064854.

SWAROVSKI. 'The Swarovski Water School'; available at: http://www.swarovski.com/ web_AA/en/crystal_society?contentid=10007.40175/ [accessed 22 September 2011]).

TAYLOR, R., BRAY, S., GANT, R. and MORRISEY, K. (2009) 'SME engagement with sustainability issues: a case study from Surrey, UK', in Corrigan, N., Sayce, S. and Taylor, R. (eds) *Sustainability in Practice. From local to global: making a difference*. Kingston upon Thames: Kingston University Press.

TIRPAK, D. (2005) *Avoiding Dangerous Climate Change*. London: Department for Environment, Food and Rural Affairs (DEFRA).

VAN MARREWIJK, M. (2003) 'Concepts and definitions of CSR and corporate sustainability: between agency and communion', *Journal of Business Ethics*, 44(2/3): 95–110.

VESILIND, P. and GUNN, A. (1998) *Engineering, Ethics and the Environment*. Cambridge: Cambridge University Press.

WARREN, M. A. (1980) *Do Potential Persons Have Rights and Responsibilities to Future Generations?* Buffalo, NY: Prometheus Books.

WHITE, L. (2006) 'The theological roots of our ecological crisis', in Gill, R. (ed.) *A Textbook of Christian Ethics*. Edinburgh: T. & T. Clark: 303–9.

WILLIAMSON, D. and LYNCH-WOOD, G. (2001) 'A new paradigm for SME environmental practice', *The TQM Magazine*, 13: 424–32.

WILSON, E. O. (1989) 'Threats to biodiversity', *Scientific American*, September: 60.

Index